MY LIFE IN PIECES

Writers, Rogues,
The Road and The Rock

Brick Tower Press
Habent Sua Fata Libelli

Brick Tower Press
Manhanset House
Shelter Island Hts., New York 11965-0342
Tel: 212-427-7139
bricktower@aol.com • www.BrickTowerPress.com
All rights reserved under the International and Pan-American Copyright
Conventions. No part of this publication may be reproduced, stored in a retrieval
system, or transmitted in any form or by any means, electronic, or otherwise, without
the prior written permission of the copyright holder.
The Brick Tower Press colophon is a registered trademark of
J. T. Colby & Company, Inc.

Library of Congress Cataloging-in-Publication Data
Clancy, Ambrose.
My Life In Pieces
p. cm.

1. Language Arts & Disciplines—Journalism.
2. Biography & Autobiography—Editors, Journalists, Publishers.
3. Biography & Autobiography—Cultural, Ethnic & Regional—General.
4. Literary Criticism—Subjects & Themes—Historical Events.
Nonfiction, I. Title.

ISBN: 978-1-899694-05-1, Trade Paper • 978-1-899694-29-7, Hardcover

Special thanks to Merce Binder for transcription.

January 2025

MY LIFE IN PIECES

Writers, Rogues,
The Road and The Rock

Ambrose Clancy

Also by Ambrose Clancy

Blind Pilot
The Night Line (with Peter Donohoe)

For Mary Lydon
... you and me

Table of Contents

Photo Index

Foreword

By Robert Lipsyte

Clancy knows he's good, really good, a common belief (and, for some, delusion) of certain Irish writers, but you have to give the devilish their due. He can uncoil a sentence like a silken rope, snap it like a whip, tie up a complicated thought. He can write long, he can write short, he can build a case, he can murmur a spooky tale. I may find this more interesting than most because Clancy is also my editor, for which I am grateful. He ups the game.

Not only that, but he teeters on the precarious plank of small-town newspapering, delivering a weekly print edition and a daily online report to a surly audience hungry for news that will enhance the value of their real estate. They regard him with suspicion. Meanwhile, he is my editor and I regard him as a demi-god. Well, at the very least one of the all-time great flies on the wall.

When you read his *GQ* profile of Jimmy Breslin, you sense Clancy's presence in the room, just as Breslin did. The great fly on the wall reporters do not totally disappear, rather they fade just enough to be able to wordlessly encourage and prod without intruding. This is an awesome gift. Even Breslin, a bubbling vat of what Frank McCourt called "begrudgery," appreciated Clancy. After the profile ran, he told Clancy to be relieved he wouldn't have to sue him. High praise from a miser of praise.

Clancy also has the eye. He froze a moment that captured The Troubles for me. This was a long time ago in Belfast. He watched a young boy, half a brick clutched in his hand, edge out of an alley, then pitch it through the window of the buffet car of a passing train.

He is a splendid travel writer, from Florence to the Finger Lakes, but never better than when he is in Ireland, where his spirit awoke. In the late 1970s, after several years as a New York cabbie, with meager success as a freelance writer, he and his wife, Mary Lydon, took the $4,000 she had earned as a freelance copy editor and bet it all on Dublin. It was romantic and pragmatic and they won. Ireland gave Clancy another home and the confidence to write a terrific novel, *Blind Pilot*, and become a successful magazine writer.

If Clancy is lyric in Ireland he's not so bad in Lawn Guyland, where he has worked these many years. It is here he can find a man "with a gait suited to a pitching deck" or a comedian who calls himself Eric Moneynipple or the remnants of Camp Siegfried, in Yaphank, where Nazis marched and postured in the 1930s. And twenty years ago, writing for *The Washington Post*, he nailed that moment, now fleeting, when the North Fork of the East End could be described as offering "the fragile, water-sourced light of Holland, the climate and soil of Bordeaux and is the only part of New England that is never designated as such, which may partially explain its feeling of aloofness and don't tread on me spirit."

His touch can be delicate and dark, in fact and fiction. Read his precise account of Shelter Island's famous homicide, recent enough to be a warm case, as well as the annual Halloween yarns he weaves. Does one also sense dark tales about himself hidden between the lines of increasingly bizarre fishing tales?

Clancy dedicated March 5, 1999, to polling barflies about new laws impounding the cars of the drunk. He is eventually thrown out of a bar, The Printer's Devil, no less, but not before he is treated to alternately aggravating and hilarious sermonettes from patrons on the evils of drink, the evils of a government trying to violate the rights to drink and told that reporters get everything wrong anyway, before being escorted out. No one actually takes a swing at Clancy, thanks in part, I think, to his appearance. He looks deceptively friendly, a compact man whose faint smile seems to offer a lack of judgment. While listening, he will be absolutely still, without affect, to allow a scene to develop to his liking, then assume a totally bogus affability, a chuckly mien when the subject needs to be nudged along, even be it other tricky writers such as *The Ginger Man's* J.P. Donleavy, *L.A. Confidential's* James Ellroy, or the late, great critic John Leonard. Be forewarned, Clancy may even assume the guise at lunch.

Let me cut to the chase here as after almost a decade I can hear him thinking, Let's cut to the chase here. Clancy's day job, being my editor, as important as it is to Shelter Island and the nation, unfortunately takes up too much of his time. I'd like him to write another novel and more long magazine pieces. But the day job is important, especially right now with an American version of The Troubles at our doorstep and Clancy's true major gift in short supply. Even beyond his eye for the wrenching detail and his fly on the wall wiles and his sense of place is his humanity, even in small towns where the stakes can be surprisingly high and an editor knowing when to dust and when to hammer can make a difference.

Clancy has a big heart along with the decency, maybe because he knows he's good, really good. Did I mention that? And the confidence to suffer fools, if not gladly, at least gently.

Thanks for that, too, Chief.

Robert Lipsyte is a former New York Times *reporter and columnist and the author of 24 books, including the memoirs, "In the Country of Illness" and "An Accidental Sportswriter." He lives on Shelter Island, N.Y., where he writes the "Codger" column for the* Shelter Island Reporter.

Introduction

Ireland, where I became a professional writer, plays a significant role in this collection of journalism spanning four decades.

In the late 1970s, my wife Mary Lydon and I, not long married, left New York and moved to Dublin. I'd been driving a cab at night and Mary worked from our studio apartment transcribing tapes and freelance editing. She scored a job from a stockbroker who wanted to write a how-to investment book. When the job was done a few months later, we had $4,000. Sitting in a neighborhood café, we decided to change our lives with a great escape. Our only language was English, and Britain didn't ring the bell. We were Irish-American. Ireland seemed foreign enough. We'd go and stay until the money ran out.

There was another reason to go. I'd had one piece published in *The Village Voice*, one in the *Soho Weekly News* and one in *The Phoenix*, the New England literary magazine. That was it, and all my other pitches for work had been rejected or ignored. But there was a guerilla war in the North of Ireland that I could go to, write about and try to sell the pieces at home. An editor at *The Voice* gave me a one-page, to-whom-it may-concern letter on the paper's stationery asking that I be given all courtesies and considerations, etc.

On a summer morning, we stepped off a ferry that had crossed the Irish Sea from Wales to Dún Laoghaire, knowing no one and with two phone numbers. It was as romantic as it sounds. Within a day, we knew we were home. Our time there bound us more strongly to each other, and we met people who made flesh the poet's wisdom that "my glory was/ That I had such friends."

* * * *

I went to the North and got close enough to car-bomb blasts to jump out of my skin, or feel the sidewalk under my shoes shivering from not-so-distant detonations. Two doors down the block from a B&B where I was staying was a gray, obscene hole of scorched timbers and black bricks where a pub, along with two buildings on either side, had stood a couple of days before.

I was alternately charmed and righteously spooked by members of the Northern Ireland paramilitaries that I engaged with, such as the Ulster Volunteer Force, the Ulster Defense Association and the Provisional Irish Republican Army. The British Army was no bargain, either, and with no charm at all. It became common, as a reporter, to be rousted by British soldiers in Belfast, in the countryside, and along the border between the Republic of Ireland and the six counties of Ulster that Britain ruled.

I was told before I went to Belfast to wear a coat and tie. Casual clothes wouldn't get me past the door to meet anyone, and the British Army wouldn't be so fast to detain—or "lift" in Ulster parlance—a journalist who looked serious enough to get dressed up. I followed this rule, which helped, I'm sure, but still ... A few encounters remain vivid.

In the Falls Road neighborhood one morning a squad of soldiers stop me. They're patrolling down the middle of the narrow street in the diamond formation, one on point, and at the rear, one walking backwards checking rooftops they've just passed. The squad is made up of a young officer commanding six extremely jittery 19-year-old soldiers, all eyes alive to the possibility that an IRA rooftop sniper can cancel their tickets at any moment. As automatic weapons are pointed at me, I'm gripping a rough brick wall, one ankle kicked sideways spreading me out as the officer searches me, finishing his frisk by pulling roughly at my crotch, a punctuation to the humiliation.

Another street, another day, another squad of soldiers, with an English officer asking me questions in rapid and condescending terms. The officer telling me, in so many words, that I was a member of a ludicrous profession. His contempt barely concealed by short joking questions fired at me so fast I can't even smile, forget laugh, and so am left looking stupid in the presence of all that quick, decisive, bristly cheer. Wrong-footed at the baseline, 15-Love, and another serve on the way.

When they left, moving on with the officer smirking, "Mind how you go," an old man standing nearby who had witnessed the roust, said to me with a smile, "Englishman barks at me the other night, 'Give me yer name.' I says back to him, 'Then what I am I to use?'"

His defiant wit calmed my anger. Just a bit, but enough.

My *Village Voice* stationery helped, although it was my American passport that always saved me real grief with the paramilitaries and the army. Once, in a car driven by my friend Niall Kiely of the Irish Times on a one-lane blacktop meandering through farm fields, camouflaged soldiers came out of a ditch ahead, faces blackened—a sniper with a good scope could easily target white faces in all that green. I was set to present my *Voice* letter when Niall quietly said, stopping the car, never taking his eyes off the approaching soldiers, "Ah, no, Ambrose. I'd show your passport to this lot."

Belfast was where I turned a corner and saw barefoot children walking in the rain on a rubble-strewn street, an emaciated woman in ragged clothes screaming at them. The faces of the poor, of the desperate, had the features of my parents, brothers and sisters.

Eight centuries of injustice, oppression, terror, bloodshed and tragedy can't be summed up in a verse or a sentence, and shouldn't be. But I'll risk it. Spending time in the North of Ireland, I started to fully understand a brief phrase: Ireland can't forget, and England can't remember.

And a stinging Dominic Behan lyric, made more painful when sung sweetly by Liam Clancy:

Come all ye young rebels, and listen while I sing,
For the love of one's country is a terrible thing.

Dublin and the North is where I first felt the rush of reporting, of engaging people, of trying to see a place in full, of realizing the accomplishment of telling stories that could mean something, no matter how small, to a reader.

I sold exactly two pieces. But for the first time, the rejections didn't bother me. I had another plan. Two years later, back in New York, a novel I was writing set in Ireland found a publisher. We returned to Dublin and I finished *Blind Pilot*. It was published in America, Britain, Germany and Japan.

Books with Irish themes were sent to me to review, and magazine and newspaper commissions followed to write travel pieces in Ireland and to do profiles. There are worse things than being pigeon-holed, and my name became an easy go-to for editors with Irish ideas.

According to Merriam Webster, the first known use of "freelance" comes from Sir Walter Scott's 1819 novel, *Ivanhoe*: "I offered Richard the service of my Free Lances, and he refused them—I will lead them to Hull, seize on shipping, and embark for Flanders; thanks to the bustling times, a man of action will always find employment."

Daring, adventuresome, yes, but the reality for freelance writers was forever defined by the American humorist and journalist Robert Benchley, who noted that the freelancer is one "who is paid per piece, or per word, or perhaps."

* * * *

Other places represented here in significant numbers are New York City and Long Island. Even though I haven't lived there in 20 years, I am a New York City nationalist, and have roots in the East End of

Long Island. Other places visited are Britain, Italy and the Netherlands with a few stops in America, and a journey to mountain monasteries set on the coasts of a remote peninsula in Northern Greece.

Also, people, places, events (and a few ghost stories) from Shelter Island, or "The Rock," as some affectionately call the place where I've worked for more than a decade.

These pieces to follow are snapshots of times and places, and it's not news that both change, with writer William J. Hogan—quoted in the pages to follow—noting: "If any man lives long enough, he becomes a stranger in his own place."

To introduce the pieces, I'll make a comment or two, to remind you that they live in the time they were written.

Somewhere I write that I had gone looking for places, but instead found people, the greatest reward of travel. But to start, we'll follow a traveler besotted by writers and their lives—which is another continuing theme—who goes looking for them, and finds places.

Part I
WORDS, WORDS, WORDS

Chapter 1
Confessions of a Literary Pilgrim

This piece was published in The Washington Post *in December 1999. Many of the writers' homes mentioned here have since been spruced up, refurbished and made more accessible to visitors. What has been lost, or gained, through deep cleaning, is up for debate.*

I was a reluctant pilgrim. Standing there in awe and terror as my buddy O'Malley pounded the great man's door, I thought: There has to be a more civilized way of doing this. An admiring letter with a subtle request for an invitation? A well-planned chance encounter on the streets of Sag Harbor? O'Malley knocked again. This was barbaric. I was ready to run. John Steinbeck might be on the other side of the door, might open it, and I would be turned to stone.

But I was also ready to go for another reason. Being there, seeing the stand of trees around the house, the cove where his boat swung at anchor, the scene, in fact, from the wonderful opening of "Travels With Charley," when a hurricane is bearing down on the author's home, this was enough, just to see it. The pilgrim doesn't expect to see the saint, and probably wouldn't be able to handle the vision if it occurred. To walk where the saint walked is the blessing.

I was 18 then—just. Saints, pilgrimages and visions were easy to apply to writers, scenes and books. Before I could get my feet moving, a beautiful woman opened the door, saying Mr. Steinbeck was not in. But then we saw him behind her and O'Malley called to him. He came over and spoke with us for a minute. I mumbled something, but O'Malley was eloquent, saying he had read all his books, it was a privilege to shake his hand. O'Malley who, the day before, seeing me reading "East of Eden," had asked, "Any good?" (meaning, Any sex?), who handled a book in the manner of non-readers the world over, turning it in his hands, wondering where the way into the thing might be.

"Nice guy," he said as we drove away. "Got the big bucks."

I looked at the house, the trees, the glint of water. It may have been a time-killing goof for O'Malley, but he'd started my steps on the road. Since then, wherever I am, I go to writers' houses. The only condition is they must be dead.

Not long ago I was walking a path curving up along the bluff overlooking the bay at Laugharne, South Wales. The path is called Dylan's Way and leads to the writing shed and "sea shaken" house where Dylan Thomas lived with his family, wrote and was happy the last few years of his life. Below, the bay was calm, there were wind sounds and soft waves, and across the way, I realized with a start of pleasure, was wooded Sir John's Hill, which Thomas saw whenever he looked up from his work. It was here, looking at Sir John's Hill, where he heard "Death clear as a buoy's bell." And here, where he wrote:

> *It is the heron and I, under judging Sir John's elmed*
> *Hill, tell-tale the knelled*
> *Guilt*
> *Of the led-astray birds whom God, for their breast of whistles,*
> *Have mercy on ...*

John Ackerman, author of the best interpretation of led-astray Dylan, wrote that, "Over Sir John's Hill" and several other poems are "marked by retrospection and meditation as well as allegory, so that a particular landscape may become legendary."

I once lived in a whole city of legend. That was Dublin in the late '70s, and now I know what Hemingway meant about the moveable feast. I was a young man, lucky, and it has stayed with me wherever I've gone. Dublin is a Vatican of literary holy sites, the Martello Tower, Sandycove, the most venerated. Joyce lived there briefly in 1904 with Oliver St. John Gogarty and an armed English lunatic. The latter dreamed of black panthers and would open fire on them in his sleep, ricocheting bullets around the stone walls of the round tower, badly rattling pots and pans and the nerves of young James.

I went out to Sandycove one summer morning, and it was there that the humor of pilgrimage began to crowd out the transcendental. In those days, the tower was a bit haphazard and pleasantly ramshackle, like Dublin itself. A bit of half-done, could-care-less. At the top were views of the "snotgreen sea. The scrotumtightening sea," where Buck Mulligan blasphemed to the morning sky. The exhibits below were strange, and one wondered if the cause was just Irish eccentricity and carelessness at work, or Dublin jackeens having a laugh. For example, one of the featured exhibits was Joyce's *tie*. It was in a dusty glass case, presented as reverentially as the thigh bone of an ancient abbot, or, at the very least, a bun in Bewley's of Grafton Street. There were two young Irishmen in shabby suits supposedly in charge of the museum, both smoking, drinking tea, ignoring everyone. A couple was studying the tie in its case, rapt. This, they must have been thinking, was once around *his* neck.

In London, I found Dr. Johnson's house by chance, wandering off Fleet Street and into the 18th century of Gough Square. Here the drill was quiet, reserve and intense worship. Visitors were greeted by a severely composed young woman whispering, "Welcome to Dr. Johnson's house." Upstairs, where the first comprehensive English dictionary was written between 1749 and 1759, it was even more quiet. Suddenly there was raucous noise on the stairs, heavy boots, a loud voice, saying, "C'mon, we'll see what's up here." Into the room strode a man in his sixties, big-chested, fresh from a beery lunch, wearing a white windbreaker over a red shirt. Emblazoned on the back was a large American flag. He turned to the stairs and shouted, "Up here, Diane, come on up." He looked around as his wife, with the same windbreaker, same flag, huffed into the room. The man approached me. Other true believers were making for the stairs in shock. I would have followed, but he was on me too quickly.

"What's this?" he boomed. I told him a little about the place. "A dictionary! You never think of someone sittin' down and writing a dictionary, do you?" He was delighted. And it wasn't just that he could tell people about it back in Tulsa. He was looking around. He was beginning to feel it. Hooked.

I visited Hemingway's house in Key West while attending a January literary seminar devoted to him. It was an odd mix of serious scholarship, cornball Americana and staying up all night for a week. There were panel discussions, slide shows, films, papers read, a George Plimpton fireworks show and a Hemingway look-alike contest at Sloppy Joe's, Hemingway's local and still one of the great gin mills of the world. Five men in their fifties, all white-bearded, posed under a portrait of Papa. They didn't look remotely like the author, but were, the photographer from *People* said, "appropriately drunk."

There were also tours of the mansion where Hemingway lived with his second wife, Pauline, and their children in the 1930s. It was here he began to acquire the weight of his legend: fishing for monsters, collecting art, boxing on piers and beaches, heroically drinking followed by machine-gunning sharks for kicks. It was also where he wrote, producing some of the last, great short stories, and that overlooked masterpiece, "Green Hills of Africa."

907 Whitehead St. is set back on a corner lot in a tropical garden. Square, two-storied, with a wrought-iron veranda, French windows, cool stone walls and a swimming pool. Hemingway had lived like a colonial governor. I trooped in one morning with a group of high school kids on a field trip, reporters, tourists and a fair number of keepers of the eternal Papa flame. Our guide was a slim, spry, elderly man, wielding a cane like a fey British brigadier, calling both men and women "honey," and making up the facts as he went along.

I was struck by the paintings in the house—the flat color, astigmatic perspective and tortured forms of the less-than-Sunday painter. This was not Hemingway's famed collection; that, along with the good furniture, had gone under the auctioneer's hammer long ago. I asked our guide, whose work was represented. "I don't know, honey. But it's the real thing." He looked at a seascape. "I think."

I heard grumbling behind me when our guide said Hemingway and Miss Mary had kept 40 or 50 cats at the house. The flame-keepers were appalled. Mary Hemingway never lived here and, one person spat, sotto voce, "Cuba is where he had the cats. Cuba." On we went, the cane pointing to a thrift-shop table. "Ernest wrote 'The Old Man and the Sea' at that very desk." The high school kids were bored, the tourists a bit wowed, the flame-keepers close to open revolt. "Cuba! He wrote that in Cuba."

"No, honey, he most certainly did not."

William Faulkner's house, which he named Rowan Oak, is set in acres of old woods on the outskirts of Oxford, Miss. Built in the 1840s, it is a good example of Southern aristocratic architecture, the kind of house that a well-to-do planter, with ideas about columned Greek temples, would design. Here Faulkner moved in 1931 to pursue his dual obsessions: creating literature and living in the 19th century. As R.V. Cassill has written, in Faulkner's best work "the tense of hope is nearly always past."

I went to the annual Faulkner festival in Oxford one August. At first it seemed a mean Southern joke to hold the event in Mississippi's blast furnace month. But it is the perfect time to celebrate Faulkner. The monolithic heat in a place of cotton and soybean fields, kudzu and "alluvial swamps threaded by black almost motionless bayous and impenetrable with cane and buckvine and cypress and ash and oak and gum" allows you to understand the inspiration for that magnificent thicket of a style that the readers of the world cherish.

To say it was hot is to say nothing. Novelist David Lozell Martin, covering the event for the *Los Angeles Times*, led his piece with an homage to the inventor of the air conditioner. There was a picnic one afternoon at Rowan Oak, where a couple of hundred people gathered on the grounds to bake and turn surly while watching vats of potato salad go green. Tubs of ice and soda became tepid ponds. When the wind blew it stirred the bone-dry woods, and resinous dust stuck to your neck.

Inside it was dark, airless, claustrophobic. It seemed the place was not well cared for. But upstairs in the half-light of the author's study, a small group of people smiled in wonder at something written on the wall. It was the plot of "A Fable" that Faulkner had put there to keep track of his novel. There were two young Frenchmen happily whispering, a couple of Russian scholars taking notes, and a young woman from Louisiana and her 10-year-old daughter, both tracing, as if it were tomb hieroglyphics, the author's list of characters, scenes, dates.

It was easy to see why we were here. We were paying respects, expressing gratitude. Outside was the landscape magically made legend and here, in this room, was where it had been done.

Chapter 2
Paper Lion

*It seems right to introduce our first individual here, Jimmy Breslin, son of Queens, who died on March 19, 2017. Eliot Kaplan at GQ assigned the profile, but it took a while to convince Jimmy to let me shadow him for a few days. Some people don't suffer fools gladly; Breslin didn't suffer **anyone** gladly. But he finally opened up and treated me like a colleague, even so far as phoning me when the issue came out in November 1987 to tell me I should be relieved he didn't have to sue me. High praise from Jimmy.*

He goes to work at nine-thirty Saturday morning of the Memorial Day weekend. He leaves the elevator and walks into the lobby of his apartment house. The young doorman says, "Morning, sir."

"Yeah. How you doin'?"

The doorman counters his scowl with a grin, and shrugs. "Awful."

He likes this, and smiles, the first of the day. As someone once said, every day is the worst day of Jimmy Breslin's life.

As he walks north up Central Park West, it is hot, jungle humid, the kind of day that is a prophesy of New York in high summer. The sky is white and gray and black, the smoldering colors of a fire in a garbage can. It starts to rain softly and Breslin looks up, furious. The writer as Ahab, ready to strike the sky if it insults him.

As he nears 72nd Street, his New York ears catch a sound—the uptown train pulling into the station below him. Breslin curses. Even if he were a track star he couldn't catch it. On Saturday mornings you can wait half an hour between trains. He's out in the street, hails a cab, settles back and lights a cigar of truly gangster proportions.

"I am one," he has written in his column, "of a half dozen or so in New York who is over the age of fourteen and does not drive a car. It is just another part of a life of noisy desperation." Now, when he's in the cab, it's like a child's first trip. He watches everything passing through his cigar smoke as the cab rattles and rolls uptown.

Yesterday, at the racketeering trial of former Secretary of Labor Raymond Donovan and seven others, a woman juror, Milagros Arroyo, had caused a sensation. The jury had been deliberating a verdict for five and a half hours when something in Arroyo came loose. She locked herself in a bathroom and demanded to see a priest. The judge put her in the witness chair, questioned her, and Arroyo responded by quoting the opening lines of the Twenty-third Psalm. After nearly nine months of trial the courtroom was in an uproar, and the attorneys were demanding a mistrial, refusing to accept an alternate juror. The judge would hear motions today in court, and Breslin would have a story.

On the Madison Avenue Bridge he looks across the river toward the South Bronx and his destination, a huge square pile of a building, something Mussolini would have liked, an example of the architectural School of Brutalism, perfect for the Bronx County courthouse. While he's waiting for a light, a nearly destroyed Pinto pulls up. The young black man at the wheel looks over and says, "Jimmy Breslin. Hey, Jimmy Breslin, right?"

"Yeah. Where you goin'?"

"Work. Down in Manhattan. Hey, great story on the polar bear kid."

The second smile of the day. "You're right. It was a great story."

The polar bear kid. Earlier in the week, on a warm night, Juan Perez, 11, had sneaked into the polar bear cage at the Prospect Park Zoo and was mauled to death. Breslin's column was from the neighborhood where the boy had lived, with an interview of an upstairs neighbor.

The column was about a brave, mischievous boy living in a home without a father in a poverty-blighted Brooklyn neighborhood, "a neighborhood of old apartment houses that are packed with people who trace their beginnings from anywhere south of Virginia to the islands in the last waters of the Caribbean." At 11, Juan was just beginning to run the streets, just beginning to be beyond his mother's control. Breslin wrote, "This was a most startling news story ... But at the same time, perhaps somebody should stop just for a paragraph here this morning and mention the fact that there are many children being eaten alive by this bear of a city, New York in the 1980s."

* * * *

The first floor of the courthouse is dim, empty, and Breslin hurries to share an elevator with one of the defendants in the Donovan case, state Senator Joseph Galiber, a tall, distinguished black man, 62 years old, looking as if he hasn't slept in days. "How you doin'?" Breslin asks. The senator shrugs.

"Where you goin' this weekend?" A strange question, a tool of the successful journalist, throwing in something offbeat, innocuous, and Galiber is almost ready to respond but is clever enough finally to just smile and shake his head.

Down a corridor, there is a wild sound buzzing off the marble walls. Turning a corner, the senator is caught in mid-stride by painfully-bright TV lights. Next to the courtroom door, behind wooden police barricades, are camera crews and photographers, at least a hundred people.

Breslin heads down another corridor and finds John Nicholas Iannuzzi, attorney for another of the defendants, William Pellegrino Masselli, a.k.a. Billy the Butcher. Iannuzzi does everything but grab Breslin by the lapels, making a point. He has on what looks like a polo shirt and a red tie wide enough to have been fashionable a decade ago. "Jimmy," he says, "I've never seen anything like it. Draggin' the poor woman around, throwin' her in the witness chair like she's a sack of potatoes. She's sayin', 'The Lord is my shepherd, the Lord is my shepherd.' Apeshit. The poor woman is goin' fuckin' apeshit." Breslin listens as if he were getting a report from a subordinate officer, looking over his shoulder, at his feet, only rarely looking directly at the attorney.

Inside the courtroom he moves around, talking to people whom other reporters, busy speaking to one another, are ignoring. One person who has information is a dwarf in a perfectly tailored suit. Another source is a man in a once-white guayaberra, a blue smudge of a tattoo on his forearm, and a ventilated baseball cap with admiral's scrambled eggs on the brim. Breslin is making notes on folded yellow legal sheets.

The judge arrives and court begins. Breslin sits slumped in the last row. Six of the eight defendants want a mistrial. Donovan's lawyer quietly says his client will accept an alternate juror. Iannuzzi shouts that "this is the sorriest spectacle I've ever witnessed." And, "I want my juror! I want my jury! I want a hearing! I protest! *J'accuse!*"

The judge calls a recess, and Breslin immediately goes to Billy the Butcher and walks out with him. Hysterics from the camera crews, falling over one another in the blast furnace of TV lights. Billy goes to the elevators and is cornered by the lights. A woman reporter with a microphone as long as a baseball bat begins to question him. She stands on the other side of the lights, four feet away. Billy says, "All double-talk legalese," and walks away, down a long corridor. No one follows him except Breslin. They both lean against a dirty marble wall in the sudden quiet. "So what do you think?"

"Jimmy, it's got nothin' to do with me."

"Come on."

"I'm just spice for their stew here."

"Donovan's going with the alternate."

"Good luck to him."

"You're taking the mistrial?"

"Yeah. Donovan's not gambling. He's a 3-1 shot."

"You sure?"

"Absolute. He's 3-1 and should be more."

"Then why don't you go with the alternate?"

"If Donovan wins, they'll never retry me. If he loses, then Donovan appeals. That takes years. They can't retry me until the appeal is over. I'll be fuckin' dead by then. There's no way I can lose."

At 60, Billy the Butcher is not doing well. His health is shot. His son was murdered a few years ago, and he has a murder trial of his own coming up after this one is through. Breslin asks him where he's done time. "Dannemora. Worst joint in the country. Fuckin' iceberg up there. Tallahassee. Another bad place."

Breslin says, "What about Tony's [Salerno] trial downtown?"

"I never met him in my life."

"Bullshit."

"I take an oath on my dead kid, I never met the man."

"You know him from the streets."

"Nah. I'm from Morris Avenue. Tony's from Harlem."

Billy starts talking about his health. "I don't know, I went to the hospital, they say my stomach's all right, no cancer there. No cancer in my body." He pauses. "Nothin' in my brain."

Poor Billy is living proof that *The Gang That Couldn't Shoot Straight*, a Breslin title that has entered the language, was not wild satire or imaginative comedy, but dead-on realism.

Breslin's late and running. Outside the courthouse he stops for more cigars at a smoke shop blaring salsa, then is out on the street hailing a taxi. A gypsy cab with a furry red interior, four pine-tree air fresheners making the cab smell like the cabinet under your sink, and a Nigerian driver. "Forty-second and Second. The *Daily News* building."

At a light the driver is giving directions to two guys looking for an auto-parts store on Jerome Avenue. The light blinks green, goes to red, back to green. "Come on, come on," Breslin says. "I'm late."

The last two words should be said to cabbies only by true sportsmen. All the way down Second Avenue, the Nigerian is running lights, lane-jumping furiously, leaning on his horn, cranking up his tape deck of African music made up of booming drums, chants and what sounds like tin cans being beaten with sticks.

Between Second and Third, Breslin gets two cups of coffee from a coffee shop and crosses the street to the *Daily News* building. The security guard says, "Excuse me, sir," and Breslin, still walking, says, "I'm goin' to work."

On the seventh floor he enters his corner office looking out on 42nd Street. There are boxes and wastepaper baskets, an old Olympia typewriter, papers everywhere, a bookcase, half-filled, the books upside down, on their sides, as if they've been thrown from across the room. He sits at the word processor, spreads his notes out, opens one coffee, lights a cigar and types his lede: *The setting was for a crap game.* In a few minutes he's lost in the story, cigar and coffee forgotten, using a rapid hunt-and-peck style, as if he wants to put his index fingers *through* the keyboard.

Nearing deadline, he answers his phone, shouts, "In a few minutes," and slams down the phone. Every sentence, except the lede, is rewritten at least once. Two hours later he's done, but still fiddling with the piece, reading off the screen, working on a sentence: *In the morning, the difference between throwing dice against a garage wall on Southern Blvd. and the game scheduled to go on in the courtroom was that there were only supposed to be two players.* His wife calls to remind him that ninety people are coming to the apartment in two hours for a wedding.

Down the hall, in the city room, he looks over the shoulder of the editor as the story comes up. If he wants, he can stop back later to make changes when word comes from the Bronx about the judge's ruling.

Exhausted, he's got to have a walk, or maybe a swim, to come down. Since six-thirty this morning, lying in bed with a telephone, three newspapers and a thermos of coffee, Breslin, 58, has been working. It's now three o'clock and he's still not satisfied. He finally won the Pulitzer last year, but it's been like this for almost twenty-five years, three columns a week, writing the central stories of his city, which are, in no particular order, the amazing thievery of the powers-that-be, the forgotten and despised poor and the fast, fierce humor of New York neighborhoods. Week after week, the life of noisy desperation.

* * * *

Three times a week, writing in what he calls "street Irish—with descriptive talent." For the price of a newspaper you can get a description of the steps of City Hall ... "with grooves worn in them from seventy-five years of people running up them and trying to leap through the doors and make a huge splash in the gravy." Or a description of Sunday in certain Queens neighborhoods as "the day belonging to the Lord in the morning and the children in the afternoon."

Breslin is one of only a few writers who have kept the faith, who have not turned cynical but are still outraged at what is happening to the poor of the city. He almost never uses statistics when writing about issues, but rather writes about the people the statistics obscure. He is one who disdains the overview, the big picture. What he is saying is that New York City is getting worse day by day for all of us, and of course much worse for those who have so much less. Unless there is a change, Breslin says, and not some hack politician's windy words of change, New York City is certain to be more grim, more violent, more at odds with itself.

But then there's the humor, the chronicling of his "daily incompetents." Fat Thomas, the bookmaker/cab dispatcher at the Four Ones in Ridgewood. Queens, who lives by the creed "Only God behaves." When Thomas hit it big with a phenomenal run one football season, he decided to look for investments. A friend in real estate knew about some property. Fat Thomas asked, "Is real estate as much fun as hookers?"

Or how about Un Occhio (One Eye), boss of all bosses, running his shadowy underworld out of a candy store on Pleasant Avenue in East Harlem? Near the store is a marble triplex, a palace whose façade is a crumbling tenement. There, Un Occhio lives with his wife,

Meenel, "who is seen only at funerals of men who have had particularly violent deaths." The *capo di tutu* i *capi* himself prefers poison to settle differences of opinion because of its simple beauty. "You give them food and they die."

Hilarious stuff, and funnier still when the Arizona State Police wrote to Breslin for information and the FBI and the Organized Crime Task Force in New York spent a month in East Harlem looking for the fictional Mafia chieftain. Recently, he wrote a piece about how real-life godfather John Gotti had received $624,000 from the Iran arms-sales diversion. Breslin received calls from investigative reporters from as far away as Australia. Daily incompetents come in suits and ties as well as blue collars.

* * * *

Two weeks before Billy the Butcher was rolling bones in the Bronx, I was home in Queens, the place Breslin has described as "the Athens of America," not for the huge Greek population in Astoria but more for the sterling qualities of democracy and gentle political debate that define the borough. Home in Queens, a place Breslin has excavated as deeply as Faulkner mined Yoknapatawpha—particularly in last year's *Table Money,* his best-selling, critically acclaimed novel of the working Irish of the borough.

My project for the day was watching the Iran-Contra hearings and attempting to figure out just what it was Bud McFarlane was saying. No easy task. As McFarlane began yet another of his drifting little speeches in the voice of a shipwrecked sailor recalling the disaster, I received a dinner invitation. It was Ronnie Eldridge, Breslin's wife, speaking in her quick, musical voice, speaking English as opposed to the *2001* computer-speak of Bud. "Look, why don't you come at seven-thirty. We're eating non-seasoned food. It's horrible. But you're welcome."

The poet of Queens Boulevard now lives on Central Park West in a spacious apartment. He lives there with his wife and various young people. When I asked where the bathroom was. Ronnie told me. "In here, off this room. Careful, there's some kid camping out in there."

She had greeted me at the door, a pretty woman with that delightful voice. Behind me came Helene, an elderly woman recently widowed. " I'm here a lot," she said. "There's always something going on."

"Jimmy," Ronnie called. "Jimmy. He's here. J.B.!" Then to me, "Come on in and sit down." She gave me a drink and talked about the apartment and the family. She had been a widow with three children and Breslin a widower with six children when they married. Not only was the number of people chaotic, but a Queens Irish Catholic crowd thrown in with a West Side Jewish family was not easy. Her children had been upset when Breslin used them and their conflicts with the Breslins as material for his column. "It's settled down now," she said as Breslin entered the room so fast he looked as if he were race-walking. He came at me, dressed in dark slacks, a blue dress shirt with the French cuffs flapping like loose sails, barefoot. He took my hand and then moved off to the side, a good jab, stick and move. "You all right?" he said, looking at the glass in my hand, and then was off. Ten seconds, tops.

Ronnie went to prepare dinner and Helene offered to help. "Did I tell you it's non-seasoned food? We're trying to lose weight. He's angling for a new TV show and TV makes you look enormous as it is." (*Jimmy Breslin's People* ran for thirteen weeks in 1986 to good reviews but low ratings due to the fact that only farmers and astronomers were awake to see it. When Breslin read rumors in the papers that ABC was about to cancel the show, he took out an ad the next day to announce he was canceling ABC.)

When the women left, Breslin came in again, rubbing his bushy John L. Lewis eyebrows, moaning, the worst day of his life. He sat on the floor, leaning against the couch. He wasn't drinking these days, he told me, looking at his toes. I asked if he missed it and he looked at me as if I were an imbecile. "Fuckin' right I miss it. And the bars. It was my only sport."

I asked him if it was true that once, after a particularly long and wet night, he had felt so catatonic in the morning that he had called an ambulance to cart him to the office. "Yeah," he said, smiling. "True. Oh, it was beautiful. Sirens. lights. But what's important is that I got to work."

He'd been working hard lately, not only on the column: he'd just finished a TV movie for CBS about New York cops, a theater in Louisville had commissioned a play, and he'd finished a novel, *He Got Hungry and Forgot His Manners,* set in Howard Beach and due out early next year. It's the story of an Irish priest who, after long service in Africa, is transferred to a parish in Queens, where he arrives with his companion, a seven-foot cannibal.

But most important, he had just announced he was leaving the *Daily News,* his base for eleven years, to write his column for arch-rival *New York Newsday* beginning in October 1988.

"Why?'

Again the look that categorized me as a poor soul. "For money. They offered me a lot of money."

"How much?"

"Big. Huge."

"How much?"

"It's a five-year deal starting off well over $400,000 for the first year and escalating every year after that [up to $1 million for the last year]. You can print it. It's good for kids in this city to know you can make big money as a writer and not just as a basketball player."

"How different is writing plays, movies and novels from the column?"

"It's the same. If you care about what you do. It's all hard. It's day labor."

Dinner was not horrible, but delicious. Scallops, red and green and yellow peppers and green fettuccine. Breslin poured the wine for those drinking, filling the glasses to the brim. The phone rang every minute and a half. Breslin leaned on the table on one arm, slumped in his chair. Remove the arm and he'd disappear under the table. Halfway through the meal his sister, Deirdre, a teacher at Fordham, arrived. The conversation was about politics—local, statewide, national. Helene asked, "Did you see that man on TV today?"

"McFarlane?" Deirdre asked.

"Yes. He looked to me like he was drugged."

"Yeah," Breslin said, getting up to answer the phone. "And I think he's a stew bum along with it. You see him goin' for the water every minute?"

Breslin's son Christopher arrived in shorts and a T-shirt, sweaty from a game of basketball after work. He's a student at Boston College, home for the summer, working as a research intern in the record business. Breslin questioned him thoroughly about his day as Christopher made short work of the scallops and pasta. "He'll support you in your old age," I said.

"Nah. I'm just concerned that he work. That's the whole thing. The job. The J-0-B."

* * * *

Another day with Breslin—the morning the column about the polar bear kid appeared. When Breslin opened the door, he was again rubbing his eyebrows, his face in mourning. "I'm punched out. Totally."

"Great stuff today."

"Yeah. that's what did it to me. Tough story to do. Took a lot out of me. The poor kid. Then I'm up half the night," he said as I followed him into the kitchen, "goin' through phone books to see if I spelled all the names right."

He was splendid in pale-blue pajamas, one gangster cigar in the breast pocket. I sat at the counter in the kitchen on a high stool. Across the room the Iran-Contra hearings were on a portable TV, an elderly woman proudly testifying about buying trucks and weapons for the rebels.

"Look at this one," he said, his face lighting up. "She'd be perfect for the Goetz jury." When Bernhard Goetz opened up in the subway and shot four Black men, Breslin was the first and, for a while, the only voice that questioned the vigilante tactics. While White New York cheered the subway gunman, Breslin was saying, Calm down, look at it squarely, look at the issue of race, look at yourselves and your delight that one kid is paralyzed for life. He quoted George Will, who, in his column, loftily examining the Goetz incident, wrote, "Let us now praise anger, and especially anger in the form of a desire for justifiable vengeance ... If you do not take Shakespeare's word for it, then take Clint Eastwood's—or else." Breslin's response was: "I got a picture of this little blond man, Will, sitting deep in a movie seat and touching himself as Clint Eastwood pulls out his gun."

The talk turned to drugs in the poor neighborhoods. Breslin worked an espresso machine— "It's decaf. If I drink the real thing, my heart goes like a trip-hammer "—with the elan of any headwaiter in a neighborhood Italian restaurant. "See," he said, deftly changing filters, "the reason everyone's pissed off about crack is that the Blacks are running their own crime. The Italians, the Jews, the Irish, all had the right to pursue their own crime." He sets a cup in front of me, sits down with his feet on the counter. "But when the Blacks do it—look out. You know about the cops in the Brooklyn precinct shakin' down dealers, breaking into places to steal? Amazing. Unbelievable. The cops never had to break in and steal from criminals. They were always paid off. Once the Blacks realize that, you'll never hear about crack again."

Just as paper has never refused ink, Breslin has never been hesitant about voicing opinions. Here are a few of his recent thunderings:

On the Pulitzer Prize: "There are only three prizes anyone knows about—the Academy Awards, the Nobel and the Pulitzer. Now, whether they're all rigged, which I think they are, they still are the prizes. And I got one. They gave me a thousand bucks, I gave that to my daughter, and that was the fuckin' end of that."

On Mayor Koch: "A bald man who substitutes comedy for government."

On the Irish in America: "Sad. They forgot completely where they came from. Like everything they went through never happened."

On the English: "The foulest race on the face of the earth."

On President Reagan: "A senile old fool."

On *New York Times* book reviewer Christopher Lehmann-Haupt: "Every time you let a German near a typewriter to do anything except repair it, he goes straight to authoritarianism."

On the possibility of ever working at the *Times:* "Jesus, that would really be giving up. That's an insurance-agency job."

We talked about his childhood, and were interrupted ten times by two phones on the kitchen wall. Every time one rang, he would groan. "Yeah? Oh, for—will you give me a fuckin' break?" The phone was slammed down. "I'm goin' nuts."

When he was 6 years old, his father, a piano player and an alcoholic, abandoned the family. His mother went to work as a substitute high-school English teacher and then as a full-time worker for the Department of Welfare.

This made me think of the column about Juan Perez, the polar bear kid. Breslin ended it with a description of the funeral of the boy's father. The father had died of drink, and the boy told a neighbor about the funeral. "I saw my father. His face was swollen. But I wasn't afraid. I looked at my father. I wasn't afraid."

And as Breslin spoke about his mother, I remembered something he had said the other night about a solution to the poverty of New York. "The only political word I ever knew was 'jobs.' If you don't have at least one person in a home getting up and going to work, you're finished. Get jobs for people, good work for them, and they'll get education and better housing. And I'll tell you, getting back to the race issue, if you had as high a number of White kids unemployed in this city as you do Black kids, you'd have jobs in a minute."

The phone again. It was his lawyer. After twenty-five years Breslin's sacking his literary agent, Sterling Lord.

"I'm firing him," he said, taking out a platter of turkey and going to work on a leg, using it as a pointer between bites, "because here I am.

I win the Pulitzer Prize. I have a best-selling novel. I've got a critically acclaimed TV show, and what happens? Nothin.' Zero. It's like a team wins 108 ball games and doesn't make it to the World Series. I got a year here I can retire on, but I don't get any help."

There were loud women's voices in the living room. "Oh, for God's sake." He got up and moved toward the door. "Goddamn kids."

Ronnie stopped him. "Now, calm down. Don't shout at her. Please?"

"Yeah. Right."

He came back with Kelly, his 22-year-old daughter, and made a call. "Yeah, I got your name from Jerry Della Femina. He says you're the man." Kelly, blonde, pretty, is pacing the kitchen, not looking at her father. "Now, look, she's a great actress. Well, she's an actress. She'll do anything. She has the distinction of being the only student in the history of the High School of Performing Arts to cut school. Yeah, I'll put her on."

Kelly took the phone into the next room. A few minutes later, she was back. "So?" Breslin asked.

"Thanks."

"Okay. So what is it, Kelly?"

"The J-0-B."

"Right."

A few hours after he finishes the Billy the Butcher column, Breslin's apartment is packed for the wedding of Pete Hamill and Fukiko Aoki. Celebrities are bumping into one another as literary New York meets political New York. Broadway says hello to prizefighters. And newspaper people, along with a few Hamills, are dug in near the champagne bar. Michael Daly, former columnist for the *Daily News,* is describing Breslin, with affection as "a beast. The man's a beast."

Chamber music drifts down a hall where people hold drinks and pick from trays of hors d'oeuvres passed by waiters and waitresses in tuxedos. The bride's mother is in a kimono, while the groom's mother seems a bit stunned by it all. Peter Maas is talking to a reporter about East Hampton in the summer and the IRA. Jonathan Schwartz leaves early; so does Pete's brother, Denis Hamill, a columnist for *New York Newsday*. A gossip column reports the next day about a shouting match between Breslin and Denis at the party. There's a quote from Denis saying, "Jimmy Breslin hasn't told the truth for years—not even to his diary." But, after all, it is the *New York Post,* so who knows whose leg is being pulled.

It's a good party, and nobody seems to be getting seriously hurt. Seeing the guests, you realize that Breslin probably knows New York City better than anyone. He has working knowledge of agents and publishers, advertising people, actors, pro athletes, television executives, the mob, and he has roots in the White working class and a commitment to the angry poor of Brooklyn and the Bronx.

He speaks with his lawyer, Paul O'Dwyer; Bob Fosse; and Cork Smith, his editor at Ticknor & Fields. Jose Torres stops by to say hello. But then, suddenly, in the middle of the party, Breslin's gone.

Down to *The Daily News* to work on the column, to make changes for the later editions.

Chapter 3
An Irish Uprising

Here is the first of three stories set in Cheltenham, England, two with literary subjects, and one a simple love letter. This chapter, on one of the most entertaining literary festivals I've covered, was published in the Los Angeles Times *in October 1997.*

"My God!" Seamus Heaney said recently in comic astonishment. "Ireland is chic!"

Yes, "Angela's Ashes" has come out of nowhere to win the Pulitzer Prize. "Riverdance" has helped public TV across America to pay the rent. The new Irish cinema has given us "My Left Foot," "The Crying Game," "In the Name of the Father." Not to mention Heaney himself, taking home the Nobel Prize in literature.

Last week, the Cheltenham Festival of Literature, the most revered annual gathering of writers in Britain, decided to find out what the fuss is about. The first two days of its nine-day conference in this splendid Cotswold town were devoted to Irish writing. "The Irish Weekend," it was called. Serious thoughts about Ireland past and present were aired; questions about identity, religion, guilt and family were asked and answered. But also, inevitably, thankfully, there was a generous amount of carrying on, and the bizarre was never far away.

Late-night incantations were performed. A case of stigmata was reported. But the essential element was time spent with people enchanted by and in awe of words, the simplest but most mysterious of things. Words in conversation, words in song, words on the page.

The Everyman Theatre, Saturday, 11:30 a.m. Rain buckets down on this city of cream-colored Regency and Victorian architecture. Meet John Walsh, columnist for the *London Daily Independent* and this year's festival director. His full head of hair is a bit wild, his eyes sensitive to light. "God," he says, "I've got a two-day hangover after only one night."

But he's cheerful. Disregarding the season, he is dressed for dinner at a beach resort—white linen jacket and a pink shirt. He introduces a discussion concerned with the church's role in Ireland today. But the three participants—Mary Kenny, Colm Tóibín and Clare Boylan—happily dispense with any mind-paralyzing sociology and tell stories.

"It's not been recorded in Rome, but my cousin Margaret Shannon killed the devil," Boylan says. "Oh, absolutely. When we were bad girls, Sister would put us in a chair facing a picture of Himself, all green flames and horns on his head. Made us sit and look at him, scaring us. But Margaret, after a time, got up, tore the picture off the wall and ripped it to pieces. So we knew, because Margaret was not struck immediately dead, the devil didn't exist."

"It's surely a post-Catholic Ireland now," says Kenny. "We've moved from the era of the family rosary to the age of the strawberry-flavored condom."

Tóibín is the comer in Irish writing these days, just 42 but already that rare professional—the man of letters who is practicing journalism, fiction and nonfiction with equal skill. He brings to mind pictures of Jean Genet, with the bald, perfectly formed head, the blunt, handsome face. But Tóibín smiles often, a thing Genet would not have been caught dead doing.

Town Hall, Saturday, 1 p.m. Paul Durcan, one figure in a spotlight, recites to a full house and holds it rapt. He's not considered the best poet in Ireland, but he is the most beloved, because of his humor and his connection to his readers and listeners.

He leaves the stage after waves of applause, the greatest reaction of the festival. Beloved, but something more, something that has come down to Celtic culture from long ago. As Robert Graves has written, "In ancient Wales and Ireland a poet was not merely a professional verse writer; he was acknowledged to exercise extraordinary spiritual power. His person was sacrosanct ..."

Backstage, Saturday, 5 p.m. I bail from a discussion of Yeats that I thought would turn my frontal lobe to tapioca. Much better to be here, with Deirdre Cunningham and her band as they prepare to perform as part of a midnight collection of poetry, dancing, music and drinks. A blowout. A hooley. Deirdre's band is described in the program as "lethal Celtic world beat fusion." And what is that, Deirdre? "Haven't a clue. Will you have a drink?" I will.

Town Hall, Saturday, 7 p.m. John Walsh, now in a chartreuse jacket, talks with Edna O'Brien in front of a sellout crowd. She is the last of the banned writers in Ireland (for "The Country Girls," more than 30 years ago) and still is storming castles of repression and ignorance. Her new novel, "Down By the River," is a harrowing tale of incest, rape and the destruction of a child, set in the rural West, where she was born and raised.

She is nervous, constantly staring at her hands, but she speaks in a strong, lovely voice. She holds the audience with such *bons mots* as, "When I was a child I thought words were alive. Really. Like other children thought dolls were alive." Walsh speaks little, as mesmerized as everyone else.

Pillar Room, Sunday, 1:30 a.m. Lethal Celtic world beat fusion is coming from every direction, even up through the floor. A pretty woman with a tambourine shouts to a man 3 inches from her: "I wish this night would never end!" He makes signs in the air with his hands.

"There," he says, "I've called on the powers. This night will never end." She throws her arms around him, beating time with the tambourine on his backside.

The Bar of The Queens Hotel, Sunday, 3:30 a.m. No lethal fusion here, where the party has moved, but everyone is still shouting. Walsh has changed jackets; this one's the color of orange sherbet. Belfast poet Ciaran Carson, who recited earlier, has not stopped merely because he's in a hotel bar and no longer being paid.

The Queens Hotel, Sunday, 1 p.m.: Tea for two with Edna O'Brien. Once a great beauty, still a great beauty. We talk of the economics of writing, literary feuds, New York, the writer in the world of film. When she speaks she looks directly at you, and comes in close. At one point she says, "Do you remember when John—did you see John this morning? He's wearing a vest with multicolored fish. When he asked me last night if I'd ever been devout, I said, 'Oh, God, yes! When I was young it was ecstasy! Stigmata! Let's always go for the high notes.' Well, it happened last night. I looked at my hands and there was blood."

A trick of the light?

"Trick of the light! No, it was blood! What do you think of that?"

Town Hall, Sunday, 6 p.m. John Banville speaks about his new novel, "The Untouchable," a story about spies. Banville is one of the leading novelists in English today. He is a small, neat man who writes in a mandarin style. He lays out some radical notions, and discusses his work habits: "One early novel of mine, the first paragraph took me eight months. Then it took me a year and a half to rewrite it." The audience laughs. Banville is surprised. He was serious. But soon he smiles.

Chapter 4
A Wild Colonial in England

The Los Angeles Times *asked me in May 2001 to cover one of L.A.'s native sons, James Ellroy, who was appearing in Cheltenham.*

The old American aphorism that says the road will make a bum out of anyone does not apply to James Ellroy.

Fresh and fit, the bestselling author of 15 books, including "L.A. Confidential," surfaced recently in this town two hours from London. Five European countries and a month of hotel rooms behind him, Ellroy was on a two-week blitz of Britain, hustling his new novel, "The Cold Six Thousand," to be published in the United States on Tuesday. "Do the gigs, do the gigs and then do the gigs," he says, sitting in the green room of Cheltenham Town Hall, waiting to give an evening reading.

For a decade of his young manhood, Ellroy was an addict of amphetamines and wines wrapped in paper bags. Speaking with him, one finds it difficult to imagine what he must have been like then, because you will rarely meet a cold-sober man with a personality more full-tilt boogie than that of the 53-year-old author. Conversation with him is like taking a carnival ride: colorful, bright, too fast, fun and almost dangerous.

Drug- and alcohol-free for 25 years, the native Angeleno seems, even sitting down, to be doing 10 things at once. As he talks about traveling, a cell phone rings musically across the room, and Ellroy, in mid-sentence, looks over and says, "That's the opening of Mozart's 40th Symphony. You know that? 40th. Mozart."

And then he plunges back to complete his interrupted thought. "Do the gigs. If I can sleep, I'm dandy. If I can't, I get a little ..." he pauses, a good actor emphasizing a line, "frazzled. Ten interviews a day, signings, readings every night. I'm in France, and I'm looking around and it's ... France. Great. Fine. Tell people not to smoke and get back some really French looks. Go to the hotel and sleep. Do the gigs."

Like a rock tour, it's suggested. "I hate rock 'n' roll. All that institutionalized rebelliousness. Kids should stop wearing black and listen to their parents. And this tour doesn't have T-shirts. Just books, man. And me. Period. Burn it down! Get it done!"

Prepare, America. The show comes to 25 cities, including two weeks in Los Angeles in mid-June.

A performer in love with his audience and his act, he glances across the room at three teenage girls, volunteers at the Cheltenham Spring Festival, to be sure they're getting it. Cheltenham is, according to Fodor's, "the snootiest town in England," and the girls, while not completely nose-in-the-air, are studiously nonchalant while reveling in a close encounter with the self-styled "demon dog of American literature" (he tends to growl and bark on occasion).

"Britons are fascinated, appalled and repelled by America. They have a powerfully ambiguous relationship with us." But the teenagers, like every other English person he comes in contact with, don't seem ambiguous; they're perfectly charmed by the 6-foot, 3-inch, 200-pound fountain of energy.

For Barbara Hillhouse, a 29-year-old who came to the festival from Glasgow just to see him, Ellroy's work "brings a whole world to me. I don't know if it's truly America, but it's a complete world." Asked about the crisis of the foot-and-mouth epidemic resulting in the mass slaughter of British livestock, Ellroy reveals some contradictions. The avatar of mayhem and extremely bad attitude says, "I hate it that so many nice animals have to die. I give money to all kinds of animal causes. I'm a vegetarian. I'll never eat an animal." He also, at times, appeals to "my seldom sought Lutheran God. I dig Martin Luther, man. He burned the world, as he saw it, to the ground. The greatest Catholic of his age, the first Protestant."

The chronicler of *noir* sleaze now lives in a tony suburb of Kansas City with his second wife, former *L.A. Weekly* journalist Helen Knode. He met her in his favorite hometown spot, Pacific Dining Car at West 6th and Witmer streets. Why Kansas City? "Quiet. I have a turbulent imagination but live a quiet and peaceful life. I listen to classical music. I work. It's the only way I could write the new novel. The story of American violence in the 1960s."

"The Cold Six Thousand" begins a few minutes after the assassination of John F. Kennedy in 1963, precisely where Ellroy's last bestseller, "American Tabloid," ended. It is a tale of bent cops, Mafia blood opera and government cover-up that ends in 1968 with the murder of Robert Kennedy in Los Angeles.

"This is the first time you'll see the real world, the underworld of that era. I take you to Cuba, Vietnam, Las Vegas. You meet the quintessential American fiend, J. Edgar Hoover. You meet Martin Luther King, Jack Ruby, Howard Hughes. My latest masterpiece, man."

Demon dog, maybe, but he really seems to be the Muhammad Ali of American letters, all brag and boast swinging from a hook of sweetness. Reviews in Britain have been overwhelmingly favorable for "The Cold Six Thousand," with the only negative reaction questioning the style. Readers will either be enchanted by the three-word-sentence/one-sentence-paragraph technique that propels the speed-bag narrative or, simply, after reading a hundred pages, be on the ropes, punch drunk.

Striding down a hall on his way to a sound check, Ellroy recalls financing his first tour himself, turning "The Black Dahlia" into a 1987 bestseller. "I figured out how I could use my mother's death, reduce it to sound bites and sell books. I addressed the exploitation of her in 'My Dark Places.'" A stunning redhead who was much too fond of

Early Times bourbon and picking up men in low bars, Ellroy's mother was found beaten and strangled to death, dumped in some bushes in El Monte on a June night in 1958. Her 10-year-old son was taken to live with his beloved father, a man spectacularly incapable of raising a child. His deathbed advice to his son: "Try to pick up every waitress who serves you."

When his father died, the 17-year-old was alone in the world. For the next 10 years, he used every drug he could find, chased by wine and vodka. He lived in parks and abandoned apartments. He stole food, jimmied coin boxes in Laundromats and broke into houses in Hancock Park to steal women's underwear. The county jail was home 25 or 30 times. "The people over here used to think I was some kind of bad man. No. I was low life, pathetic, a buffoon."

At 28, he was a barely burning cinder. Pneumonia, abscesses on his lungs and auditory hallucinations was the pit where he decided to make his stand. "I realized I wanted things. Women. Then one woman. I wanted a decent life. I wanted to write books." Los Angeles, Ellroy has written, is his "mythtown." Myth in the older understanding of the word, as a serious attempt to describe a particular place and a set of calamities that shows the community the underlying moral faults and motivations that define them.

Fictionally, he has moved away from L.A. with his last two novels, but he has kept his hand in as a writer for *GQ,* doing pieces on Mexican boxing and, this fall, profiling District Attorney Steve Cooley.

His sound check is a recitation of a long, obscene and very funny poem boasting about his writing and his sexual prowess. A British camera crew for "60 Minutes" is delighted. The soundman, in the sharp accent of East London, says fondly, "Ah, he's gobsmacking."

There are 150 or so people for the reading, a young crowd, in an ornate room of red-veined pillars and creamy molding. Ellroy has them from the moment he takes the stage. "Good evening, peepers, prowlers, pederasts, pets, panty sniffers, pugs and pimps. I am James Ellroy, the foul owl of the death growl, the white knight of the far right," and continues with a rhymed couplet concerning his penis. The room is rocking.

(Asked earlier about his politics, Ellroy replied, "My opinions are all over the place. If there is a political model, it's newsman Bill O'Reilly," the shout-maestro of the Fox News Channel's "The O'Reilly Factor.")

Afterward, a line snakes through the tall corridors of Town Hall to get books signed by the author. He stands, disarming everyone who approaches with his chatter, making everyone part of the show. To a tall, pale boy with dreadlocks: "Hey, the Rasta man!" Softly, to a shy, bearlike, auburn-haired young fellow: "Come on up here, Red. Give me that, and I'll put my name on it." To a man in his 40s who wants a book signed for his son: "Why? The boy some kind of junkie?"

The last book is sold and signed, and he says, "Is that it?" He growls. "I want more. More. More."

Chapter 5
Mirth & Misery

When I was in my teens, my older brother Jack returned from a trip to Ireland and handed me a well-read paperback of "At Swim-Two-Birds," saying only, "Read it and we'll talk."

Years later, my editor at the Los Angeles Times, *Tony Lioche, and I were talking about "The Third Policeman," and when a biography of the author was published, I was on my way to Dublin for the paper. From August 1998.*

Mention his name—or, rather, any of the three names he used—and it's like one of those codes used by secret societies. If you get a blank stare, you know you're dealing with one of the uninitiated. But if there is an immediate smile (always a smile), you know you're in the company of a fellow member, another admirer of Brian O'Nolan, or Flann O'Brien, or Myles na Gopaleen.

A good case can be made that after James Joyce, Myles (the name Dubliners use) was Ireland's greatest modern writer. But even though all his books remain in print 32 years after his death, he is not well known outside his native country. Now, however, a penetrating biography by Anthony Cronin, "No Laughing Matter" (Fromm International, 1998), is raising interest in Myles' life and work as the author of five novels and a remarkable newspaper column that ran for 26 years and endures in three collections. A new edition of his first novel, "At Swim-Two-Birds," was published last week by Dalkey

Archive Press. In March, the only film based on his fiction was shown at the Dublin Film Festival. The screening sold out, forcing a move to a larger theater, and *it* sold out. That the first cinematic expression of this quintessentially Irish work was made by an Austrian, in German, titled "In Schimmen-Swei-Vogel," would make perfect sense in Myles' world.

All his work glows, not just with euphoric language, but with deadpan hilarity and a commitment to irreverence driven by skepticism of anything remotely serious or somber. ("If university education were universally available and availed of," he wrote, "the country would collapse in one generation.") But the biography reveals this writer of splendid comedy to be essentially a sad man of many gloomy demons, not least his firm belief in Manichaeism, the ancient philosophy that human life is a battleground of Good versus Evil and that the latter always has fresh troops.

Myles took a well-developed Irish pleasure in bitterness. Much of it was directed at himself: He systematically drank himself to death, seven months shy of his 55th birthday.

On a recent mild Saturday afternoon, Cronin—who was a friend and drinking companion of Myles—came to the Westbury Hotel here to speak about him. It was a First Communion Saturday in Ireland, and the hotel's spacious upstairs lounge was packed with celebrating families. Cronin suggested the bar and settled in for talk and coffee.

"That's such a loaded word, 'friend,'" he said. "He had no friends, really. But I suppose I was, yes, in a way. I was somebody he found it possible to talk with ..."

At 73, Cronin has become a grand old man of Irish letters with an international reputation; he is an active and influential player in the blood sport that is Dublin's literary life. Perhaps his own finest book is "Dead As Doornails" (Poolbeg Press, 1976), a portrait of literary and bohemian Dublin in the 1940s and 1950s. One chapter starts with a description of Myles as "a small man whose appearance somehow combined elements of the priest, the baby-faced Chicago gangster, the petty bourgeois malt drinker and the Dublin literary gent."

Creating Literature in a Second Language

Brian O'Nolan was the name he was born with, in 1911 in the Ulster town of Strabane, near the Donegal *Gaeltacht*, or Irish-speaking area. Irish Gaelic was the language of home, yet four of his five novels would be written in English. Like Beckett and Nabokov, he did much of his most important writing in what was a second language to him.

"His English, especially in 'At Swim,' he treats with that care and scrutiny people used to give Latin in the 18th century," Cronin said, sipping coffee. "It was kind of a remote language because he read English before he was allowed to speak it. He also, like most people in this country, has fun with English. We take it as a rather marvelous invention which hasn't always been here."

The O'Nolans moved to Dublin when Brian was 11, and he entered a school run by the Christian Brothers, of whom he later would write: "Though they were not by any means uniformly savage, the worst of them were scarcely human at all ... I would not be bothered today to denounce such people as sadists, brutes, psychotics, I would simply dub them criminal and expect to see them jailed."

He entered the Irish civil service and in 1939 published "At Swim-Two-Birds" in England, under the name Flann O'Brien. "There were rules in the civil service about publishing under your own name, easily circumvented by a *nom de plume*," Cronin explained. "Even though everyone knew who the author was."

"Flann is a very rare name," he continued. "I've only known one other person named Flann. It's delightful, though; it has a real literary ring to it, doesn't it? Perfect."

A man politely eavesdropping on the conversation said, "You know, now, my father was from East Clare, and there's a church out there, St. Flannen's. Did you know that?"

Cronin smiled. "I didn't. But I'm sure Myles did."

"At Swim" attracted little attention, though it was noticed by Graham Greene and by Joyce himself, who said the author was "a real writer, with the true comic spirit." He called it "a really funny book."

It actually is three books in one, each with its own opening: The protagonist is a writer who creates characters who start to plot against him and eventually start writing about *him*. Over the course of "At Swim's" 315 pages, we come to know "The Pooka MacPhellimey, a member of the devil class," mythological Irish heroes, bone-idle students and Shanahan, arguably the greatest barroom bore in literature. There is wise humor throughout. In a dissertation on evil, the author says: "Put a thief among honest men, and they will eventually relieve him of his watch."

It's a "book of amazing virtuosity," said Cronin, "far beyond the compass of most novelists." Dylan Thomas read it and called it "just the book to give your sister, if she's a loud, dirty, boozy girl." But it sold precisely 244 copies over the next dozen years, until it was issued in a small American edition that sold moderately. Flann O'Brien's other novels were equally challenging. "The Third Policeman" is a strange, chillingly funny description "of the world of the dead and the damned, where none of the rules and laws (not even gravity) hold good." O'Nolan completed it in 1940, but when it was quickly rejected by a publisher, he kept it in a drawer, telling people he had lost it on the train. It finally was published posthumously in 1967.

In 1941, he published his only novel in Irish Gaelic, *An Beal Bocht*, a searing satire that Cronin calls "an astonishing description of the human condition. Human life reduced to the basics. Funny, oh, God. But it's much more than just a joke."

More than 30 years would pass before it would be translated into English as "The Poor Mouth." Meanwhile, aimed at the limited Gaelic-reading audience, *An Beal Bocht* brought in practically no money and became O'Nolan's third commercial failure in a row. He claimed he didn't care, that he had achieved his goal of creating a masterpiece in his beloved mother tongue.

And he wrote no more fiction for 20 years. Never far from a perverse worldview, he seems to have decided, Cronin said, that if the English publishing world rejected him, he would reject it, with silence. "A tragedy," Cronin continued. "There was no publisher or agent fussing over him, advising him if the next thing to do was the right thing."

Finally, the success of a new edition of "At Swim" spurred him to write two short novels: "The Dalkey Archive," in which the eternal war of Good and Evil rages especially fierce; and "The Hard Life," whose characters and themes include Jesuit Father Kurt Fahrt and a plot to enlist the Vatican's support of public lavatories for women.

Flann O'Brien "was an Irish realist, not an Irish romantic," said Cronin. "If he owes any of his popularity to his Irishness, it is not because he presents the place in a rosy or picturesque way. And if he is, right enough, an Irish humorist, he is certainly not an 'Oirish' one."

At Home, His Columns Hit a Nerve

Among the people of Ireland, however, O'Nolan was best known and loved for the column in the Irish Times that he wrote as Myles na Gopaleen (Myles of the Little Horses).

"He got the name," Cronin said, "from a book by Gerald Griffin, very famous in the 19th century, called 'The Collegians,' which was then turned into a play and then an opera, 'The Lily of Killarney.' So 'Myles na Gopaleen' isn't as abstruse as it seems. Well ... maybe it's more so."

The column, which first appeared in October 1940 and ran until O'Nolan's death, "was almost holy writ to intellectual Dubliners," said Cronin. "Its humor became their humor, its mode of response to many sorts of situations, public and private, became their mode of response."

It was so ingeniously elastic that anything could appear in it; it was a machine with many moving parts. To name just three: the Plain People of Ireland, a cunning group, "fond of a drop," who engage cliché and faked ignorance to make their points; Keats and Chapman, a couple of wandering beyond-effete poets who go to great lengths to produce epigrams disguised as puns; and The Brother, a hapless but arrogant figure who has an answer (usually wrong) to all the problems of life.

Myles was not only the writer, but also a figure in the column who had been everywhere, done everything. He could, on occasion, be a publisher announcing a new book: "Limited edition of 25 copies printed on steam-rolled pig's liver and bound with Irish thongs in a desiccated goat-hide quilting, a book to treasure for all time but to lock away in hot weather." He had been Einstein's partner, studied music with Scarlatti, ran colleges, huge corporations and banks. At home he was known as Sir Myles, or "The Da."

He would produce three or four of these columns a week, often writing them in batches on Sunday afternoons, "hammering them out on his Underwood typewriter," Cronin said, "with scarcely any hesitation or apparent agonizing."

But he wasn't paid much for them, and in 1953, financial disaster struck: Because of his constant lampooning of politicians (including his own immediate superior) in his column, the civil service forced him to resign. He took a small pension and tried hustling work as a freelance writer but didn't have much success. Cronin's book quotes heartbreaking letters that O'Nolan wrote begging publishers for work.

A Life That's Tragic—and Comic

His life became one of awful routine. Delivering his column to the Times office early in the morning, he would retreat to the pub and nearly every day of the week had to be helped home by midafternoon. He never traveled, had acquaintances but few friends, had no interest in food, art, music or anything really except pounding out another column and getting to the pub to start drinking all over again.

"When licensing hours changed in Dublin for closing time," Cronin recalls, "everyone knew the new rules except Myles. But he always knew exactly when opening time was."

He was married in his late 30s, but, Cronin said, "I could uncover no hint of sex in his entire life." His wife, Evelyn, moved them into a one-story house with no stairs for her husband to climb or fall down.

His life can be viewed as tragic, but he seemed to live in a world where comedy was inescapable.

Consider the first Bloomsday pilgrimage. In "Ulysses," Joyce had traced a day in the life of fictitious Dubliners Leopold Bloom and Stephen Dedalus. June 16, 1954, was the 50th anniversary of that day, and Myles decided to gather some friends to follow Bloom and Dedalus' steps through the city.

"The plan was an ambitious one," recalls Cronin, one of the five men involved. "The cityscape was to be traversed almost in its entirety."

Two horse-drawn black carriages, the kind still used at funerals then, were hired and the pilgrims assembled in the morning at a friend's house, next to the Martello Tower where "Ulysses" begins. Spirits were high and became more so when, as Cronin says, the host "gallantly set out a tray of drinks." One led to another; the pilgrimage never made it past the first pub mentioned in the novel.

Later that night the friends found themselves in a suburban pub. The landlord, spotting the carriages and Myles dressed in black, came over and said, "Nobody too close, I trust?" Myles said it was a friend, a fellow by the name of James Joyce. The publican inquired if he meant the local plastering contractor. "No," grunted Myles. "The writer."

"Ah, the sign writer!" the publican exclaimed, happy to have solved the mystery. "Little Jimmy Joyce from Newton Park Avenue! Sure, wasn't he sitting on that stool there Wednesday last."

Even when Myles would try to be serious, comedy sought him out. He was the rare writer who could recognize it and bring it into the world. Even his death had a wink about it. As the last sentence in Cronin's biography notes, "He died peacefully and rather unexpectedly on 1 April 1966. April Fools' Day."

Chapter 6
A Post "Graduate" Life

For the Los Angeles Times, *May 2002.*

Charles Webb works in the wee hours, rising about 2 a.m. and writing on a laptop until nearly 6. Creating things that will have an audience beats cleaning houses, acting as caretaker-manager for a New Jersey nudist colony, picking fruit or clerking at Kmart, which is what the author of "The Graduate" was doing, among other things, during a 25-year publishing drought.

And when he's done working and goes to the windows of his apartment, this son of Pasadena, now 63, looks out on the cool and mostly wet mornings of Brighton, on the southern coast of England. It certainly beats a trailer park in Ojai, or a three-year stay at a Motel 6 in Carpinteria, both of which he's called home.

With a handsome new edition of "The Graduate" just published by Washington Square Press –the play based on the book now running on Broadway—and a well-received novel, "New Cardiff" (his first since 1976) published last year and now out in paperback—Webb has made a remarkable comeback. He and his wife Fred even have some financial certainty after years on the margins of minimum wage, maxed-out credit cards and bankruptcy, due to the six-figure, movie-rights sale of "New Cardiff."

His agent, Caroline Dawnay, speaking from her London office at PFD Ltd., Europe's largest literary agency, said, "It's been the fastest turnaround this agency has ever known. From acquiring the rights to releasing the film will have taken slightly less than a year—a great tribute to Charles' talent." The movie, to be renamed "Hope Springs," will open in October and stars Colin Firth, Heather Graham and Minnie Driver.

It's good the check for the movie sale arrived. Webb receives nothing from the new edition of "The Graduate," or from the play, which grossed more than $14.5 million and, though receiving poor reviews in New York, had an advance sale there of $5.3 million, the record for a non-musical. The theatrical rights were sold not long after the book's original publication in 1963, and the novel's copyright was given permanently to the Anti-Defamation League of B'nai B'rith in 1991. Reached by phone in Brighton, where he moved to get away and experience a new culture, Webb said, "Though neither Fred nor I are Jewish, we gave the rights to the ADL because we felt they had influenced us in a profound way, to understand prejudice in all of its forms and victims."

He and Fred are no strangers to the grand, and sometimes eccentric, gesture. Married in the 1960s, they divorced to protest the ban on gay marriage (only to remarry to smooth the emigration process to Britain in 1998), and Fred, formerly Eve, changed her name in solidarity with a support group of men named Fred who suffer low self-esteem. "True story," Webb said, "but the original impetus was for other reasons. 'My father always wanted a boy' would be closer to the mark, although my father-in-law already had two of them, so his appetite was seemingly insatiable in this regard."

The author speaks about success and failure in the laconic manner of an aristocrat who would find it bad form to complain or boast about anything, a man equally at home in a cowshed or a palace. Never bitter, Webb seems amused by most things, but added to his charm and courtesy is a survivor's iron confidence. Asked perhaps one too many personal questions, he responded with a gentlemanly but prickly sense of humor: "Well, what do you think of this? Next time you're at your dentist, what if you said: By the way, I'd be interested in knowing more about your wife. Can I see a picture of her? Is she your first wife? Have you ever been sued? Are you straight or gay? Do you have affairs? How much money do you make?"

Born in 1939 to the son of a successful doctor and, "I suppose we'd have to call my mother a homemaker," Webb boarded at a prep school in Santa Barbara and then went on to Williams College in Massachusetts. He won a writing prize at graduation that allowed him enough money for the two years it took to write "The Graduate." Mike Nichols' 1967 film soon transformed his creation into part of American cultural history.

Reading the novel, one is struck by how Buck Henry's script merely transcribed it, almost scene by scene, line by line, but with two notable exceptions: The word "plastics" is never mentioned, and the novel doesn't demonize Southern California. (The film's first line, also not in the book, is a pilot's announcement, "Ladies and gentlemen, we are about to make our descent into Los Angeles.") Webb said, when asked about this, "If I'd grown up in Peoria, it would've been the same book. I'm happy it's out again."

The roots of his distinctive style can be traced to a trip to London during his college years, when he saw "The Caretaker," by Harold Pinter. "It was the one piece of writing that moved me more than anything else. The dialogue, characterizations, it really stood out, an electrifying experience." In "The Graduate," you can see Pinter's influence, especially the sense of menace beating at the heart of ear-perfect exchanges. Question marks are eliminated where they would normally be employed, which adds a note of alienation between characters who aren't terribly interested in answers anyway but are conversing by rote, barely hearing one another.

The novel holds up well because of its stripped style and the absence of politics, historical events, brand names, fashion or any reference that would place it in a particular era. It's a good bet that certain young people will always understand this tale of youthful inertia, chronicling a few months in the life of a young man with a first-class education but no ambition and less hope, at sea in a culture he finds grotesque, honest enough to say: "I don't see any value in anything I've ever done and I don't see any value in anything I could possibly ever do. Now, I think we've exhausted the topic. How about some TV." Shipwrecked in the real world, he embarks on an affair with his father's law partner's wife, one of the great villains of American fiction, Mrs. Robinson. It is only when he falls in love with her daughter, and then loses her, that he sees the course he has to follow.

"Benjamin is part of a long line of naive, confused, innocent heroes in the coming-of-age tradition of Holden Caulfield," said Morris Dickstein, Distinguished Professor of English at City University of New York, author of "Gates of Eden," the seminal study of 1960s culture, and the just-published "Leopards in the Temple," an examination of postwar American fiction. "'The Graduate' is a generation-gap story, pitting the unspoiled freedom of youth against the sterility of their middle-class families. Its point of view is that older people live unhappy, materialistic, sexually frustrated lives and impose their boredom on the young. That's why it touched a nerve in the '60s. It's a declaration of independence, of generational rebellion in the name of greater innocence and purity of motive."

Six other novels followed, none approaching the success of "The Graduate." Asked if one of them, "Booze," a story of an alcoholic artist, was in any way autobiographical, Webb said: "I've never had that particular problem, though I had a lifelong smoking habit. I finally kicked it, working in Hackettstown, New Jersey. I had to. Any drug limits your perceptive horizons. And at that point in my life, I'd drifted into this job at Kmart, which on one level I thought of as a great lark. But it was a horror show. I felt I was limiting my clarity of mind. To see my way out of it, I discovered a connection: I'm either going to keep smoking and stay here forever, or quit and leave the job. The day I quit Kmart was the day I quit smoking."

Webb speaks of the years without an audience as a "hiatus" and "not wanting to be distracted by the publishing process." He referred to the new novel, a love story and comedy of manners about an artist, Colin, and two women he's involved with. Colin hasn't worked in a while and says, "Some artists go for years without doing any work. It's common with creative people." But then later he says, "I've lost my art, and I don't know what to do." And finally, a startling admission: "I've been leading a secret life, the life of someone slowly losing their sanity."

He's completed a screenplay with the working title "Home School," and is in the middle of a play. He doesn't read much. "Every writer is supposed to provide a list, aren't they, of what they're reading. After writing and thinking and thinking about writing, when I'm done for the day, I'm not much interested in more fiction. I watch 'Eastenders,' this great soap they have over here. In the States, I was addicted to 'All My Children.' Brighton's interesting. It's like the West Hollywood of Europe. Getting a perspective on one's self by leaving one's culture is important. I felt like I was soaked in all things American."

He paused. "It's always good to go away."

Chapter 7
The Novelist at Home

A visit to Ian McEwan's home in Oxford, for the Los Angeles Times *in May 1999.*

Ian McEwan, winner of last year's Booker Prize, Britain's most prestigious literary award, for his novel "Amsterdam" (Nan A. Talese/Doubleday, 1998), has lived in this small university town for 15 years. But there are other places he wouldn't mind calling home, he said recently, standing in his workroom, a high-ceilinged space looking out on a narrow street and a long oval park, garden colors shining in the wet, gray afternoon.

"I could live in France. I could easily spend a year or two in Manhattan. And L.A., I like it there. I like the architecture, actually."

Admiration of Los Angeles architecture from a man who lives in an 1852 limestone townhouse in a city renowned for its classic buildings, streets and parks? Is this proof of the popular image of the novelist's perversity? Perverse being one of the kinder press descriptions. For years he was "Ian Macabre" in the tabloids. When his work took a new turn in the 1990s with the novels "Black Dogs" (Doubleday, 1992) and "Enduring Love" (Doubleday, 1998), London's daily rags renamed him "Ian Makesyouqueasy."

But he's serious about his admiration for the look of Los Angeles. "There's a wonderful book on L.A. by, oh, what's-his-name? He taught me to see the city in terms other than a tottering Hollywood sign on a scrubby hillside." McEwan reveals himself as not a perverse but a precise man, as he moves to the shelves for the second time in 10 minutes to find a book to illustrate a point.

There is no denying he has gone against the mainstream from the beginning, when his early work consisted at times of incest, child murder, sexual games ending in ritual killing, detailed descriptions of dismembering a body, subjects that astonished readers and made his reputation. But it is precision, not the labels of grisliness or prurience, that has allowed him to make a successful career as a novelist. The quality is apparent in everything he does and surrounds himself with, from the beautiful prose and flawless plots of his 10 books, to his highly polished Giorgio Armani glasses, and the neatness and elegance of his home.

He runs the house by himself, living with his two teenage sons from his first marriage, with visits from his second wife, Annalena McAfee, a journalist who lives in London.

"It's tricky," he said. "I have to be here because of the children, their school, their world. I don't really want to remove them from that. My wife's hours make commuting difficult. We sort of patch it together. We've invented a name for it—telegamy. Sexual relations at a distance."

Slight, wiry, at 51 he has an athlete's quick grace and sureness of movement, kept fit by serious hiking, tennis and skiing. His eyes are bright, amused and surprisingly kind. In contrast to his quirky reputation, McEwan is a welcoming host, at ease in a long sweater and khakis, explaining the art in his workroom. He speaks in a light, cultured voice, and his conversation is thoughtful, expert on a hundred topics, often outrageous and funny. He picks a small ivory ram off the top of his computer screen.

"A gift from a hiking friend. He was impressed by my goat-like tendencies." Here, every morning at 8:30, after he's sent the boys to school, McEwan works in longhand, sometimes switching to the word processor, not breaking until 1 o'clock.

"A daily routine of waiting, watching, moving slowly. Patient. If I can get those four, five, six, eight hundred words down before lunch, I don't really mind what happens the rest of the day."

Started Out With Tales of Violence

His first collection of stories, "First Loves, Last Rites" (Random House, 1975), published when he was 24, were diamond-hard tales of violence, sexuality, adolescence as a theater of cruelty, and here and there a psychopathic narrator. "I was astonished at the fuss," he says. "I'd been reading 'Lolita,' 'Naked Lunch,' 'Celine,' 'Portnoy's Complaint.' Part of the premise of serious literature is that anything can be expressed."

"Amsterdam" is something of a departure, a short novel about two friends, a journalist and a composer, who make a pact to help the other die if they ever come to suffer a debilitating illness. It is a devastating comedy of manners. "'Amsterdam' is an Evelyn Waugh tribute novel," McEwan says. And, like the best of Waugh, "Amsterdam" is a pitiless dissection of a generation, McEwan's own. At one point, the author skewers his contemporaries with a sly riff: "To come of age in full employment, new universities, bright paperback books, the Augustan age of rock 'n' roll, affordable ideals, they consolidated and settled down to forming this or that—taste, opinion, fortunes."

Is there anger in this indictment? "The baby boomers are now presidents, prime ministers, heads of corporations, graying novelists," he pauses, and smiles, "entrenched like any other generation. No worse, no better. They've got their claws on the levers of whatever operates the machine that distributes power. They haven't become desperate. They've become Machiavellian."

The doorbell rings downstairs, and McEwan excuses himself. At the door is an elderly woman with the screech of a Michael Palin character in a Monty Python skit. "I've come for the sea shells," she states.

"Sea shells? I'm sorry, I . . . the sea shells . . . I am sorry, but I'm not sure. . . ."

"They're not at home, and I've come to see them," she says.

It becomes clear. McEwan's neighbors are named Sichel. He invites her in to wait for them. Upstairs it is noted that this could be the opening of a McEwan story.

"Yes," he says in a whisper. "Now, how do I murder her?"

Mr. McEwan Goes to Hollywood

McEwan has also written for the movies, most notably "The Ploughman's Lunch" with Jonathan Pryce and the screenplay from his novel "The Innocent," which will star Anthony Hopkins, Isabella Rossellini and Campbell Scott.

"20th Century Fox asked me to write a 'bad seed' movie. I said, yes, phoned my agent and asked, 'What's a bad-seed movie?' He explained, and I said I'll do it on one condition: no sulfur and brimstone. It had to be a story about psychological realism. They agreed. All executives were delighted by the script. Until the guy who gives the green light said, 'Where's the sulfur? Where's the brimstone?' We all got sacked. But, you know, it's a novelist's duty to go to Hollywood. You would never, in an average bourgeois life, see people behave so badly. Spectacularly badly. It's like being in the court of some extraordinary Italian prince. People are meant to behave badly. They do it with such a flourish. I went to Hollywood and saw all Shakespeare's plays lived out."

Always a man of the Left, especially during the Thatcher years, McEwan can't help telling a story that goes against the grain. "I was once invited to speak on a panel. The topic, 'Eroticism and the Left.'" He rolls his eyes. "I was asked, among these worthies, I suppose, to be the one who would talk dirty. My point was that the erotic was the possession of no ideology. Many people, for example, have fantasies of being dominated, and this might run right against their politics. Then came the foot-stamping and angry clapping in the hall. People muttering, 'Get him out of here.' I continued, saying you might want to get Nelson Mandela out of prison but that wouldn't stop you fantasizing about being handcuffed to the bed and flogged before sex. I was hustled off the stage to sounds of 'Get him out before we beat him up.'"

Downstairs, the unexpected guest is again speaking in her high-pitched, insistent tone. The Sichels have arrived. The novelist takes a turn in his garden as a light rain falls. "Well, at least she didn't move in," he says.

His words written for the day, his talent recognized with the Booker Prize, and his house in order, Ian McEwan seems able to handle it even if she had.

Chapter 8
In London Paging All Bibliophiles

Sometimes freelance writing can seem like stealing. Being paid a fee and expenses to poke around bookstores is one of those experiences. For The Washington Post *in January 2004.*

London is one of the most secretive cities. The purpose of exaggerated English politeness is to hide rather than reveal. Silent parks wait, concealed just a few steps off streets running black and red with taxis and buses. Empty squares lead to cobblestone mews proceeding through shadows.

It gives everyone a gentle thrill of anonymity—everyone, because London is the multi-racial capital of Europe—and heightens the city pleasures of privacy and solitude in the midst of millions.

In most places, reading is a distant second on the list of most enjoyable private, solitary acts, but in London the gap narrows. Since the rise of the popular theater in the Elizabethan era, when Modern English was formed by poets into the most flexible and expressive of tongues, Britons have rightfully prized their language above all their other gifts. Reading and the collection of books approach obsession here, and to find the passionate heart of this world, walk along always-jumping Charing Cross Road and enter a quiet alley flanked by a café and the top-hat-and-bowler-strewn display window of Lipman & Sons Ltd.

Cecil Court (pronounced Seh-sill) runs a short distance to St. Martin's Lane, but more than a dozen shops stand stacked as tightly as books on a shelf, all honoring anything printed on paper.

Here are antiquarian and second-hand bookshops devoted to nearly everything: children's literature; books in Italian; "The Witch Ball" (for anything to do with music, opera or ballet); shops selling autographs, old cigarette cards, ancient bank notes, posters and all manner of treats, if you have the patience to entertain your vice. And that word is not too strong, considering that Richard Davenport-Hines's "Vice: An Anthology" grants 12 pages out of 600 to the topic of "Reading" (almost the same number as "Alfresco Sex").

In P.J. Hilton, near the middle of the short alley, a high-ceilinged front room no more than 10 feet square has a pleasant aroma of paper, glue and leather. When proprietor Paul Hilton is in the below-street-level warren of the shop with some of the 8,000 shelved books—there are 4,000 more housed elsewhere—it is so quiet the ticking of a wall clock sounds clearly, admonishing that there are so many books and such a brutal lack of time.

Hilton, a small, calm man with perpetually amused eyes, specializes in English and American literature, and translations into English of European masterpieces. "I've learned to stick with what I like," he told a visitor. "Whenever I buy art books it's a disaster." He also specializes in antiquarian religious books, which he also personally collects. "It's a bit of an obsession," he said with conscious understatement, pointing out a Bible on a top shelf that could serve as the cornerstone of a building.

"A woman came in recently and wanted to buy that, but the husband refused, saying, 'Not me, I'm not lugging that thing all over London today.' "

Business is good, he said. "One must have enthusiasm in the book trade. People will stand for anything. They'll even put up with rudeness and inefficiency, but never indifference," said Hilton, the soul of competency and courtesy.

Across the alley, the door to Pleasures of Past Times was slightly opened, and when a visitor entered and closed it, owner David Drummond, at his post behind a tall counter, said, "Would you mind leaving it ajar? I find it more welcoming."

If you can't kick a bad theater jones, Drummond, 73, who has been on Cecil Court since 1967, can help with his incredible stash of theatrical collectibles, including posters, playbills, photographs, autographs, manuscripts and books on the arts of make-believe. The tiny shop is a gold mine of books on acting, plays and anything related to the performing arts, from toy theaters to everything you don't know about the circus.

He spoke about his own work on the London stage and bit parts in film and television. "When people ask if I was an actor, I tell them, 'I'm an is, not a was.' I still keep my Equity card up to date."

A man browsing through the more than 3,000 objects asked if there was anything on fish. "Fish in the theater?" Drummond paused. "Afraid not, and we don't have anything on angling." The man said he wasn't interested in fishing but "the animal." Drummond, with precise timing, looked silently at the man for an extra two beats, before politely directing him to another shop on Cecil Court.

There are few raconteurs as agile in conversation as Drummond. Ask him his theory why Dr. Jeckyll, of novel and horror movie fame, should be pronounced "Jeek-el," or why Grimaldi is the father of clowns. And be prepared for a dazzling verbal tour, with inevitable diversions from the main path, guided by one of the more witty Londoners.

It's worth the trek to go to Highgate, 20 minutes north of central London, and visit Fisher & Sperr to seek out J.R. Sperr and his four floors of books, numbering almost 40,000. Fisher, like Marley, is dead, but Sperr, at 90, seems far from it. His shop is probably the greatest of antiquarian and secondhand bookstores in London. Superbly organized, every shelf holds treasure, from a Coleridge first edition worth $14,000—"My friend lives in a house Coleridge lived in here in Highgate," Sperr said, as if the 19th-century poet had moved out a week ago—to a French encyclopedia, complete in 35 volumes, valued at close to $80,000.

Sperr showed the masterwork in a back room, explaining that they were books that changed the world. Originally commissioned by the *ancien régime* in 1750, the first few volumes greatly disturbed the powers that were. "Like all good writing and research, they exposed myths the royalty wanted to maintain," Sperr noted. Banned from continuing their work, the authors went underground and took 30 years to complete the encyclopedia, which Sperr maintains was one of the causes of the French Revolution.

(A close student of the Revolution, and a book-crazed resident of London, is buried a short walk away in Highgate Cemetery. Stop by to see the grave of Karl Marx, topped by a massive bust, and the legend on his tombstone: "The philosophers have only interpreted the world in various ways—The point however is to change it.")

The building of the bookshop dates from 1670, and it once had a large back garden. "It's all been taken over by books," Sperr said, leading the way to rooms of shelves behind the main shop.

"We're at the highest point of London here, and my lounge has a view looking out over the whole city below," he added happily, with the certainty of a man who knows that even a flower garden withers in comparison to being surrounded by books, a chair to read in and a long view of a beloved city.

Chapter 9
Dublin Books

A ramble around Dublin was another assignment where I kept looking over my shoulders for the robbery squad. This was April 2009 for The Washington Post.

Ireland is a nation whose most revered object is a book.

That would be the Book of Kells, and you could do worse than visit Trinity College in Dublin, and pay homage to the 1,200-year-old masterpiece, a hand-drawn manuscript of the Gospels where the distinction between word and image disappears. (Go early in the day, since getting a later look can be similar to standing in a Dublin bus queue gone wrong, with urgent elbows and hips gently but inevitably moving you out of the way.)

After bending your knee at the great Book, it's a treat seeking out contemporary Dublin temples of the printed word. You'll set out for places and find people. Make your way to the Georges Street Arcade. Step out of a delicate rain greasing the pavement into a glass-canopied bazaar crowded with shops and stalls selling everything: coins, stamps, cards, jewelry, vinyl records, clothes of every era and description. If you're concerned about a future decision, there's a tarot card reader who can stop you before it's too late.

If you're hungry, there's a four-stool chipper (a fish-and-chips counter) with one customer bending the ear of the counterman, who has the empty expression of one who has heard it all before. But if you're hungry for books and conversation, there's the small, crisply kept Stokes Books, where Peter Conway considers every visitor an honored guest. That includes a fellow just leaving, looking as if he'd dressed in the dark with clothes found on the floor that morning. "People come in, you'd think they're beggars," says Conway, eyes dancing. "But, no! They're readers, aren't they? Not getting out much."

Asked if Stokes sells only used books, Conway holds up a hand. "Not used, please," he smiles. "Rare." Some are rare indeed, such as an early edition of "Ulysses," a steal, Conway notes, for about $6,500. Story follows story. Speaking of Stokes's mail-order business, Conway says, "The largest amount we ship to the States goes to Texas." He pauses, before adding, "Texans are very Erin-udite."

Between tales of his father's adventures in the silk trade (really), Conway takes a call, and when asked about his accent, replies, "I never had the advantage of an underprivileged background." You take your leave when another call comes in, and Conway cups the phone and reminds you not to be a stranger.

Leopold Bloom, James Joyce's Dublin voyager, poses a test to himself: how to cross town without passing a pub. An equally difficult challenge would be crossing Dublin without passing bookstores or places of literary significance. On Duke Street you'd be stopped twice, by Davy Byrnes pub, where Bloom has a lunch of a gorgonzola sandwich and glass of burgundy (still on the menu), and across the street, David Cunningham's Cathach Books, perhaps the city's most beautiful bookstore.

Mellow light falls on polished shelves, and a mural of Irish literary giants circles above the stacks. Elegant editions by those exalted masters gazing down are available. Catching the eye recently was a $10,000 first edition of "Dracula" by Bram Stoker (who lived nearby on Kildare Street), with a creepily simple cover, an innocent yellow background with lettering the color of dried blood.

Take some time with ancient maps and prints. You might find yourself enchanted by an exquisite chart of Kinsale Harbor by one Capt. G. Collins from 1693.

Thomas Spain is leafing through bound copies of the *London Illustrated News* from 1854. A question about the Dubliner's unusual surname sets Spain off on a history of his family and its "checkered past," coming to Ireland from France in the 12th century. "We're mentioned in that book," Spain says, pointing to an annals of the Huguenots. Books are an issue in Spain's marriage. "I've taken to sneaking books into the house, my wife saying, 'We can't eat books, you know.' "

Asking Cunningham to wrap up the volume of Victorian journals, Spain is puzzled someone would ask about his interest in newspapers more than 150 years old. "Look deeply enough into the past and you're no longer here, but there," he smiles, and steps out clutching his time machine.

Regan Hutchins, manager of The Winding Stair, a bright, laid-back shop on the River Liffey, uses a boxing term when speaking of competition with monster bookstore chains. "We punch a little above our weight," the young Corkman says, meaning that dedicated customer service creates an edge. "When someone mentions a book, we go first to the stacks before the computer."

Hutchins also doesn't fear competition from electronic books. "I'd rather take Sean O'Casey or Jane Austen to bed without an electronic device."

Hutchins, of course, has a story. Teaching in Budapest, he heard of an opening at The Winding Stair. "I fell off an airplane in Dublin one morning with a very tatty CV, and here I am."

The Winding Stair, with bargains on art books and new releases, is named for the Yeats poem: "My soul. I summon to the winding ancient stair/Set all your mind upon the steep ascent ..." The shop does have a spiral staircase leading to one of Dublin's finest bistros, also called The Winding Stair. Reservations are a must. Ask for a window table, looking down on the river, "always going, never gone," as author David Lozell Martin has it. Browsing in the bookstore and then ascending the stairs for sensational food are not-to-be-missed Dublin events.

Through a nondescript door on Dawson Street, down a flight of stairs, into a narrow corridor haphazardly crowded with books, a dazzling 18th-century drawing room opens up. Welcome to De Burca Rare Books. It's the kind of room that initially makes you lower your voice in the presence of an antique library table on a sea-green rug, a tiled Georgian fireplace and a mahogany mantel flanked by portraits of Edmund Burke and George Washington. Here are globes, prints, historical documents, including some by Cromwell and William of

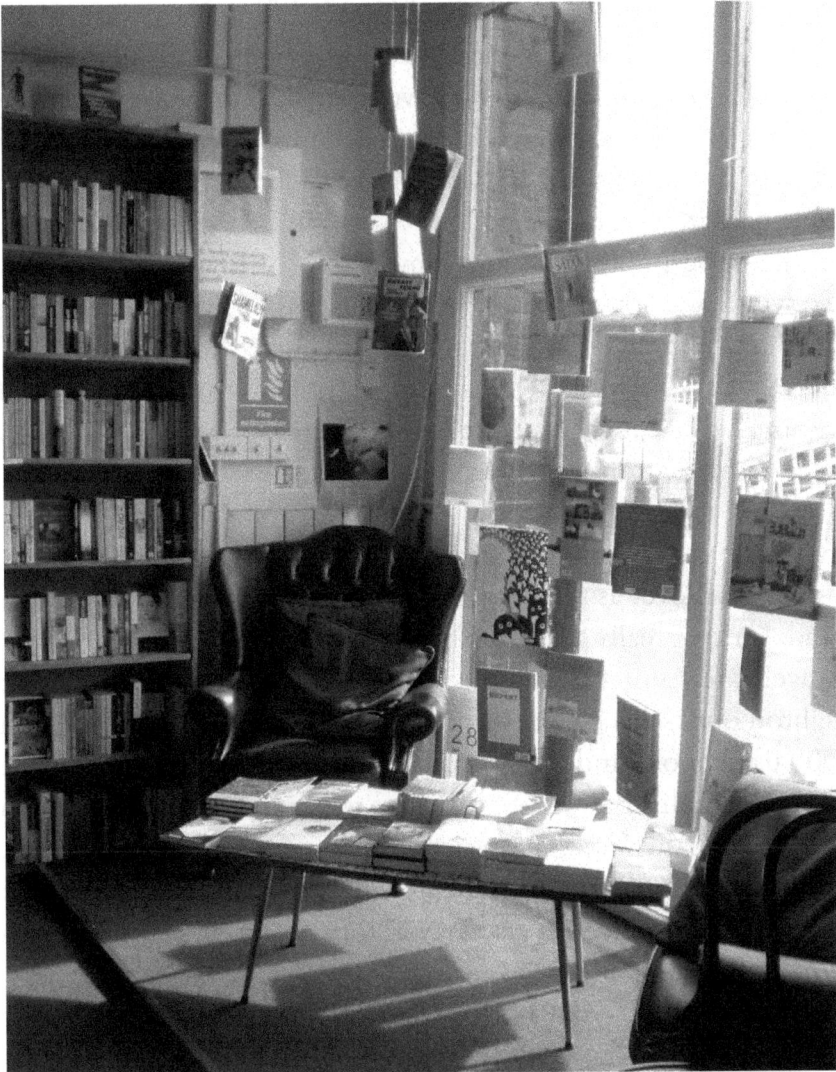

Orange, and, above all, exceptionally printed, bound and preserved books.

The effortless hospitality and buoyant wit of proprietor Eamonn De Búrca, typical of his country, allows you to stop your whispers. Offering tea, he asks, "Strong, medium or weak? I like it so you can trot a mouse across the top of the cup."

From here and his other shop just south of Dublin, De Búrca sends antiquarian books on Irish topics to every continent. He also publishes books under his own imprint. "Here," he says, lifting a heavy tome, one of a five-volume series he has published. "It's a book of Irish genealogy from 1650," De Búrca says. "You have to be mad or brave to publish something like this." Or clever. He rounded up 1,000 subscribers who pledged to pay about $825 each for a set of the series. Every subscriber but one paid in full on publication. "A man in Belize," De Búrca says. "But I'll not be going out to find him."

Conversation flows from one topic to another, eventually leading to De Búrca himself. "I had an unorthodox entree into bibliomania," he begins. Leaving his native County Mayo at 17 for England ("All the young lads went there or the United States for work"), De Búrca worked construction and "was a salesman, a barman and finally a policeman."

When he came home, he started from scratch dealing in books, something he loves as much as he does his native county, in western Ireland. "I never really left Mayo," he says. "Spiritually, I'm still there."

Travel a few miles down the coast to Dun Laoghaire and visit Naughton Booksellers, a basement cave of a Georgian townhouse with 20,000 used books, indexed from "Antiquity" to "Zoos." Across the road from Dublin Bay, it looks toward the dramatic Hill of Howth looming across the water. A long jetty reaches out through the harbor, the place where, one wild night, Samuel Beckett wandered alone, later saying he discovered his literary vision, or in Beckett-speak, a "memorable equinox."

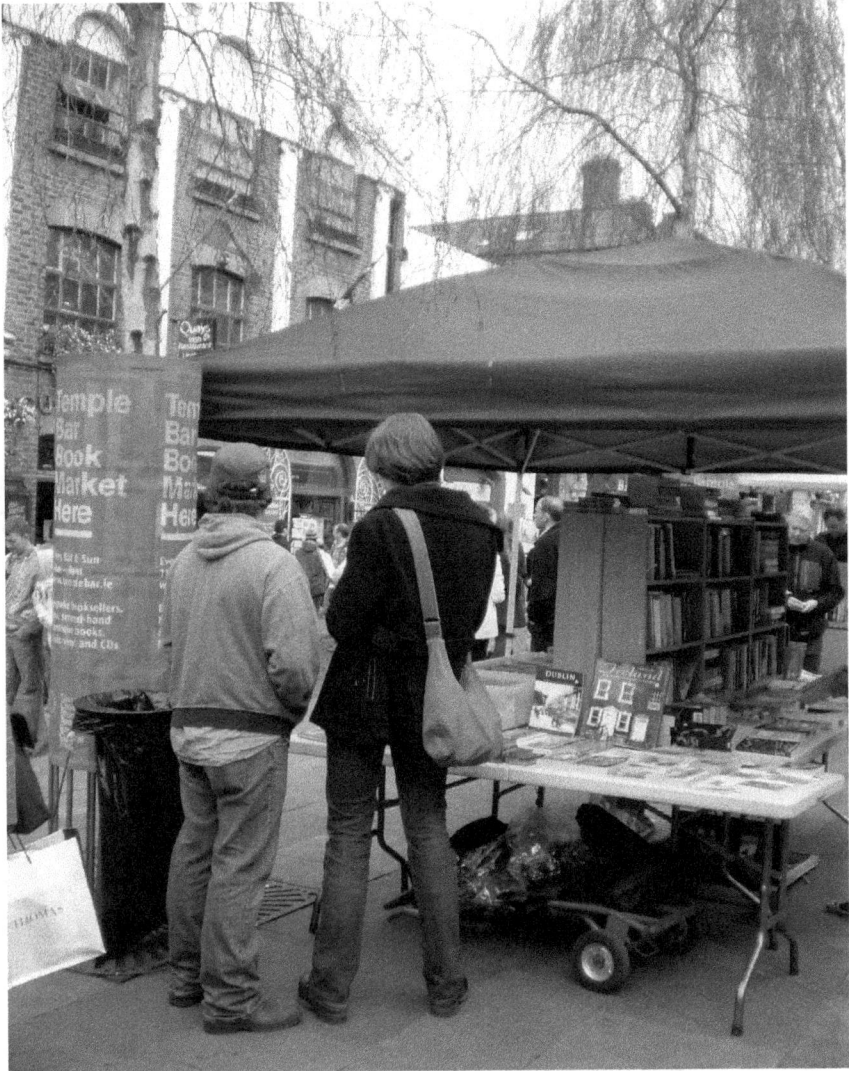

Naughton Booksellers is reached by opening a blue wrought-iron gate in a fence with rosemary fragrantly pushing through. A path leads past daffodils, a patch of lawn and pots of flowers.

The shop is open again after closing a few years ago. Michael Naughton, who runs it with his mother, Susan, says they had gone to an online-only business. But customers kept showing up to browse, forcing the Naughtons' hands.

It seems Dubliners, some of the tech-savviest people on the planet, need bookstores. Not an online add-to-the-cart experience, but a place where actual books crowd actual shelves, welcoming book lovers to share the printed and spoken word.

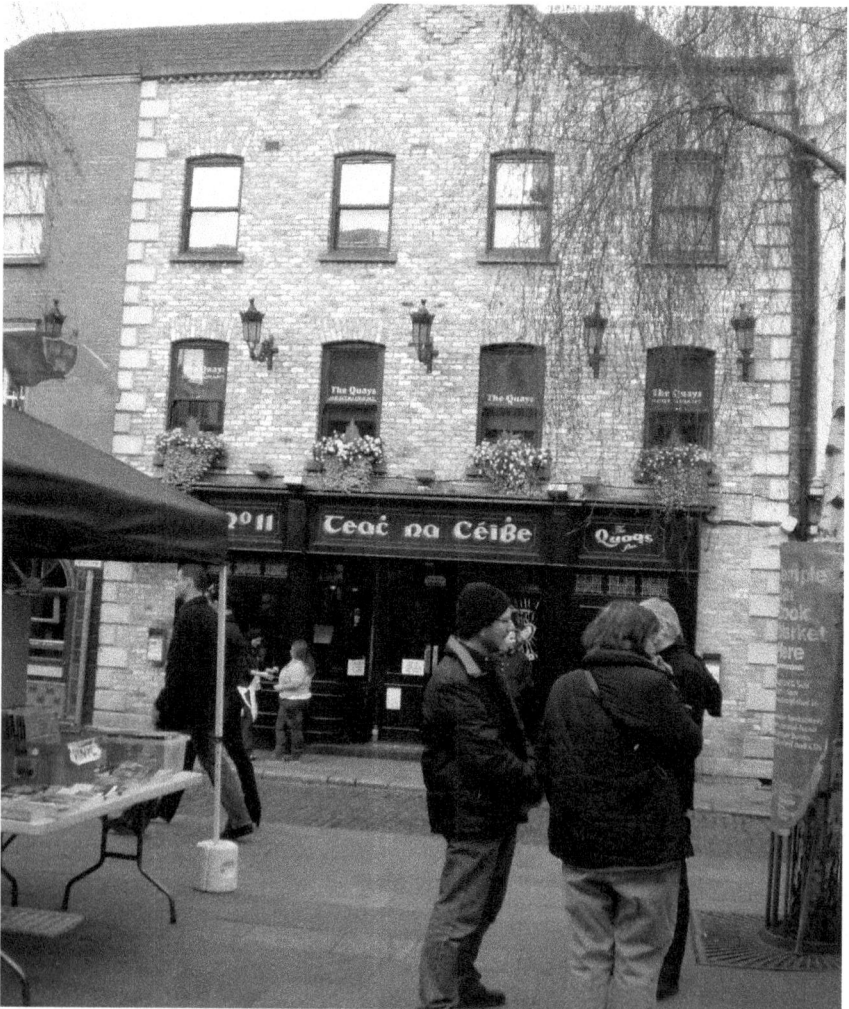

Chapter 10
Meeting Mr. Donleavy

The hook for this piece was news that one of the most famous and best-selling novels of the 20th Century was about to be filmed after years of false starts. It wasn't, and in the piece you can get a hint why. GQ editor Eliot Kaplan commissioned the story in July 1990. It was a gift, gratefully accepted, of two days at a manor house on an estate in Ireland in mid-summer with excellent companions.

No one will ever know the great relief to have people shut out. Or a walled-in garden. Walls forty feet high and I think the three-foot thickness for strength. Hundred acres of it. Boxwood mazes for me to get lost in.
—J. P. Donleavy, The Ginger Man

I was in Dublin, asking around for opinions on J.P. Donleavy, fellow citizen and author of, simply, one of the greatest novels of the 20th century. Some responses:

"Bastard. Did you see that thing he did on Ireland?" said the novelist.

"A bit of a chancer," said the journalist.

"Dreadful writer," said the former government official.

"Bollocks," said the broadcasting executive.

"Insane, isn't he?" said the lawyer.

Many younger readers are not familiar with Donleavy's work. That will change. After years of false starts, the screen adaptation of his 1955 classic, "The Ginger Man," will begin filming, with Arthur Penn directing, late this summer in Dublin. "A Singular Man," based on his 1963 novel, is in preproduction, with Ben Kingsley and Tina Turner being discussed for the leads. And eight other Donleavy novels have been reissued in handsome editions by Atlantic Monthly Press, which also just brought out the new, "That Darcy, That Dancer, That Gentleman," the third title in his Darcy Dancer trilogy.

Casting "The Ginger Man" has been an embarrassment of riches for Robert Mitchell, who along with Philip Donleavy, the author's son, is producing the movie for Bluebird Films. Several popular young American and English actors are up for the title role. Mitchell told me about being in a New York club recently when he was approached by a hot young star: "This girl was hanging on his arm, begging him to take her home and make love, while he was reciting whole passages of "The Ginger Man" at me."

Donleavy himself has no clear idea how many copies of the book have been sold. Since its appearance, thirty-six years ago, there have been something like eighty-five printings. Twenty-five million copies would be a fair guess. But the number of people who have read it is far greater. It's the kind of book that is passed on. As Donleavy told me, "I've never known anyone to have a copy. It's always been given away. Or stolen."

V.S. Naipaul once said of "The Ginger Man," "It is one of the books which reveal their quality from the first line. On every page there is that immediacy all good writing has." Donleavy's style has been called Joycean, and it's true that he shares some things with the master. They are both primarily comic writers, both have a lyrical gift, both write perfect dialogue. But Joyce had many styles, while Donleavy has stayed with one: the use of the short, telegraphic phrase, often without a verb, that Joyce developed for his stream of consciousness, or interior monologue. Donleavy grafted on his own innovations, writing in the third and first persons intermittently, and scattering his tenses. It sounds like an awful concept, like some kind of mind-numbing "experimental" prose, but it works. Also one of Donleavy's many trademarks, the little straggling haiku at the end of chapters.

From the opening page of "The Ginger Man" to the last, we are in the mind of a young man in trouble. With everyone. With everything. He is Sebastian Dangerfield, an American who attends Trinity College Dublin and for most of the book affects an upperclass English accent. He is desperate, crazed, perpetually broke, telling friends that he is off to see his "broker" (pawnbroker) or "accountant" (bookie). He moves at speed from one disaster to another (all of his own making), giving himself nautical instructions when things are going particularly badly: Don't worry, don't despair, save hair. Heave to, head into the wind, sails aback and I'll ride this out even though most decks are awash and I'm taking water amidships."

Along the way—through blitzkrieg monologues, catastrophic drinking bouts, sexual acts on piles of turf, orgies in gloomy wet basements, houses literally coming apart at the seams—Dangerfield holds forth on Ireland, "this English amusement park" or "shrunken teat on the chest of the cold Atlantic. Land of crut. And the drunk falling screaming into the ditches at night ..." He is forever analyzing the country: "I have discovered one of the great ailments of Ireland, 67 percent of the population have never been completely naked in their lives."

Every Irish person has known a Ginger Man. He is the one who just by showing up produces smiles and expectations, who gives license, bringing orders that care, caution and consideration *must* be thrown to the winds. He provides the certainty that there is not enough time and, when you're tired and looking for bed, that you'll have more than enough time to sleep in the grave. You can't sit and brood—there is much too much experience waiting to be captured, too little time to waste before chasing down the night and catching it by the throat. Too many weak benedictions of dawn to see through kitchen windows.

"The Ginger Man," in all his forms and guises, makes you wonder if you should laugh or cry.

Near the end of the book, we get another clue to what all this desperation is about. Dangerfield is running from death the way you'd run out of a house on fire. This theme pervades all of Donleavy's work. The triumph of his characters is that, in the end, they do escape, and somehow death is overcome, either by running from it or running toward it. Or is there a difference?

The last lines of "The Ginger Man" — "Come here till I tell you … On a winter night I heard horses on a country road, beating sparks out of the stones. I knew they were running away and would be crossing the fields where the pounding would come up into my ears. And I said they are running out to death which is with some soul and their eyes are mad and teeth out.

God's mercy
On the wild
Ginger Man."

* * * *

The featureless, prosperous market town of Mullingar, County Westmeath, on a sunny summer's day. A man at the train station, on learning where I was bound, said, "Ah, the great writer," a touch of contempt lighting his tone.

Then he'd met the author?

"No, I couldn't say that."

He'd read his novels?

"No," he said, and then repeated what every creative writer has heard too many times: "I never read novels. The wife does, you know." I nodded. Good that the wife is holding up the fiction end for the family while himself is busy at night with Schopenhauer, Kant and the rest.

The cab ride took twenty minutes through the sort of day in the country that makes you begin to believe Donleavy's contention that the universe is ruled by "a smiling benign God who sports a thick Irish brogue."

We turned off the road onto a lane, between two stone gatehouses, and entered a dream. Up a hill, amid lush greenery, stood a two-story gray mansion: Levington Park, built in the 1700s by a wealthy man for his mistress, Donleavy would tell me later. The driver turned between two stone lions in front of the house and parked next to Donleavy's black 1972 Daimler Sovereign.

The distaste and violent bitterness that many Irish feel for this man they've never met is because of Levington Park. Less than a hundred years ago, their ancestors would have delighted in running the residents of country mansions out into the night and putting torches to the symbols of their oppression. Like elephants, like loan sharks, the Irish never forget. To their everlasting fault, Irish people distrust success—even success absent of any trappings—in their midst. Most reactions to Donleavy are, I think, poisoned by this feeling. A partial list of writers who have suffered it includes Yeats, O'Casey, Beckett, Frank O'Connor, Sean O'Faolain. It's the matter of a critic, or of an average citizen, feeling someone has "put on airs," and Donleavy, living like a duke, is easy prey.

* * * *

Entering the front hall, I was greeted by Suzanne Fetherstone-Haugh, the pretty, athletic young woman who lives with Donleavy. She took me to the sitting room and went to fetch the author. Two school-age girls at the piano ignored me, an easy thing to do in a room that size.

Paintings, drawings and watercolors were everywhere, most done by Donleavy, who often has exhibitions in London and Dublin. His *Evening Standard* Drama Award sat on the mantel of the marble fireplace, reminding me that he is a successful playwright as well. The award is a female figure holding the masks of comedy and tragedy. Someone had capped her head with the wire from a Champagne cork.

A handsome man, fit at 65, with a lean face, close-cropped thinning white hair and a white-and gray beard, James Patrick Donleavy entered the room, dressed in a tweed jacket with leather patches at the elbows, cuffs and lapels, tan trousers, stout shoes, a checked waistcoat, an ascot and, spilling from his jacket's breast pocket, a yellow handkerchief adorned with fox heads. He then told me he couldn't understand the fuss that people made about his wardrobe. He's obviously vain about his appearance, feuding with the novelist John Irving about several things, not least, I think, Irving's criticism of his clothes. (When I talked with Irving later he said he admired "The Ginger Man." What about Donleavy's more recent work? "Oh," Irving said wickedly, "has there been any recent work?")

Donleavy has an extraordinary voice, rich, musical, perfectly clear. His accent is one of the strangest you'll ever encounter. Part London, part Irish aristocrat—and, sneaking in now and again, his native New York. We had been talking for five minutes or so when Donleavy noticed I was distracted by Alain, Suzanne's 6-year-old son, who was rattling around the room over the floorboards in a low-slung tricycle, shrieking. The author seemed to have been unaware of the commotion.

"Ah," Donleavy said, gently but firmly, "Alain, would you mind taking that outside? You'll find it's much more fun on the terrace." The boy nodded and roared out of the room. I was puzzled. Was this the man who wrote so tellingly, so lovingly, about paranoids, madmen who left havoc in their wake, who drank themselves silly at every opportunity, were oversexed as rabbits, would threaten to strangle a crying infant, reveled in fistfights and general chaos? Through the better part of the two days that I spent with him, I would see a glimpse of the satanic grin, the occasional wild gleam in the eyes. But when, I wondered, would Mr. Hyde fully appear?

Born in 1926, of Irish-immigrant parents, Donleavy had a fairly conventional American childhood, growing up in the Bronx. After serving in the Navy briefly at the end of World War II, he was accepted at Trinity College Dublin, and set off to a time of his life that formed him not just as an artist but as a person. Overnight, he found that he was an aristocrat.

Now, carefully, ever so carefully, buttering a scone in front of the fireplace, he said, that if you were at Trinity College, it conferred upon you a social status in Dublin. "It gave you a right and a privilege. It meant that at some stage, after you'd sown your wild oats and rampaged around Dublin in pubs, you were going to be a famous barrister, a famous doctor, a judge, a governor of a country. That was implicit and part of you as a student, and recognized."

Having social status and a bit of money wasn't a bad thing in Dublin in those days. Coming from America, and a life of relative comfort, he was stunned by the city's "thronging mass of poverty. Dublin at the time of Thackeray was known to have the worst slums in Europe. And it was that bad when I was there." Sipping his coffee, he continued, "As a medical student, I would have to spend afternoons down in some dark basement of a hospital, going over autopsies. It was horrible. And walking down an evening street in those days, out of an entrance to a building would come a procession of people with a little white coffin on their shoulders. A child's death. That was common. Death just walked through the streets. Children wore rags. It was appalling."

One of the first persons he met in Dublin was the playwright, poet and rebel Brendan Behan. "Behan looked like a street boy," he remembered. "He never made any compromise at all with being, as it were, respectable. If he entered a pub in a new suit and someone said 'Brendan, you've got a new suit,' he would reach for his pint of Guinness and just pour it right on top of his head. And if anyone then remarked 'Well, the suit still looks pretty new,' he would get off the stool, go out the door and roll around in the gutter back and forth. Get up and come back in again."

A favorite meeting place of the time was an enormous labyrinth in the basement of a Georgian house. The Catacombs attracted a broad assortment of people—not just artists, but students, revolutionaries, wealthy folk slumming, and those for whom slums were a way of life— and every night, after closing time, drinking, singing and every other sort of revelry occurred. Upstairs was a respectable dentist's office. Someone had stuck a note to the gate leading to the basement:

"EXTRACTIONS UPSTAIRS. INSERTIONS DOWN BELOW."

Two fellow Americans at Trinity became friends. One, a student of literature trying to unravel "Finnegans Wake," was George Roy Hill, later to be the accomplished film director of "Butch Cassidy and the Sun Dance Kid," "The Sting," and many others. The other was Gainor Crist, later to be immortalized as Sebastian Dangerfield, The Ginger Man. Crist fascinated Donleavy. "He came from a sort of Midwest-Brahmin background, but he never had any money," Donleavy said. "Anyway, when he went to Europe, his aunt thought, 'Oh, wonderful, my nephew is attending Trinity College. What does he need over there? Oh, yes, he needs a subscription to *Fortune* magazine. And, I know, he'll need a nice dog!' I came to this tiny house he was living in, and there he was in this rented chair, *Fortune* open in his lap, holding a Great Dane. He'd sent his tweed suit out to be dry cleaned, but in Ireland in those days there was no such thing as dry cleaning, so they immediately washed it. He could barely get into the thing, it was so shrunk. There he was, in this *astonishing* suit, which was constricting his breathing. Then he was leaving, carrying the Great Dane, and I said, 'Gainor, where are you going?' And he told me he was going to have a family portrait done. He couldn't afford to feed the dog—he could barely afford to feed himself—and here he was spending money on a photographer."

More and more, Donleavy realized he wasn't suited to the medical profession. He had begun to paint, but was surprised that many people were attending his exhibitions not for the artwork but to get the brochures, written by the artist. So, the 24-year-old Donleavy left Dublin and moved to a small cottage in County Wicklow, where he began to write seriously. He continued working for seven years in Ireland and later in America, on what would become "The Ginger Man."

But no reputable house in the States or the United Kingdom would publish the bawdy book. One publisher in Boston, after reading the manuscript, said, "There's libel and obscenity in that book, and we would be tarred and feathered were we to publish it." He was wrong. There is no libel, no obscenity. There is only great comedy, great sadness, great beauty. In short, there is nothing less than life between the covers.

Finally, the Olympia Press, a tiny English-language publisher in Paris, agreed to print the book. Donleavy received 250 pounds ($700), dished out from a satchel in the basement of a vegetable shop. When he eventually received a copy of the finished novel, he was horrified. "The Ginger Man" was included in something called The Travellers Companion Series, along with such immortal works as The Whip Angels, White Thighs, Rogue Women and The Sexual Life of Robinson Crusoe. Thus began, perhaps, the longest litigation in publishing history—twenty-five years, resolved with a particularly Donleavyian flourish. "You're now looking at the proud owner of Olympia Press," he laughed. When he heard the firm was in bankruptcy and put up for auction in 1970, he bought the whole thing, lock, stock, and Travellers Companion Series.

Later that afternoon at Levington Park, with kids chasing one another through the halls, Donleavy, dressed in a gray warm-up suit, showed me an amazing sight. In a room off the drawing room, a long table was piled high with every manuscript he had ever written. When asked why, he tried several responses. One was that he was worried about fire at the other end of the house. The next was that Mary, his second wife (from whom he's been divorced now for two years), comes by when he isn't home and takes things. And last was that some "man from Sotheby's" is cataloguing the manuscripts.

Sitting in an Eames chair by the window, Donleavy writes mostly in long hand and then gives the pages to his secretary for typing. She tapes her page to the bottom of the original, and then he corrects it. She types a new draft and tapes it to the bottom of the previous draft, and so on. "Some of these can stretch across this room." Donleavy noted. "The man from Sotheby's said he's never seen anything like it."

He took me for a walk around the property, past the sauna and the indoor swimming pool, a courtyard with a large cistern full of goldfish and out to a stone shed, where a newborn calf stood with its mother. Then he started talking about Joyce and "the Mullingar connection." He'd been investigating a report that Joyce spent time at Levington Park. "I can't completely prove it, but I'm working on it. I spread rumors all the time in newspapers and magazines. If they're published enough times, they'll be taken as truth."

I promised I'd help him spread the rumors, and I just have.

Back at the house. Dream time once more. Red roses spilled from a trellis sheltering the terrace, allowing the sun to shine through haphazardly on the stone walkway. Rebecca Donleavy, a girl of 12, was reading at a shaded table on the veranda. We walked through a small orchard, talking about the scripts Donleavy has written for "The Ginger Man" and "A Singular Man." None of his work has ever been filmed, but not for lack of interest. For one reason, thirty-six years ago "The Ginger Man" would have been too racy for the cinema. Plus, Donleavy refuses to sell if everything is not right. His old friend George Roy Hill, he told me, had once been interested in doing "The Ginger Man" but finally decided not to; he wouldn't want the responsibility if he botched the job. Robert Redford, also a friend, had wanted to do "A Singular Man," but they could never work it out. "One's life is enriched by fooling around with show business," Donleavy said.

Once, when Donleavy was in Paris, a Hollywood producer showed up in Mullingar and waited a week for him to return. The author treated him cordially and negotiated for two days for the rights to "The Ginger Man." At the end, Donleavy asked for one more clause: "If after seeing the film I don't like it, the project is canceled."

We passed a pen holding chickens and turkeys, bred for Donleavy's table. For all its gorgeous parklands, Levington Park is a working farm of 180 acres with a herd of 70 cattle. Up a pathway bordered by yellow roses, we came upon Rory, Donleavy's 10-year-old son, with a cricket bat and a tennis ball. "Shall we take it down to the pitch?" Donleavy asked the boy.

The "pitch" was an open area of grass near the orchard. We banged the tennis ball around for forty-five minutes. Rory trying to teach us the proper cricket stroke and bowling technique. After a while he gave up and swung the bat baseball-style, as Donleavy and I had. The author is a remarkable athlete for his age, going back on the ball like an experienced outfielder, sure-handed, showing off with long runs and over-the-shoulder catches. "You've played this game before," I told him as he belted a long drive into some hedges. Taking a vicious practice cut, he said with mock amazement, "Of course. I was an American kid, after all."

We finished and walked back to the house past the high gray walls of the garden. The clouds were changing their shapes, and a breeze brought perfume from the rose garden. Long ago, writing "The Ginger Man," the author had his poverty-doomed hero fantasize about a place exactly like this, a walled-in garden. Now, Donleavy is that rare man who got what he wished for, a splendid isolation, a comfortable garden to get lost in.

* * * *

At Canton Casey's pub, on Market Square in Mullingar, we sat in a corner and ordered pints. The barman and the patrons treated us with a stiff politeness, quite unusual in an Irish pub.

I asked Donleavy about his critics, and about his infamous reputation in Ireland, but he courteously refused to talk about it. One of Donleavy's mistakes was writing his best book first, producing a masterpiece right out of the gate. He has written several excellent books during his long career, but they've always been judged, unfairly, against the brilliance of his first effort. He did mention that last year's "A Singular Country" had received mixed reviews, the bad ones because they had missed the point.

The book is a sly comedy about the state of modern Ireland. Many people disliked it because the style swings between the voice of an outrageous stage Irishman (perhaps that "smiling benign God") and the vernacular of a countryman holding forth in a pub. The latter is ear-perfect. Just spend some time in Canton Casey's and you'll see what I mean.

The next day, in our corner again at Canton Casey's, pints in front of us. Donleavy happily munching on Sam Spudz Hunger Buster chips, telling me Gainor Crist stories. Crist dating a woman working for Churchill during the war and had the phone number of the command center. "The most guarded sort of place in the British Empire during the war, and Gainor would constantly phone up because he'd lost his shoes." Crist in New York, working as a V.I.P. public relations man at the airport. If he didn't like some celebrity on his way to London, Crist would put him on a plane for Tokyo.

A group of young women came in, each one eyeing Donleavy before going behind a cut-glass partition. "I'm in touch with this vast network of readers all over the world," he said. "Just this morning I got a fan letter from a banker in a small Ohio town. A banker! It's been a rare case that I could ever go to any city and sit down on a bench for more than twenty minutes without someone coming up to me."

"Excuse me," one of the young women said, coming up to him, "are you J.P. Donleavy?"

"Yes, I am," he said with a smile.

"I'm so glad to meet you," she said, shaking his hand, and returned to her group. We heard shrieks and laughter. Twenty minutes later, she returned with a copy of "A Singular Country. "Would you please sign it?" she asked.

"I'd be delighted," he said and looked at the price. "Good God! Did you pay that much?"

She shrugged. I asked the author, "How much will you get of that?" The young woman tried to answer for him. "Enough for another pint?"

"Yes" Donleavy said. "Barely."

"Would you write," she asked, "To Jim, you owe Marie twenty massages?"

"Certainly. Where's Jim?"

"Ah, he's just over there," Marie said. "He's too shy, you know."

She thanked him and left, clutching the book to her breast and returned to more shrieks.

Donleavy sipped his pint and said, with all the rascally panache of one Sebastian Dangerfield, "I should have told her that if Jim doesn't live up to his end of the bargain"— he raised a finger, an ominous tone —"then steps will be taken."

God's mercy on the singular squire of Levington Park.

Chapter 11
Maestro John

I had read John Leonard everywhere he was published, and fell for his incandescent style immediately. When he was literary editor of The Nation, *I sent him a fan letter and some clips and he assigned me three books to review. I then convinced Tony Lioche at the* Los Angeles Times *to do a profile. This appeared in April 2002. John died in 2008 from lung cancer.*

On Sunday at 6:50 a.m., John Leonard may be one of the few intellectuals in Manhattan on his way to work. Or, perhaps, the only member of the literati even awake at this hour, except, of course, for those who still consider it Saturday night.

"In my drinking days, I thought I was a night person," the 63-year-old Leonard says, walking on an empty West 57th Street to tape his spot as media critic for CBS' "Sunday Morning." "But it was just the booze. When I stopped, I realized that I liked going to bed and getting up early."

The massive CBS Building squats on a long block sloping down toward the Hudson River, gleaming in the bright morning. The writer calls his Sunday critiques, which usually run four to six minutes, "sermonettes." And he is something of a political chaplain, using wit to put across liberal orthodoxy from his 1960s active service in the antiwar and civil rights movements. But Leonard can never quite be pigeon-holed, calling down God's wrath on American magazines, for example, from what seems a conservative pulpit: "Why should we shrug our shoulders at the glossy triumph of the kind of scratch-and-sniff journalism that, between pornographic ads for vodka and dot-coms, postures in front of experience instead of engaging it?"

Or calls for plagues on both political houses by arguing that they have sold out to the ruminations of one man, "the gnome of the Fed, Alan 'Chuckles' Greenspan." And he is the rare intellectual, on the left or the right, who not only admits to watching commercial TV, but enthusiastically praises it as "weirdly democratic, multicultural, utopian, quixotic and rather more welcoming of difference and diversity than the audience watching it." Leonard is as happy quoting Karl Marx as he is Ed Sullivan.

In his 10th book, a recently published collection of essays titled, "Lonesome Rangers: Homeless Minds, Promised Lands, Fugitive Cultures" (he's fond of subtitles; his last book, "When the Kissing Had to Stop," pulls a rollicking 36-word train behind it), the author describes himself as having once been "the young man from the provinces," that 19th century avatar of ambition, talent and cunning, who comes up to the Capitol burning to make good. Leonard's province was postwar Southern California, Lakewood, to be precise, where he grew up "word-drunk and moon-maddened."

Walking quickly through the narrow CBS corridors, he points out "the Edward R. Murrow Room, the only place we could smoke." He smiles nostalgically, "Yeah, that was the Black Lung Room." A locomotive smoker for more than four decades, Leonard, feeling perfectly fine, went for a chest X-ray late last year and in January found himself on an operating table having 40% of his right lung cut out. Practically race-walking though the maze of the building, he talks about the difficulties of working without his beloved Tareytons. "I've got to find a new dance at the keyboard."

Lean, long-faced, terrier-quick and nervous, Leonard responds to questions tentatively at first, searching, like all good writers, for the proper opening. After a false start or two he plunges ahead and speaks the way he writes—intense, amused, on wide-open throttle.

"I first went on the air back in the '70s doing book reviews for local news. But," he says with a wicked grin, "when I talked about a biography of Leon Trotsky they suddenly didn't want me anymore."

More than 40 years ago he arrived and "hopped" onto the pogo stick of a New York career, working for *The New York Times* for 16 years, including five as editor of the Book Review, which he transformed from the Buckingham Palace of American letters (either you were asked in, turned away, or, with excruciating ceremony, thrown out) to something open and inclusive. He has been literary editor of *The Nation*, and in his 19th year as the weekly TV critic for *New York* magazine, and has had the CBS job for 13 years.

In addition to the books (including a novel set in Long Beach, "Crybaby of the Western World"), he's written for everything from "the old weekly *Life* before it died for *People's* sins," to *Playboy* and *TV Guide*. He describes what he does as "sorting the signals of an overheated publicity culture, manufacturing opinions instead of widgets."

A subversive with a smile on his face, Leonard lays landmines for sleepwalkers strolling through a book review, a magazine column, a TV appearance. He believes politics and culture are two sides of the corporate coin, and in the Orwellian notion that professing no politics is in itself a political act.

His work succeeds because he's funny and not, like most of his peers, merely clever. Part of his technique is long lists, providing souped-up rhythms with juxtapositions that are revelatory and slapstick at the same time. In "Lonesome Rangers," names are roller-coastered together to make a point about the absurd, yet age-old, practice of living vicariously through manipulated images of celebrity: Chaucer and Edith Wharton, Helen of Troy and Jodie Foster, Plutarch and Liz Smith. It jolts a reader into the recognition that chronicling celebrities is as old as storytelling, and now American media is perfecting the coverage of personality to the point of deafening overload, drowning out information about the real world.

It's curious to learn that Leonard began on the opposite pole of politics, working for William Buckley's *National Review*. Twenty years old and writing captions for UPI in New York, he got a call out of the blue from Buckley who had seen something Leonard had written for an academic magazine. Soon he was in Havana covering the first weeks of the triumphant revolution, close enough to hear the firing squads in the sports stadium.

Pouring coffee, Leonard remembers, "I was one of what Buckley calls the apostates. He hired Garry Wills, Joan Didion and Renata Adler, and thought the charismatics of his personality would take care of the politics. But he had no illusion about me from the start." (Reached later, Buckley said, "John was with us a year or two, drank deeply but insubstantially of conservative doctrine, and went off to distinguish himself." Recalling that in 1975 Leonard went to Moscow, "I think they gave him a potion that put the finishing touches on his apostasy, leaving him otherwise as we found him, a dazzling writer, and a nice man.")

At the studio, Charles Osgood, the host of "Sunday Morning," glides in, looking like a benevolent but befuddled country doctor who has lost his way. Asked about Leonard, he takes a second and then, in that rumble of a voice, says, "Very simply, and most importantly, John Leonard elevates the American discussion."

Leonard goes on the set and sits next to Osgood. He crosses his legs, folds his hands in his lap and is still. One take and he nails it. ("John never misses," the stage manager says later. "Letter-perfect every time.")

His piece this day is about the re-release of "ET: The Extraterrestrial." Twenty years ago seems like a century, he tells his audience, when aliens were "friendly and playful," seeking communication. Now aliens want to "abduct our children and steal our sperm. It's as if our imagination of the other has regressed to the darkest days of the Cold War 1950s, when sci-fi films were full of pods, blobs, body snatchers and collectivized Bolshevik killer ants."

You can tell America's mood and prophesize its political future, Leonard goes on, by examining its entertainment. Paranoia in fantasy mirrors something closer to reality in the body politic.

Twenty minutes later he's walking on a block on the Upper East Side toward a townhouse he shares with his wife, Sue, and "ten or twelve thousand books, we're not really sure." In an upstairs sitting room he talks of how he was formed by a vanishing act, a central theme of "Lonesome Rangers." His mother took 8-year-old John and his younger brother from Washington, D.C., to California, leaving behind her husband, "a very gentle Irish drunk. My mother decided she couldn't stand it anymore and set out to find something, as far away as possible from everything. She's an extraordinary woman, 82 now, still living in Lakewood on Nixon Street, which, as a lifelong Democrat, has always irritated her."

Downstairs in his office, he talks of how the process of writing has changed from when he was editor of the student paper at Woodrow Wilson High School in Long Beach. "My whole writing life they've been removing senses. You had ink, you had paper, you had tactility. I was at *The New York Times* when they closed down the linotype machines, put down carpets, took away the sounds of typewriter keys, carriages and bells, and made paper disappear. But once I started with a computer I realized I was back where I began in high school, that it was a doodle until I chose to make it into a sentence. Once that happened, it restored something in me that had been lost. Playing."

In one essay in "Lonesome Rangers," Leonard examines Elizabeth Hardwick's work, but could be writing about himself, creating literature as somehow playing at jujitsu: "We have been thrown by our own weight, tumbled into deeper meanings, rueful reflections, and surprise perspectives."

Chapter 12
Smoldering Ashes

Tony Lioche and I were talking once about Frank McCourt's "Angela's Ashes," and I told him a few things about Limerick. He suggested a story for the Los Angeles Times *on the city and the reaction of some folks to the runaway best seller. From September 1998.*

On a quiet Sunday afternoon at W.J. South's pub—all mahogany, frosted glass, marble and mirrors—an old fellow at the bar was contentedly sinking a pint of Guinness when a photographer's flash whitened the room.

"I don't like my picture taken," the man snapped, glaring. Assured that he hadn't been included in the shot, he turned away, still angry. Asked his name, he said "Martin, and that's all I'm givin.' The worst thing to happen to Limerick was that book. And the next worse was the likes of you fellas. This isn't a pub anymore, it's a bloody disco. Try and drink a pint in peace and here's another Yank or Englishman or God-knows-who after your opinion. Opinion about a book!"

"That book"—"Angela's Ashes"—a coming-of-age memoir by Frank McCourt is set amid the horrific poverty of Limerick in the 1930s and 1940s. It is one of the publishing phenomena of the century. Winner of the Pulitzer Prize, it has been on the hardcover bestseller lists for nearly two years. Sales are so strong, there is still no American paperback edition. The numbers of copies sold worldwide, in English and in translation, are "like the national debt: I can't begin to understand it," McCourt said recently from his home in Manhattan.

A film version, produced by Scott Rudin and David Brown and directed by Alan Parker, will include Emily Watson and Robert Carlyle, star of the "The Full Monty," as McCourt's parents.

"The whole thing," the author said with comic gravity, "has gotten out of hand entirely."

* * * *

Beyond the numbers of editions and copies sold, there is another sure sign of McCourt's success: the appearance of *searbhas*, the Irish word for begrudgery. "A defining national trait," McCourt said. "They should put the word on the Irish flag. Oh, the snipers are out in Limerick, you can be sure of that."

South's pub features prominently in the book as the neighborhood "local," the place where the family's meager finances go, mostly for drink for McCourt's ne'er-do-well father. The current owner of South's, David Hickey, says there have been many visitors lately, from the world over. Proudly, he shows a picture of a Chinese journalist who dropped in a month ago.

The people of Limerick, Hickey continues, have three opinions of the memoir: "Pro, anti and against the whole debate itself. Deep down, I feel, it's a true book, or 75% to 80% true, and that's a good percentage for memory. The anti crowd says it never happened, the poverty that McCourt describes. Or they say he never should have written about his family that way, you know, his mother being sort of a prostitute. That did not go down well. The pro people say it's a great book, and something that should be said. There were poor people everywhere in Ireland in those days. Everywhere. Don't I remember it," says the 60-something-year-old. "The women in the old shawls and ragged clothes. Toilets in the yards, the smell, Jesus. And cold. And hunger. And some who went through those times have a sense of shame about it. Limerick people take everything so personally, you know."

* * * *

Thin skin isn't all that the people in this city of 150,000 are accused of. Many Irish look at Limerick as forbidding, insular, clannish, hopelessly provincial. It was a grim British Army garrison town for more than two centuries; unlike other Irish cities of its size, it was without a university until 25 years ago. If young people wanted higher education, they had to leave. Meanwhile, culture was defined exclusively by the Church.

"Angela's Ashes" seems to some people just one more black mark against their city, a reaction that hasn't been confined to barroom arguments. Last year, after the University of Limerick awarded McCourt an honorary doctor of letters, comments by phone and letter began to flood in, including anonymous threats.

"The response was overwhelmingly favorable," recalls Colin Townsend, dean of Humanities. "But then there were some saying McCourt had fouled his own nest, that sort of thing. We even got a letter from a convent of nuns in Florida, letting us know what a scurrilous book it was and that giving the author a degree was absolutely disgraceful."

Were the threats taken seriously?

"Enough to get in touch with the police," Townsend replies. "At every event there was security. But it all went smoothly."

* * * *

These days, with its world-class university, and benefiting from Ireland's powerhouse economy, Limerick in many ways has been reborn. The filthy, crowded "lanes" where the McCourts lived are long gone, having been replaced with new housing or gentrified into pleasant rows of brick houses and flower boxes. The poor don't live there anymore.

Indeed, there is a social safety net now, and life for the poor has been eased somewhat since McCourt's boyhood days. But poverty still exists: The poor are still ghettoized, and it is still a struggle to escape. In what ironically are called "estates" such as Southill and Weston on the edges of the city—bleak, graffiti-scarred neighborhoods that are drug-plagued and violent—the dole still passes from one generation to the next like patrimony. And now there are the added scourges of addiction and crime.

In Weston—where the graffiti is about soccer ("Leeds United"), nationalist politics ("Brits Out") and rock 'n' roll ("Metal Rules")—Josephine O'Reilly, 68, invites a visitor into her immaculate home to talk about "that book." She grew up in the lanes before moving to Weston in the early 1950s.

"It was nice then," she says in a clear, musical voice. "We had some beautiful neighbors." Seated at a table in her small, tidy garden, she waves a hand in the direction of the street, shaking her head. "But now these drug people. It's very frightening. I had a car, but it was burned out, right outside there. If they can't steal it, they burn it. If they can't have it, you can't have it."

Still, O'Reilly—who "knew the McCourts, I lived on Windmill Lane with them"—was horrified by the book. "The way he wrote about Angela, his own mother! I think it's a pity. She was a very good woman. I can't see her doing anything bad. And Pa Keating taking a child into a pub, young Frank for a pint, it was a crime to do that sort of thing. I don't believe it a'tall."

She speaks of Malachy McCourt, Frank's brother and author of his own bestselling memoir, "A Monk Swimming." "He was on the radio here in Limerick, a call-in show, Malachy was. I phoned in and said, 'Your brother has wronged your aunt, Aggie Keating.' Malachy said she'd once hit him in the head with a bottle. I said, 'Well, I'm sure you deserved it.'"

When Josephine was 9 years old, her mother died at age 36, leaving a husband and five children. The family lived in one room "and a very small room at that. Right after my mother died, my grandmother stood me on a stool and taught me to wash on an old washboard. At 9 years old I had work."

Asked if her reaction to the book might have anything to do with memories of her own hard times, she answers indirectly: "I can't really be bitter or cross. He's telling the truth in a lot of ways. But why write a book about Limerick showing it in that light?"

* * * *

The call-in radio show of which Josephine spoke is "Limerick 95," a late-night program hosted five nights a week by Gerry Hannan, easily the most dedicated and vocal critic in town of Frank McCourt's memoir.

Hannan is the author of "Ashes," a self-published book ("I paid for the entire excursion myself") dedicated to "all the people who grew up on the lanes of Limerick and were perfectly happy during their childhood." Hannan was born in 1959, well after the lanes were gone; nevertheless, he claims on the book cover that these are "real memoirs." The 383 pages, he says proudly, took him "only six weeks to write." Some say it shows. But sales have been brisk in Limerick—nearly 8,000 copies and climbing.

"I have no ax to grind with Frank McCourt," Hannan says. "And I don't begrudge him the success he's had with his book. But I genuinely feel he was unfair to his contemporaries. I wrote my book to defend the people of the city I love."

At midnight on a Monday, from his studio on the third floor of a downtown building, Hannan broadcasts yet another program on "the controversy." Caller Jim, who describes himself as "a country man down to the ground," says he has not read the book but heard it is "indecent." Caller Terence, "67 today, and lived every day of my life in Limerick," says that McCourt "hasn't a bloody clue. He makes Limerick sound like a third-world country, for the love of God." Hannan asks Terence if he had a happy childhood.

"Happy? If you wanted some help from the church, from the St. Vincent de Paul Society, they'd come, wouldn't they, to your place and say, 'You're not poor. Sell that chair. Sell that table.' "

Hannan moves quickly to a new caller.

Chapter 13
Celtic Skelter

I've reviewed for The Washington Post, Newsday *and* The Nation. *Here's one from March 2000 for the* Post.

THE PENGUIN BOOK OF IRISH FICTION,
Edited by Cohm Toíbín, Viking. 1,085 pp. $40

THE TRUTH ABOUT THE IRISH,
By Terry Eagleton, St. Martin's. 181 pp. $19.95

Colm Toíbín is the leading Irish writer of his generation because he is what was once called "a man of letters," meaning he can move among various literary arts and odd jobs and be professional, knowledgeable, and above all, entertaining.

A journalist and critic of influence, a brilliant novelist, and an author of several works of engaging nonfiction, he now has edited a handsome, densely packed, 1,000-page anthology covering Irish fiction from Jonathan Swift to 32-year-old contemporary writer Emma Donoghue. His long (59 footnotes) introduction is no gentle greeting or awestruck homage, but a literary legal brief of what Irish fiction is and is not. You have to admire his courage. He might be in for it this time.

A similar selection of American or British fiction would most likely be greeted with mild interest and polite discussion before professors carted it away to strip quotes and embalm it. To do what Toíbín has done is to jump over the ropes into a blood sport. Irish fiction, he eloquently explains, has been seen not just as art or the way we live now but as the nation itself.

Commenting on the wild new writing coming out of Scotland, he says, "Books are written, as in Ireland in the old days, to replace a country." Defenders of the sanctity of Irish letters, as pugnacious and pea-brained as the Citizen grilling Bloom about nationhood, will be ready and waiting.

The battle over "The Penguin Book of Irish Fiction" will not be over anyone's being left out (almost everyone made the cut—there are 91 entries, save Tóibín himself, suffering from false modesty—it will be over why some writers are included and why some are given more space than others. The editor will be roughed up by the nationalists asking, Why Iris Murdoch? She's English, surely. Well, all right, she was born in Dublin, but does that make the Irish-born Duke of Wellington—who said that because you were born in a stable doesn't necessarily mean you're a horse—an Irish general? And Bram Stoker is Dublin-born, but isn't that moldy creepfest "Dracula" (127 pages worth excerpted here) about as Irish as some Ricean blood-on-the-bodice porn? Benedict Kiely gets only one story; Frank O'Connor, the Irish Chekhov, is given only a brief stroll of nine pages; but Tóibín's man John McGahern, who he declares has "produced the most impressive body of work of any Irish writer in the second half of the century," gets a gallop of 45 pages.

It's fun if weapons are checked at the door and everyone realizes that it is the editor's party. He can invite anyone he pleases. And a close reading of the introduction will prove that everyone present here belongs because "the purpose of much Irish fiction, it seems, is to become involved in the Irish argument." Stoker is part of that argument, Tóibín maintains, and is uniquely Irish. "If you want to know how love can lead to marriage, read Jane Austen; but, if you want to delve into the secret and dark unconscious of an embattled ruling class, read Bram Stoker."

Toíbín uses Stoker in his essay to explain something Roy Foster calls "Protestant magic," an obsession distilled into art by Anglo-Irish writers such as Charles Maturin, Joseph Sheridan Le Fanu and Elizabeth Bowen. These writers went Gothic with a purpose, explaining, by the means of controlled narrative and grotesque imagery, a doomed class. Remote, decaying mansions in gloomy climates, madness and violent history hidden in the attic, tightly wound aristocrats surrounded by a peasantry they can't begin to understand, a peasantry eager to rise some night and burn their houses to the ground and send them into exile. This material, a good beginning of horror stories, went through the mill of Anglo-Irish history until the grease of privilege dried up and the engine stuttered, seized and stopped for good in the early 1920s. Credit Toíbín for seeing this contribution to Irish literature and including the startling, wonderfully written selection from "Dracula."

About Joyce he is equally good, and brings some news. Some think that Joyce appeared as a kind of literary virgin birth, but Toíbín has found sources proving a debt of patrimony to George Moore, of all people, not only in the unearthly beauty of the last paragraph of "The Dead," but in Molly's solitary bedtime ruminations. Joyce's gift was, Toíbín maintains, to offer "sanctity ... to ordinary experience—and also to memory, love and sex, to companionship, to long, shapeless days and city life, to men half down on their luck, to song." All four of Joyce's books are represented, with "The Dead" and the Cyclops chapter of "Ulysses" reprinted in complete form.

The anthology's greatest success is that, when you turn to something you're familiar with to read an opening line, the result, time and again, will be a lost hour or two given over to the pleasures of the Irish argument. And reading an unfamiliar author is like finding treasure. This is especially true of Donoghue's extraordinary story "Going Back," which ends the book, about a gay Irish woman in England, arguing with herself and her native country.

Toíbín has relied on Terry Eagleton, professor of literature at Oxford, to stand with him and hold his coat as he makes his case about

Irish fiction. Eagleton, the author of books like "Literary Theory: An Introduction," has now cut loose and written a fine, fast and very funny meditation, "The Truth About the Irish," an A-to-Z ramble with "Alcohol" leading off: "The Irish tend not to say 'he was drunk.' But 'drink had been taken.' This is a pleasant way of implying that you were drunk but you didn't do it yourself."

There are only two missteps. The entry "Fairies" says that there are none—they went to San Francisco. This is grubby, stupid and doesn't belong. Neither do the 10 cartoons littering the pages, captioned sketches with all the wit of tea towels bought by hapless Americans on a coach tour.

But any writer who can begin a paragraph with, "The playwright Brendan Behan, whose only resemblance to Adolph Hitler was that he too started off as a housepainter," may be forgiven everything.

Part II
LAWN GUYLAND

Over the past 20-plus years, I've worked for five Long Island papers, and am still at it as editor of the *Shelter Island Reporter*.

One of the great chroniclers of his home region, writer and editor Nick Buglione, has written about the accent of Long Island with dutiful research and wit. He wasn't the first, but maybe he's the best, at perfectly rendering the sound of the place where I live as Lawn Guyland.

But hey, like, you know the Island, am I right? Tabloid treasure. Suburbs of demonic teens, serial killers, Howard Stern. Mix with robber-baron heirs on vast Great Neck estates paralyzed in an F. Scott Fitzgerald hangover, add the Hamptons' celebrity-rutting season tracked by safaris of the nouveau obnoxious, desperate to be invited to the latest party by Mephistopheles in the shape-shifting form of an L.A. super-agent.

Is that Long Island? Let me answer quietly —No.

Does everybuddy tawk like dis? No.

Here are some views of the region I love.

Chapter 14
Tales From The Graveyard Shift

I went to work for Long Island Business News *in 2005 and stayed for seven years. An old friend, Gregory Zeller, was an editor there, and recruited me. The money was better—way—than where I was working, and* LIBN *was and still is one of the best regional business papers in the country. When I was there,* LIBN *was led by publisher John Kominicki, a rarity in that he was a publisher who had come from the editorial side of the business. He was also one of the best journalists I've ever known. He gave me a weekly column on start-ups, and another weekly column on strategies to grow a small business. I edited the second section of the paper, and also did lots of features, with John and Greg letting me—for the most part—do what I wanted.*

This is from November 2009.

Even the simplest things—eating, sleeping, being with the ones you love—require discipline and strategy. For most, it's unhealthy, and in some cases, it's fatal. Even the word is ominous—the graveyard shift.

Ominous and misleading. During the wee hours it can get alive to the point of deafening at that bakery or popular pub. But for all the negatives, there are those who wouldn't have it any other way. Take Neil Maguire, rumbling up Port Jefferson's hills behind the wheel of his boxy milk van at 2 a.m. "I love this job," Maguire said, smiling, looking out on residential streets so still the parked cars seemed asleep. "I love the night."

Maguire has been working on Suffolk County's North Shore five nights a week, from 10 to 6, for 19 years. But catch him quick, he's a vanishing breed, one of only 12 milkmen left on Long Island, bringing milk, juice, eggs, butter, rolls and bread in the middle of the night to waiting porches. Maguire has about 200 customers and makes about 60 deliveries a night. He's lost a third of his customers in the last two years due to the crumbling economy and the many college-age kids who have flown from nests. "Those high school boys can do a half-gallon of milk like it's nothing," he said.

Now 55, Maguire has been a tool-and-die maker, worked on oil rigs off the coast of Louisiana, and dealt blackjack in Atlantic City. But in taking this job, Maguire immediately found not just something to love but a new persona. "Out here, I'm Neil the Milkman," he said with the smile that seldom leaves his face. He's invited to boozy parties he has to decline— "Come on in, Milkman. Are you my daddy?"—and when he was reported as a suspicious person a night shift cop he knew laughed and asked if he could buy a roll. "I love the solitude," Maguire said, hustling out of his van with half-gallon glass jugs of milk. Back behind the wheel he pointed out fellow nocturnal creatures: deer, foxes and owls hunting above darkened suburban lawns.

Statistics vary, but from 10 to 15 percent of Americans are on the job at two in the morning, either working a regular or a rotating shift. And the ranks are swelling. Even before the recession forced people into second jobs, the graveyard shift was claiming new recruits at a rate of close to 5 percent a year.

Another stop. "This guy works for a car dealership and pays me every three months when he sells a car," Maguire laughed. "If people are late paying I leave a note saying, 'Holy cow! You forgot the moo-la.'"

Maguire's wife, Eileen, also works a night shift as a medical technician, so they're not separated by work schedules and have no trouble with sleeping or eating schedules, Maguire said. They're the rare ones. People who work at night disrupt the circadian rhythm, or the body's inner clock. The negative effects include eating and sleep disorders, diabetes and high blood pressure, plus psychological problems stemming from isolation.

A veteran bartender, who didn't want to give his name, said working nights is especially bizarre in winter. "You never see the sun. You get up in the afternoon, take a shower, eat and go out, and it's already dark," he said. "It's like living in Norway."

What's more frightening: The International Agency for Research on Cancer, part of the World Health Organization, has characterized night shift work as a "probable carcinogen" because hormone development, which suppresses tumors, is disrupted and the immune system is weakened by haywire circadian rhythms.

But don't talk to Harold Alcaide about getting sick. "I could get hit by a bus if I walked out of here now," Alcaide said. His attitude might be because he's 27 and can't imagine being anything else but the overnight DJ on radio station Party 105.

Alcaide, like Maguire, takes on a night-world persona when he gets behind the microphone, Sundays through Fridays, midnight to six. He's "Humpty," broadcasting "rhythmic Top 40," meaning hip-hop, power ballads and anything with bass lines felt as well as heard.

At 3:30 a.m., Harold wouldn't be hit by a bus on Veteran's Highway in Ronkonkoma, where Party 105 shares studios with La Nueva Fiesta 98.5. Vets is a frantic thoroughfare during the day, but at night it is deserted, with sporadic squad cars flashing down DWIs. It's also empty inside, with Alcaide not just alone in the studio, but in the whole building, where he stays for La Fiesta until 10 a.m. And he's not finished working on Fridays, instead going to another job, where he produces traffic spots for two all-news stations. He lives, or rather sleeps, at a Bay Shore apartment.

Eating smart takes a disciplined strategy. Leaving the station at 10 a.m., Alcaide tells himself to shun junk and hit the gym so sleep comes easily. It also doesn't hurt to be in shape for his grueling week.

Listeners called and Humpty put them on the air, one from a woman involved in self-love as she spoke and a stripper calling to dedicate a song to her daughter. The DJ just shook his head. Asked about people acting strangely during a full moon, Alcaide smiled. "People are weird, moon or no moon," he said. "I figure 95 percent of people are drunk or something else."

Sam Thomas disagreed with Alcaide about the full moon. "People get weird and stupid," said the Metropolitan Transit Authority police officer who works 7 p.m. to 7 a.m., four nights a week. Recently, he responded to an alarm at an LIRR station. "Full moon. Guy's smoking pot alone on the platform watching me coming," Thomas said. "He had 8 ounces on him and a scale. Another night he would have thrown it away."

Thomas' wife, Sondra, works during the day. Do they ever see each other? "Not much," said Thomas, who has been on the graveyard shift seven years. "Sleeping you can get accustomed to," he said, "Eating you never get right."

Police work is dangerous in the middle of the night, Thomas said. "But I'm six-four and 265 pounds," he said. "People don't push the issue."

After policing trains and stations, Thomas' day isn't done. He's on his way to his business, Bellmore's Personal Training Institute. The second job isn't only for income. "People with high-intensity jobs retire and they're dead in five years if they do nothing," Thomas said. "I like being busy."

Busy is an understatement for what's happening at 4:30 a.m. in a house rising above Jamesport's main drag. Seeking shelter from a wind with teeth, a visitor comes to the back door of Junda's Pastry. Knocking on the door or rattling the window does nothing to the seven people furiously working inside. Someone finally looks up and the door opens to the smell of fresh bread and the sound of Dominican merengue blasting out of the bright room.

Owner Christopher Junda is of Polish descent but said he likes all music and all people, including his crew, which is mostly Latino. They've been working since three, transforming 300 pounds of flour, 50 pounds of sugar and five cases of butter into strudel, pies and bread.

Asked about life on the graveyard shift, Junda says, "Sucks." He calls to a baker, "Right, Nicky?"

Nicky smiles and shouts, "Totally."

Up at 2 a.m., breakfast is a cup of coffee for Junda. Baking until noon, he then works the front of the shop and makes deliveries until 6 every day except Monday. It's hard on friends and family. "People want to relax with you, have a glass of wine, but you're either asleep or exhausted," he said. It takes effort to make a life outside work. "Or be a hermit," Junda said.

Would he do anything else? Junda is amused by the question.

"Why would I want to?"

Chapter 15
Ball Geezer

One afternoon in the late 1990s I saw an unfamiliar tabloid on my newsstand in Queens—the Long Island Voice. *Like it's long gone sister, the* Village Voice, *it was lively, on target about most things, and filled with excellent reportage and writing. I sent some clips to the editor, John Mancini. He invited me to lunch and offered me as much freelance work as I wanted, plus a column. John has worked for every daily in New York City and anyone who has ever worked for him immediately lights up at the mention of his name. Lately he's gone straight and is teaching. Following are a few of the* Voice *columns and stories, which put into action the idea that you don't get paid much in journalism, so you should have some fun. I'll interpose these strays with longer takes on Long Island.*

From July 1999. Somewhere, I hope, George Plimpton is smiling.

Once you've made it as a ballboy for the US Open, you're a ballboy for life. Gary Spitz, a 35-year-old lawyer from Long Beach who's working his 20th Open, tells why: "The best seat in the house. Twenty thousand screaming fans. It's exhilarating."

He's talking about making it, not about *trying* to make it.

I'm no ballboy. I'm a ballgeezer. On this day at the National Tennis Center at Flushing Meadows, 228 people will try out to fill about 60 spots as ball retrievers. Standing on the sideline at the net of a court, I wonder if any of the other hopefuls have trained on red meat and wine.

I follow instructions from supervisor Dorian Waring, an in-shape, middle-aged woman who first worked a court in 1976 at Forest Hills. Waring's coaching me now: legs spread wide as shoulders, hands clasped behind back, head up. It dawns on me that tennis is the only sport that requires servants in short pants.

But I can't afford stray thoughts. I have to focus on stray balls. I eye a 16-year-old kid with a live arm standing at the baseline with a basket of yellow balls, ready to throw them rapid-fire into the net while I run, stoop and pick up, keeping from breaking bones or blacking out.

The writer George Plimpton once went four rounds with Archie Moore. For a long time after his encounter with the light heavyweight champ, Plimpton said he heard Chinese music playing in his head. But raising my hands whenever I hear a doorbell is preferable to this: I am about to be embarrassed before a crowd of more than 100 people standing 10 feet behind my clasped hands. Aged 14 to 20, they are obscenely fit, gloriously tanned, confident as gods, silent as judges—brutal youth.

I heard their snickers, superior laughter, jokey condemnations of another geezer, Kenny Kramer, "the original" Kramer, who tried out a few minutes ago, in imitation of the actor who imitated him on Seinfeld.

I turn to my coach Waring, and say, nodding toward the boy at the baseline ready to throw tennis balls, who is grinning like a horror-movie hangman, "Tell that kid to take it easy on me."

"Sure," she says. Then she yells, "Make him run! He's from Long Island!"

The kid makes like Nolan Ryan and is about to deliver ... and like a true geezer, my mind wanders. I think about the oldest ballboy to work the Open. "The guy's become mythical," Gary Spitz had told me. "About 10 years ago a man from Arkansas showed up, 55 years old. He made it, worked the tournament, kept to himself and then just disappeared. No one's heard from him since."

In the early afternoon, there was a long line of kids in the main plaza waiting to register. One of them was Victor Pelaez, a 16-year-old student at St. Francis Prep in Flushing. His older brother has been a ballboy the past two years, so Victor gave it a shot. "It's something to do," he told me. "And they pay you." Is he a tennis player? "Nah," Victor replied. "Basketball, man. Baseball. Real games."

If he was trying to impress 14-year-old Meredith Berman, who was standing behind him in a tennis skirt and top, it was a bad move. Meredith looked at Victor, but she didn't see him.

Meredith is attending a camp this summer at the tennis center and in the fall she'll enter Great Neck South High. Why was she trying out? "You're close enough to touch Andre Agassi."

The oldest tryout today was Joyce Hartley, a 49-year-old registered nurse and grandmother from Sayville who explained to me, "I've always been competitive. I motivate myself, give myself goals."

Kramer had arrived with his publicist and photographer. He was all legs, long gray hair, enormous teeth and a baseball cap on backwards, quick with the quip. "Speed," he said, reading from the requirements for the job. "Hmm. Don't use it anymore."

When Laura Spencer of WABC-TV threw a ball, Kramer went for it like a spaniel, making Spencer happy by falling down. But hot-dogging didn't earn him a ballboy job. Waring had lectured us: "Go hard. Don't give up on a ball. No showboating. A good ballperson should be invisible out there. Be quick, be ready, be focused."

Back to the present: The future Cy Young winner smokes one into the net and I'm off. Strange, but I've forgotten how to run. I reach down, pick up the ball and head for the sideline. Why does one leg feel shorter than the other? I wheel and throw a perfect one-bouncer to a kid in the far corner. I congratulate myself, but am brought out of my reverie by Waring's shouts, "C'mon, Long Island! Move it!"

A ball into the net, and I'm off again. Why am I running like Rain Man? Up court, down, stop, pick, run. I hear nothing from the crowd. I'm in the yellow chasing zone, responding to Waring's commands. Finally, heart booming, winded, I go to the end lines and throw balls the length of the court. Nothing to it. Cake.

Waring grades me. **Speed:** Adequate. **Footwork/Agility:** Adequate. **Throwing ability:** Good. **Hands:** Good.

Grandmother Joyce Hartley made the cut. When they told her, there were tears in her eyes.

I ask Waring, "Could I do this?"

"Only if you know someone important," she says.

Chapter 16
Driver's Dread

In January 1999, according to The New York Times, *"Starting within the next month, the cars of people arrested on drunken driving charges ... will be seized on the spot and later forfeited if the drivers are convicted, Police Commissioner Howard Safir announced yesterday." In 2002, the law was found to be unconstitutional.*

For the Long Island Voice, *March 1999.*

Eighty people were killed in alcohol-related traffic accidents on Long Island in 1998. Do Long Islanders oppose the government taking away cars from those accused of DWI?

What better way to answer that than to talk with drinkers, drivers, the people who catch them and the people who defend them? We devoted Friday night, March 5, to bar-hopping and cruising with a cop to try to figure it out.

This cold night was even colder for drunken drivers—for the past two weeks, Long Island police have been seizing their cars right on the spot, in Nassau for the first offense and in Suffolk if they've been convicted of driving while intoxicated within the past five years.

8 p.m., Rothman's Steak House, Oyster Bay

Just talking about the new crackdown could give a seizure to any DWI lawyer. "The impoundment of vehicles is politically correct but constitutionally incorrect," declares Oyster Bay attorney W. Adam Mandelbaum, who says he's represented nearly 700 drivers pinched on DWI charges since beginning his practice in 1981. The 46-year-old Mandelbaum came to Rothman's in alpha lawyer's gear—double-breasted pinstripe, subtle gray tie with matching pocket handkerchief and gleaming wingtips.

This particular evening, the restaurant and bar are packed. It seems like every country club on the North Shore must have had kitchen trouble and sent its members here. An enormous moose head gloomily stares from the wall at the buzzing crowd. The dark interior of the bar is matched by Mandelbaum's view of what's going on.

"I don't really believe the government gives a rat's ass either way about driving while intoxicated," he says. "They're using it as an easy moneymaker, collecting fines."

It's a numbers game, all right, but the only magic number you need to know is 0.10. If you're caught driving with your blood alcohol level at that mark or higher, you may want to have a more detailed conversation with someone like Mandelbaum. By then, however, it may be too late to save your vehicle. You may have to prove your innocence to get it back.

"If they really care about DWI," Mandelbaum says of the authorities, "they'd implement the interlock ignition system, which mechanically forbids anyone from operating a car if the blood alcohol is at a certain level." Such systems, in which a motorist has to pass a mini-Breathalyzer test before an electronic sensor will let an engine start, have been used sporadically in pilot programs on Long Island and around the country, even in states where vehicles are confiscated. Although courts have sometimes ordered such machines installed on repeat offenders' vehicles, technical problems have reportedly kept them from coming into common use.

It's the human element that worries Mandelbaum. When Mothers Against Drunk Driving is mentioned, he only gets more heated. "If Nazism ever comes to America, it will come under the guise of Mom and apple pie," he says. "DWI forfeiture laws are a symptom of a growing tendency on the local state and federal level to destroy the constitutional rights of U.S. citizens. Most people are sheep. And sheep get caught by wolves."

9:45 p.m., The Printer's Devil, Port Jefferson

If you want to find the confluence of drinking, driving and the law, this may be the place. A restaurant and bar, The Printer's Devil might better be named The Conflict of Interest.

It has been owned since the late 1980s by Suffolk County District Attorney James Catterson and his wife, Lola. The public record of the place has been controversial ever since Catterson, a Republican, was first elected in 1989. A month after the election, he claimed to have transferred stock in The Printer's Devil to his wife. But three times this decade, he filed papers with the State Liquor Authority naming himself as sole owner.

While he told the SLA he owned The Printer's Devil, he swore every year from 1991 to 1997 in front of the County Ethics Commission that his wife is the sole owner of the bar/restaurant.

Two years ago, Catterson applied to the SLA for approval to transfer the stock. His office said he had waited to file with the state agency those eight years because of an oversight.

In any case, one of the Cattersons sells booze to potential motorists and the other one arrests them and takes their cars away. You could call it synergy. Or the ultimate in paranoia for the bar patrons: drinking in a place owned by the DA. We didn't meet the DA or Mrs. Catterson, but after speaking with a couple of their patrons and a manager we did have the distinction of being thrown out.

Who owns the place? Brian I'd-Rather-Not-Give-My-Last-Name says he doesn't care. The 41-year-old lawyer from Port Jefferson is drinking a beer from a bottle at the bar. It looks like he's beginning to feel no pain, but he's not worrying about a DWI: He says he will walk home. Brian knows the blood-alcohol limit for intoxication and he knows that, according to guidelines handed out by the authorities, four drinks in an hour would classify a 200-pound person as hammered.

Should a district attorney own a bar? "This D.A. should," says Brian. "I know him personally, and this is a guy who would prosecute his own mother if he was convinced she was guilty of a crime. His integrity is unquestioned. There's no conflict of interest."

In Suffolk County, there are 6,000 miles of road, 1 million registered vehicles, and only scattered modes of public transportation. Last year, 57 people died of alcohol-related crashes. That number led the state. And, since 1989, the district attorney or his wife has owned and operated a bar. Six years ago, Catterson didn't prosecute his mother, but one Joseph Dunbar, who drank at The Printer's Devil, among other places, on an August afternoon and evening and later that night, struck and killed pedestrian Daniel Darppraicone, 25, of Port Jefferson. The DA's duty is to investigate crimes. Catterson did just that, saying (at the time) that Dunbar had had only "a shot and a beer" at his place. He also pointed out that it was several hours after drinking at his bar that the crime took place.

Phillip Marsh, sitting on a stool, says he doesn't know what the legal limit is but adds that he never has more than one drink in an hour. Marsh, a 38-year-old executive with Macy's of Roosevelt Field, also doesn't know of Catterson's connection to the bar. "You can't have it both ways," he decides after being told of the link. "Coming out saying you're in favor of strict DWI laws and then making money selling alcohol to people who drive? I mean, nobody who ever drank here didn't jump in a car and drive away drunk? I'm surprised, yeah."

As the conversation continues with Marsh, a big guy wearing a rugby shirt requests a word in the corner. He identifies himself as Pat Campbell, the bar manager. Apparently you don't have to be a potentially drunken motorist to be paranoid. After learning that an article is being prepared on DWI and related issues, Campbell says, "This is none of your business."

"It's not?"

"I'd rather you not ask questions here."

"Why?'

Noticing a tape recorder, Campbell grabs it and the hand that holds it. "What, are you taping this?"

"Is that a problem?"

"Not for me, but maybe for you. I'd appreciate you don't ask any questions here. Do you understand?" With that, Campbell leaves and Marsh asks, "What was that? You can't talk to me?"

Campbell, now behind the bar, says, "No questions. Didn't you understand what I told you? I tried to do this nicely, but that's it. I'm asking you to leave. Understand? Don't make it hard on me. Or hard on you. Do you understand?"

"You're throwing us out?"

"I'm asking you to leave. Understand?"

10:50 p.m., Bee Jay's, Hempstead Turnpike, Uniondale

Out front the marquee sign reads: Happy Hour, Mon.-Fri., 4-7, All You Can Drink, Tap Beer, $5.

This appears to be a paranoia-free place, and no one seems to be getting overly happy or stupid. The bartender, Brian Servat, is busy serving drinks, making change, putting out platters of pub grub. He's 21 years old, works 9 to 5 as a graphic artist and tends bar on Friday nights. He knows the 0.10 limit, but adds, "I think one drink an hour can put some people over."

"A drink an hour?" a big, bluff guy at the bar puts in, "I'd get really thirsty."

Is this new seizure policy fair? "I can see one or two drinks and driving," Brian says. "They shouldn't take your car for that. But if you're driving around totally fucked up, yeah, take the car away."

Barry Fineberg, the owner of Bee Jay's, comes over to chat. He's a portly, friendly man of 50.

"I'm dead against these seizures," says Fineberg. "On constitutional grounds, and the idea that punishment doesn't fit the crime. For a first offense? That's too much. People learn from their mistakes. People

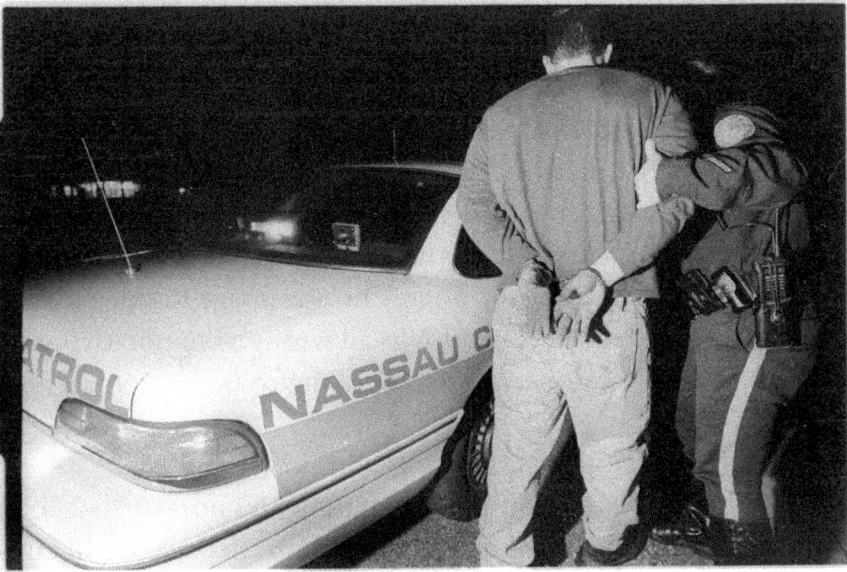

should get a second chance. And on Long Island, if you don't drive, you're stuck."

11:20 p.m., Monterey's Grill, Hempstead Turnpike, Uniondale
Carl Bishop, 20, a student at Nassau Community College, is tonight's good Samaritan for his friends. He's the designated driver. He knows all about the new DWI seizure policy. "Oh yeah, it's gotten my attention, and my friends," says Bishop. "Everyone's talking about this new thing, taking cars. I don't think it's fair, really. Repeat offenders, yeah. But the first time, no. And just being arrested? In the United States, you're innocent until proven guilty. But the new law has rung some bells."

Susan Ronaldson, a 26-year-old waitress from Brooklyn, stops to chat on her way inside to meet a friend. She voices the opinion of every woman, without exception, who is asked this Friday night about the seizure of vehicles. "Take their license, take their car, throw them in jail," she says. "Rights? What kind of rights do we have if some drunken idiot kills us or our families? If it stops people drinking and driving, do it."

Peter O'Donovan, who works at Monterey's, notices the interviews in the parking lot and, in the foyer of the bar, wonders what is going on. He agrees to be interviewed, but a well-put-together man in a short-sleeved shirt, head shaved, approaches quickly. Identifying himself as the manager, but not giving a name, he relieves O'Donovan. Pleasant, courteous, he stands in the door like a parked truck and says, "Sorry, but you can't come in. There's no advantage for me to let you in here tonight. Reporters get things all wrong. I'm not saying you, but most of them. I don't want you talking to my customers about drunk driving."

"What about going in and buying a drink?"

"Sorry, I don't want to offend you, but, no, it's not worth it to me. Go down to McHebe's you know, that white-trash bar. They'll talk to you."

Midnight, McHebe's, Fulton Avenue, Hempstead

If you have a bad headache on a Friday night, come here. You won't be able to tell if the pain is coming from your head or the sound system.

Nicole Demmy, 23, a special-ed teacher from Bayside, shouts over an eyeball-shaking bass line, "They shouldn't be on the road. Absolutely take their cars away. They've got a weapon that kills. Take the weapon away."

Jason Ruggiere, a 21-year-old student at Hofstra, disagrees. "What about the preamble to the Constitution? Did we forget that? Life, liberty and the pursuit of happiness. Drunk driving is serious, but the Constitution and freedom are serious, too. Why give so much power to an individual cop?"

The manager, a guy in a torn flannel shirt and backwards cap who's holding a Budweiser says, "Last interview, pal. The boss says you gotta go. Something about the fire marshal, I don't know. But you're out of here."

1:15 a.m., The Ground Zero, Newbridge Road, Bellmore

Under a cold moon ducking through clouds, the band that just finished playing here shivers in the parking lot, instruments and drum kit boxed and waiting. Maryanne Turndahl, a 21-year-old patron who works in a doctor's office, hurries to her car. She fails the first test: What's the legal blood-alcohol limit? She replies, "It's like 0.15, 0.16 alcohol in your blood. But everyone knows if they can drive safely or not. Don't kid yourself." She's in favor of DWI car impoundment. "Great idea!" She says. "Take these drunk jerks off the road, lock them up, take their cars, absolutely. They're killing people, putting people in wheelchairs for life. Rights, yeah, we all have rights not to be killed by a drunk who decides to drive."

1:45 a.m., Bulldog Arms, Bedford Avenue, Bellmore

Overhearing a question to a bartender about the new vehicle seizure policy in Nassau, Ciaran Hearns, 38, says, "It sucks. Big time." Asked if he knows the legal limit, he says, with a smile, "I don't, but I know I'm well over it." Hearns, who says he's had five pints of Guinness in three hours, doesn't look worse for wear. "But I'm not drivin' tonight. Or any night I have a bit too much. The new law has made an impression, no doubt. I don't believe in driving drunk, in hurting someone or yourself. But I'm a carpenter. I have my whole livelihood in my van. Take my van, because of the judgment of a cop, and I'm struggling to feed my family. They've gone too far."

2:10 a.m., East Meadow Plaza

People are spilling out of Zachary's and Chelsea Street. It sounds like a riot going on. Nassau County Police Officer Billy Staker, 33, wheels his '91 Ford Crown Victoria out of the parking lot, saying, "If you're a fisherman, you go where the fish are. If you're a highway patrolman assigned to SET, you go where the deewees are." (SET is Sobriety Enforcement Team; "deewee" is cop-speak for DWI.)

Staker, like the rest of his unit, works alone. He's been a cop for eight and a half years, the last four and a half as a highway patrolman in Nassau. Tough, no nonsense, he loves what he's doing. The radio traffic is non-stop. "Domestic disturbance at a McDonald's ... suspicious vehicle at ... large group of youths throwing garbage ..." To which the unflappable Staker simply says, "Ah, Friday night."

If you commit a traffic infraction but are sober, you could do much worse than to be stopped by Billy Staker. For close to two hours on this Friday night and Saturday morning, patrolling along Hempstead Turnpike, the LIE and other roads, he stops cars for broken tail lights, erratic lane changes, failure to signal, even a couple of speeders just a few miles over the limit. He cuts them all slack, giving only warnings.

"I'm not out here to just write tickets," he says. "I'm out here to find the drunks."

One exception is a Blazer clocked on the patrol car's radar at 85, passing the parked Ford Crown Vic on the LIE. "Look at that!" says Staker. "This guy is really ballsy. He could see me sitting here. He's getting a ticket for speeding. *And* being stupid." The driver is sober and takes the summons silently.

It's a pretty straightforward job to Billy Staker, one in which political games about the issue of drunken driving seem far, far away. "My job is to get drunks off the road. To protect the public. I want to do it the safest way I can," he says. "Someone gets belligerent, I want to talk with them, not dance with them on the sidewalk or on the highway. Someone's upset, I say, 'Please take a seat in your car while I check your license.' Then I call in other cars. Bottom line, at the end of the tour, I'm not goin' to the hospital. And I don't want to send someone to the hospital. I'm not out here to be a cowboy wrestling with people."

Cruising Wantagh Avenue at a little after 4 a.m., he questions whether the new seizure rules have had an effect. "Too early to tell," he says. "But it's been slower, for sure. We'll have to wait and see." He does a quick U-turn and climbs to 60 the other way. "That car, see that Thunderbird?" he says. "He's doing 47 in a 30 zone."

At Laurel Lane the speeder slows. Staker hits the lights and the car pulls up next to a Dunkin' Donuts and stops. A young guy gets out of the car and looks back sheepishly. He's dressed in sneakers, jeans and a Polo Sportsman sweatshirt. There's a person sitting shotgun and two people in the back seat. Checking the driver's license and registration in the patrol car, Staker says, "These are OK, but I can smell alcohol and his eyes are glassy. He says he knows a cop in the Eighth Precinct. That might help with speeding. But not this."

On the sidewalk, beginning a field sobriety test, the soon-to-be ex-motorist looks cold and bewildered. He gamely tries to follow Staker's calm, easy instruction. Back in the patrol car, Staker says, "His balance is way off, he's having trouble following directions. I'm going to PBT him." This is the Portable Breath Test, a gadget the size of a beeper with a straw to blow into. The driver registers 0.13. Staker asks him to sit in his car for a minute and then radios for a tow truck and another squad car.

The driver is asked to step out of his car and Staker tells him he's being arrested for driving while intoxicated. The driver shakes his head and then hangs it as he's handcuffed behind the patrol car. He'll be taken to 1490 Franklin Ave. in Mineola—police headquarters. The car is searched, and three passengers are let go. Gary Wagner of Bellmore Towing and Recovery, on his fourth police tow of the night, hooks up the Thunderbird and pulls away.

The ex-passengers use the phone at Dunkin' Donuts. "You got a pen I can borrow, man?" says a tall fellow with uncombed hair and bloodshot eyes. "They got the car, oh, man, I've got to call his girlfriend. The car, wow. We only had three or four beers, right?"

Chapter 17
The Un-Hamptons

For The Washington Post, *August. 2000.*

The North Fork of Long Island, the extreme northeastern tail of the fish-shaped island, a two-hour drive from Times Square, is a long, lovely peninsula reaching up toward the Connecticut coast, a place of vineyards, orchards and farms. Coming onto it from Riverhead, the county seat, the landscape changes as dramatically as if you had taken a journey across water to another island. There are farm stands at the edges of open fields under a new sky. There is a feeling of separation and independence.

It has the fragile, water-sourced light of Holland, the climate and soil of Bordeaux, and is the only part of New England that is never designated as such, which may partially explain its feeling of aloofness and don't-tread-on-me spirit. The Main Road, Route 25 (there are two west-to-east roads; the other is Route 48, but always called the "North Road"), is dotted with spare white churches with slim spires, well-tended cemeteries with 17th-century graves and memorials to those who fought against "the rebellion—1861-65." In Robert Lowell's poem "For the Union Dead," a bittersweet homage to his home region, he writes:

On a thousand small town New England greens...
The stone statues of the abstract Union Soldier
Grow slimmer and younger each year—
Wasp-waisted, they doze over muskets...

And there he is in the center of Southold, perfectly described.

The northern side of the slender finger of land is bounded by Long Island Sound and runs in a more or less straight line of tall bluffs descending to pebble beaches. It is unlike any other saltwater bathing. Two or three strides off the beach and the bottom falls away. Not as rough or powerful as the sea, but as silkily cold and clean, the Sound is usually a startling blue and, far out, the deep channels are feathered with whitecaps. The vista extends to the austere coast of Connecticut, and normally is empty except for a fishing boat or two. You are almost always spared the idiot howl of the jet ski. Early morning or near dusk, the ivory-colored pebbles and bleached driftwood turn rainbow tints.

The south side of the peninsula is made of coves and wide necks of woods and farms crossed by creeks and salt marsh, all proceeding east through a series of bays to the Atlantic. During Prohibition, the North Fork was money in the bank for bootleggers. Ships from Canada would anchor at sea and offload hooch onto small quick boats that would then run west in through the bays. Trucks waited on unlit farm roads. The thirstiest city in the world was 75 miles away. Today, it's not hard to understand the smugglers' strategy. Streets run off the Main Road south from villages like Jamesport, become country roads and end in sand.

There's no parking lot; leave the car alongside the low dunes. Bring a lunch—there's nothing but a wide beach and the gentle swell of Peconic Bay. The water is noticeably warmer, shallower and easier to swim in than the Sound, perfect for kids or anyone who wants to splash around or have a good float.

People who come and stay on the North Fork never speak of it as simply moving house, but as explorers making a discovery. The sculptor Robert Berks and his wife, Tod, moved here in 1966 and still speak of it as the place choosing them, not the other way around. In his studio, a soaring old schoolhouse rising from the table-top fields outside Orient, Berks, 78, has created more than 300 sculptures, about 100 of which are in public collections on four continents. At least a dozen are in Washington, including the John F. Kennedy monument at the Kennedy Center and the massive, joyous Albert Einstein Memorial at 21st Street and Constitution Avenue.

In the garden behind their 1888 house, Berks says, "I first saw this part of the world from the water, sailing down the sound and coming around Gardiner's Bay to Greenport. We summered in the area for a few seasons, then put down roots here. This light"—his hands take in the arch of milky blue sky—"is like northern Europe, the Netherlands, parts of France. The weather is different from the rest of Long Island. Winds moving west to east have 90 miles of salt water to pass over. You're aware of the sea, always."

Tod Berks walks through the garden, pointing out peach and plum trees, keeping an eye on two cats hunting through meadow grass. "It's true the light is Dutch, but also you have the Dutch sense of long, long space. There's a freedom about it ... If someone asks why are you here in the winter, then you know they don't understand it."

When the English first settled here in 1640, coming down from Rhode Island and Connecticut, they called the North Fork "the garden of New England." In the last quarter-century, it has been transformed from crops of potatoes and root vegetables to a thriving wine industry, greenhouse agriculture, sod farms, tree nurseries and small organic farms.

Becoming "certified" organic is as time-consuming and arcane as taking holy orders, Karen Lee explains at her farmstand out in the open green fields near Peconic. She and her husband, Fred, have owned and managed the 200-acre Sang Lee Farms since 1987, producing greens for Asian markets from Canada to Florida. They have recently gone retail as well, selling salad greens, potted herbs, cut flowers, heirloom tomatoes and ornamental peppers.

The Lee family originally had farms in places the North Fork locals call "up island," meaning anywhere west of Riverhead, but Karen says they've settled here for good. "It's very beautiful. Quiet. The beaches are beautiful, the air is fresh. The work is all-consuming, but the three children work with us, we're outside all the time. It's a good life."

Standing in the fermenting room of his winery, Ternhaven Cellars, Harold Watts pours some of his formidable Claret D'Alvah and talks wine. President of the local wine council, Watts has the only winery in Greenport, the old whaling village.

Once as important as New Bedford and Nantucket in its day, then a pleasantly sleepy backwater for almost a century, Greenport now is in danger of coming down with a case of the cutes, with twee candle shops and one too many places with names like "Shoetique."

Watts, a droll man taken to wearing flat caps indoors, is asked about the overpowering and delicious smell in the fermenting room. He explains that the French oak barrels allow the wine to "perspire" through the wood. "Every so often we have to top off the barrels with about a liter. So what we're doing now is breathing wine." Which is not the most terrible way to spend an afternoon. Asked about the casks, he talks about wine snobbery, how people can go on forever about which forest in France produces the best oak, how it's cured, etc. He rolls his eyes. "And they haven't even begun to talk about corks. Try some of this rosé. A nice picnic wine, you can drink it all afternoon. You might have trouble standing up, but ..."

In some taste competitions, the North Fork wines have come out ahead of venerable French vintages, most notably scoring well with Rieslings and Chardonnays. There are 23 vineyards and wineries, and all have tasting rooms where you can sample the wine for free. Even if you know nothing, you'll never be embarrassed; the tasting rooms are mostly devoid of wine twits and bores. You can drink a little wine in comfort and learn about it if you want. But be careful: Two or three tastings won't help you navigate the country roads any better.

People are proclaiming the North Fork as the next Napa, and serious money is coming in: A Chilean wine consortium recently bought Laurel Lake vineyards and an executive at New Line Cinema bought a vineyard in Cutchogue.

Watts swirls some merlot in his glass and holds it to the light. "And the prince. Have you talked to the prince yet?"

Sitting shotgun in an SUV, Prince Marco Borghese tours his newly acquired winery, Hargrave Vineyard. The rows of his 85 acres roll away softly with the land on a late afternoon. The sky is clear with just a single reef of purple cloud moving north over the Sound. At the end of each row, yellow roses are in bloom, placed not just for aesthetic reasons but because they're important to the life of the vineyard. The roses are sentinel plants: Molds and pests will appear on them before attacking the vines.

The prince's title comes from the 16th century, when Pope Paul V (born Camillo Borghese) endowed it to heirs of the Borghese clan. "But in America there are no titles. I'm Marco." He, too, came to the North Fork and discovered where he wanted to live. "I'm here by way of accident. I was not in the market for a vineyard. I was over in the Hamptons, visiting friends, and they asked if I'd ever been to the North Fork. So we took a tour. It reminded me of where I grew up in Italy, north of Florence, although here it is so much flatter and, where I was raised, our estate was all hills. But the feel, the sense of place, was the same. That was Thanksgiving of '98. By October of last year we had a deal to buy this property.

"It's a solid place to live. I love the ample expanse of things—vegetables, fruit, fish. The sunsets are truly magnificent. And this wine we all are making. We made wine in Italy when I was a boy. When I bought the vineyard, two cousins called and said, 'I hope you make better wine than we did.' That's no problem. This wine is far superior."

Walking or getting out on a bike is a pleasure here, not just because of the lack of hills but any route you take off the Main or North roads puts you immediately in a pastoral landscape. Take New Suffolk Avenue (a grand name for a blacktop road) where it begins across from the Presbyterian church cemetery in Mattituck.

You pass modest homes on either side and a greenhouse alive with flowers set near a field of potatoes sprouting greenish-white buds. Close to a bridge over wetlands, a swan is nesting while her mate gallantly rises at the approach of a stranger, displaying enormous wings in warning. Under a sky scoured bright from last night's rain, straight vines seem to be in motion as they dip and flow, and at the next turn of the road, the view opens out to more wetlands and Peconic Bay.

A salt creek runs with a cross tide between marsh grass. Working the grass are red-winged blackbirds, each darting wing revealing a sudden patch of yellow in the scarlet. A cloud covers the sun, turning the creek black, and a snowy egret stops his jerky feeding in a tide pool, looks around and goes stone-still.

The road ends at the boatyard in the village of New Suffolk. Up along an inlet, as a barefoot man in jeans and no shirt takes apart a 75-horse Evinrude in his front yard. Down at a gray ramshackle dock, another sunburned man guts a bucket of porgies, throwing offal to a mob of wheeling, shrieking gulls.

Out of town, in Wickham's peach orchard, squat sturdy trees stand in rows on grass speckled with daffodils, the same land the family has owned since the middle of the 17th century. The orchard extends all the way to their farm stand on the Main Road in Cutchogue. Bees float in the warmth of midday as the pink blossoms barely move in the salty breeze.

There is a sharp thin call made by an osprey beating upwind over the orchard. The hawk flashes in a turn and rides down the wind. Watching it glide off toward the bay, you realize there is nothing more important to do than stand here, eyes and ears open.

Chapter 18
When the Whole Car Is Loaded

For the Long Island Voice, *December 1998.*

There are storied trains with legendary names—the 20th Century, the Super Chief, the City of New Orleans, the Orient Express. And then there's the Long Island Rail Road's legendary train. Let Nikki Browne tell you.

"The Drunk Train? Oh, man. Any train after 1 a.m. on Friday or Saturday night, that's the Drunk Train. People are either passed out or partying. And from Thanksgiving to New Year's?" She shakes her head. "Awesome."

It's after midnight on a Friday in Charley O's at Penn Station. People are three deep at the bar and the noise is approaching ear-bleeding levels. Browne, 23, has come in from Farmingdale after her shift at UPS and is nursing beer from a bottle, looking out at the crowd under the Big Board. She's waiting to hook up with a friend and take the subway to the Village. Will she take the Drunk Train home tonight? "If something better doesn't happen. Those late trains can be fun."

How does Browne define fun? "People get different. Some guy stripped in front of me. When he got to his underwear I thought he'd stop, but ... They threw him off and his clothes after him. It can get really loose. I had sex on the train once. In the bathroom."

Bill Clinton-type sex? She shakes her head. "Intercourse-type sex. Cramped. But great." With a stranger? Browne is offended. "Of course not a stranger. He was a friend."

To the regular commuter, the LIRR is a necessary evil or blessing, a rarely changing chore. After midnight on the weekends, people aren't dwelling on the job or home, but travelers either continuing the party or trying to figure out how the night went so terribly wrong.

At Penn Station, you can refuel to keep laughing or drown your sorrows for the ride home. Every pizza joint, deli and convenience store has big plastic ice tubs holding mortar-shell-sized beer cans for sale. The place is well patrolled by police, but no one is told to stop drinking, not even a couple of staggering oafs near the schedule kiosk who think it's the height of comedy to pour beer down the insides of their shirts.

With one exception, people hanging out think that security at Penn and on the trains is adequate. The exception was Patricia, in town with her friend Susan to shop and go to Radio City. Both well-dressed, in their late 20s, they sometimes dread the ride home.

"Teenagers throwing up in the aisles," Susan says.

"And," Patricia puts in, "there are some really weird guys around here. The cops could do a better job."

"Come on," Susan says, "You've dated weirder guys than these."

Patricia laughs. She looks at a man sleeping on the floor, curled up next to a pillar next to the ticket line. Her smile fades, "They could do better."

Raymond Devlin, a conductor rushing to work a late train, says, "The mood during the holidays is usually festive and good. But it gets intense and," he rolls his eyes, "the people coming from the office parties—they can't handle their liquor."

Joe McLaughlin, 47, a computer consultant who often works late in the city, agrees that Christmas brings out the amateurs. Chugging a scotch on the rocks at Charley O's before hurrying to a train, he says in a gravelly rumble, "You can get some lethal bores, man. Last year, for two weekends running, I got stuck with"—insert the name of a washed-up ex-NFL player here—"on the way home. He was living in the Land of the Lame—the Five Towns—and he'd get on, completely trashed, and beg me to talk with him."

David and Jackie, both 16, are waiting to make a phone call. He's a pocket Marilyn Manson, she's in black with Doc Martens and a spiked necklace. They've just been to an Anthrax concert and, like the stylish Patricia and Susan, are dreading the ride home. "The bathrooms are sick," Jackie says. David watches the crowd under the Big Board, his mascara-panda eyes wide. "Lot of strange people down here."

On the train to Long Beach, it's a rowdy departure. Law students break open 12-packs of Bud. People are howling, nearly paralyzed with laughter. After Jamaica, things settle. There's no sex, but something close to it, as people sprawl on top of one another, groping, giggling.

Some voices bravely carry above the racket, more forlorn than joyous. A sweet but wildly off-key voice is struggling through "O Come All Ye Faithful" until she is hooted into silence.

The Drunk Train hurtles through the night. Lights flicker and go out, and then flash on to staring eyes. The doors slide open for the last time and the smell of low tide fills the train. It's the end of the line.

Chapter 19
Nazis In Yaphank

For Long Island Business News, *May 2007.*

Lucille Stroud recalls when Nazis marched through the streets of Yaphank. Yes, Nazis. In Yaphank.

Every place has a past that, if examined, will at best be embarrassing and at worst reveal horror. Yaphank, which some see as a future Melville of corporate headquarters and glittering office blocks, is no exception. For a time, hate was out in the open in the village, glaringly so, and hate's poison was expressed with pride as it sought legitimacy.

Stroud remembers Yaphank as a peaceful, rural place set along a lovely reach of the Carmans River. And she remembers a sleepy Sunday morning in the 1930s when all that was broken by the pounding sounds of marching feet and blaring martial anthems. A special train from New York, regularly scheduled and leaving every week, delivered up to 1,000 people from the city to Yaphank, where pro-Nazi families rallied and vacationed at Camp Siegfried, named for the dragon slayer and savior of Germanic mythology.

Stroud, along with other neighbors, watched American Nazis on Main Street in full uniform singing the "Horst Wessel Song," a fascist marching staple. The would-be storm-troopers flashed the stiff-armed salute under large swastika banners, parading every Sunday from the station to Camp Siegfried.

"Many of us felt a great deal of tension," Stroud said, looking back.

Rising above one of the village's lakes, the camp was a 54-acre retreat of open parade grounds and nature trails with a large restaurant, inn and meeting hall. Bungalows and camping grounds were available for weekend and summer visitors.

From 1934 to 1940 the camp was owned and operated by the German-American Bund, or federation, an organization loudly promoting Hitler and his violently anti-Semitic policies. Yaphank streets were named for the Fuehrer and other Nazi chiefs. A nationwide phenomenon, the bund had 25,000 dues-paying members and an untold number of supporters at its height. There were up to 15 Nazi retreats similar to Camp Siegfried across the country. The Bund's energy was fueled by a sense of resentment and humiliation borne by German immigrants, fleeing the chaos of their homeland after World War I to come to the United States, according to Commack's Marvin D. Miller, 72, the author of "Wunderlich's Salute," the only book about Camp Siegfried.

After Germany's capitulation to the Allied powers, impossible war reparations were demanded of the German people and grinding poverty was the daily condition for a once proud and prosperous middle class, Miller said.

"There was starvation in Germany," Miller said, partly due to a shipping blockade imposed by the victorious allies.

By the 1920s, German politics had descended to street brawls and armed militias. The rise of Hitler and a sense of order, whether real or imagined, inspired the new German immigrants to organize here, Miller said.

The Bund's seriousness of purpose is revealed in Miller's title. In a Riverhead courtroom in 1938, a Camp Siegfried fuehrer, named Wunderlich, was on trial for violating a state civil rights law. Asked to give the Nazi salute, Wunderlich proceeded to do so. When the prosecutor asked if this was an American salute, Wunderlich responded, "It will be."

But why was a foreign, fascist ideology accepted in such an all-American place, once heralded in a patriotic Irving Berlin revue entitled "Yip Yip Yaphank?"

Miller, a teacher who gives a presentation of his research at libraries, noted that Camp Siegfried's heyday was during the depths of the Depression. Yaphank, a bone-poor farming community, was mostly isolated from the dark politics of the greater world and residents gladly sold farm products to Camp Siegfried and rented out spare rooms and even barns when the overflow of visitors to the city became too much for the camp to handle.

By 1940, the Bund was finished as any kind of force in America, its leaders discredited and jailed on various charges. America was opening its eyes to the gallant Battle of Britain and the charnel house of Hitler. In a few short years, the deadly legacy of the Third Reich would become clear.

Little wonder, then, that Miller pushes history as an essential social necessity, expressing astonishment that no Long Island secondary school books refer to Camp Siegfried.

"We have to understand what has happened and what can happen in our own backyards," the author said. "The danger wasn't an ocean away. It was right here."

There is danger in forgetting history, but perhaps more peril in attempts to erase it. Take the 1995 resolution in the Suffolk County Legislature to expunge the names of Yaphank streets named for Hitler and his lieutenants—long since changed—from all official records. Edward Romaine, Suffolk's county clerk at the time, cautioned that it would be illegal to do so and the matter was dropped.

Stroud, who is a member of the Yaphank Historical Society, recently attended a "Victorian High Tea" at the magnificently restored Hawkins House near the river. She, too, believes firmly in history's teachings. "Children have to be taught the past," she said simply.

Yaphank today, although often besieged by traffic, remains a peaceful and quiet community, with the historical society vigorously restoring homes and bringing the past alive.

Forsythia is alive in the winter-damaged woods. Around a curve is a sign next to a private road that reads, "German American Settlement League." Another sign says, "No Outlet." Up the narrow road the parade ground opens, watched over by a large Bavarian-styled building. A tall flag pole flies the Stars and Stripes, and just below it is the German tri-color.

A lone man flying a kite on the open grounds asked a recent visitor if he needed help, and then, politely, noted that the site is a private community for members and guests only.

Chapter 20
Monster Trucks: Fumes With a View

For the Long Island Voice, *February 1999.*

I have seen the future, and it's loud and smells awful.

Saturday afternoon, three hours before the US Hot Rod Monster Jam at the Coliseum, connoisseurs of cacophony and nitro-methane fumes had a chance to see their beloved machines at rest. This was the "Pit Party"—several thousand people on the dirt floor of the arena staring at the monster trucks.

"Wow," Melinda Stein said, staring up at the bile-green Liquidator, which was perched on 5-foot-high, 700-pound tires. "This is really ... weird." Stein, 29, a social worker from Manhattan, was here because her father-in-law was connected to the promotion. "I don't get it." She was the only one who didn't. The hot-rod people, some walking around like stunned believers who suddenly find themselves center altar in the cathedral, others giddy at being in the presence of the objects of their desire, were not what Stein had expected. Bikers, guys in cowboy hats and jacked-up seekers of strong sensations were few and far between. "They're mostly," Stein said, looking around in wonder, "like, *families.*"

Paul Christopher, 42, a state court officer who works in Kew Gardens, had brought his wife, Jeanine, and two sons, Ryan, 12, and Joey, 9. "This is our fourth year in a row," Christopher said. "When we noticed Ryan watching videos of monster trucks over and over and over—"

"For hours," Jeanine put in, happily.

"—we thought he should see it live. And now Joey's into it."

Ryan's favorite? "Grave Digger," he said, pointing at a truck with a ghoul in a shroud rising out of a derelict cemetery painted on its side. "I like it when the cars get crushed down in the dirt," Ryan said, pushing his little fists toward the floor.

Charlie Pauken, 32, driver of Grave Digger, stood nearby, methodically signing autographs. Vendors of T-shirts, flags and programs did a brisk business, with the skull-and-crossbones flag the most popular. Drivers signed autographs non-stop for an hour and a half in the shadows of their fiberglass trucks.

Pauken has driven monsters for 12 years and never been seriously hurt. "Shook up, you bet. Bell rung and gong bonged. But you can roll one of these and walk away. Now the quads—you can definitely get messed up on those."

Behind the Carolina Crusher ("Have you driven *over* a Ford lately?") was a row of the quads, four-wheel blown Japanese motorcycles. Sitting astride one, in a black jumpsuit, was Michelangelo Cravotta, 24, owner of a used-car lot in Riverhead. (Later, in the show, for reasons unclear, he would be introduced as "Mad Mike Angelo from Philadelphia.") When asked what it took to handle one of the wicked little bikes, he said, "Big fucking balls." There was no argument. "And write this down: If you race a quad, tell your wife or your girlfriend to be ready to wipe the drool off you when you're sittin' there paralyzed." A word to the wise.

Bobby Cox, 34, a.k.a. "Hot Rod," was teasing the driver of Bear Foot about something, and signing autographs. Cox, from West Virginia ("Almost heaven, man") was dressed in overalls, a checkered flag bandana and wrap-around shades. How would he describe what he does?

"Comedy. I'm the comic relief. I fill the downtime. Last night the CO2 levels got so high in here we had to stop the show to get some air in. I had to entertain the folks with ad libs for a while."

Truck-jam comedy relief is only a part-time thing. Bobby is really a rodeo clown. "This is like a vacation from rodeo. There's no brakes on a Brahma bull, man. And I'm not runnin' around shit-scared."

At eight o'clock, the Coliseum was packed in anticipation of the races and car crushings.

Conscientious parents were fitting their children with ear-plugs. Down on the floor, the emcee, a burly man with a brush cut wearing yellow and black overalls, wandered around in the dirt raving into a microphone. If he had been doing this on a street corner, he would have been fitted for a straitjacket. The crowd loved his act, especially when he insulted Hot Rod. "When he drives, he's got a tiger in the tank and a jackass behind the wheel."

Low rumblings were heard behind a black curtain. The lights went out, and especially creepy metal rock blared. Spotlights ran around

the arena and settled on the black curtain as Grave Digger burst through. The monster truck posed in the light. People screamed through the smoke.

Chapter 21
Being King, As In Peter

In early December 2009, I went to Washington for LIBN *to shadow U.S. Representative Peter King. A Republican, King retired from Congress in 2019 after representing his Nassau County District for 28 years. He was an unusual politician: the only Long Island representative who had a national reputation as a conservative who had some not conservative ideas, such as being pro gun control, pro union and pro Irish Republican Army. This piece, published in December 2009, is also a snapshot of politics in the early days of the Obama presidency.*

It had started quietly in the Washington office of Rep. Peter King, but now at 10 a.m., a week after Thanksgiving, the volume was approaching a roar.

"It's the full Ginsburg," said Kevin Fogarty, King's chief-of-staff, happily scanning requests from almost a dozen media outlets that had to talk to his boss—immediately, if not sooner—about the White House party crashers. Translation from Capitol-speak: The full Ginsburg occurs when the Washington media pack seeks out a single person who sprints to accept. The term comes from William Ginsburg, Monica Lewinsky's lawyer, who swooned before every notepad and embraced every camera pointed his way.

The gate-crashing story was growing whiskers after more than 10 days on the news cycle, but King had found a way to spruce it up and make it sexy. And in the process put the Obama White House on the run.

Full volume, throttle or Ginsburg—take your pick—is exactly the way the nine-term Seaford Republican likes to live. It's why he's the only Long Island representative with a national reputation, one of the few members of the House who has international visibility, due to his loud, decades-spanning voice supporting the Nationalist side of The Troubles in Ireland.

King's refueling of the gate-crash saga was textbook, something he does in his sleep these days. As the ranking Republican on the Homeland Security Committee investigating the incident, King had the choice of picking only one witness, and masterfully chose Desiree Rodgers, the White House social secretary.

He let everyone know he wanted to question her under oath and ask her why there were no White House staffers checking lists with the Secret Service when Tareq and Michaele Saliah swanned past everyone for their troublesome photo op at a White House gala.

The White House responded that it wouldn't be necessary for Rodgers to come to the Hill, and King pounced, wondering publicly what the White House was hiding.

Seven newspapers from across the country joined several digital news outlets, plus CBS and ABC, all banging on his door for quotes and face time. "*En fuego,*" said Fogarty, King's top aide for 12 years, as he carried the requests into the congressman's high-ceilinged office.

On his own

For a man who thrives on tumult, King is a model of personal stability. His staff is small by congressional standards and has been with him a decade or more, which some say is the sign of a good boss. He and his wife, Rosemary, have lived in the same Seaford house for 40 years, raising two children along the way.

Sitting behind a massive desk with a view of the Capitol dome floating in a rainy sky, King was reading e-mail correspondence from the Saliahs "proving" they had actually been invited to the state dinner.

"Hey, here, you gotta read this from the wackos," he said in the fast, pavement-hard tones of his native Queens, tossing the printout across the desk.

King, who at 65 keeps in remarkably good shape by boxing regularly, had started out a week ago by throwing a few mild jabs at the White House over staffers' handling of the affair.

"Now they're stonewalling," he said, moving from behind the desk, pleasantly surprised at how effortlessly he was throwing off balance an inexperienced White House.

Tempest in a teapot? No way, King said.

"You're talking about the security of the president, and the Secret Service shouldn't take all the heat," he said.

He walked quickly down the marble halls of the Cannon House Office Building, heading for a meeting of the Republican House caucus. Asked if the Republican leadership was directing him on the issue, he shook his big head.

"I haven't heard a word from them," he said, as minority leader John Boehner, his permanent tan almost orange under TV lights, strolled past with a nod. "They see the Democrats playing defense, and so they're saying, 'Let him go.'"

The independent
House Republican leaders have learned that giving King free rein may actually be the only way to deal with him.

He is, after all, the man who said the GOP's romance with Christian evangelicals was turning the party into "barefoot hillbillies who go to revival meetings."

Roy Blunt, former Republican House whip and now running for a Missouri Senate seat, stepped out of TV lights in the Cannon Rotunda to talk about King after shooting a "Holiday Message to the Troops."

Had he ever had to whip the man from New York's third district? Blunt smiled diplomatically. "I like Pete," he said.

"I met his sister one time, and told her, 'Your brother is smart and courageous. But that courageous part is the most difficult part for me.'"

Blunt was gone before he could answer if it was courageous to label Newt Gingrich "road kill on the highway of American politics," a classic Kingism.

Al D'Amato, King's political rabbi when the young man was making his bones in the Nassau Republican machine, once tried to act as peacemaker between Gingrich and King. During a sit-down at the Washington pub, The Dubliner, D'Amato straightened Gingrich out: "Look Newt, Pete's a guy who might shoot you in the front, but he'll never stab you in the back."

True, but King has often strayed from the GOP reservation. He was one of only four Republicans to vote against Bill Clinton's impeachment, in part because of Clinton's commitment to bringing peace to Northern Ireland. The other part: King's disgust at the hunger for gossip he said has consumed American politics and society. It's the same reason he isn't baying for Rep. Charles Rangel's blood, unlike almost all of his GOP colleagues, as the powerful House Democrat scrambles against ethics charges.

"Jesus had 12 apostles," King said. "One betrayed him, one denied him and one doubted him. That's three out of 12. And these guys were the cream of the crop. Come on, stop being so sanctimonious."

He unfailingly supports labor unions, pure heresy for conservative Republicans. He castigated President Bush about paltry homeland security resources for New York and crossed Bush again by supporting Democrats who were demanding that the administration drop a Dubai company's control of six American ports.

He was one of the few Republican House members who voted with Democrats to curb corporate off-shore tax havens, a bill introduced by Rep. Richard Neal, a classic Massachusetts liberal Democrat.

Neal used the word "courage" again when asked about King, adding he has known and liked him for more than a decade.

But isn't "likeable" what politicians do?

"Oh, no," Neal laughed. "You'd be surprised."

Being independent brings admirers, but it has cost King a chance at a Senate seat. In 1999, he was ready to run against Hillary Clinton when Rudy Giuliani dropped out of the race. He thought he could win because his support of Hillary's husband took away the "vast right-wing conspiracy" she could hang on a Republican challenger. He had name recognition and was pro-union in a blue state.

But Gov. George Pataki, head of the New York GOP, knew he couldn't control King and tabbed Rick Lazio to take on Hillary. She won going away.

Since then King has flirted with running for governor or taking on U.S. Sen. Kirsten Gillibrand, but thought better of both ideas. A friend and adviser told him that turning a Senate seat in New York from blue to red was not just quixotic, but crazy.

The adviser wanted him to run for governor, noting that in tough economic times even liberal states will elect a Republican. Take, for example, William Weld's tenure in Massachusetts.

"But Peter would have to raise $40 million and face the inevitability of Andrew Cuomo," the friend said. "It was too much."

Picking a fight

The week after Thanksgiving, King moved through the basement halls of Cannon on his way to a vote, the crowded tunnels resembling New York City's subway system, with low ceilings, gray light and rushing crowds of young aides briefing representatives on the run, all the while scrolling through messages on their BlackBerrys.

What had put extra bounce in his already quick step was the White House swinging wildly again and missing. Press Secretary Robert Gibbs, reacting to constant lobs from reporters, said the reason Desiree Rodgers wouldn't testify was government's fabled separation of powers.

"I've called Clinton White House staff up here and they've testified," King said dismissively. "That isn't going to work."

King has always found a survivor's instinct in being a moving target. If it's not just the boxer's skill, then perhaps it's a practiced way of ducking the contradictions.

He'll tell you what a mediocre student he was, proud to be a "dese 'n' dems" guy, but he holds a degree from a prestigious law school and easily quotes Daniel Patrick Moynihan and the Victorian writer and politician Lord Thomas Macaulay. King himself is the author of three well-written and executed novels.

A loud and frequent critic of British torture and internment of Irish Republicans when few Americans were, he also wholeheartedly supported the Bush administration's policy of detention without trial for suspected terrorists and so-called "enhanced interrogation techniques."

Where contradiction ends, controversy takes over.

Michael Jackson's corpse was barely cold when King trashed him, labeling the entertainer a pervert and a child molester during a video shot in front of an American Legion Hall.

He's also infuriated Muslim-Americans by saying 85 percent of the nation's mosques are led by extremists.

Ibrahim Hooper, communications director of the Council on American-Islamic Relations, gave a derisive laugh when King's name was mentioned.

"We regard Congressman King as the nation's leading Muslim basher," Hooper said. "He's been an individual who has been most noteworthy in promoting hostility towards the American Muslim community."

King has at least one Muslim defender. Golam Mehraj, a Bangladeshi Muslim living here, is a director of Bangladeshi Associations Overseas, with a constituency in Queens and Nassau.

"Peter King is a man who believes that all religions are against violence and killing, but believes we should fight the small minority that promotes global terrorism," Mehraj said.

But then, terror is real to King. On Sept. 11 he watched the Pentagon burn from the roof of his Washington apartment house.

More than 150 people from his district died at New York's Ground Zero.

The survivor

He comes from a place where a good fight is always welcomed, Sunnyside, a mostly Irish neighborhood by the Queensboro Bridge, the son of a policeman and a homemaker, the grandson of immigrants from Inisbofin, an island off the coast of Galway where life was grim and bleak and poor. "Nothing romantic about it," he said.

Those roots have made King a streetwise, corner-of the-mouth Irishman, the kind who says with a shrug of the shoulders that he's seen it all and finds most of it amusing, while never forgetting there are things worth fighting for. Smart and not just wised up, he knows if you have a chip, you might as well wear it on your shoulder.

The first in his family to attend college, Peter studied history at St. Francis in Brooklyn, a small school educating the sons of the Irish and Italian working class. While going to college full time he also worked full time, loading and unloading trains in the vast yards on Manhattan's west side, working every shift in every kind of weather. Question why he supports unions and he'll let you know he owes them for supporting him as a young man.

The first great jump in King's life was going to Notre Dame law school. Had he ever traveled before? "I think I went to the Bronx once," he smiled. Tom Curtin, a lawyer from Morristown, N.J., remembered meeting the kid from Queens on their first day in South Bend. "That accent," Curtin said. "I couldn't understand a word he was saying—and I'm from New Jersey."

Curtin saw the politician in King even then, when the young New Yorker became chairman of the school speaker's bureau, bringing in lawyers from around the country. "We always suspected it was really a way for Pete to get himself good summer jobs," Curtin said with affection.

At Notre Dame, King met and fell in love with Rosemary Wiedl, a girl from Atlanta—friends thought they must have communicated by sign language—and they moved to Nassau County to start life together. He became a foot soldier in one of the last great political machines, Nassau's GOP powerhouse, serving on the Hempstead Town Board, as county attorney and then rising to comptroller in 1981. The only election he lost was when he challenged incumbent Democrat Robert Abrams for state attorney general in 1986.

In 1992, King took on a millionaire Democrat for Congress and squeaked by, winning by four percentage points. He's never faced a serious challenge since, making New York's Third District one of the safest Republican seats in the country.

But that could change. If Democrats control the state Senate after the 2010 election, the threat is real that King could be gerrymandered out with the new census figures.

It would be a dangerous game, however, with two liberal Democrats, Carolyn McCarthy and Steve Israel, on his borders. Cut into either of their districts and it could cost them votes.

At a recent Saturday morning meeting of fire chiefs at the Jericho firehouse, state Sen. Carl Marcellino said Democrats would be stupid to go after King. But that won't stop them, he added.

"They'll target Pete," Marcellino said, as King circulated easily among the chiefs.

Asked earlier, King had said he didn't care if he was redistricted.

"I'll win anywhere," he said.

Making it look easy
Back in Washington, a Cuban-American technician from CBS was setting up equipment in King's office while chatting with the congressman about boxing. King noted that the legendary Cuban Olympic champion, Teófilo Stevenson, was an unusual Cuban heavyweight since he didn't just rely on punching power but could box with the best of them.

The technician was so absorbed by the conversation that he stopped working at one point and sat down to talk.

The brawl between the White House and King was still hot, with the administration unable to get past the issue. Reporters were looking for a response to King's charge that previous administrations allowed staffers to testify on the Hill when serious issues were at stake.

Robert Gibbs countered by saying, "I don't think even Peter King would have the audacity to put the Saliahs in the same trifecta as Watergate, 9/11 and some financial deals."

Bad move. King's immediate response: "The only audacity I had was 'the audacity of hope' that the White House would be honest. Unfortunately, they are more interested in covering up and stonewalling."

Later, taking questions from CBS's Elizabeth Hartfield, King spoke forcefully about the need for the White House to take ownership of the security breach. After five minutes, she thanked King and asked if there was anything he wanted to add.

"That was all off the record," he said earnestly, pausing, then finally smiling to reveal the joke.

Walking down the hall, Hartfield was asked how the interview had gone.

"Wow, he's fantastic, a total sound-bite machine," she said. "He makes it easy."

Chapter 22
And Now ...
The Hardest Working Comic On
Long Island!
Mr. Glen Anthony!

My assignment was to find the worst comedian on Long Island. I found someone better, Glen Anthony, miles from the worst, but just maybe the busiest. For the Long Island Voice, *November 1999.*

What's it like for a comedian to bomb?

Glen Anthony has to sit down to talk about the trauma of stand-up. "OK, you ready?" he says. "You fall asleep somewhere. You wake up. You forget where you are. And you have no clothes on. Then you stumble through a door stark-naked. A spotlight hits you, and there's five hundred people staring at you. And you have to stand there for 45 minutes. Does that give you a feel for it?"

Think of Dudley Moore on his worst day. Add a marble-mouthed riff with echoes of Brooklyn, a black-and-white jumpsuit, sneakers, a particularly aggressive cologne. Ladies and germs: Glen Anthony, professional comedian, at home.

Sitting in a small alcove off the dining room of his spotless Smithtown house, dead-center on a brocade couch, dwarfed by its enormous pillows, Anthony says, "If I knew how painful it was going to be, I never would've done it. You have to go out there and take the arrows." Is he talking about the fake ones you put on your head to try to make people laugh? Maybe.

Anthony, 45, retreats to a home that is like a haute bourgeois fantasy in overdrive. The dining room has a baronial-manor theme with a two-ton table and high-backed chairs. He has earned this abode by being, not Long Island's best comedian, certainly not its worst, but perhaps its busiest.

"The thing," he says, "is to do everything. Senior shows, comedy clubs, conventions, firehouses, stags. Every kind of audience you can get your hands on. Some comedians make a mistake by only doing their act. That's stupid. The only time you can just do your act is when you're famous." Which Anthony is not. He adds, wistfully, "Then, you don't have to go looking for them."

Before he was Glen Anthony, he was Enrico Ponzini of Bay Ridge, Brooklyn, a kid who sang lead in the church choir and could also wail on guitar, piano, bass, drums, sax and harmonica by his early teens. When he decided to sing professionally, he was warned by an agent, "If I say I got a singer here named Enrico Ponzini, it's strictly Sons of Italy shows."

It was time to find a new handle. "I always wanted a short name. Brad? Cliff? Derek? Scott? I picked Glen. Anthony was my father's name. I know, very mayonnaise, you know what I'm saying? But I use another name in the comedy clubs. You ready? I just developed it, great name, greatest you'll ever hear. You ready? Eric..." he pauses "... Moneynipple." Ba-da-boom.

Anthony describes the day he left singing to become a stand-up comic as a huge moment, Paul blinded by grace on the road to Damascus. "I was at a place called Kutscher's, upstate, I'm rehearsing a band, it's awful, getting worse and worse," he recalls. "Opening for a comedian. I watched his act. I'll never forget it." His voice becomes a hush. "A tall resplendent guy in a tuxedo. I thought, What command! What majesty on that stage! Just one man in a spotlight. And I said" — he's whispering now — "Jesus Christ, that's what I want to do." Silence.

Who was the comedian?

Back to the rat-a-tat-tat delivery. "I always forget his name. I'll think of it. I want you to write it down when I remember it. Bob Nelson! No, no, Bob ... I'll think of it."

Since that Catskills epiphany, he hasn't had time to look back. He's a pro and he rarely bombs. If one block of material isn't working, he switches to another. The absurdity-of-life block: "How come nowadays when a man talks to a woman about sex it's harassment. But when a woman talks to a man about sex it's three dollars a minute?"

The nothing-works-for-me block: "I saw an ad in the paper: If you have a drinking problem, call this number. I called, it was a liquor store."

The my-father block: "My father goes to the doctor. Doc says, 'Do you have mutual satisfaction with your wife?' My father says, 'We don't need it. We got Allstate.'"

After talking about something called the collective comedic intelligence ("I should write a book!"), Anthony gets practical, describing his "train-wreck theory of comedy." An example: "Old man takes his girlfriend, an old lady, home to his apartment. He's performing oral sex on the living room floor and says, 'You're very dry tonight.' She says, 'You're licking the rug.'"

He waits for his guests to finish laughing. "Now, why did that happen? I led you down a track. Three people involved. He's licking the rug, she wants sex, and you're wondering where's this going, what the hell's going on? And it all hits at once. Train wreck."

Some of his best wrecks are preserved on videotape. In one you see Glen Anthony, gorgeous in a tux, pinkie ring, big watch, working 750 people in Jersey. He's slaying them.

"See that tux," he says quietly, always the analyst. "You wear that thing, you can say shit and make it sound clean."

Chapter 23
The End Is Here

This is truly a faded snapshot of Montauk from September 2002 for The Washington Post. *But go in late autumn, or winter, or early spring, and you'll find what is described here.*

If you can make your way through the traffic of the Hamptons—clogged day and night, even now in the off season, by SUVs with the attitude of armored personnel carriers—you will be rewarded.

Past the town of Amagansett, the road runs through scrub and dunes, the prevailing southwest wind brings scents of salt and pine. Every now and then shacks appear with signs that say only "Lunch" or "Clam Bar." A village of two streets passes and soon the road rises and drops among thick trees before proceeding through open moors giving views of the limitless sea. A tall lighthouse commands the last bluff.

This is Montauk, 120 miles from New York City, the extreme southeastern tail of the long fish-shaped island, where T-shirts say "The End" or "The Last Resort." But those who stay for even a few days find themselves referring to it, along with the locals, as simply and tellingly, "out here." The beaches rival the Caribbean's, the sport fishing is equal to anyplace in the world, and the feeling, even in high summer, is of off-season, removed, away from it all.

Simplicity is Montauk's charm. The village business district is barely three blocks long and ultra-chic resort shops have not made it this far east. There are 10 public beaches, and you can get passes from your motel or inn for all of them. The New England tradition of renting

151

beach cottages by the week or weekend is here, with Burcliffe by the Sea and Lenhart's Cottages sharing space along Old Montauk Highway, most with fireplaces and views of the sea.

The majority of visitors are from Long Island and New York, but the throttled-back pace of Montauk slows people down, and going native is easy and almost instantaneous. September through October is called "the beautiful season," as the light changes to windowpane clarity. Surfcasters, saltwater fly fishermen or anyone with tackle and dreams come for what is known as "the run," when striped bass with big shoulders and bad attitude are easy pickings.

Winter can be bone-cold one day, sparkling and mild the next, and blowing half a gale the third. The land and sea take on the color of driftwood and gulls: gray, whiter than white, black. Beaches can be walked for miles without encountering footsteps, and long walks are perfect excuses for hot toddys in quiet bars.

In Montauk Village, the Shagwong Restaurant sits in the middle of one of the commercial blocks. The facade is half-timbered Tudor, built by Carl Fisher, who purchased most of Montauk in the 1920s. Fisher had become rich turning 3,500 acres of pestilential mangrove jungle into Miami Beach, and his dream for Montauk was to make it the "Miami of the north." Kindly, providence provided the Wall Street crash of '29 that wiped out Fisher and kept Montauk a backwater. All that's left of Fisher's fantasy is an incongruous office building, the palatial Montauk Manor, now condominiums, and the faux Tudor front of a couple of blocks of the main drag.

But the Shagwong Restaurant has survived as a lively place of dark wood, stuffed fish, whale's teeth and men off the boats cracking lobsters and pounding down Budweiser. Lilting brogues come from everyone who serves you. At times, being in Montauk is like being in County Clare—powerful land and seascapes all around you and mist-soft voices asking, "Are ye all right, then?" Years ago, cops and firefighters and other blue-collar Irish from the city discovered Montauk and built simple second homes. Kids from Ireland come every summer to wait tables, tend bar, clean motel rooms and live the beach life.

Author and journalist Russell Drumm stopped by at the crowded bar one night not long ago to talk about his home for the past 35 years. One of America's finest writers of the sea, he is the author of "In the Slick of the Cricket" and "The Barque of Saviors." The former is the story of a five-day, shark-hunting sail out of Montauk with the legendary Frank Mundus, the model for Quint, the not-all-there captain in "Jaws." (Mundus is revered in Montauk for capturing the individualist spirit of the place. Drumm described him at one point as standing on a dead whale 40 miles out at sea feeding gingersnaps to circling Great White sharks.)

"I came out here in the late 1960s to surf," Drumm said. "Montauk is in the top three places on the East Coast. When it gets big, it can be dangerous. The swells come out of very deep water and we have rock reefs. Between Ditch Plains and Montauk Point are some of the most beautiful surf spots in the world, with backdrops of those pristine moorlands. We're really fortunate—almost three-fourths of Montauk is either state or county parks."

In his work, Drumm has described his home town as having the "feel of an outpost." He recalled his time working as a commercial fisherman. "Fishermen are a breed apart. There are reasons people want to leave the land and make their livings out there on the water. It's not quite sociopathic," he grinned, "but antisocial to a certain extent. Montauk has always been a defensive position, from the time the Montaukett Indians settled here. They viewed this place as a natural fortress, easily defended, and could see their blood enemies, the Narragansetts, from far off rowing across Block Island Sound to battle. In every one of our wars this has been a defensive position." He smiled again. "And so we're all a bit defensive."

The earliest white settlers used Montauk as grazing land for livestock from the 17th century to the 1920s. The good grassland needed only one fence, across the isthmus that begins east of Amagansett, to keep in up to 3,000 head of cattle and sheep.

Montauk's tie to those times lives at Deep Hollow Ranch, the oldest working cattle ranch in the country.

Drumm described how some people go over the edge out here—a perverse tribute to the, at times, overwhelming wildness of sea, shore and sky combined with the fact that there is no farther place to go. "In the fall and especially winter, lost souls get on the train in New York and ride until the last stop, Montauk. They wander around for a few days and either find their way back to the station or kill themselves, a lot of them out near the lighthouse. It's probably because it's literally the end of the road."

Tom D'Ambrosio, executive director of Montauk Point Lighthouse, greeted a visitor recently saying that lighthouses "are magnets for everyone. I'm not sure what it is, except there's an immediate sense of romance and attraction. You want to go to them." Perhaps the attraction begins with language, when two of our more evocative words form one that describes a place ensuring safe passage.

In 1792, the Second Congress under President Washington authorized construction of the 110-foot beacon. It was built between June and November of 1796 and still operates, the light visible from 19 nautical miles away. Unlike a lot of American lighthouses, this one has exhibits that are presented (on the ground floor) in museum-quality fashion. History here is not rusting anchors and dim-lighted rope knots under glass, but clean and crisp charts, graphics and a small but remarkable collection of sparkling cut-glass lenses. One hundred and thirty-seven iron steps spiral to the crow's nest. You might get winded, but blame it on the view; even mountaineers will have their breath taken away.

Fifty yards out, shrieking gulls wheel above a wide circle of baitfish driven to the surface by blues feeding on the run, hammering into the school. One boat slowly circles, lines out, hooking the bluefish. Beyond, the open ocean rolls in long swells, as if it's breathing. In "Montauk Point," Walt Whitman wrote: "I stand on some mighty eagle's beak," reminding you of another reason to climb a lighthouse

and look out over the water all the way to the horizon—liberation from solid ground, a feeling of flight.

Sitting on one of the long, beautifully carved wooden benches at the Depot Gallery, formerly the railroad station, is Percy Heath, president of the Montauk Artists Association. Heath's career is the history of jazz for the past 50 years. His powerfully fluid bass lines anchored everything from big bands to hard bop to the "new traditionalists." His legend is secured by his work with the Modern Jazz Quartet, where his bass, in the words of producer Ira Gitler, "was utilized as another voice as well as a rhythm instrument." He still plays, using a cello more and more these days, as well as painting, to express himself.

"What do you think of our station?" he asks. The old depot was built in 1944 from a Stanford White design and has been turned into a stunning art space and the association's headquarters. Construction has begun upstairs to create studios, dark rooms and offices.

Striped bass brought Heath to Montauk. "I followed the stripers all the way out from Far Rockaway to here, the summer of 1963. When I saw this place, I told the quartet not to book during the summer because I have to be here with my wife June and three boys. That was it," he said. "We rented for 26 summers and have been here permanently since 1989."

Asked if there have been big changes, he smiles. "Everyone thinks they discovered Paradise when they get here, and then watch it get less beautiful with time. There was a fellow named Sam Cox I met out here the summer of '63. He said, 'Percy, Montauk is ruined!'" Heath laughs, a man who understands that, just as in music or painting, perspective is everything.

A man visiting the gallery overhears the musician talking about fishing. Soon a detailed conversation is flowing about rigs, bait, boats and the art of surf-casting.

Painter Lorraine La Vista stops by to explain what artists mean by "Long Island light," the quality that attracted, among others, Jackson Pollock, Lee Krasner and Willem de Kooning. "It's bright light, clear, but the colors are muted," she says. La Vista grew up in Westhampton, New York, and has been in Montauk 18 years. Her work uses the media of undiluted watercolor and oils, her subject the natural loveliness and sense of quiet "out here." Montauk suits her. "I'm up at 5, get a cup of coffee, wander around my yard, and then I go to the easel. But I'm really working all the time in my head, solving problems."

Heath talks about the facilities for teaching art that the association is preparing on the second floor. He then pauses and looks out the gallery door at the dappled light of a sleepy summer afternoon. "I've been around the world nine times. And I don't want to be anyplace else but right here."

Chapter 24
Life In One Long Meal

For the Long Island Voice, *July 1999.*

If you go for a drive with Mario Andretti, you toss him the keys. Go out to eat with Ron Beigel and Ken Keith, you let them pick the place and order the meal. The way you might check out movie or TV listings to plan your week, these two plan where they'll eat. It's not a now-and-then diversion. It's week in, week out.

Every week. Planned and with a purpose.

We're sitting at the bar of Waterzooi, a bistro on Franklin Avenue in Garden City. Keith says that since the place is Belgian, we'll drink beer. This does not simplify things. Waterzooi has about 125 different types.

We choose. Keith, a lawyer from Rockville Centre, takes a sip from a goblet foaming with cold brown stuff. He says, softly, "Wow." Without another word, he hands it to his partner.

Beigel sips, nods his head, "Yeah."

Keith says, "Made by Trappist monks. Which reminds me. There's a new place opening in Manhattan. Someone described it as a monastery run by aliens."

Beigel has only one response: "When are we going?"

Friends for more than 20 years, they are collectors of restaurants. Beigel, 47, is a real-estate closer and *Long Island Voice* contributor.

Keith, 46, is a criminal-defense specialist who is not shy about marketing.

"I'm thinking of a new phone number," he says. "How's 1-800-ARRESTED?"

Beigel is more laid back, but just as intense when it comes to restaurants. Closing real-estate deals in the City and on the Island allows him to scout places where Keith and his wife, Bari, and Beigel and his wife, Ellen, can dine on Saturday nights. At times the two guys will eat without their wives, and sometimes one of them, guiltily, will eat solo. This can cause conflict. "It's like committing adultery," Beigel says, "Like, 'What? You ate Malaysian without me? How *could* you? After all we've been through?'"

"We're addicts," says Keith. "We are 'we gotta' people. Gotta have perfect dumplings. Gotta have ribs that fall off the bone. Gotta have tastes that jump off the plate."

We are joined by the noted Long Beach boulevardier and wit, Kirk Condyles. Soon we are knee-deep in mussels. They're so delicious I throw some on my shirt and notebook trying to get at them. The best food I've ever eaten is, of course, free food. No matter. This Belgian stuff is, as Mr. Condyles says, a bit stunned, "incredible."

Keith is spooning rock-shrimp ravioli on my plate, explaining how the obsession began. "I'm a Queens kid, like Ron. Haute cuisine was Hamburger Helper. Variety was Kraft macaroni and cheese. Then, years, ago, I went to a place called The Quilted Giraffe. That was it. Struck by lightning. It's been the quest for the Holy Grail, the two of us chasing restaurants. Oh, man, did you try this wild boar?"

Besides Beigel's scouting, they read everything they can and "sometimes we'll just go out fishing for restaurants." There have been rough seas at times. Beigel, all over a soft-shelled crab, says, "I've had stuff put in front of me that would scare children out of a week's sleep. Remember that Chinese place in Flushing? But it's like the old saying: My worst sexual experience, in retrospect, wasn't really all that bad."

Another diner, Doris Atlas, noticing the commotion at our table (shouts, wild laughter, passing plates), stops by. Asked where she's from, Doris says, "Fort Lee." Simultaneously, the guys say, "Great sushi in Fort Lee."

Our waitress, Katherine, brings more liter bottles of beer and serves it like champagne—the label shown, wire cage undone, cork popped. "The Island's coming along," Beigel says. "It's becoming more ethnically diverse, so the food's more interesting. We found a great Vietnamese place—now closed—in a Bethpage strip mall. Stan's Soul Kitchen in Uniondale—you can get it as good, but you've got to go to South Carolina."

The problem with Long Island, Keith says, is sometimes there's no place to walk off a good meal. I don't need a walk. I need to be hosed down. I have a feeling I'll never have to eat again. And, if I do, never as good as this. Everyone passes on dessert except Mr. Condyles, who decides he will indulge only if the treat is on fire. Katherine obliges and brings out a *crème brulee* and a blowtorch, firing it up at our table.

Drinking a cappuccino, Beigel says, "We're in a place a couple of years ago, one that Ken had gone to by himself, cheating on me. We're looking at the menu and he says, 'Have the feet. The feet are good.' I look at him. 'The chicken feet,' he says. And I think, 'Has this gone too far?'"

So is there a dark side to a life spent pursuing restaurants? Beigel thinks it has something to do with the psychology of collecting. "Ken has a whole basement full of pinball machines. He collects what are called 'coin-op items.' I collect old records, TV and movie memorabilia," he says. "It's fun, but it's serious." Both of our eaters seem to believe in the British writer Richard Davenport-Hines' code that "cheerful vice is preferable to a stubborn virtue."

"I don't know," Keith says, "For me, food done right is everything. It's instant gratification, instant education. Instant culture."

He opens his hands. "Everything."

Chapter 25
Trane Tract

My colleague at LIBN, *Henry Powderly III, worked next to me in the newsroom. We were both early birds (as in really early) and would hang out before hitting the keyboards. Henry, a sax player along with being a superb writer and editor, would play some music on those early mornings. Coltrane was a favorite. "As good as coffee," Henry would say. One morning he said, "You know he lived on Long Island."*

"Really?"

"Yeah. So, when are you going to his house?"

From May 2008.

By the time he got to Dix Hills, for someone not yet 40, he had lived several lives, passing through the fires of physical and spiritual turmoil and coming out the other side stronger.

An addiction to narcotics and alcohol had buried him to the point where he would forget to bathe or change his clothes, and was seen on a Greenwich Village park bench blitzed by heroin, holding a wine bottle.

When he moved to Long Island, a broken marriage was behind him replaced by another as strong as an anchor. It was here that three of his children would be born. He had endured a decades-long search for a flawless means of expression, and by the time he arrived at the address on Candlewood Path he had transformed his art as completely as Picasso had changed his.

Living from 1964 to 1967 in Dix Hills, he created an enduring masterpiece, and trailblazed new territories for others to follow.

And here John Coltrane died, two months shy of his 41st birthday.

* * * *

Coltrane moved both critics and colleagues throughout his prolific career.

Recorded in 1965, "A Love Supreme" remains one of the best-selling jazz albums ever. It's a culmination of his ambition "to uplift us and even change us," as author Eric Nisenson wrote. "Some of it forces us to redefine the very meaning of beauty."

In the jazz clubs, Coltrane produced sounds no one had ever heard, "sheets of sound," critic Ira Gitler famously dubbed it. Solos could go on for nearly an hour, prompting Coltrane's friend Miles Davis to ask why he went on so long. Coltrane answered: "It took that long to get it all in."

The music wasn't "difficult," but a means of emotional transportation, according to writer Dan Morgenstern. "If you let yourself be carried by it, it was an absolutely ecstatic feeling," he wrote. "And I think that kind of ecstasy was something Coltrane was looking for in his music."

A voracious reader and dedicated student of all religions and all music, Coltrane listened to Hindu chanting, the music of Central African Pygmies and Bach concertos.

He was "an authentically spiritual man, but not innocent of carnal imperatives," writer Nat Hentoff slyly observed, adding that music for Coltrane was "a way of self-purgation, a healing art."

For any saxophone player, from professional musicians to Sunday players, Coltrane is Everest. Always there. But even rock-and-roll musicians owe a debt of gratitude to Coltrane. Jerry Garcia, Eric Clapton, Bono, Carlos Santana, Sting and many others have acknowledged his influence on their work, which would make Coltrane smile. He disliked the term, "jazz," believing music is music, with no boundaries, only open frontiers.

The world of music, and not just the world of jazz, went into shock when Coltrane died so young with so much left unfinished. Keith Jarrett, the eloquent pianist on and off the bandstand, summed up the aftermath of Coltrane's passing. "Everyone felt a big gap all of a sudden," Jarrett told an interviewer. "But he didn't intend to leave a gap. He intended that there be more space for everybody to do what they should do."

* * * *

The wrought iron fence at the entrance off Candlewood Path needs work, a preview of the condition of the derelict split level ranch found at the end of a long drive framed by trees. Steve Fulgoni greets a visitor next to the house. A bent TV antenna tilts from the roof like a desecrated crucifix.

Fulgoni, an amateur saxophonist who sells musical instruments in Deer Park, has dedicated a large part of more than 10 years to restoring and preserving Coltrane's home, an idiosyncratic house, which had a recording studio in the basement and a circular stained glass window off the living room leading to a meditation room.

Fulgoni's quest resembles a detective story, beginning in 1997 when he moved from Seaford to Dix Hills. Fulgoni "felt an immediate connection to John" after his first saxophone lessons. He read a biography noting the musician's move to Dix Hills, but it didn't give an address.

"Every six months or so I Googled 'John Coltrane, Dix Hills,' hoping something would turn up," Fulgoni said. In July 2002 he hit pay dirt. Up popped a story by Art Rice from a music magazine recalling his stint as a delivery boy for a pharmacy, delivering medicine for the children to the Coltrane house. Rice remembered the musician as being especially kind. He also recalled the day he went to the house and found "four or five guys sitting around in suits." Coltrane was dead of cancer.

Fulgoni contacted Rice and got directions to the 3.4-acre property on Candlewood Path. He drove by dreaming about someday going inside to witness where "A Love Supreme," Coltrane's magnificent, spiritually-themed suite, was composed. Dreams began to come true in 2003 when Fulgoni, historian of the Half Hollows Hills Historical Society, added Coltrane's house to the historical register. He discovered a developer had purchased the property to subdivide it and raze the house. But through sheer perseverance Fulgoni and others persuaded the Town of Huntington in May 2004 to make Coltrane's house a landmark.

Open space preservation funds were used to purchase the property for $975,000, with the grounds designated as a town park and the house given to a nonprofit, managed by a board consisting of Fulgoni, John and Alice Coltrane's son Ravi and his wife Kathleen Hennessey. The goal is to restore the house exactly the way it was when the Coltranes lived on Candlewood Path, and "have a very strong educational component with the home," Fulgoni said. "We want to partner with school districts. We also see it as a repository for musical artifacts and memorabilia so people can come, see, touch and feel where John Coltrane lived and worked."

Huntington Councilwoman Susan Berland was a champion to preserve the house. She noted she wasn't a Coltrane fan in the beginning, "but now I am." Berland praised Fulgoni's persistence and remembered receiving e-mails from Herbie Hancock and fans as far afield as Japan, urging preservation. Her vision of the house and grounds is a balance between the needs of the community and people who want to visit a place where a 20th century American genius lived and worked. "I don't see any concerts on the lawn," Berland said, but did envision weekday class trips and weekend hours for the general public that are not be a burden on the quiet neighborhood.

Berland is working with the Long Island Power Authority to get a right of way at the rear of the property leading to the service road off

My Life In Pieces

the Long Island Expressway, she said. Buses and cars would park in the back "and there would be no traffic at the front to affect the community at all," Berland said. "This is doable." Extensive renovations are needed for both the interior and exterior of the structure. Fulgoni is calling on general contractors, plumbers, electricians, carpenters and home improvement companies to volunteer goods and services. He also seeks support from other Long Island businesses to help preserve the home of one of Long Island's most honored and revered residents.

Helen Harrison, director of the Pollock-Krasner House in Springs, said Fulgoni's efforts have an advantage because "historic homes are a dime a dozen, but people like Jackson Pollock or John Coltrane are iconic American figures." She added that any effort must begin with the family of the artist. "Will they dedicate any income to the preservation of the house?" Harrison asked. "If the family is not interested, no one else will be, I can promise you."

Alice Coltrane gave $25,000 to the not-for profit before she died a year ago. "It's been difficult since then," Fulgoni said. One of Coltrane's record labels, Impulse, which is today part of Verve "has supported us in different ways," Fulgoni said. He believed more support will be on the way. It would seem only fair that Impulse kick in. The label released "A Love Supreme," and profited so much from the album that a book about Impulse is titled, "The House That Trane Built."

Michel Cogswell, director of the Louis Armstrong House in Queens, said preserving Coltrane's house "of course should be done and it's going to happen." Cogswell, who advises Fulgoni and the board, noted that after a master plan is in place, government funding will begin to flow. "Then corporate and private foundations can be tapped. Once opened you can get earned income from a gift shop and other sales."

What's left of the Coltrane's influence in the house is striking, with a dramatic carpet in the living room of orange, red and yellow stripes. There's a perfect circular hole where the stained glass window once was, placed so morning light would filter through the meditation room. Fulgoni led the visitor up to the second floor guest bedroom

165

where "A Love Supreme" was composed. It's a simple, bare room, with a dormer window looking out on thick woods.

He explained that after a long road trip in August 1964, Coltrane decided to kick back for a while, but his obsessive creativity drove him upstairs to work on a new composition. He rarely left the room for five days. When he emerged, he told Alice, "I finally have it. It's come to me in music."

The woods were winter gray and bare, but for those five August days, the composer looked out on full summer.

"Coltrane transcends music," Fulgoni said. "If you listen to him, you've got to be moved."

Chapter 26
Smooth Operators

For the Long Island Voice, *November 1998.*

Two hours before the Islanders' face-off, I'm standing in a puddle of water with Al Saxton in a big room under the Coliseum. Saxton, a weather-beaten man in his 60s, is talking about how he once had a nine-month gig operating cranes in Nigeria. "This is better," he says, slapping a hand against one of two gleaming new ice-smoothing machines—a.k.a. Zambonis.

He fires up a Pall Mall under a "No Smoking" sign, inches from two propane gas tanks strapped to the big blocky machine. Flicking ashes, he comments on how painful propane is to the skin if it leaks. "Pretty flammable, too," he says with a grin. If something leaks now—Mission Control, Al and I have lift-off.

"Seventeen years I've been doing it," Saxton says. "But I'm not the guy. He's the guy." He points at Rich Larkin making his way toward us across the concrete floor. He's the Zamboni guy.

Larkin is even more a part of the Coliseum than the retired numbers and Stanley Cup banners hanging in the rafters. He was here first—25 years ago, in fact. For fans who come as kids and get hooked on Islanders hockey, Larkin has always been "the bald guy, the Zamboni guy," because for years he was a solo act, slowly riding the ice between periods. Now he and Saxton run both machines, preparing the ice in five minutes or less.

Larkin is—there's no other word—passionate about Zambonis. He shakes my hand and gives me some history. Fifty years ago come January, Frank J. Zamboni, a rink operator out of Fairmount, California, was watching a crew resurface the ice. This involved a bunch of guys dragging a big blade around, sweeping the shavings, spraying water and then taking squeegees to the whole rink.

Orville and Wilbur in the bike shop, Bill Gates in the garage—presto!—Frank J. would find a better way. He got an army-surplus jeep, put studs in the tires, strapped on a movable blade, water pump and industrial-strength squeegee, and indoor-skating history was made. Frank J.'s invention has also hypnotized countless hockey fans around the world (patents are in 81 countries) who, after the speed, splash and crunch of a period, gaze on the droning Zamboni slowly creating its pattern, leaving a cold sheen, making everything right once again. Visual Prozac for even the most tightly wound fan.

Saxton slapped the machine. Larkin puts a hand on one like he's petting it. "These new Zambonis are quicker, more efficient, cleaner, easier to handle," he says. "But the theory can't be improved on. You shave it, bring up the chip to the tank, put down hot water and squeegee. How thick is the ice? Don't worry about it, you won't fall through."

"No ice fishing either," Saxton puts in.

"Couple of inches," Larkin says, "more or less. We keep it at about twenty or twenty-two degrees for hockey. Hard and fast. Figure skaters want more traction for jumps, softer when they fall, about twenty-four to twenty-six degrees."

What's he seen out there? "Blood, oh yeah, lots of it. Paper airplanes made from programs. That's a problem. Screws things up. Coins, lots of them."

"Bullets," Saxton says. "We got a whole collection over there in a jar. These geniuses throw bullets out on the ice and hope they go off when we go over them." He points a finger to his temple and twirls it.

Any accidents? "Never ran over anybody. Never hit anything. Never a problem," says Larkin. "Some sweetheart hit me in the neck with a paper clip shot out of a slingshot. Try that sometime and see how it feels. But most people are great."

Best memory? "No contest. You know the booze, Black Velvet? I once rode around the ice with Miss Black Velvet." Larkin smiles, "Just the two of us."

"Santa Claus is fun to carry at the holidays," Saxton remembers.

"Yeah," Larkin says. "But Miss Black Velvet ..."

Saxton runs one of the machines quickly for the pre-game skate. The fans aren't in yet. Ushers and maintenance workers who have seen this hundreds of times will stop and stare at the man riding around the rink.

Fifteen minutes before face-off, when the players have left the ice, Larkin and Saxton drive the Zambonis up one level and park single file in a tunnel with hockey nets hanging from the walls.

They've changed into green, purple and gray zip-up sweaters and shiny black pants. Up on the Zambonis, they're quiet as two men wheel in a stretcher stocked with first-aid gear.

A huge corrugated steel door slowly grinds open and the tunnel fills with pounding music and whiter-than-white light bounding off the ice ahead. Kids in caps lean way over to look down the tunnel where the Zambonis wait.

Larkin winks, Saxton touches his eyebrow with a finger, and they glide out to the arena.

Chapter 27
Passion Fruit

For Long Island Business News, *March 2007.*

John Rena is a banana man, a term used with the same pride you'd get from a dock-working longshoreman. At times, the work is not dissimilar. Though Rena is an owner of Suffolk Banana Co., a no-show driver can mean he has to take to the road himself, humping 200 or more 40-pound boxes to supply a route.

"A banana man is just about done when he gets to be 60," says Rena, meaning he has 18 years to go.

Tom Chumas, 81, nods his agreement. Chumas is a fellow banana man and Rena's mentor. He was done about 15 years ago, but still comes by the company's Yaphank warehouse now and then for conversation. Chumas was in the business all his working life, taking over from his father, who started Long Island Banana in 1929 in Patchogue, finally selling the firm to Rena and two partners.

The partners run a warehouse in Lynbrook, and Rena operates Suffolk Banana in Yaphank. That peel-able finger of yellow sweetness you buy in your local market—"The number one fruit in America, and the cheapest," Rena says—almost certainly passed through one of the company's Long Island warehouses. "We deliver bananas as far west as Jersey and as far east as Montauk," Rena boasts.

Along with general manager Donald Hemberger and 15 employees, Rena moves as many as 1,500 boxes of bananas a week. The price of bananas fluctuates daily, he says, but the average wholesale price over a year is about $15.50 a box.

Ready to go bananas? OK, then. Bananas grow as plants, not trees. Part of the same horticultural family as lilies, orchids and palms, bananas were mentioned in Buddhist texts from 600 B.C. They were spread to the rest of the world when Arab warriors brought them from India to Palestine and industrious merchants found suitable growing conditions in Africa and elsewhere.

The word "banana" comes from the Arabic word for "finger," and a bunch is referred to as a hand. About 100 million tons of bananas are cultivated annually, with India as the world leader in production.

In the Americas, where the fruit arrived at the beginning of the 16th century, the banana hasn't just been a nutritious, easily digestible fruit, but a fuel powering history. Consider "banana republics," those impoverished countries virtually owned and operated by United Fruit Co., which dictated American foreign policy in Latin America from the end of the 19th century until the 1970s, resulting in coups, juntas and military dictatorships to suit American financial interests.

Bananas are still on the political page. Just this month, federal prosecutors revealed that Chiquita, an Ohio-based company, paid $1.7 million in protection money from 1997 to 2004 to a Colombian guerrilla army the State Department has designated as a terrorist group.

The fruit Rena sells begins its life in Central and South America, growing on enormous plantations owned by companies such as Chiquita, Bonita, Del Monte and Dole. Picked in the tropics when they are still "grass green and hard as rocks," Chumas says, the bananas are then given a chilled field bath to take away their tropical heat, because controlling temperature is crucial to ripening. The fruit is then labeled with stick-on company labels, but there is no difference in quality by brand.

"A banana is a banana," he says.

Wrapped in plastic and boxed in the fields, the fruit is transported by train to waiting ships. A few days later, they're picked up in refrigerated trucks at the Port of Newark and driven to Lynbrook and Yaphank to be stored and ripened.

Chumas recalls the days when he went with his father and brother to Brooklyn piers to buy bananas on stalks, not in boxes, and store them in cool Patchogue basements to ripen. Back then, a banana man had to be on the lookout for unwelcome visitors that had hitched a ride to the States.

"Snakes and tarantulas, they were very common," Chumas says.

Ripening was once an art. Bananas are constantly evolving, so the trick is to get the hands to stores where they can be purchased and eaten within a week's time. In the past, timing the chemical process that turns a starch into a sugar involved a certain seat-of-the-pants skill, constantly monitoring and adjusting storage temperatures to keep the fruit between 58 and 64 degrees.

Lower than 58 degrees and bananas "get a chill."

"It doesn't hurt the taste, but they turn gray and no one will buy that," Chumas says. "I wanted the fruit to ripen when I wanted it, not when the fruit wanted it."

That romance is gone, replaced by ethylene gas rooms that allow consistent ripening. In the Yaphank warehouse, Rena shows off large ripening rooms behind yellow—what else?—hydraulic doors, each with a machine releasing the gas.

A banana man to the bone, Rena sells other varieties of fruit – "I have to," he says—and he's a patriot when it comes to personal taste.

"There's nothing like a Georgia peach," Rena says. His friend nods.

Chapter 28
You Can't Get There From Here

For the Long Island Voice, *October 1999.*

Captain Kidd, who is said to have buried treasure on Fishers Island, was just the first of many buccaneers to invest in the place; later pirates had names like DuPont, Whitney, Luce and Firestone.

But any of you can still make easy money off the island. Try out this bar bet: Name the Long Island community you have to leave the state to enter. Pay up only if someone says Fishers Island.

Shaped roughly like a fishhook, 11 miles long and never more than half a mile wide, it is slung under the Connecticut coast out in the Sound four miles from New London. But it is some 15 miles northeast across the water from its government in the Suffolk County town of Southold. New York and Connecticut fought for title to the tiny island for two centuries, until 1879 when New York produced an ancient document from the Duke of York that the Nutmeg State couldn't match. Call Fishers from Suffolk, it's a local call. From nearby New London, it's long distance.

Getting there isn't easy. There is no direct ferry service from Long Island to Fishers. You take an hour-and-a-half ferry ride from Orient Point to New London, across Long Island Sound, change boats and chug another 45 minutes to Fishers.

On a September day, with Hurricane Floyd storming up the coast driving sultry weather north, the Cross Sound Ferry was just another

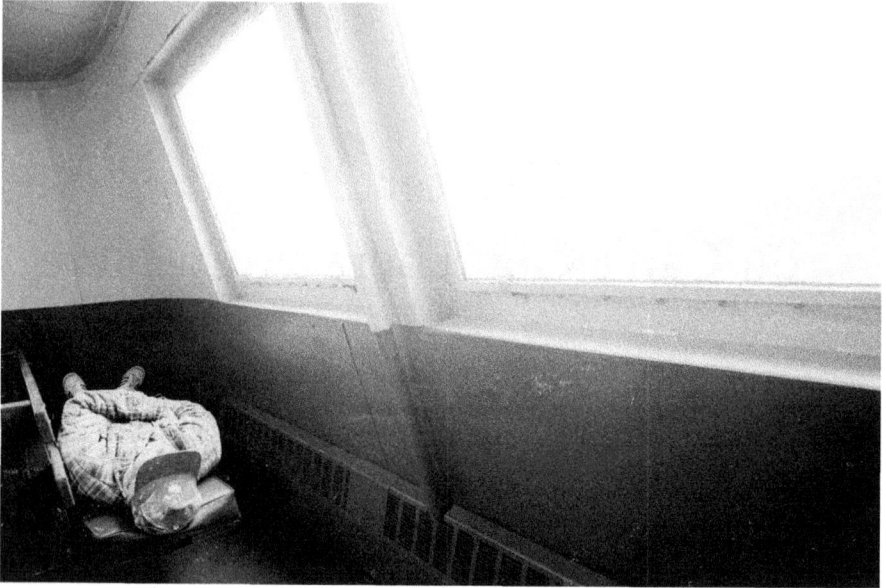

commuting Wednesday, packed with business people going to Connecticut and points north, families taking a late summer vacation and students starting school in Boston.

The New London terminal was modern, bustling, efficient. But down the waterfront, the Fishers Island ferry was quiet, with no terminal, just a few cars and trucks lined up in a muddy yard. A handful of people waited for the rusted old bucket that would take us across.

On board were construction crews and landscapers, some hung over from whatever nightlife New London features. There was a man hauling stone for a private estate, mocking his buddy who was trying to light a cigarette in the wind with shaky hands. Nearby was a young man in pale white slacks, a pink polo shirt, yellow socks and brown velvet loafers.

The loud guys standing in work boots and the young fellow in the uniform of the Protestant leisure class was Fishers in a microcosm.

About 280 year-round residents work to maintain the comfort of about 4,000 summer people of vast and venerable fortunes. Captains and crews get along well, from all reports, both realizing their mutual dependency.

Fishers has always been a vacation spot, used by the Pequot tribe as hunting and fishing grounds and as an escape from hot summers. It was named by the explorer Adrian Block in 1514 when he passed through this narrowest part of Long Island Sound, where it races to meet the Atlantic. A certain Mr. Fishers was a favorite member of Block's crew.

There is no supermarket, no ATM, no bar (except the VFW hall), one restaurant and an inn with just a few rooms. There is no movie theater after Labor Day, no UPS or Fed Ex delivery, no video store, no fast food, a coffeehouse that opens once a week.

"There's some rigor to living here," said Kathleen Koehnen, superintendent of the K-through-12 school, in her bright office. It is one of the finest public schools in the state, blessed by a stable and wealthy tax base. Seventy-five students are educated by 14 teachers, one of the best ratios in the world. "It's beautiful," Koehnen continued. "But lonely. And the people who live here want to live here. If they don't, they go off. You can't say that about many other places."

Allison Scroxton, 21, bagging groceries at the one small shop, said, "We all are kind of happy when the summer ends. There's a sense of relief. And then come spring we're all eager for the people to be back and summer starting."

A woman, hearing Allison's last name, said, "I didn't know you were a Scroxton."

"Yes, ma'am, Mrs. Browne." Their conversation, with its air of defined borders, in sharp accents, could be from another country— the lady conferring with a tradeswoman.

The year-rounders live on the west end, about one-third of the island, while the remaining two-thirds is tracked by narrow, winding roads where extraordinary estates and a world-class golf course and country club are hidden by trees, bushes and stone walls.

Summer ends on Fishers with the suddenness and finality of a door slamming. The man in velvet loafers and Mrs. Browne might be the last birds of summer. The yacht club's clubhouse was open but empty, chairs stacked against a glass case of cups and trophies. There was no one, not on the grounds or on the network of docks. No one working on boats. The silence was interrupted by the creak of wood and the rattle of chain.

In a small cemetery, Dan Cole was doing "tree work." The fit, red-haired 31-year-old was in a Red Sox T-shirt and shorts. "It's real quiet in the fall and winter," he said. "The churches do social things sometimes." As he buckled his harness, preparing to climb with a saw, he added, "I like working alone. Working on trees can be art, you know, shaping them, sculpting them."

The evening ferry was crowded. Work crews lugged six-packs aboard, quickly setting up a game of stud before the boat disembarked.

The dealer's chant tolled the cards, "Jack no help, trey to the fives ..."

A prim couple sat quietly, dressed for a night on the mainland. The ferry cut out through a warm rain, scattering gulls and cormorants. On a hill above the ferry dock two teenage girls shared an umbrella and watched. They waited until the boat was just about to clear the western end before turning their backs and walking away.

Chapter 29
Inconvenient Truths

For Long Island Business, *August 2008.*

I'm a liar. And Joel Reicherter found me out.

I was caught while sitting in the office of his elegant Lloyd Harbor house in the wooded hills above Long Island Sound where his company, University Polygraph, is based. Two bands across my chest to measure breathing, palms rigged up to measure perspiration, and a blood pressure wrap on my forearm were all attached to his laptop. I was caught fibbing about a "pick a card, any card" trick.

What made it even more magical was I was found out by not even saying a word, but silently answering "no" to a series of questions. Later the polygraphist showed me my chart. When I lied about my card, my rates of perspiration, breathing and blood pressure rose significantly.

Reicherter's comfortable living comes not from card tricks, but primarily from working with attorneys and through seminars, college teaching and government work. Every year he is a featured player training federal agents at Fort Jackson, South Carolina. All government agencies from the CIA to the U.S. Postal Service use polygraph testing, Reicherter said. At the top of his field, Reicherter even went Hollywood when he coached Robert DeNiro in the polygraph scene of "Meet The Parents." But his reputation stands on his doctorate in physiology and some high-profile cases, such as his part in Martin Tankleff's long search for justice.

In 2001, Reicherter spent four hours with Tankleff at an upstate prison at the behest of attorneys who were considering taking on the young man's case. Tankleff had been convicted of brutally murdering his parents in 1988, when he was 17 years old. When the attorneys received the polygraph report they took his case. After 17 years behind bars, he won a right to a second trial late last year and on July 1 all charges against him were dropped.

Before meeting Tankleff, Reicherter looked at the evidence and was convinced Tankleff was guilty. "I was shaken when he passed."

So much for instinct. But it makes Reicherter's case that the polygraph is an instrument of science, and not of parlor tricks. Simply put, the polygraph measures breathing, heart rate and perspiration. When we lie, what Reicherter calls "the mind-body agreement" breaks down and physiologically we are altered by the untruth.

Since the polygraph came into popular use in the 1940s, there has been a debate whether the device belongs as a stage prop for turbaned conjurors with lovely assistants or, as Reicherter maintains, a scientific tool. Doubters point to a report issued by the National Academy of Sciences in 2003 that stated polygraph data lack scientific validity. Polygraph data are only legally admissible in New Mexico. The results are admissible in every other state only on the condition that all parties agree to it, which never happens. In New York there is no licensing or even certification for polygraphists. This convergence of facts tends to keep the use of polygraphs in the shadows.

Reicherter said as a scientist working with the polygraph he struggles against amateurs in the field. "You and I could right now put an ad in the Yellow Pages and we're immediately polygraphists," he said.

Reicherter came to his life's work of exploring the murky world of truth and lies from the bright classrooms of academia. While teaching physiology to nursing students at Farmingdale State College more than 20 years ago, he noticed that some of his students were also taking a course on the uses of polygraphs. He went to sit in for an hour, became fascinated, and attended every class. The teacher became his mentor and the two went into business together, using the teacher's initial contacts. By 1988, Reicherter formed University Polygraph on his own.

Robert Bornstein, professor of psychology at Adelphi's Derner Institute of Advanced Psychological Studies, puts little store in the polygraph. "It doesn't measure honesty and it doesn't measure a person's attempt to deceive," Bornstein said. "It only measures a level of physiological arousal."

Asked how accurate a polygraph test is, Reicherter bluntly said he couldn't answer the question. "If I'm given good information about a crime, it's very accurate," he added. This is especially true if Reicherter has information shared only by the perpetrator of a crime.

Miller Place attorney John Ray, who practices criminal and civil law, said he and a majority of his colleagues use a polygraph with prospective clients to judge truthfulness. If someone fails, will Ray represent him? "Absolutely," he said, noting that everyone is entitled to a defense. If the client passes however, he will make the results available to the prosecution. Ray only uses reputable examiners. "You get what you pay for," he said.

More and more, Reicherter is taking on what he calls "domestic matters," which amount to about 25 percent of his business. Sometimes the issue is stolen money. More often it's someone accused of stepping out on his or her spouse.

Although he's a physiologist, his work offers a front row seat to human psychology. "I've gone to women and said, 'Good news, your husband isn't cheating on you,'" he said. "Almost always her response is she doesn't believe the test. But if I say, 'Bad news, it looks like he's cheating,' they're happy. They've been proven right."

It's a testament to some people's ignorance of the polygraph and their arrogance that adulterers would willingly get strapped up and questioned. A guilty person will often be the first to volunteer themselves to be wired. "They hope their accuser will think if they're willing to take the test, they must be innocent," Reicherter said. But very often their bluff is called. "I have a 50 percent cancellation rate," he said. "I'm about equal with dentists."

The polygraphist said humans' relationship with the truth is not a close one. "I've seen clinical studies where we lie multiple times a day," he said, with deceptions ranging from fibs—you have a headache and answer you feel fine when someone inquires—to making up an excuse to get out of a dinner party with bores.

Being dishonest might be one of the components that separates us from the rest of nature. "Everybody lies," Mark Twain wrote. "Every day; every hour; awake; asleep; in his dreams; in his joy; in his mourning."

Chapter 30
Finding His Center at The Fringe

For the Long Island Voice, *August 1999.*

It's estimated that there are 75,000 actors in New York City. Joel Manaloto, attending an average of 10 plays a week, is on his way to seeing every single one of them.

Born in Lakeview and raised in Baldwin, Manaloto, 25, is the rare person who can make a living from his obsession. He's a casting director, specializing in non-union productions. That means he casts, for the most part, credit-card-financed indie films and plays so off-Broadway they're done in candlelit basements seating a dozen people on broken furniture.

His weekly average of plays goes up with the August 18 kick-off of the Third Annual New York International Fringe Festival, an 11-day orgy of avant-garde theater in 20 venues on the Lower East Side. One hundred and seventy-five productions will run from 3 p.m. to midnight every day. Fifteen foreign countries are represented and 30 U.S. cities, presenting everything from a Tom Waits-William Burroughs-Robert Wilson musical to "King Lear" to soon-to-be classics titled "My Penis" and "Geek on Smack."

Manaloto will see 30 of them, including one of the most eagerly anticipated—"Notes From Underground," Dostoyevsky's magnificent rant, adapted and directed by Michael Gardner, and cast by Manaloto.

"Producers, I've found, are mostly from Manhattan, mostly raised upper-middle class," he says. "Actors are mostly from the suburbs, or anywhere in the country except New York. I can connect to both worlds."

He's been busy doing that. In the past year he's cast 22 films and 37 plays. "All I do all day is something I want to do. I got an undergraduate degree in finance from NYU and went on for a masters in film," Manaloto says. "But even in business school I lived with and hung out with actors. I bummed around for a year. Then last year I was temping, typing at Sloan Kettering Hospital from 9 to 5. By 4:30, I was beat. Not just beat. Beaten. Now, though, it's not unusual for me to go 20 hours straight. It's what I want to do."

He lives in three worlds: an apartment on the Upper East Side; the rabbit warren of clubs, cafés and theaters off-off Broadway; and Baldwin, which he still refers to as home. "I go every six weeks, like clockwork, to stay for three days. I have this fear of my body collapsing, so I go home. And get my hair cut at Dominick's in Oceanside, where I've gone since I was seven. He always asks the same question, 'What're you doin' home?' I say, 'Getting my hair cut.' And he never believes me."

Early on, a connection was made between theater and money. "When I was eight my father took me to see Andy Gibb in "Joseph and the Amazing Technicolor Dreamcoat." Andy was sick and his understudy played it. What a career, you know? Wow, understudying Andy Gibb? But my clearest memory was my father saying, 'I paid 30 bucks for this ticket. You better appreciate it.' Casting, I use 98 percent of my business degree and two percent my film degree. I can make a living. It's a huge range. In the last three months, for example, I've had things that paid $65. And I've had things pay $2,250. I've never turned down a job because I was offered too little money. I've never been refused a job because I asked too much. I don't turn down work. The toughest thing I had was for an industrial film. They needed a sumo wrestler who wasn't in the Screen Actors Guild. I combed the city and came up empty. Lots of sumo wrestlers but all in SAG. An agent told me the only thing in New York harder to find would be a non-SAG midget."

Did he get his man? Manaloto nods. "A former football player at the University of Alabama. Huge Korean guy. He could even act a little."

Young actors revere DeNiro; young directors, Scorcese. Who does Manaloto idolize? "Francine Maisler. She cast "The People vs. Larry Flynt." Think about it. Courtney Love. The guy who played Woody Harrelson's brother was Woody Harrelson's brother. Flynt as the judge. James Carville. That's where casting is a creative act."

Is there a casting couch for casting directors? "Not this casting director. I love actors, but I try not to get involved with them. I get tons of mail. Chocolates with the resumes and photographs. An actress sent her picture, an invitation to a show and a condom. My response was to sit and stare at it for half an hour."

Chapter 31
Thrills and Spills on
The Gambling Cruise

For the Long Island Voice, *September 1998.*

Get too loud, rude or hostile in a casino in Atlantic City and a couple of large men named Junior and Sonny will throw you into the parking lot.

But what happens if you behave poorly on a casino boat three and a half miles out in the ocean? The question is put to Bill Tietel, owner of the Midnight Gambler II, in his office along the funky Freeport waterfront. He almost smiles.

"We haven't had any problems with the public since we opened in April," he says. "I run honest games for honest people. I like winners. They'll always be back."

For $15, the boat will take you out beyond the three-mile limit, where gambling is legal. There are two trips daily, 11 a.m. to 4:30 p.m. and 7 p.m. to midnight. On Friday and Saturday nights, the boat returns at 1 a.m.

This Friday night, we glide out of the slip for the 45-minute sail to gambling waters. The $10-million boat, 135 feet long by 36 feet wide, capable of carrying 500 people, has a lower deck with a bar and ranks of slot machines, a middle deck with a bar, two crap tables, a roulette wheel and blackjack and poker tables. The top deck is open, with hard plastic chairs and tables.

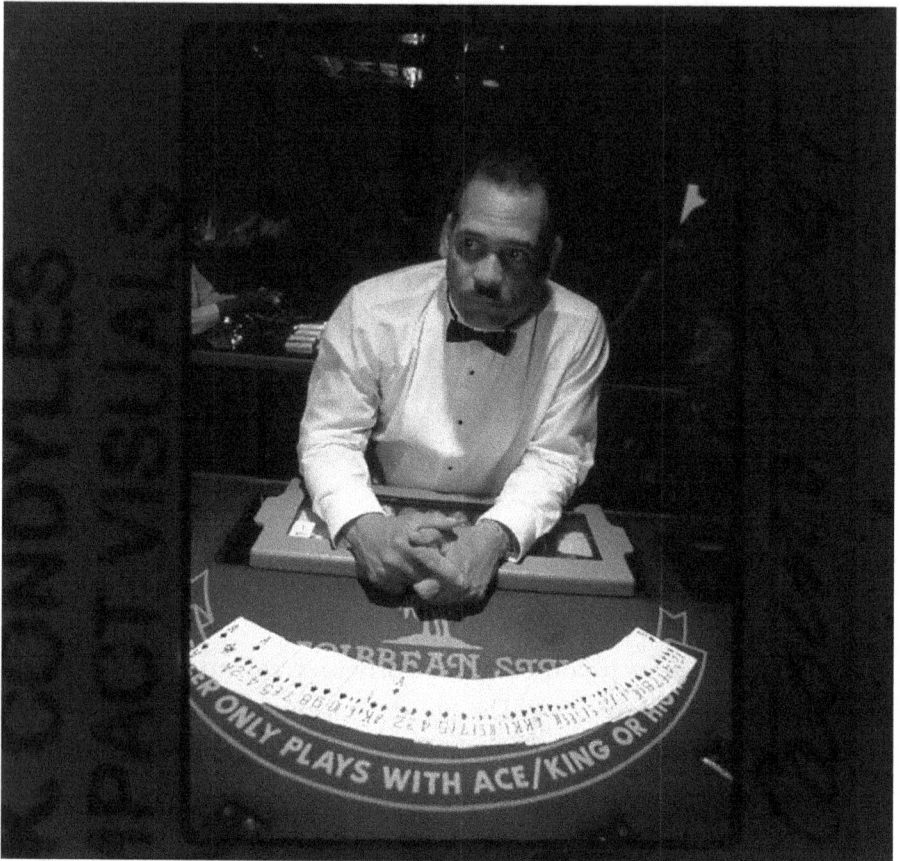

Most of the 184 customers sailing tonight are up top watching the sun sinking over the South Shore. The fashion, with few exceptions, is what is worn at amusement parks on hot days. Some people are disappointed there is no music, no dancing. They miss the point. This is an enterprise devised to separate you from your money, not one designed for comfort or entertainment.

Watching the dealers set up the crap table at about 7:30, is Zoose, a 30-something lawyer from Brooklyn. He's a regular at the table, coming out at least once a week, tonight with about $600. He's with Harry Steiper, 75, another regular, a jolly man with slicked-back white hair. Gina Scudes, a petite woman carrying a rum and Diet Coke, smoking a Newport, comes into the room. She's laughing. She gets a hug from Harry.

"My girlfriend," he says.

She shrieks, poking him. "I'm here every day," she says. "Sometimes twice. It's like my second home, like 'Cheers.'"

She sings part of the TV show's theme song. Zoose says, "Marry me, Gina." She screams, shaking her auburn-streaked hair. She has to think when asked about her job. Giggling, she finally says, "Oh, waitress." She's got $1,000 to play with tonight.

An hour later, Bob Scagnelli, in a Ranger jersey and shorts, standing at the crap table, orders a drink from a passing waitress. "These dealers suck," he says. Scagnelli's a mailman. "Don't get me disgruntled." It's difficult to tell if he's kidding.

Cutting through the loony-bin buzz at the blackjack tables, we find Gina Scudes letting out rebel yells. A crowd has gathered to watch her play $125 a hand. There's also noise at the crap table. Zoose is up $200. Steiper is losing but insists, "I'm building."

It's 10 p.m. and an ashen-faced man in a Yankee cap sits on steps in a corridor. There are trickles of vomit at the sides of his mouth. Downstairs, near the ladies' room, a woman sits, sweat at her temples, hand to her forehead. "About 10 percent, maximum," Captain Gregory Koon, 48, says in estimating the number of seasick passengers on every trip.

Koon shows the security room, off the darkened bridge. It's a closet with monitors, racks of VCRS. He moves a joystick, and a camera zooms in close enough to see the dirt under a fingernail at the blackjack table. "Someone claims he fell on my boat? I've got a tape if he did or didn't."

Just after 11 and there's trouble at the crap table. "Fuck you!" Bob the Mailman is yelling at the dealer. "You don't know what the fuck you're doing." A pit boss immediately points a finger. "You relax! Go cool off." Bob stalks out.

Precisely at midnight, the captain announces the casino will close in 15 minutes. Someone asks, "What'd he say?" Zoose, who has lost close to $500 in half an hour, answers him, "He said: Iceberg dead ahead."

The casino is closed and the bars are crowded. Some people are wandering around as if they'd just witnessed a serious accident. Gina Scudes is laughing at the bar, still working her rum and Diet Cokes and Newports. She has broken even, which is as it should be. Harry Steiper and his friend Zoose are broke, but they have fought the good fight and even had a few laughs along the way.

Bob the Mailman says, "I'm never coming back. These dealers are fucking morons. I'm going to Atlantic City."

Chapter 32
No One Loves A Loser:
Al D'Amato Is Defeated

Al D'Amato, from Island Park on Long Island, was a career politician in the Nassau County Republican machine for years. He was elected to the U.S. Senate in 1981 and served until 1999, defeated by then Congressman Charles Schumer. After his loss, D'Amato opened Park Strategies, a lobbying firm. For the Long Island Voice, *November 1998.*

Grim visions—full moon over the Hilton on Sixth Avenue in Manhattan on Election Night, a blue- and pink-lighted ballroom with dirty tinsel hanging from the ceiling, lots of Republicans getting oiled at three bars, attending the political wake of Senator Alphonse M. D'Amato.

Most are in full cry, trying desperately to boogie to a demented sound mix—Madonna followed by Benny Goodman morphing into K.C. and the Sunshine Band fading to the Everly Brothers. A little after 9, some faces are sullen, staring at nothing, with cellphones clutched to ears, getting the news that the networks have projected the senator, Long Island's own, will go down—and big.

Stew and Ray and Larry are drinking Coors Light from the bottle, scoping chicks, talking about them in a brand of macho White-boy lingo. In their early 30s, dressed in dark suits, silk ties, proud to show off power suspenders, they work, Larry says, "on the Street."

Asked about issues in the campaign, Stew says, "Issues? You mean the abortion thing? The gun thing? Who gives a shit? It's the bucks, my friend. The bucks. Alphonse respects the Street. We're the engine of New York, and he knows it."

Two men confer near the photographers' platform, one with a cellphone to his ear, listening. He punches it off and says, "We could go home now." His friend nods. He has a good tailor, but not skilled enough to conceal more than 300 pounds. He rubs his close-cropped hair that looks like it has the texture to clean barbecue grills. Where's home? he's asked. "The Island."

Is he a long-time D'Amato supporter? "I support this," he says, and cups a hand to his crotch. "You don't want to ask me no more questions." He moves toward the door like a boat weighing anchor and slipping away.

At the foot of the stage is Georgette, a stylish woman in her late 30s, with her companion, Peter, a man in his 60s, made comfortable, he says, by "real estate and investments." And politics? Peter grins like a skull. "How can you make money in politics?" If every man over 40 deserves the face he has, what could Peter have done? Strangle children?

Georgette is having a good time, keeping the beat to Tina Turner's "Simply the Best." In politics, she says, "You have to energize your base." She turns and wiggles in a circle with a wicked smile.

The crowd is overwhelmingly White. Here and there are some Black church ladies in big hats. Some Orthodox Jewish men hang together at the edges of the crowd, including Chaim Lebovits, 23, from Williamsburg, Brooklyn. "Senator D'Amato saved us," he says. "When no one cared for us, he saved us!"

Bob Franklin, in town from Seattle on business, has wandered into the hotel ballroom by mistake and has taken advantage of the bar. What does he think of D'Amato? "A massively insecure little dirtbag. The only thing he knows how to do is to answer his phone when money calls." He looks out over the crowd. "There's not one sane person in this room."

The music stops around 10 p.m. and the TV screens are bringing bad news. D'Amato is doomed. People leave, others stay and drink and cheer televised images of Newt Gingrich and Dan Quayle. Stew and Ray and Larry are still pounding the Coors Light. Their instant analysis is harsh. "Loser," Larry says. "Gone. That's politics. When you lose, it's too bad, but—you're a loser, right?"

Chaim Lebovits says, "I don't believe in so-called 'projections.' He stood by me. I stand by him. He saved us!"

After Schumer's victory speech is aired, a frightening thought has entered the minds of reporters and the remaining Republicans—D'Amato could keep us here all night. But around 11:30, the theme from—what else?—"Rocky," and white-out TV lights envelope us. Suits fill the stage, Ed Koch and Rudy Giuliani shamelessly jockeying for position.

D'Amato gives a strange, rushed, jumbled and pathetic speech, beginning by apologizing for keeping everyone waiting. There had been elevator trouble. Was this a final deception? Had he simply stayed upstairs in a fit of pique. Bouncing on his toes, still in campaign mode, he's reciting phrases as if even he's sick of hearing them. "It's great to be a New Yorker ... It's great to be in the Empire State ... My New Yorkers ... We've come a long way ... To make this state a better place ... People of every stripe ... The little village of Island Park ... My mama ..."

Only one person out of hundreds seems upset, a young woman in tears. Everyone else is ready to clear out as fast as the defeated senator.

A transparent fraud to the end, a hustler, a bully and a clown, Al D'Amato took a fall under tinsel and a full moon. But the word is, the senator will stay on the gravy train, lobbying his former colleagues. Not a loser after all.

Chapter 33
Time Machine:
Test Driving a DeLorean

For Long Island Business News, *January 2007.*

Off Montauk Highway in West Sayville, the legends are silent in the morning sun. If you weren't looking, you'd never know they were there: more than two dozen DeLoreans, one of the most storied cars in automotive history. Compared to the pickups crowding the curved driveway, the low-slung, stainless steel masterworks look fast, even standing still.

Of some 9,200 DeLoreans manufactured in 1981 and 1982, 6,000 are believed to remain, each offering something more than beauty and performance. They're at once inseparable from their larger-than-life creator and linked forever with an Irish guerrilla war, a videotaped drug bust and the magic of time travel.

The West Sayville lot adjoins a long, low garage of crisp white doors. The interior, although shadowy and reeking of motor oil, has the appearance of a tidy laboratory, the polar opposite of Doc Brown's eccentric digs in "Back to the Future," the film trilogy in which the DeLorean gained widespread fame. Four more of the vehicles are up on lifts or in various stages of repair on the shop floor.

Welcome to P.J. Grady DeLorean Sales, Parts, Service and Restoration. Mechanic Mike Pack apologizes for his oil-stained palms when a visitor reaches out to shake. Asked if this is the largest De

Lorean dealership in the area, he nods. "This is the only dealership on the East Coast."

P.J. Grady is not limited by geography. It takes in DeLoreans from as far away as Colorado and California, at times as many as 50 of the gull-wing-doored sports cars. Pack himself has owned three. "I like their looks, the aesthetics of the car, the history, everything," he says.

Cinematic time machines may be the perfect fit for this obscure South Shore spot, where the business' namesake opened a Pontiac dealership in 1914, one of the first car dealerships in New York. Current owner Rob Grady, P.J.'s grandson, says the garage has always sold and repaired cars, from Chevrolets to Cadillacs and other GM vehicles. On the basis of a prototype, Grady's brother, Paul, moved the company into DeLoreans in the late 1970s, before the first commercial vehicle ever rolled off the line. "He just liked the cars," Grady says.

Business is good. Grady sells only about five cars a year, but he's always busy in the repair and restoration business. In addition to style, a DeLorean is a practical, everyday car, getting about 30 miles to the gallon on the highway, he says. One in good condition will set you back $30,000 or so.

Dream machine

Any discussion of the automobile turns instantly to its charismatic creator, John Z. DeLorean. Born into an immigrant family in a hardscrabble patch of 1925 Detroit, DeLorean studied engineering at a technical college before joining the auto industry. In less than two decades he rose through the ranks to become vice president of General Motors, where he was responsible for several Motor City classics, among them the Pontiac Firebird, the Grand Prix and America's first muscle car, the GTO. Says classic car consultant David Brownell: "He had gasoline in his veins."

Six-feet-four, movie-star handsome and sporting *la dolce vita* appetites, the much-married DeLorean walked away from a $650,000-a-year job in 1973 to make his own automobile. He promised an "ethical car," his vision focused on safety, durability and fuel efficiency.

It was to be a car that would be affordable and, most importantly, sexy. DeLorean raised a portion of the necessary capital, then sweet-talked the British government into pouring $140 million into a factory outside Belfast. Forget that the British were embroiled in The Troubles. DeLorean promised to put the Northern Irish to work, Catholic and Protestant alike.

A prototype was ready by 1977, but the car went through years of design tinkering; it wasn't until 1981 that the first "DMC-12" rolled out of the Irish plant. The price: $26,000. The gull-wings were an improvement on the doors of a venerable Mercedes sport coupe. The stainless-steel skin guaranteed the body would never corrode. Powered by a rear-set V6, the sleek but boxy roadster would top out near 135 mph; aficionados claimed that even at those speeds, a good DeLorean felt like it was just getting started.

The timing, as it turned out, couldn't have been worse. Car sales withered in a U.S. recession, and not everyone shared DeLorean's dream. There were complaints about the cars being underpowered and bad press about performance. Crippled by low sales and the need for more capital, it was all over within two years.

In October 1982, DeLorean was busted in a Los Angeles airport hotel trying to peddle 60 pounds of cocaine to an undercover federal agent for $24 million. He promised to deliver 220 pounds more, allegedly to finance his lifestyle and bankroll a restart of his car company. DeLorean did 10 days in jail before walking on a $10 million bond, a stay that would prove to be his only time behind bars. He beat the rap by claiming entrapment.

When he died in 2005 at age 80, one of his homes—worth $2.5 million—was awarded to his attorney by court order. The judge was quoted as saying the lawyer deserved the prize for "pulling off the legal miracle of the century."

Easy rider

As he tosses you the keys of a gunmetal-gray DMC-12, Grady reflects on the DeLorean criminal saga. "At first I thought it would affect us adversely," he says, "but in retrospect it didn't hurt at all."

The door floats up soundlessly. Slipping inside, there's a feeling of sitting in a roomy, gray-leathered cockpit. A leather strap hangs down, and with a pull the gull-wing shuts with an agreeable click. The car was one of the first to feature unified interiors, Grady says, noting the two-seater's seamless construction and lines from door to dashboard. And there's the window within the window, which Grady said is handy at a toll booth.

Asked where the flux capacitor is kept, the dealer gives a look that says please ask me a question I haven't been asked a million times. Then you drive. A car that is power everything has no power steering, which keeps your attention from drifting. Manual steering offers a better sense of control and provides the feel of the road coming up through your hands. It's a smooth ride. Grady says it's comfortable even on 1,000-mile trips.

Opening it up a little, the car responds with a growl. A comfortable and fun ride, and a real treat for exhibitionists. Idling at a light or cruising slowly down Montauk Highway, passersby can't help but stare.

After all these years, the car still looks like the future.

Chapter 34
Home Security Blues

For Long Island Business News, *August 2012.*

It wasn't long after we moved in, when Mary noticed the miniature video cameras attached to trees on our neighbor's side of the fence. Two of them aimed at spots along our gravel driveway, which snakes about 50 yards from a sleepy road to our house under the trees. Our neighbor's house, set on the road, is shielded from us by that fence and a stand of bamboo 20 feet high.

We'd already noticed the dog.

The brute doesn't howl—that's left to some forlorn creature way in the distance behind us—but does something beyond howling, something wrenched from his unholy depths. He's enormous, white, one of those Arctic breeds, but this boy wouldn't be caught dead pulling a sled. No, he's the one the Innuit sic on the polar bear. I mean he's big.

If he's patrolling the semi-hidden backyard—a pool, pool house, basketball court, sprawling patios—and I take the garbage out, he starts his thundering one-way conversation: I hear you. I'm on duty. I'm a big dog. Big dog, big dog, big dog.

But then I realized the wolf in wolf's clothing is inside most of the time, and after raising his alarms, he quickly shuts up.

Our neighbor's handsome spread also has spotlights on all night, making the front lawn suitable for small plane landings. When we first moved in on a snowy February day, we both thought the only downside would be the Klondike Demon, briefly but piercingly reminding us that if we were nuts enough to climb the fence he'd make short work of us.

If that was the only problem with our paranoid neighbors, we'd be fine. But then, thinking about the coming summer evenings in our garden, we looked at each other and said at the same time: "Parties." With that amusement park next door, it could be a sleepless summer. "Imagine," Mary said wearily, "what kind of sound system they have." We decided the only thing to do was make nice and they'd invite us over for the all-night swim/dance bacchanals. But even though the lights burn night and day, through the weekends, there's never been a sound. Once every three months or so they have guests over. Very, very quiet guests.

I met the neighbors once. Sort of. One afternoon we lost power. To find out if it was just us the Long Island Power Authority had picked on or everybody was included, I walked down the driveway—past the little cameras—across the lawn and up on to their porch. After knocking several times, I was about to leave, when the door opened halfway revealing a slight, middle-aged woman. I introduced myself as her neighbor, hand out to shake, which she didn't seem to notice. No issues with power she said, since if LIPA failed they had their own generator that automatically kicked in. I looked past her and saw a man down a hallway holding a choke chain around the neck of the Alaskan Assassin, who was growling, quivering with rage.

Who are they? Who knows?

I thanked her for her time and walked off the porch. She'd been pleasant, barely. Better, I thought, than a woman neighbor in Greenport who, the morning we moved in and Mary introduced herself on the sidewalk, replied: "Why would anyone want to live here?"

I once worked with a guy who had the same ideas as our neighbors, if a bit down market, who said, "I got a really big fence, a really big dog and a really big gun." Swaggering, a homesteader taking care of his own. This cowboy wasn't from South Dakota, but Main Street Southold.

Oh, for the days, old timers say, when you never had to lock your doors. That would be now, if you accept some truth. Serious crimes are lower in the U.S. than they've been in 20 years, with murder down by half and robbery off 10 percent in 2010 from the year before. That's according to research by James Alan Fox, a criminologist at Northeastern University in Boston. Quoted in *The Christian Science Monitor*, Fox said the plunging crime pattern "transcends cities and U.S. regions ... We are indeed a safer nation than 20 years ago."

But we're putting our money where our myths are. A recent Gallup poll found Americans believe crime is spiking out of control, and according to Dallas-based Park Associates, a market research outfit specializing in technology, we're paying $10 billion annually for household security. That's slated to rise 30 percent in four years.

Good fences make good neighbors, Robert Frost wrote. But we discovered recently no fence is completely neighbor-proof. Last week Mary went into the kitchen and saw the dog on our back porch looking through the screen door. When he saw her he rose up, playfully putting his front paws on the door, a puppy nodding his head, wagging his tale. He then bounced away to the back yard and stood, looking silently at some landscapers, until the neighbor lady stormed into the yard with the chain and led him away.

He was looking over his shoulder at Mary standing on the porch. "I felt so sorry for him," she said. "I wanted to wave."

Part III
NEW YORK, NEW YORK

"The true New Yorker secretly believes that people living anywhere else have to be, in some sense, kidding."

So said John Updike, and even though I'm not all the way there, I know what he's talking about. I was born in Brooklyn, and when I was four, our large family moved to a little river town of 8,000 people in Southern Illinois. That's where I grew up.

I went to school in St. Louis and we spent a year in Chicago before moving back to New York when I was 18. As Dublin did later, New York seduced me immediately, and I gratefully succumbed. I went to school there, got married and worked four years on the streets of the city as a night line cab driver. Those years gave me an extensive education of the city and its people. New York is still my hometown, even though I've been gone now more than 20 years.

Chapter 35
In Harlem, A Neighborhood Finds Its Groove Again

For The Washington Post, *April 2002.*

The beauty is immediately apparent when you come up out of the rattling claustrophobia of the subway. European-wide boulevards open the sky and give uninterrupted views stretching a hundred blocks to the glass towers of midtown. Side streets of tall sycamores, restored brownstones and a reserved stillness are a relief from the rest of Manhattan, which is never prouder than when boasting of its insomnia. Take it easy, say the lovely blocks of Striver's Row, Mount Morris and Sugar Hill. Take your time. You're in Harlem.

You will hear references to "Spanish Harlem," which is also known as El Barrio, and "Italian Harlem," which has evaporated to a couple of restaurants feeding minor celebrities. But just say Harlem and New Yorkers will point you toward the area of Manhattan that runs roughly from Broadway east to the Harlem River, and 110th Street north to about 155th Street. Boundaries aside, like any true community it is a place that allows for imagination and desire.

"I knew the Dance Theatre of Harlem was one of the great companies of the world. But I was happily surprised at Harlem as a place of beauty," said Laveen Naidu, a choreographer for DTH. He never removed his eyes from his charges: students levitating through the dusty light of a rehearsal studio at the company's home on 152nd Street.

"Look at them," he said, nodding toward the bodies soaring past. "From all over this country—from Argentina, Brazil, Europe and three blocks away—they all want to be here. Something new, something fresh is happening."

He was talking about the "Harlem Renaissance," which is a result of capital flowing uptown, and middle class people moving to this Manhattan neighborhood, reclaiming parks, streets and buildings. The arts revival, with new or refurbished galleries, fine shops, restaurants, clubs and small cafés, recalls the first Renaissance, between the two World Wars, when a vibrant movement of art and politics transformed Harlem, New York, and the country, forever.

Harlem's Heritage

When you spend time in Harlem, the first stereotype dispelled is that the neighborhood is somehow menacing. There is an air of hospitality, a small-town atmosphere. If you're not afraid of New York, don't worry about Harlem. Heed the directions of Duke Ellington and Billy Strayhorn and take the A train, like Annelies Boogaerdt, who was strolling down Lenox Avenue one morning last month, taking a break from her work with the Dutch consulate downtown.

"When I was a girl in Holland, this place meant poverty and crime," Boogaerdt said as church bells filled the air. "I first came intrigued by its connection to home—you know, Haarlem is a Dutch town, New York was first New Amsterdam. And I found it such a pleasant place. I love discovering the architecture—like that," she said, pointing at a church on the corner of 123rd Street. The home of the Ephesus Seventh Day Adventists (built in 1887 for the Reformed Low Dutch Church) is a sandstone Gothic beauty with a broad tower and masterfully carved monsters.

"The people are welcoming," Boogaerdt continued. "I go to the Apollo, I go shopping, church services on Sundays for the singing. I bring friends from home and tell them if you go to church you must do three things: Dress nicely, put something in the plate when it passes and stay until the end. My friends are always amazed at Harlem."

In 1658, the Dutch settled Nieuw Haarlem as farmland on a fertile plain running west from the river to rocky heights. Two hundred years later it had descended into such a horrific Irish shantytown that a health inspector reported conditions were "rank with filth and stench, and the consequence is that mortality holds high carnival there." But with the arrival of elevated trains in the 1870s, Harlem developed into one of the finest areas of the city for all classes, provided they were white.

This changed in 1901, when an African American real estate agent, Philip A. Payton, persuaded a few landlords to rent to black families. Overcrowded communities migrated uptown, as well as rural folk from the South and the Caribbean. Soon Harlem was the "Capital of Black America," and has remained so.

Part of its appeal is its sense of integrity and continuity. The Italians are mostly gone from the Village, the Irish are barely there in Hell's Kitchen, and Jews are few and far between along the Grand Concourse of the Bronx, but Harlem has more than a century of shared history and layers of memory.

The most enduring memory is of the original Harlem Renaissance. Artistic expression—Black America's life raft in an ocean of troubles—found safe harbor in Harlem. Musicians, painters, sculptors, activists and intellectuals set up shop. Writers like Claude McKay and Countee Cullen (who would later teach the young James Baldwin high school French and connect memory with inspiration) chronicled the new city within a city.

Hearing the news, one Midwestern kid rejected his father's advice to study in Europe and chose Columbia University instead. "More than Paris, or the Shakespeare country, or Berlin, or the Alps, I wanted to see Harlem, the greatest Negro city in the world," said Langston Hughes. Although well-traveled, the poet never left his dream city, and became as important a contributor to American literature as Walt Whitman.

From the mid-1950s, Harlem spiraled into decline. Bad economic times were worse uptown. As the saying goes: "New York catches a cold, Harlem gets pneumonia." Unemployment, moronically ugly "urban development," despair and narcotics (especially the pathology of crack in the 1980s and early '90s) turned parts of the small town into a spooky urban wilderness. But people are breathing easily once again, in safety and hope. A former president locating his office on 125th Street has accelerated momentum in the neighborhood, but it is really people like Donna Lewis who keep the gears turning.

Originally from Cincinnati and a world traveler, the young woman opened Home Sweet Harlem Café two years ago on 135th Street. "Light fare, and I use organic products whenever I can. We're providing a healthier alternative in Harlem," said Lewis one late afternoon, keeping an eye on Michelle Hawkins, a neighborhood kid who was doing her homework while her father worked in the shop next door. "My silent partner," she said, as Michelle beamed.

Lewis had installed a new pressed tin ceiling and elevated nooks in the windows flanking the door. There are fresh flowers on the tables and coffee flasks on an antique stove. "My grandmother always had coffee ready for visitors, so when I saw that stove, I knew where the coffee would go. I love remembering her every time people ask for coffee by saying what she said: 'On the stove, help yourself.'

"I was taught as a child that a community is only as strong as the strength put into it. I own property here. I'm an entrepreneur who walks to work. I want people to see me and my café as something solid, an investment in our future."

Another world traveler settling in is painter Dianne Smith. She's lived as far afield as France and Italy, but her home and studio are now in a restored building on 130th Street.

"I was living in Beverly Hills," she said, rolling her eyes and taking a seat on the studio floor. "I wasn't painting and had to get out, and I'd always wanted to live in Harlem. My early work was Afrocentric, I had to paint that way, but what I'm doing now ... it might not look it, but it's inspired by where I live."

Her abstracts, which resemble land or seascapes inhabited in dreams, have definite horizons. Her art, like the best of modern work, is concerned with analyzing forms, not reproducing them, and her subtle, expert melding of color holds the eye.

"Sometimes I work all night," she said. "Or all day. It's comfortable here. Home."

Smith shows at a downtown gallery in the hot art district of Chelsea but also at the World Africa Gallery in the Brownstone complex. Entering the Brownstone is part-time travel to a glamorous past, part Fellini experience, with unexpected and delightful spaces in period surroundings. Three floors offer clothes, jewelry, scarves, fine art, a beauty parlor, massage therapist, even a bridal shop, all run by radiant women who act more like visiting neighbors than merchants.

Through a narrow foyer past a carved wooden staircase, the rooms open out with clothes on racks and tables. Princess Jenkins presides here (asked if that is her given name, she said, "Even then they knew"), selling style under 20-foot ceilings and stained-glass windows. Shopping in Harlem is finding bargains and fun, and the Brownstone is the place to start.

Around the corner on 125th Street, evening settled with crowds browsing, bargaining with street vendors, filling the chicken joints and the discount stores. Starbucks and Disney have come to the signature street of Harlem, but the bright vertical neon of the Apollo Theater still announces the proud tradition of celebrating more than 70 years of African-American musical arts. Hip hop now shares the stage with R&B and '60s soul, but the chorus girls, the comics and the audience on Amateur Night are a tribute to the past that is still right on time.

Beyond the brightness of 125th Street, looking west, were yellow lights dotting the parlors on Sugar Hill. Above them was a fairy tale castle of turrets and towers gleaming against the darkening sky: the great keep of City College, crowning the heights above Harlem.

Masterworks and Words

Over on Convent Avenue, Sherman Edmiston was showing a couple of visitors his gallery, the Essie Green, before closing for the day. The gallery, considered one of the finest dealers of African-

American art in the country, shows "Black masterworks" in a generous space of oriental rugs and rich wood tones. Vivid but unobtrusive lighting reveals the genius of Romare Bearden, Jacob Lawrence, Charles Alston, Allen Stringfellow and others.

There are works here that will put you back $200,000 and attract clients like AOL Time Warner chief Richard Parsons. "We help collectors," said Edmiston, closing up and heading down the block for dinner. "And people who want to start a collection. But if you're not in the market but serious about exploring this art, you're welcome. It's not just about beauty, excitement, mastery of form. It's as much about heritage."

Born in Harlem Hospital, Edmiston has lived all over the city but has been here since 1989. Greeted warmly at the Sugar Hill Bistro on 145th Street, he settled in behind a stupendous Manhattan cocktail and said, "You know six degrees of separation? In Harlem it's more like three."

Physician Dineo Khabele is one of the owners of the Sugar Hill Bistro, which is a bar, nightclub with music (Wynton Marsalis often sits in) and a comfortable, elegant restaurant of three upstairs rooms. The diners were an integrated crowd (the norm in upscale Harlem nightspots). The partners opened, Khabele said, "because we couldn't find anything like it in the neighborhood."

Khabele was born in Africa, raised in the States. "I was fascinated by Harlem growing up, its deep culture, the sense of fun, music, fashion, excitement. We're re-creating it here."

Langston Hughes wrote: "I, Harlem,/ Island within an Island,/ but not alone."

And that heartfelt notion lives in the comment of a waitress at the Lenox Lounge one late night. She handed out a menu of bar food as the Richard Clay Quartet was doing its damnedest to blow the roof off, and was asked what was good.

"Everyone," she said, taking in the packed room, "being here tonight."

Chapter 36
A Day At the Races

For Newsday, *April 2002.*

Neil Kavakos and Henry Tantillo got out to the Aqueduct earlier than usual a couple of Saturdays ago to ensure they would get their favorite spot.

They figured it would be crowded. One of the world's great horse races, Wood Memorial, would be run for the 78th consecutive year at the America's legendary "City Track," the only one in the country you can get to by hopping a subway. But, for the two Forest Hills neighbors, Wood Memorial Day would be amateur day.

"New Year's Eve is amateur night for drinkers," Kavakos, a retired owner of a travel agency, explained. Tantillo, also a retiree, completed the thought, "And today is amateur day at Aqueduct for horseplayers."

The two men say they go to the south Queens landmark every Wednesday and Saturday. "His wife lets him out for good behavior," Tantillo teased. His friend rolled his eyes as they made their way by elevator to the top floor of the 110-foot-high structure, and entered the Skyline Club, a spacious place of comfortable chairs, an espresso bar and subdued lighting, looking like the lobby of an old-fashioned but still upscale hotel.

Bill Haig, another regular, had saved seats at semi-partitioned "handicapping tables" that faced a bank of TV monitors. There are more than 1,500 of these sets throughout the track, giving odds, up-to-the-minute information and replays of races, as well as broadcasting the 10-race Aqueduct card and simulcasting action from Florida, Arkansas, and Kentucky.

The retirees were three out of 20,103 that day filling the halls of the track, a complex that sits on 192 acres. Horseplayers sat or stood and studied racing forms, some kibitzing with friends; others silent and dedicated as military codebreakers, focused on the weights, times and ages, fractions that would reveal a winner in the thicket of numbers.

"I just come to make a donation," Tantillo, who bets no more than $2 a race, handing out coffee and cake.

Kavakos, who budgets about $100 a day for wagering said, "It passes the time."

Without looking up from his racing form, Haig scoffed, "I'm not here to pass the time."

"Study long, you study wrong," Kavakos needled.

Haig smiled, "Lots of ways to lose, only a few to win. Everyone's got a system, and no one's right."

Horse racing is one of the simplest and most natural of sports. Five thousand years ago, when horses were first domesticated, someone must have declared his horse faster than his friend's horse, with the friend then asking if he wanted to bet. In New York, the sport goes back to the time of the Dutch settlers, racing their mounts at Bowling Green and Hempstead Plain.

The original Aqueduct opened on September 27, 1894, with 700 fans and six bookmakers giving odds. The track took its name from a large overhead pipe, 10 feet in diameter, that originated in Nassau County and made its way across the grounds to supply water to Brooklyn.

Even then, Aqueduct was the track without pretensions. The old clubhouse and grandstand was torn down and rebuilt beginning in 1956, and the Big A reopened September 14, 1959. In New York racing circles, they say Belmont Park is just that, a beautiful park to take the kids, and Saratoga is a county fair. Aqueduct is down-to-earth, practical, as tough and tender as the borough it calls home. The city track that has the scale, complexity and popularity of a city itself. On race day, 300 miles of electrical wiring provide power. There are close to 2,000 employees, including 170 security officers, and a full-time doctor and nurse who, along with 10 emergency medical technicians, runs an infirmary of 10 beds.

You won't go hungry or thirsty at the Big A, with seven bars, 21 grills, delis and concession stands, including New York's largest restaurant, Equestris, which can serve 1,600 diners. Like everything at Aqueduct, Equestris is inexpensive (the track has a better way of taking your money) with a rib-eye steak going for under $20.

Views from trackside dining are spectacular. In the distance, more than 10 stories above the grounds, you can see clearly the eleven barns of the backstretch, the trim houses of South Ozone Park, planes gliding into nearby Kennedy, and miles away, the façade of Belmont Park.

At 1 p.m., Aqueduct was as noisy, busy and bustling as a city at lunch hour, but the track had been in business hours before the first post time. Anthony Trotta was at the track barbershop at 8 a.m., cutting hair and giving shaves to horsemen after the morning workout. He would run the barbershop until mid-afternoon.

"Tony," a man said getting into the chair, "tell us about all the celebs who've been in and out of here."

"Ah," the barber responded. "After 24 years of haircuts, everyone's the same to me."

It was so quiet that you could hear the soft rumbling of the 18 escalators churning throughout the track. One floor below, Sal Sciara, clerk of scales, was checking the big Toledo in the scale room. This is a serious job, taken seriously by Sciara. Everything has to be right, to weigh jockeys and their gear before and after races. Next door was the jockey's changing room. A few of the athletes were reading papers or going for coffee in the lounge, a big room of pool tables, couches and a food counter. Two of the diminutive men had last night's Yankees game on video, but they barely watched, slumped on couches, speaking softly to each other about horses.

Down the hall was the silk room, where Louis Olah is in charge of dispensing riding attire. A former jockey, for the past 36 years Olah has worked here, a narrow room filled floor to ceiling with a dizzying riot of vivid color. Look quickly and you feel you've fallen into an abstract painting. But eventually, patterns emerge of stripes, hoops, stars, and other logos. "Four thousand silks," Olah said, "and no two the same."

Thoroughbred owners hand the silks (really made of nylon) over to Olah, who must keep them clean and organized for the jockeys' valets to claim before the races. The silks, for the most part, belong to old familiar names from America's leisure class, but a few pointed out by Olah break the mold. There's George Steinbrenner's blue with a brown sash and brown hoops on a sleeve. Basketball Coach Rick Pitino's white with green shamrocks hangs nearby.

The maroon with white sleeves and stars belongs to Sheik Mohammed Bin Rashid, minister of defense of the United Arab Emirates, owner of eight horse farms from Kentucky to County Kildare, whose other hobbies include camel racing and falconry. Olah approves. "You got the money," the little man said, "why not play a bit?"

Jim Zito works in the horse identification room down the hall, a job as important as any at the racetrack. Thoroughbreds who arrive at Aqueduct must be the horse racing form says they are. Zito is out on the backstretch by 8:30 a.m. taking photos, comparing them with other photos and checking marks to identify horses. There are various ways one horse is different from another, the simplest being color and markings or individual cowlicks, but the surest way for Zito is checking out what track slang calls chestnuts or "night eyes."

"These are calluses inside the horses' legs," Zito explained. "It's the best way to identify a horse. Like fingerprints, no two are alike. You know, all thoroughbreds are tattooed on the inside of the upper lip, but tattoos can be altered. And sometimes you can be mistaken, peeling back the lip of a big powerful animal when he's feeling fractious."

Upstairs at 10 a.m., men guided long flat brooms across approximately 1 million square feet of floor area. Hawkers of racing forms, programs and newspapers quietly set up shop. At the Hello Deli, three bartenders had coffee before going to work, silently checking the form. Most employees play the horses; it's hard to avoid when they're running all day long in front of you.

Richard Giacalone, operating the press elevator, was marking a program. The Maspeth resident has worked here 21 years. "I don't go crazy," he said. "A race or two. I don't have the power to go crazy," he went on, using the track word for finances. "Even if I had the power I wouldn't go crazy."

Around 4 p.m., a few minutes before the running of the Wood, the three retirees in The Skyline Club placed their bets. They watched the race on the TV monitors, as is their habit, rarely going out to see the horses in the flesh. They are old hands and have seen it all before. But it is something not to be missed for those who have never experienced it.

There's the lone, long bugle call, then the fire alarm bell of the starting gate, and the bunched pack of loping colors on the distant backstretch under a high, darkening sky. But the best part is the slowly rising sound, 20,000 voices cheering the magnificent animals on as they turn for home, a sound unheard in any other sport, becoming suddenly the single, urgent and roaring voice of the city track, splitting the afternoon wide open.

Chapter 37
Jazz All Night

For The Washington Post, *December 2010.*

Before the house band started shaking up the bar of the Lenox Lounge one recent evening, a patron ordered a "Billie Holiday," which the drinks card described as rum mixed with cherry brandy and cherry juice.

The bartender looked at the guy, waited a beat, and deadpanned, "Tryin' to go home with a headache?"

That's the atmosphere at the Lenox, a wised-up, welcoming place in the heart of Harlem.

The club, which opened in 1939 and has hosted jazz royalty ever since, is actually two places. The Zebra Room, in the back, has jazz and comedy acts and charges a cover and a minimum. But a spot at the bar up front, which has live jazz several weeknights, doesn't cost anything.

It's said that Wednesday is the new Saturday in New York, but that's not true. Every school night of the week can be Mardi Gras, especially in jazz clubs where the price of a beer is your ticket and you don't get the vibe that you're sitting in on some reverential rites, which is often the case at the pricey places.

On Wednesdays, the Nate Lucas Organ Trio performs in the Lenox bar, with musicians sitting in and neighborhood regulars taking the mic to shout the blues or make love to a ballad. The crowd is black, white, Latino, Asian and mixed-generation in this perfectly preserved art deco dream that pays homage to the curve, from the sign out front to the recessed lights to the tiled floor.

One night, comedian Paul Mooney was in the Zebra Room laying down his paranoid, harebrained and occasionally hilarious invective on world history and pop culture. A hint: White people don't emerge in a positive light, but then, neither does anybody else. Although Mooney did note the strength of Patti Labelle's pipes: He heard her when she performed at the Garden, "and I was in Cincinnati."

While Mooney raged on about proving that O.J. didn't do it, Lucas and his rhythm section were cooking in the front window of the bar. It was packed three deep, with the door open to the street and people gathered outside, listening.

Sitting in was 15-year-old jazz guitarist Solomon Hicks, fresh from an appearance at the Apollo around the corner. The kid flashed long lines that had the crowd applauding before he slowed down to chugging eight-bar blues.

"Only 15," one guy said to his friend, who replied, "No way, those fingers are 100 years old."

A beautiful young woman from Spanish Harlem said she'd taken a fancy to drummer Matt Baranello, especially the way he "scowled" during his blistering solos. After Baranello kicked the bass drum, machine-gunned the toms, hushed the high hat and crashed the ride cymbal, whoops of appreciation filled the Lenox. The drummer's scowl melted to a smile as sweet as that of a schoolboy presented with his pie.

If you're out in Manhattan, one place to keep your motor running is the 169 Bar on the Lower East Side.

Two general rules of thumb for finding quality jazz acts without paying through the nose: 1) You can hear the music from half a block away, and 2) From the outside, the establishment looks like a perfect place to get stabbed. But the 169, on a narrow street where the Lower East Side meets Chinatown, is where happiness, not evil, presides. Even James Washington, built like a garage door, sitting on a sidewalk stool, was a peaceful presence. What does James do? "I look out for the owner's best interests." A guy in a top hat strolled to the entrance, getting a nod from James.

Through the open door, soul jazz barreled out of the little club. The full-size sound was the work of petite Adrienne Hindmarsh, sliding, mixing and punching rhythms out of a Hammond organ. She and husband Josh, who backs her on guitar, are New Zealanders who live across the river in Queens. They get by with weddings and she sings in some bars. The 169 is home, though.

"This place is the best," Adrienne said.

You'll find the owner, Charles Hanson, at the far end of the bar every night of the week. The New Orleans native was a bike messenger who got clipped by a limo a few years ago and won a $100,000 settlement. He turned the 169 from a sleazy dump into a club with music every night and never a cover or a minimum.

Hanson is a happy man, he will tell you, and it's not hard to believe. "I live upstairs," he smiled. "I don't even have shoelaces for my shoes anymore."

Everywhere you look, your eyes are delighted. The pool table has leopard-skin felt. Instead of a stuffed moose head over the mantel there's a Tyrannosaurus rex. Soft-core 1970s porn on TV, a huge fish swimming solo in a backlit tank and go-go dancer Cate Winter, 24, who can't dance a lick, but that's not the point. As the Hindmarshes set sail on another groove voyage, a guy at the bar said, "This place reminds me of when drugs were fun and sex wasn't perverted."

Crosstown, master sax player Ned Goold sat in a booth at the Fat Cat, a pool hall 22 steps below Christopher Street that hosts jam sessions after midnight. The basement room has two dozen pool tables, 10 netted ping-pong areas and a beer and wine only license, and is open until 5 a.m.

Goold has been around, spending close to two decades playing tenor with Harry Connick's band, and currently gigs at upscale Manhattan clubs. At the Fat Cat, he plays what he loves, improv bop, the music created by Charlie Parker, Dizzy Gillespie, Bud Powell and other geniuses in places like this.

Here, you know if you're getting through, Goold said. "It's kind of like playing on the street," he added. "You have to earn your audience." Once he was onstage, it didn't take Goold long. In a minute, two bearded, long-haired Dostoyevsky anarchists looked up from their chess match in the pit of old couches, tables and stools to hear what was happening.

Goold's tenor sprinted scales, paused for fat, perfectly timed bursts, and then was off chasing notes in front of a rhythm section that included his 19-year-old son Charles on drums. Players with horn cases stood and sat, listening, sizing up the talent, waiting to sit in.

At quarter past three, a skinny young man wheeled a stand-up bass through the crowds of Christopher Street, disappearing down the steps to the Fat Cat, gently bumping his bass before him, hurrying to earn an audience.

Chapter 38
A Working Holiday

For the Shelter Island Reporter, *Thanksgiving 2021.*

I got to the garage in the early afternoon and took a seat on the bench in the drivers' room. The cabbie next to me had two rolls of paper towels and an industrial-size plastic jug of Lysol. When I asked him what they were for he looked at me as if I truly had been born yesterday.

New Year's Eve certainly turned out to be Amateur Night for those drinking before they turned pro. But it was also a nightmare of people from Omaha coming to New York to see the ball drop and thinking a yellow cab was some kind of tour bus where a friendly driver with amusing patter would show them the sights. And no one had told those farmers that tipping was mandatory.

Still, I worked a couple of New Year's Eves. You did make good money, even if it produced cabbie PTSD that could last into March. About Thanksgiving, I should have listened to my friend Donahoe, a former cabbie who scored a job as a police photographer. Low man on the totem pole, he was assigned to pull the 4 p.m. to midnight tour one Thanksgiving, shooting mugs in the basement of the precinct house.

"The usual parade of skells and knuckleheads, but now and then there'd be a regular person standing with the height numbers behind him, looking at the camera like he was about to be hanged," Donahoe said. "It was, like, an uncle who'd been invited by some family member who thought he'd finally make up with a relative he hadn't talked to in years—and who hated him. But too many cocktails and it all started over again. Fist fights, and you know, at Thanksgiving you have those serving forks? And knives? It was awful, these guys in nice clothes with blood on their shirts, asking me what came next, you know? What could I tell them?"

Mary and I got married in August and on Thanksgiving, figuring we could use the money and then have a long weekend, we had the meal and did the family thing and I got to the garage about four in the afternoon to go to work. There were just a few guys waiting for cabs to come in off the day line when I took a seat on the bench next to Fitz to pass the time. Fitz was an old guy ("old," younger than I am now) who was one of the great raconteurs. Everybody talked and listened to him; everybody, from the young Black and Latino and White guys to the old cabbie wizards like himself.

Fitz was an immigrant, who came to America as a young man and achieved the dream. He started out selling insurance and worked his way up to running his own agency in Queens, getting married and starting a family. But then he lost it all—the family, the business— through years of betting on slow-running horses. Finally, coming to his senses at rock bottom, he got help and started over, driving a cab. He helped some other guys in the garage—D.J.'s as they're known, "degenerate" gamblers—to find help.

"What do you think you're doing?" he greeted me. "Get out of here. Don't you have a home to go to?" I told him I'd heard it was a good night to work. Lots of happy and generous people foregoing the subway or bus and splurging on cabs. Plus, all the restaurant workers and everyone else punching clocks on Thanksgiving would be ready to treat themselves by hailing a cab home on the holiday.

"But you didn't answer my question," Fitz said, and told me a story.

One Thanksgiving afternoon he got a fare 20 minutes out of the garage on Park Avenue, an elderly man, holding a bouquet of two dozen roses, impeccably dressed in a three-piece bespoke suit, camel's hair topcoat, leather gloves and a felt fedora at a jaunty angle. "The smell of those flowers in the cab," Fitz said. "The smell of money." The old gentleman gave him an address in Little Falls, New Jersey. Any trip beyond the city limits automatically meant the fare on the meter when the destination was reached would be doubled.

"I told him about double the meter and he knew all about it. I thought, 'I'm gonna be rich tonight, mining gold in Jersey.'" The dapper old gentleman was going to his brother's, he said. He and Fitz chatted about Thanksgiving, a pleasant conversation between two men with the gift of gab, covering everything from the proper way to cook a turkey to whether the Lions had a chance against the Packers. "He directed me to Little Falls and then started to direct me through the streets," Fitz said. "It was already dark when he said, very quietly, 'Here. Here we are.'"

It was a cemetery. The passenger directed Fitz in through the gates. "I saw him in my mirror slumped in the back, his face white as a sheet. Staring straight ahead." The passenger told Fitz to stop and wait for him, got out and climbed a hill with his bouquet, stopping at a grave. "After a while I could see his shoulders heaving," Fitz said. The bouquet was hanging down from his hand, touching the ground. Fitz waited 20 minutes before he got out and went up to the man and put his hand on his shoulder. He had pulled himself together by then, putting the flowers on the grave, drying his eyes.

Back in the cab the man apologized, saying he was alone today— some kind of old family dispute—and had suddenly wanted to be with his only brother, who had been kind to him. He had somehow neglected to express his love for him when he was alive. "I'm alone and so is he," the man said. Fitz suggested a cup of coffee. "We went into a diner, sat and talked. He was a terrible old man, really," Fitz said. "Tossed his life away by not paying attention to those nearest to him."

On Park Avenue the old gentleman paid the double fare. "And stiffed me on the tip," Fitz said, with a smile.

"Prick," I said.

"Where's the wife today?"

"Home," I said.

"What are you doing here?" Fitz asked, his voice soft. "Do you have to work today?" I took the subway home, and going down the hall to our apartment, I saw the light under the door.

It was then I realized I'd forgotten to ask Fitz why he was working on Thanksgiving.

Chapter 39
New York's New Bohemia

For The Washington Post, *June 2001.*

At precisely 5 o'clock, a hydraulic construction platform glittering with tinsel rose above the narrow street carrying Reverend Billy over the crowd. Rush-hour taxis slowed to squeeze through as the reverend, a handsome man with a shock of oak-colored hair, began to testify, his strong Midwestern voice pouring through a bullhorn.

"Oh, children! Stop the visual pollution of our neighborhood! Praise be! Architecture, not advertising!" Cheers, applause, whistles. Students swelled the crowd, joined by office workers spilling out of the subway and older folks carrying groceries in knit bags. Everyone was smiling.

"Stop the Disney-fication of downtown! Mickey Mouse is the antichrist! Can I get a witness? Join us! Join the Church of Stop Shopping!"

A young woman in a floppy Afghan hat and a Mexican serape, holding a finger in one ear, a cell phone at the other, was saying, "It's not a riot, it's like a—a party. Where? I'm on the Lower East Side."

She was standing in the new bohemia of New York, where the confluence of fresh notions of fashion, theater, art and politics stream together. Often all of these elements are fused within a single person, like Reverend Billy, who most of the time is Bill Talen, an actor, performance artist and social activist. One of the most beloved figures on the Lower East Side, Talen is also representative in that he is an exile, one who has escaped Somewhere Else, who believes in life as periodic self-reinvention, and has found the place that encourages him to do it.

The Lower East Side now can be defined roughly as Canal Street north to East Houston Street, the East River west to Lafayette Street. You'll know it when you see it. It's a place that reminds you that the arts are handmade; they don't spring fully born, enclosed in shrink wrap. And a place where something remains of an older New York that has faded elsewhere in the city during the Giuliani era—small shops as opposed to merchandise hangars seething with too-hip-to-live surliness and pop music; good and inexpensive restaurants where you can eat without the suspicion you're attending an event of some kind; nightlife that's fun, untamed, but not the eighth ring of Hell.

The people who engraved an identity on the Lower East Side were Eastern European Jews who flooded in from the 1880s to the 1920s. Their sense of humor was a nonchalant wise guy's stance, the shrug of the shoulders of the down but never out, a delight in irony, the courage of David laughing at a puzzled Goliath. The style was soon adopted by all of New York. Now it's all-American.

In the 1950s, the neighborhood became increasingly Puerto Rican, "the *Loisaida*" in Spanglish. Now young people are coming for cheap rents and a more vivid lifestyle, moving in with the newest impoverished exiles, the Dominicans and others from all over the Caribbean. But the old Jewish neighborhood is still there in the 19th-century synagogues wedged between tenements, in the delis, specialty food stores and shops where New Yorkers still come for bargains.

Get there early to watch the district slowly awaken. Through the narrow streets, the breeze carries the smell of still-warm Italian bread and espresso; turn the corner and there is the aromatic tang of Chinese breakfast soup. The tenements are rarely higher than five stories, so the sky can be seen whole, not in patches. In Harlem you can look south and see midtown towers. Here, look north in the mornings from Essex Street, and see the sunlight striking the top of the Chrysler Building 60 blocks away, a gleaming spire from a distant city.

The "callers" along Orchard Street are softly touting clothes in front of shops. "Ri' here, ri' here," Georgie is cooing. "I got the leath-uh, the leath-uh, forget the weath-uh, I got the leath-uh for less, you got to try the bes'." Georgie is a plump man in a white jumpsuit. He stands in front of Adler's, riffing to the almost empty street like a musician tuning up, fiddling with notes for his own pleasure. Coats and women's clothes flutter like flags from the fire escapes; shops overflow, blocking the sidewalk with luggage, backpacks, crates of underwear, socks, belts, shoes.

The old comfortably shares breathing room with the new. Next to a little button shop is Skella, an immaculate, light-filled space with clothes designed and made by the proprietor, Deborah Skell. "Fashion comes from the street, from young people," Skell says. "We're not close to the street, we're on it." She's a woman who has lived in different places with different lives, and now has found her home. One of her most popular designs is the "bustle skirt," the bustle made of soft, sexy folds, with deep pockets that brings to mind a liberated Victorian.

Around the corner on Rivington Street, Jenny Lee Sheriff waits tables in her small café, a pleasant place with magazines and newspapers on a rack and people quietly reading. Some have oversize cups of sensationally rich, frothy hot chocolate. "Beautiful, pure chocolate. I get it from Economy Candy." She points through the windows to a place down the block. "I thought about a café for about 10 minutes, had one conversation, and the next thing I'm signing a lease. 'Head-spinning' is an understatement."

Why, she's asked, are there no signs, no name over the door? "It's like a lot of the new places. There's a kind of need for anonymity, which is very weird, I know, if you're in business. But we're doing really well. People know we're here."

Staten Island, just across the harbor, is the Elsewhere Sheriff has left. "After living here, it's really hard to spend any time there now," she says, proving that traveling great distances sometimes has nothing to do with geography.

By mid-afternoon, the streets begin to truly awaken, and sculptor Heather Nichol gets ready to leave her studio on Mott Street to wander her neighborhood. The studio looks four flights down to an old church and a green cemetery sheltered by tall trees. Her latest project seems to swim above the floor, a series of cloth structures lit from within, dimming and brightening, producing sounds of women whispering, giggling, sighing. On a wall is some new work in glass: gray-green ideas about breasts hanging from aluminum tongues. Like everything she does, they are highly crafted, perfectly finished statements about gender, beauty and mystery.

Walking east across the Bowery, she says, "I've been in New York 20 years and always lived within a 10-block radius of where I am now." Originally from Canada, she came to New York to study art and design. "So much is happening here. Like, just recently I woke up to realize Mott Street was the handbag boutique capital of the world. I can walk in just a few minutes to Chinatown, SoHo, the Village. There's so much to see every day."

There is public art everywhere. On the wall next to the Marz Bar, near Second Avenue, the mural changes almost monthly, painted by the artists found drinking inside. Off Delancey Street, a five-story glowing green helicopter descends through jungle to Angkor Wat. Near where Nichol is heading, a big, brilliant yellow-and-red painted wall advertises "Schapiro's Kosher Wines."

By early evening, the Lower East Side starts to hum as the bars and little restaurants fill with people home from jobs uptown. A good place for a drink or a meal, and always conversation, is Baby Jupiter on the corner of Orchard and Stanton. Like Sheriff's café, there is no sign. Asked about the name, a bartender says, "No clue. If it makes a difference, I can find out."

At the moment, it doesn't seem to matter. A life-size sheet-metal shark cruises above the tables where people are taking time over their meals. In the back room, the band is setting up, the guitarist strumming a sweet lament. By 9 o'clock, the windows will be rattling.

In a storefront on Ludlow, Bob Berger, executive director of the Collective: Unconscious theater company, is prepping a screen for a silent black-and-white video documentary about Detroit that's running tonight. Tomorrow they're doing Bertolt Brecht's adaptation of "Antigone." Berger is Cape Cod born and bred and looks more suited to wrestling fish into a boat than running an avant-garde theater.

"We're the only small theater and performance group in the world to have a contract with the Department of Defense," he says, smiling. About a year ago, Berger came up with the idea of taking cockpit voice-recording transcripts from major airline emergencies and performing them in a completely realistic manner. The result is "Charlie Victor Romeo," electrifying theater that has won two Drama Desk Awards. The show has been videotaped by Air Force crews and used as training for pilots.

"It's crazy," Berger says. "We're this little company on Ludlow Street, doing our thing, and now we're getting e-mails from the Pentagon thanking us for saving lives." He looks around his little theater. "Crazy."

"The Lower East Side is the R&D wing of American culture," says John Clancy, whose Somewhere Else is St. Louis. He is the artistic director of the Present Company Theatorium (and this writer's nephew). "Theatorium is a mid-19th-century term from this area when the theater district was the Bowery. It meant a place where you could see a dog act, some Shakespeare, a minstrel show, jugglers, a lecture. All kinds of performances. We're re-creating that idea here. Everyone's sharing a dressing room upstairs, going out later, influencing each other."

After the show, a pub crawl is in order. We head for an all-night pharmacy circa late 1950s. On the left as you enter, there's a counter of greeting cards, key chains and candy. A floor of tiles marked Rx. Large mirrors advertising Squibb Pharmaceuticals, a four-pose photographic booth and a soda counter. But something is not quite right. The soda jerk is wearing a black slip with a mandala tattooed across her back. She's not jerking sodas but pulling beers and pouring whiskey. This is Barmacy, where they "serve tonics for stress relief." Part of the fun is watching the other patrons. Nobody seems to notice.

At the Parkside Lounge on Delancey, young white folks and older Latinos hang together in the spacious back room where the Latin Vibe Sextet is making everyone move. There is no cover, no minimum. Eddie Rivera turns his conga over to another player and takes a break to get some air. "No place like this," he says. "And I'm from the Bronx, man, where we know how to play. No rip-off, all mellow. You never want to go home."

On Norfolk Street, across from a razor-wired lot, a hole in the wall (there's no sign, just a scrawled number) reveals metal stairs going down deep below street level. It's a haphazardly lit brick tunnel so narrow you must walk single file, coming out into an alley closed off at the far end. Looking at the deep shadows, you have the feeling you are about to meet your end, and not peacefully. But climb another flight of metal stairs (the only way out except back from where you came) and through an unmarked door and you're in, as my nephew says, "the coolest bar in New York."

Lansky Lounge is softly lit, in some places by clustered votive candles, and drinks are served in long-stemmed, wide-mouthed cocktail glasses. A woman slinks by in a cloche hat and a foot-long cigarette holder. There are two levels—the one above the bar has booths sporting white tablecloths. Here you can get a bowl of corn chowder, a grilled sirloin with fries, cheesecake and Irish coffee at midnight. John looks at candlelight through his glass and says, "You know, the entrance, that walk through the labyrinth, and then coming in here—before I lived in New York, this is what I thought it'd be like."

E. B. White wrote of three New Yorks: one of commuters who give the city a sense of restlessness; one of the native-born who provide continuity; and the city of newcomers who fuel New York with passion. The last are "strangers who have pulled up stakes somewhere and come to town, seeking sanctuary and fulfillment or some greater or lesser grail—the city of final destination, the city that is a goal."

Another round at Lansky's and there's talk of heading to Katz's, the madhouse Jewish deli, for monstrous pastrami sandwiches and a liter of diet ginger ale (Bill Clinton's order when he's in town). Or maybe falling by Meow Mix, the lesbian bar. Back on the street, there are couples strolling, and groups of five and six all talking at once, making their way to another place before the night ends.

Chapter 40
Queens For A Day

For The Washington Post, *November 2002.*

There are certain Manhattanites who are convinced their lives are episodes of "Friends," and we who live in Queens are living the life of the TV fat guy with the foxy wife, deliveryman's job and goofball father-in-law.

True, Queens' first and last association with a nose-in-the-air personality was when it was named for an English queen, Catherine of Braganza, in 1683. According to some, we're not real New Yorkers but residents of an "outer borough" (might as well be Outer Mongolia), "bridge-and-tunnel people" (human moles) whose idea of a cultural evening out is steel-cage wrestling followed by dining at the troughs of Sizzler.

Am I over-amped? What do you want? This is New York.

It's envy, really. Our instincts tell us that the black-clad boulevardier really dreads one more evening with Countess Anorexia at the newest tapas/sushi place and would prefer to have pizza out of the box and a couple of cold ones with the deliveryman's wife.

But when Manhattan's Museum of Modern Art closed for renovation in June and moved for at least three years to a refigured staple factory off Queens Boulevard, 17,000 people showed up for the first weekend. Discovery (we were here all along) is happening to us. And it is, as they say from Sunnyside to Douglaston, all good—even when it's not.

MoMA's bold move (call it MoMA QNS now) has accomplished several things; not least is the blurring of class distinctions. A significant advantage for Queens is that it has brought attention to four of the most exciting art venues in the city, places that couldn't be imagined anywhere else: P.S.1 Contemporary Art Center, the Isamu Noguchi Garden Museum, Socrates Sculpture Park and the American Museum of the Moving Image.

Besides the arts boom, MoMA's journey across the East River opens visitors to a New York seldom seen in the flesh: neighborhoods thriving in the most ethnically diverse county in the nation, where approximately 40 percent of the 2.2 million residents are foreign-born, and the public school system has identified more than 100 languages and dialects.

Take the 7

To get to Queens, people will tell you to "take the 7." The No. 7 subway begins under the corporate sterility of Times Square and ends in the world's newest Asian city, Flushing. Once on board one of the distinctive red cars, you've gotten real. In the 1920s, tunnels were dug and elevated lines constructed by off-the-boat Irish, Germans and Italians, and the 7 has been running 24 hours a day ever since. Today it carries 400,000 New Yorkers daily and transports off-the-plane visitors arriving at the new Ellis Island, Queens' John F. Kennedy Airport. (This is the same train that nitwit John Rocker, when he was a reliever for the reviled Atlanta Braves, didn't want to ride to Shea Stadium for games against the beloved Mets. The clueless yokel thought the 7 didn't look quite American enough.)

After Grand Central Terminal, the 7 travels under the river and two stops later comes up to become an El, rising above rail yards, loft buildings and rows of taxis parked in lots as orderly and bright as sunflower patches. The jade-green Citibank Tower soars above the long, back-city view. As you approach the 33rd Street station, stand on the right side of the train and look across the rooftops to a MoMA sign with letters jumbled together. Then, with the movement of the approaching 7, it magically assembles itself. (Hope for a wildman of an engineer—the effect is even better at speed.)

The museum's new home is a boxy, bright-blue building just down the street from Queens Boulevard. On one corner, a Nigerian woman in traditional gown and headdress sells fruit next to the luckiest greasy spoon in the city. "We ran out of pork chops by the afternoon," the owner grins, remembering MoMA QNS' opening day.

Without carpets or cramped galleries, 20th-century masterworks have become truly modern again. A painting as iconic as Picasso's "Les Demoiselles d'Avignon" jumps out at you, shocking in its freshness and primitive energy.

Putting sculptures by Giacometti, Brancusi and Duchamp all on one low, simple platform on the raw concrete floor spotlights their individual talents while producing a visual poem that explains how revolutionary the modernism movement was, and continues to be. Decades of reverence heaped on famous works is not even an afterthought; the only consideration is the things themselves.

Ciao, Manhattan

If you had left the 7 a few stops before, at Vernon-Jackson, you'd be in the last undiscovered Italian neighborhood of New York. (Well, not for long.) Hunter's Point is centered on the tall, slender steeple of St. Mary's and still has storefront bakeries that stack semolina loaves in the window. On fine days you'll find two retirees, Rudy Bassachi and Butch Carrado, at a table under an umbrella outside of Paris Sandwich and Donut on Vernon Boulevard.

Rudy, who worked as a longshoreman from the time he was 14, talks about the old days when the piers just a couple of blocks away were humming with life. "Then everyone went and forgot us," he said one recent morning. "Now the young people are coming, the big museum came. Being forgotten, then being remembered, is a good thing"—he held up one finger for emphasis —"and a bad thing."

"All good," Butch disagreed. "This is a neighborhood to be proud of."

Individual skyscrapers across the river are framed at the end of tree-lined streets and views up the narrow avenues are of the turreted Queensboro Bridge. Hunter's Point is bounded by the Long Island Expressway and the Queens-Midtown Tunnel, the river and factory streets of cobblestones and weeds showing through the macadam. Even though new businesses have arrived, notably a Brazilian café and a French bistro, the neighborhood retains the welcoming faces, the respect for food, family and tradition, and the comforting isolation of a mountain village.

In Butch and Rudy's day, if you didn't go to St. Mary's Catholic School, you went down the block to P.S.1. Built in 1896, the enormous Romanesque revival building steadily fell into disrepair, and by the 1970s the deterioration was complete. The Museum of Contemporary Art then took over, transforming it into the school you always wanted to attend.

Skylights have been cut into the ceilings, and the young, unfailingly polite and helpful staff is dressed not in museum-military fashion but in hip-hop togs, the T-shirts as long as the droopy shorts. Now associated with MoMA, P.S.1 is dedicated to the new and experimental, so the quality of work is often uneven. Some exhibits are merely baffling, while others make you despair at the personality and mind that produced such confusion. But there are treasures here.

Every part of the school is used as art space, and the old place provides countless opportunities for clever presentation. A recent example is a series of photos by Enrique Metinides, gruesome and heartbreaking images from Mexico City. P.S.1 had the wit not to glass and frame these catastrophic pictures but to attach the naked prints to the walls with straight pins and bulldog clips, like students' work in a classroom.

Sculptures and Ethnic Stew

Farther down Vernon Boulevard is Socrates Sculpture Park, named in honor of the large Greek community of Astoria. Through an arched entrance, a field dotted with sculptures, running the gamut from monolithic to whimsical, stretches to an old collapsed pier. Once an illegal dump site, the park was reclaimed by artists as a place to work and exhibit. There are usually sculptors working in outside studios here who love nothing more than being interrupted to discuss their art.

The park looks out on what 17th-century Dutch river pilots named *Hellegat* (Hell's Gate), the place where the East and Harlem rivers meet, a wicked confluence of perilous tides and hidden rocks. In late afternoon, light swirls in Hell's Gate eddies. People home from work come then, to picnic and watch their kids playing on the sculptures.

Find your way back to MoMA QNS and walk two blocks east on Queens Boulevard and another two blocks north to reach the Isamu Noguchi Garden Museum, now in temporary quarters in a loft gallery while the museum proper is undergoing renovations. Noguchi (1904-1988) was, simply, one of the great artists of the 20th century, whose protean imagination mastered sculpture, drawing, architecture, interior design, furniture and theater. He moved in the 1960s to this light-manufacturing district to be near materials he was using then (sheet aluminum and commercial slate), continuing the ancient tradition of sculptors setting up shop near quarries.

His mission—to bring nature into the gallery, to eliminate barriers—is realized here, with stands of bamboo, granite rocks and "The Water Stone." The monolithic stone with water sliding down its sides is a fountain, a sculpture, a great lump of beautiful rock, solidity turned liquid. The long windows near the museum's little café give on to low, cube-shaped buildings, and just above the rooftops you can see the rolling cars of the 7 snaking into a turn as it heads for Jackson Heights.

As recently as 1914, Jackson Heights was known as the "cornfields of Queens." The only connections to corn now are the fresh tacos sizzling in oil at one of the stand-up streetside taco bars. Take the 7 to 74th Street-Broadway, walk downstairs and you've entered the Third World, with a couple of happy exceptions: It's a safe neighborhood, and there's no grinding poverty.

Residents stroll by in straw cowboy hats and guayaberas, turbans and saris. Banners for check-cashing joints are in Hindi and Spanish, and shopfronts with names like Tibetan Yak are next to Kebab King. Puerto Rican botanicas hedge their religious bets by placing crucifixes within Stars of David. The old urban-American myth of an ethnic stew peacefully cooking in the melting pot is alive like nowhere in the country, including that colossus across the East River.

Ask Mike Shehadeh. On Steinway Street, he can be found regularly in Egyptian Coffee Shop 100% Inc., smoking a hookah and downing cups of muddy Turkish coffee. "I love Queens," said Shehadeh, who emigrated from Jerusalem as a boy. "I have a business out on the Island, but this is the place I came to 23 years ago, and this is the place I always come back to. The whole world is here, you know?"

If you're in the neighborhood, don't be shy about entering the clean, narrow café that leads to a patio under the sky. That cliché about Arab hospitality is true at the coffee shop; the welcome is warm, the patrons are interested in you and pleased to explain the hookahs, beautiful objects of fabric and gleaming metal. Pipes are rented with a new, cellophane-wrapped mouthpiece. Sweetened by flavored charcoal, the tobacco is mild to begin with and the water softens the taste further. A good smoke.

Another place to cool out from the mad swirl of color, sound and people is La Boina Roja (the Red Beret), a pretty and inexpensive Colombian steakhouse. It's friendly but quiet, and after a meal, no one is upset if you linger over coffee. The management wants you to savor the Colombian brew, and if you ask about it, the padrone, if he's around, will take a seat to explain why Colombia is to coffee as France is to wine. Two cups of this stuff and you're ready to swing with the dazzling flow of Broadway just around the corner.

Hollywood Meets Chinatown

A few blocks away is the American Museum of the Moving Image, a unique institution in the United States. Before Hollywood was Hollywood, Astoria was Hollywood, so this lively museum is perfectly placed. Next door is the vast Kaufman Astoria Studios, where a lot of the television you watch is produced. There are 95,000 artifacts here that tell the story of movies and TV, from flip books to digital imaging.

AMMI is dedicated to showing how it all works, but it never forgets that a large part of our love for the most popular art is the schlock, the camp, the glamour and the purposeless fun. Kids have a difficult time leaving once they start creating their own animation or re-scoring soundtracks of terminally serious action/adventure flicks with Road Runner effects.

There are more than 500 screenings a year, from masterworks of European and Asian cinema to programs closer to home, such as: "Directed by Martin Scorsese: A Complete Retrospective." Most are shown in an ultra-comfortable theater with easily the best sound and projection facilities in New York. And you won't have to put up with

Queens' favorite indoor sport, behaving in a public theater as if you're in your living room.

Last stop on the 7, Main Street-Flushing. Only out-of-towners find the name funny (biggest plumbing job in history, flushing Queens, ha ha). The Dutch, settling here in 1643, named it *Vlissingen* and the English gave it its current name, which now means, for most New Yorkers, Chinatown without the tourists.

Fred Fu, president of the Chinese Business Association, explained how the sleepy neighborhood was made new 25 years ago by Taiwanese immigrants coming for work, and the United States' steadily improving relationship with mainland China added to the boom. "That street"—he pointed up a crowded lane alight with neon Chinese characters—"had three restaurants 15 years ago. Now there are 19. In a five-block radius, there are 60 restaurants and every cuisine of China."

One of these, Sun Young Spring on Main Street, picked because of a bathroom need and general hunger, was a happy revelation. Unpretentious and inexpensive, it will make you wonder at the quality of the takeout most of us eat. This was creative food, delicately and expertly prepared, and the helpful staff was eager to help a non-Chinese navigate the menu.

Outside, under the El, markets sell live turtles and buckets of fish heads, and melons overflow from bins out to the sidewalk. Fresh mango juice is squeezed and poured over crushed ice in front of you, while nearby newsstands do brisk business selling all five Chinese papers published in the metropolitan area. Chinese bookstores are quiet, filled with browsing scholars ranging in age from teenagers to elderly men. Tea cafés, where juice is frothed with tea, are hangouts for young people in the hippest American clothes, working cell phones, looking out on the teeming bazaar of Main Street.

Fu pointed at the lighted rim of Shea Stadium in the distance. He's involved with merchants to promote attendance at the ballpark, while the Mets management is encouraging fans to go to the new Asian city before or after games. "There's a little creek out there, they call it the Flushing River, I think," Fu said. "Big deal. Nobody here in Queens believes a river can separate us."

Part IV
PLACES

Chapter 41
Losing and Finding Our Way on The Holy Mountain

For GQ, *November 1989.*

I can always blame Jack, I thought, as we rested against our packs on the dock at Ouranopolis, a shabby little port in northern Greece. Blame my brother if in the next four days we drown in the Aegean, fall off a cliff, break our legs in the mountains and die of exposure, or go mad. It was *his* idea, wasn't it? His idea two years ago when, talking with him about travel writing, I mentioned that there didn't seem to be many bizarre, and undiscovered places left, places difficult to get to but worth the effort.

I know a place, he said. Mount Athos, the "Holy Mountain," one of the holiest places in Christianity, where twenty monasteries, a thousand years old, are set along the wild coasts of a remote peninsula, a peninsula that is its own republic within the Greek state, where no women are allowed, in fact, no female *creatures* are allowed, and there's only one way in and one way out, by boat, and once in, you have to hike from one monastery to the next, where the monks take you in to feed and shelter you, where masterpieces of Byzantine art, centuries old, beyond price, are in churches, where ...

And so, on a raw morning last November, watching our boat make its way toward us through the Aegean, I thought that every journey begins in apprehension. My physical fears were nothing, really, a joke, a mask for other concerns. I wasn't sure what I would find. I was afraid that Athos would change me.

"It will be on your head," I said, turning to my brother, using a family phrase.

"Oh, come on," Jack said. He straightened his pack and smiled, quoting from *Two Gentlemen of Verona*: "A true-devoted pilgrim is not weary/To measure kingdoms with his feeble steps."

* * * *

The monastic republic is approximately thirty-six miles long and varies in width from five to eight miles, ending where Mount Athos soars directly from the sea to over 6,000 feet. The Holy Mountain (as Athos and the whole peninsula is called) is dedicated to the Virgin, who according to legend, was so taken with the beauty of the place that she asked her Son to give it to her as a garden, "and a haven of salvation for those seeking to be saved."

The seekers, the day after Election Day in America, besides Jack and me, were two Serbian hikers, a few men going to work in the primitive logging trade and some monks going home. We had surrendered our passports to the captain on leaving Ouranopolis, along with another document from the Ministry of Northern Greece. This is required of all non-Greek men. Your passport is returned in Karyes, the capital, when you're issued an Athos passport, good for only four days. (It had been recommended that we also get a letter from our employers or "a responsible person" to testify as to our worthiness.)

It was a two-hour sail to the port of Daphne, a jumbled grouping of hovels clinging to a dock at the base of a steep hill. There, a crippled bus took us up to Karyes on a high, switchback dirt road overlooking the sea. Without a word of instruction, we were dropped off in a courtyard, and we walked to the administration building.

Karyes is a town of brick buildings, red slate roofs and narrow cobbled streets. We saw no people, not a soul, but many cats and a few tired mongrels, all male of course. There was no sound of radios, of engines, voices, no sound of children. This was a place where no one had been born since the year 885. We trooped along in the bleak silence, past ramshackle buildings, through the emptiness. "This isn't the end of the earth," Jack said. "But you can see it from here."

Waiting in a large stone-floored room of the administration building was colder than standing in the street. Two elderly monastic policemen wearing grimy caps entered the room, conferred with each other, eyed us carefully and then left by separate doors. In a few moments they reemerged, conferred again and left quickly through different doors. As I was making a note, Jack whispered to me, "Kafka. Write 'Kafka.'"

"More like the Marx Brothers."

After a few more turns of the farce, one old man let out a burst of Greek and began pounding on a bench. Jack, who speaks the language, told me the policeman was merely telling us to have a seat and wait. An hour later we received our passports.

We crossed Holy Ghost Street and entered the one inn of Karyes for tea. In the dark, squalid room, a mentally disabled man took our order. There was only one other patron, a very drunk young workman drinking wine and slurping soup near the fire. Another man came in and sat next to him. As drunk as his friend, he suddenly began to sing, loudly. The soup eater ignored him. The singer went quiet and then laughed, and stopped just as suddenly, now staring. Jack looked over at the couple.

"Wow," he said, shaking his head. "Down-and-out on Holy Ghost Street."

It was an easy hike to our first monastery, walking a dirt road that reminded me of West Virginia in the fall, if the mountain hollows could reveal views of the sea. An hour and a half out of Karyes, we rounded a bend to see Stavronikita below us, across half a mile of woods draped in mist: Stavronikita, a castle with a tenth-century tower built on a headland over the Aegean. Looking down on the sight, we found ourselves whispering in the quiet, the only sound the seashell murmur of faraway surf. I thought of Nikos Kazantzakis, who, visiting Athos as a young man, had the impression that he had entered "a colossal church composed of sea, mountains ... roofed at the top by the open sky instead of a dome."

We were greeted by Father Theologus, a handsome young monk dressed in the Orthodox habit: a fezlike black hat, black cassock and the sturdy black shoes worn by policemen the world over. The monks never trim their beards, and their long hair is carefully gathered in a neat bun just below the back of the hat.

He served water and sweet, sticky Turkish delight before checking our Athos passports and registering us in a large book. After some conversation there was a pause. The monk, with a tinge of embarrassment, asked, "Who won the election in Washington?" Jack informed him that Dukakis, the son of Greece, had lost. He nodded and shrugged in resignation.

We were then taken to church to hear vespers. (The monks of Athos spend approximately eight hours a day standing at prayer, which explains the cop shoes.) Candles and dim lamps revealed icons and ceiling-high frescoes. There was the bland smell of burning wax mixed with pungent incense. Veiled monks stood in stalls, bowing from the waist, chanting prayers. In the theatrical gloom, all the elements of spookiness were assembled for our modern eyes. But there was only a sense of beauty, mystery and order.

The frescoes, made in 1546, were quite beautiful. Byzantine art is almost solely religious and confined to a rigorous style. Jesus and the saints stand in vivid colors, their features elongated, as in the work of El Greco, who was trained as an icon painter. Their long, delicate fingers are posed in the Byzantine blessing, the tip of the thumb lightly touching the tip of the third finger. Mary and the female saints give a blessing of the palm held vertically in front of the body. Byzantine Christ is not portrayed as Jesus meek and mild but as a man who suffered and a God who judges. Even the Infant Jesus is not presented as a child but as a miniature man. And Mary is not the pretty girl down the street, the Mary of Raphael, but the Mother of God, who looks like no one. Very few figures look like anyone you'd ever meet. It is an art that seeks transcendence above all else.

A silent dinner was served in the refectory by the light of kerosene lamps: hard, tasteless bread, olives and lentil soup cooked with garlic and onions, presented stone-cold.

That evening Theologus came to visit us in our sitting room, a lamp-lit place at the top of the monastery with a three-sided view of the sea. As he entered, another monk was passing in the hall, beating an oblong block of wood with a mallet, calling the community to prayer.

Theologus seemed hungry for news of "the world," as the monks call everything except Athos. We noted that we had seen many more young monks than old ones, and he told us that of the 1,300 or so men on Athos, half had come in the past ten years. The world held interest for him, he said, because he was the librarian, but for most monks the Holy Mountain was more than enough.

I kept waiting for a question from him, to which I had no answer: Why have you come? To say I'd come for the adventure, or to look at art and architecture, wouldn't satisfy him, I knew, and didn't begin to satisfy me. But the question was never asked, not by Theologus or any monk we met in the four days we were out of the world. I asked myself the question many times—in churches, through silent meals of awful food and while hiking the difficult trails in the mountains—before I had the answer.

* * * *

Our breakfast was a cold quiche of rancid cheese, hard bread, olives and water. Theologus gave us directions to the monastery of Vatopedi and told us it was only a two-and-a-half-hour hike. It turned out to be closer to six. We found that the monks have a different sense of time, or no sense at all. They are men who live by the bell, from sunrise to sunset, one saint's day to the next.

The trails of Athos are rock strewn, rugged and narrow. We hiked single file up along the ridges, past sheer drops, above empty capes and bays, the channels running aquamarine and purple, the wine-dark sea of Homer. After two hours we came down into a grove of olive trees and rested on a stone wall over a dry creek. The wind was blowing so hard that brown sea foam filled the air. "Olives," Jack said. He was sitting on the wall, smoking a cigar, pointing to the trees, the delicate silvery green leaves fluttering in the gale. "Olives are a sign of hope and dreams, since it takes 20 years after planting for trees to bear fruit. It means you're settling down, dreaming of a prosperous future."

"I'm dreaming of dinner," I said, picking a leaf from a tree.

"'Hold fast to dreams/For if dreams die/Life is a broken-winged bird/That cannot fly.'"

"Shakespeare?"

"Langston Hughes. Let's go, dreamer."

Vatopedi, seen from the mountains, is a great walled medieval city on the sea. It was founded in the second half of the tenth century and has been raided and looted through the centuries by pirates, crusaders and Catalan mercenaries. The enormous courtyard, with weeds growing between cobblestones, was empty when we walked in.

Cold, hungry and exhausted, we were stunned to have entered a fantasy, a dream castle of colors—green, Chinese red, cream and yellow—with towers and turrets all around us, a fresco on a wall of an eye in a triangle, a statue of a man with a scimitar seemingly suspended in space high upon a tower.

A French monk of Greek descent finally greeted us and gave us water, before inviting us to church. The bum-at-the-mission tactic, I told Jack. Sermon Before Soup. We sat in the stalls in the half-light, too tired to have any sense of the extraordinary mosaics and frescoes from the fourteenth century or of the huge gold chandelier bright with candles.

Although Vatopedi seemed to be the poorest monastery we visited, it was by far the most hospitable. When we asked for coffee in the kitchen, an old layman directed us to a dingy room and brought some muddy Greek coffee and a brazier of coals, both warming us immediately. Father Stephanos, a gruff old Bulgarian, showed us to our room. It was at the end of a long, high-ceilinged corridor, a room of marble—floor, walls, ceiling—with a wood-burning stove. Dinner was at seven.

Dinner. We were both starving, but the thought of another monastery meal was not pleasant. I took out a small can of Danish paté from my pack, spread it on crackers and offered one to my brother. He held it like a jewel in his hand, staring at it, saying, "This is the first food I've seen in two days that doesn't look like it's already been eaten."

But dinner in the little room off the kitchen (we were the only pilgrims) was superb. Hot tomato-and chick-pea soup, mounds of pomme frites, hot cheese-and spinach quiche and good, rough red wine. Two well-fed young monks from Cyprus served us and spoke to us, Jack translating. We learned that there are only thirty monks at Vatopedi; thirty men rattling around in a place that could house 2,000 in comfort.

After dinner we stood on a balcony overlooking the courtyard. Occasionally, a monk would pass on his way to church, his footsteps faint on the cobblestones. Then silence. Silence dominates Athos, in the monasteries and on the mountain trails, where the call of a bird is an event. Jack was reminded of descriptions of monasteries in the Himalayas: the isolation, the wind, the emptiness, the quiet. It was easy to understand why the lack of sound is paramount to the meditative life. The seeker needs a place where he can understand, as Rilke put it, "the endless news growing out of silence."

We were up at first light, and one of the Cypriots gave us bread and tea. We asked directions to the monastery of Zographou and several monks gave us several versions. The only thing they agreed on was that it was "a two-and-a-half-hour hike." We set out in the cold morning, shipwrecked before we had set sail.

Hours, miles, of hiking, all uphill, to the mountainous spine of the peninsula. I have no sense of direction and wasn't worried (Jack was in charge), but my brother kept checking the sun and cursing the one map we had, a primitive thing torn from a book. There are no reliable

maps of Athos trails. You just ask directions, hump your pack and have faith.

Near two o'clock, deep in the woods, Jack threw down his pack, sat on it and lit a cigar.

"Wandering lost upon the mountains of our choice."

"Emily Dickinson?"

"Auden. Really, man, we are two lost cowboys. Get ready to sleep up here tonight."

We both knew the rule that all monastery gates close at sunset. Without another word we started up the trail again. At each abandoned stone cell built by hermits, I felt something sink in me.

Sleep in one of those? How cold would it be tonight? Why had I come?

Around four o'clock we came to a dirt road. Salvation. A road has to go somewhere. My big brother punched me on the shoulder. "O ye of little faith. Would I get us lost?"

Our road was a feather bed compared to the rocky trails. We could walk side by side. My legs, a second ago jelly, returned to muscle and bone, and my pack was again a friend and no burden. For the first time all day we were hiking downhill. I was whistling. And up ahead was a remarkable sight. A pickup truck and, even more startling, a man (the first human we'd seen that day), coming from behind a tree, zipping his pants.

Jack greeted him, and the man at first was a bit reserved, perhaps because we were two ragged men appearing out of the wilderness grinning like souls who had slipped their moorings. His name was Adonis. A big fellow with the weathered face of a handsome pirate. Being Greek, he finally joined us in our joy out of sheer politeness. Suddenly Jack's face dropped. What was the matter? "He says it's fifteen kilometers to the nearest monastery."

"So?"

"So? Christ, man, that's ten miles."

Before real panic set in, Jack struck a deal. We threw our packs in the bed of the truck and sat next to him in the cab. Adonis accepted drachmas.

This was *his* road. Jack translated: Adonis had made it himself. Took him only ten hours. Jack thought he might have been on the mountain a little too long. But we didn't challenge him; it was a day of miracles. In the open dashboard was a bottle of clear white liquid. Ouzo, Adonis told us, and didn't so much as offer a drink as insist on it. I took a belt that went straight through me. God's own booze, even if there was a slight aftertaste of bathtub.

It was a happy journey down Adonis's road to the monastery of Docheiariou.

You enter Docheiariou through a tunnel-like entrance in the walls, up into a courtyard where orange and tangerine trees blossom. A small monastery and one of the most beautiful we visited with, four stories of turrets, balconies and galleries. But, for all that, it had, as Jack put it, "all the amenities of a stable." The food we were given was something in a cold tin bowl that I couldn't identify. We found a room by ourselves (the monks told us nothing) near the top of the monastery, with no heat, no light and broken-down camp beds. We went to sleep with our clothes on.

Breakfast was something I could identify—garbage. Afterward, we started walking up along the coast to the monastery of Xenophantos, where we were hospitably greeted, and realized that Docheiariou was an aberration.

At Xenophantos, coffee was served along with Turkish delight in a warm, clean common room. A young monk came and asked if we would like a tour. He showed us the courtyard and took us into a church, an unusual church by Athos standards, in that it was sparsely decorated, very bright, with whitewashed walls. The monk showed us two large mosaic icons facing each other on bare pillars. They were Saint Demetrius and Saint George. Tall, slender figures made in the thirteenth century, of ground gold and silver, catching the light, as bright as the day they were finished.

The question I had been asking myself since arriving on Athos was finding an answer as I looked at the mosaics. It was nothing mystical, there was no religious experience, just the beginning of an answer, really. In Yeats's poem "Sailing to Byzantrium," he writes:

O sages standing in God's holy fire
As in the gold mosaic of a wall,
Come from the holy fire, perne in a gyre,
And be the singing-masters of my soul.
Consume my heart away; sick with desire
And fastened to a dying animal ...

Some questions have answers that cannot be voiced or written, just as some poetry is understood completely but cannot be explained. A poet, an icon artist, can consume your heart and that is enough; in fact, that is the purpose. By wondering why you have come to a place, you already know the reason is somewhere within you.

There was a boat we could catch, the monk told us, that ran down the coast to the monastery of Dionysiou. Wonderful things could be seen there, he said. I followed my brother down to a white stone dock, where we waited, silently, in the clear windy morning.

Postscript: *My father could pun at will. After any remark, uttered by anyone, he could make a pun, some good, some funny, most appalling. Fortunately, he almost always kept this annoyance to himself. And Jack, as you've just read, could quote poetry. He, too, picked his spots. It wasn't showing off, it was honoring an experience with spoken truth hinged on rhythm.*

A scholar with multiple advanced degrees, author of two books, he also had been a successful business owner in Silicon Valley as well as a teacher of political and economic theory. He was an adventurer, making journeys to the rainforests along the Mexico/Guatemala border to hike in to see Mayan ruins—I was along, as worried and exhilarated as on the Athos trip—as well as tearing across the U.S. on 24-hour drives so we could see the Little Big Horn and Shiloh.

He had set foot on every continent. After going to Antarctica with our sister Liz, he said there are two kinds of people in the world. Those who say, after you've told them you've been to the South Pole, "Wow!" And those who ask "Why?"

(To the latter, Liz always responds, "I went for a wedding. I've got family there.")

His presence always, and his memory now, his encouragement from the time I was a little boy, his love for me, have always helped me nurse Langston Hughes' injured bird.

His toast was, "Happy days." We toasted a lot, and saw a lot of dawns on city streets. One late night in New York, I said I had to get some sleep.

"Sleep?" Jack said, and quoted Benjamin Franklin: "There will be sleeping enough in the grave."

Since his death in October 2019, I've had one of his favorite Dylan Thomas verses running in my head like a melody that won't let you go:

Oh as I was young and easy in the mercy of his means
Time held me green and dying
Though I sang in my chains like the sea.

Happy days, beloved Jack.

Chapter 42
Peggy's Place in Venice

This piece was published in The Washington Post *in the spring of 2000. We had spent a month in Venice at the end of 1999 as the clock ticked toward a new millennium. The Serenissima took no notice of the calendar, or of us.*

Venetians are a somber people, the most serious of Italians. Theirs is a city of shutters, practical in keeping out light and cooling rooms, but also proof that they value the inner life and discretion. It's telling that they introduced masked revels to Europe. Their Mardi Gras might be as depraved as Rio's or New Orleans', but please close those shutters and lock the door. Venetians wouldn't be caught dead carrying on in the street, even at Carnival.

Famously tolerant, they treasure the visitor who, unlike themselves, is uninhibited, publicly eccentric or just entertainingly strange. Lord Byron, making moves on everything not tied down at both ends and, as a matter of course, swimming home up the Grand Canal. Richard Wagner, taking rooms and insisting the wallpaper and curtains be changed to blood red; then, undone by hypochondria, getting a bad case of the frights by gondolas reminding him of hearses. Fredrik Rolfe, English writer and professional house guest, renamed himself Baron Corvo, went to Venice for a short stay and never left, besotted by a city full of muscular young boatmen whom he tirelessly pursued, rhapsodized about endlessly, and even tried to become one of, with the unfortunate result of often falling or being knocked into canals.

One of the last great characters to conquer the buttoned-up Venetians was Peggy Guggenheim (1898-1979), the self-confessed "art addict" and patron, who spent the last 30 years of her life in this floating dream of a city. Her extraordinary collection of 20th-century art, which she assembled in Paris, London and New York, finally found a permanent home at her palace in the Dorsoduro district on the Grand Canal.

Guggenheim left her house and collection to the Guggenheim empire of museums with just a few provisions: It should stay intact; it should stay in Venice; and, if Venice were to sink, the collection should be placed somewhere nearby so the public could enjoy it.

An example of her celebrity in Venice, and the awe the average person had for her, is a remark made to a young Englishman and his wife when they came to live in the city in 1973. Phillip Rylands had just arrived to study Renaissance art when, after agreeing on terms for a flat, the landlady said, proudly, "You'll never guess who we had to dinner last night." Continuing in hushed tones, "Peggy Guggenheim's gondolier."

Soon after, Rylands was introduced to her at a British Consulate party. It was the kind of party, he said, where guests scouted people for their own soirees. Rylands and his wife were soon at Guggenheim's palace, mingling with Gore Vidal, Paul Newman and Joanne Woodward. "After all," Rylands, director of the Peggy Guggenheim Collection, said recently, "everyone comes to Venice eventually."

And, eventually, most everyone went to Guggenheim's. Her collection represents a concise history of modern art, from cubism through surrealism to abstract expressionism, and every school and ism in-between. Under Rylands' energetic direction, it has become by far the best museum of modernism in Italy, and one of the great small museums of the world.

More than 300,000 people visit the palace annually, and the average time spent is close to two hours. The reason for the lengthy stay can be partially explained by visitors to Venice relieved after staring at their 90th *Madonna con bambino* and 50th *San Sebastiano* pincushioned with arrows. But it is also a lovely, light-filled place with a welcoming garden and café, easygoing, elegant, as pleasant as the days when Guggenheim would open her house on summer mornings to the public, with unaware house guests in pajamas and nightgowns sleepily wandering among the visitors.

Aerial views of Venice are always something of a shock; they reveal a city of hidden gardens, trees and open spaces. Passing Guggenheim's glass and wrought-iron door off the six-foot-wide street, you would never suspect that a small courtyard with a distinctively Venetian wellhead leads up to a long, wide garden. Two huge trees stand in a floor of marble, stone and brick. Immediately you get a sense that this is far from an average place; some unique personage had settled here. There is an emaciated Giacometti figure near sturdy bushes, a bright Brancusi bronze seemingly lit from within, a huge Byzantine throne.

You're drawn upward to an entrance hall where you can see through to the traffic on the Grand Canal. A Calder mobile shimmers down from the ceiling flanked by two large Picassos. Turning to the right, you're drawn along again at the sight on the far wall of a Magritte oil, "Empire of Light," the most popular picture in the collection. Some of the original furniture is in the dining room off the hall, giving the place a feeling of still being a home, not a museum. And in each of the spaces there is a photograph of how the room appeared when Guggenheim was in residence.

Everywhere you look, your eyes are greeted by masterpieces by Braque, Leger, Moore, Motherwell, Mondrian, Klee, de Kooning, Bacon and Chagall—modern masters of every decade and every European country and America. What makes a visit to the collection such a tranquil experience is the personality of the garden, café and house, but also the way the art is arranged; it all has breathing space and is allowed to speak to you without another work eavesdropping.

Built in the mid-18th century, the Palazzo Veneir dei Leoni is also known to the locals as "the unfinished palace" because it consists of only a basement and one long ground floor. No one is sure about the leoni (lions), but a former resident kept panthers and threw parties entertained by a naked pianist covered in gold paint.

Guggenheim kept the palazzo's spirit alive by placing an equestrian statue directly on the Grand Canal, with the ecstatic rider sporting a fully erect phallus. The artist, Marino Marini, made the phallus so that it could be unscrewed, adding to Guggenheim's reputation by gossips wondering what she might have used it for. It's fun to stand inside and look through the windows today, as the owner once did, and watch people's reaction to the statue.

In another city, there might have been outrage, or at the least, embarrassment, but in Venice people were charmed. Guggenheim was originally worried she might offend the prefect of Venice, whose palazzo was directly across from hers, not just by the statue but also by her habit of tanning herself on the flat roof. When asked about his neighbor, the prefect simply replied, "When I see Mrs. Guggenheim sunbathing on the roof, I know spring has come to Venice."

Guggenheim's Uncle Solomon had the real bucks in the family. Her side was eccentric at best, with some members completely unhinged. One grandfather married his stepsister. Her favorite aunt was, in Guggenheim's wonderful phrase, "an incurable soprano." An uncle "lived on charcoal," and from his general appearance and teeth looked like a coal miner coming off a 12-hour shift. He also kept pieces of ice in a zinc-lined pocket, took whiskey before breakfast and didn't go near real food unless absolutely necessary. Her father, Benjamin, drowned in the Titanic disaster while traveling with his mistress and male secretary. Both men changed into evening clothes to meet their watery fate.

Peggy Guggenheim could charm anyone, even dazzling the legendarily dour Samuel Beckett, who upon meeting her in Paris immediately took her to bed for three days straight, interrupting the tryst only to go out for more champagne. She was also considered by some to be a rich ditz and dilettante who was more interested in getting to know artists sexually than helping them survive or promote their work. The truth is she wasn't as wealthy as her lifestyle would indicate, and was no dimwitted bimbo with a taste for the less polite side of town. She did, indeed, have a healthy sexual appetite and many affairs. And she was thought of as vacant between the ears because of sexism.

Keeping a melange of tiny yapping terriers didn't help. Venetians, who adore dogs of all sizes (watch where you step), called her "*la donna americana coi cani*" ("the American lady with the dogs"). Fourteen of her furry "babies" are buried next to her in the garden, with names and dates engraved in marble.

But beyond getting silly about lap dogs, she had a curious conversational tic, Rylands remembers, of asking a question and appearing not to listen to the answer. Her friend Gore Vidal explained it by saying that there was "something cool and impenetrable about her. She does not fuss. She is capable of silence, a rare gift. She listens, an even rarer gift."

A serious student of art, well-schooled in the Italian Renaissance, she wore her learning lightly, and had the vision to see that what conventional wisdom of the day considered junk, was genius. Guggenheim financially supported Jackson Pollock when critics considered his efforts to be the work of a madman. For that reason alone, she is considered one of the most important figures in 20th-century art.

When Guggenheim came to Dorsoduro in 1947, it was known for its students, artisans and artists, in Rylands' phrase, "not the most fashionable district." (She supported several neighboring painters with monthly stipends and provided studio space in her home.) But Venice changes less than most places. It is still possible, as British art historian Hugh Honour has written, "to walk for a couple of hours from one architectural masterpiece to another without being offended by a single eyesore." What does sting the eye is the ubiquitous graffiti, most of it the result of morons with access to Magic Markers. But in Dorsoduro, which seems to have more university-aged people than the rest of the city, the wall scrawls often have the wit of budding Keith Harings and Basquiats.

There are just a few aspects of her old district that Guggenheim would not recognize today but would certainly approve of, like the terribly serious *signorina* featuring nose studs and fuchsia or cobalt buzz cuts, but with sensible shoes, hats and gloves, of course. Henry James said that the most useful faculty to employ in Venice was the ability to get lost. This is still important in Dorsoduro, discovering the pleasures of following your nose through a labyrinth. Humpbacked bridges lead to squares where wash hangs on a line above portable fish markets watched closely by cats and gulls. Watery light plays tricks on old plaster, voices and footsteps of people somewhere unseen remind you that the ancient city is real, not a museum, or a romantic illusion, but a human place, busy with itself, operating somewhere outside your notion of time and, if you just follow this little canal, to that little street—didn't we just pass that café 10 minutes ago?

To get lost, in more ways than one, is what brought Guggenheim, and countless others, to Venice. To find a sense of what life was like then, and is more or less the same now, start at Ca' Rezzonico, the incredible 17th-century palace where Robert Browning died, and where a plaque quotes the poet:

Open my heart and you will see
Graved inside of it, 'Italy.'

Follow the long narrow street away from the canal, past frame shops, a chic deli with barrels filled with wine bottles, a working-class café, into Campo San Barnaba, a busy crossroads of Dorsoduro. Nearby on a small canal is a floating fruit and vegetable market, giving on to a quay where a students' pub quietly pulses with 1960s soul or ominous techno. Back on the Campo, take Calle Lunga past small stand-up cafés, lace and needlework shops, a painters' supply store window glittering with granulated pigments, a patisserie specializing in a Venetian treat—doughnuts stuffed with zabaglione.

Your eye will be drawn to a storefront of exquisite miniature sculptures of bookcases, street scenes, rooms and fine pencil and pastel architectural drawings. The door is usually open (especially late at night) to the studio of Ahmad Eddine. Stop in, and if you are the slightest bit simpatico, the 36-year-old artist will pour you a glass of arrack, the fiery liquor of his native Lebanon, and talk about his work.

Five minutes away, near the flagpole in Campo Santa Margherita, you'll pass what looks like an expensive haberdasher with fine leather jackets hanging on a line in the window. What stops you is a leather sock, bra and a pair of hands holding a human brain, and then the sudden realization that they are all made of wood. Step into Loris Marazzi's studio to the smell of a pine forest, the heady aroma of the Dolomites, where the wood for Venetian church statuary and altars has been harvested for centuries. It is a special kind of hardwood that naturally ages to the rich color of tanned hides.

Ankle deep in chips and shavings, Marazzi, 27, says, "It's not such a great or strange thing to be an artist here." He pointed at the wide campo, his gesture indicating the district, the city itself. "You're respected along with the café owner, the woman who sells you fish. Art is natural here."

Guggenheim knew that about Venice. It was the most natural place for her to be. As for her personality and the effect she had on her beloved city, Phillip Rylands has written: "Most probably, to adapt Voltaire's *bon mot* with regard to a rather higher personage, if Peggy had not existed it would have been necessary to invent her."

Chapter 43
A Separate Country

The Burren in County Clare is a place I've returned to many times, always finding something new along with what I hope has remained the same. This story for GQ *in July 1990 recounts a visit back after years away, and introduces the reader to Christy Browne—teacher, environmental activist, storyteller and friend. Snapshot: Clare has since remembered the Great Famine with monuments and memorials.*

There was music along the street. A faint, insistent sound of fiddle and pennywhistle and the muffled thump of a handheld drum sounding through the busy main street of Ennistymon, County Clare, a little market town set above the falls of the River Cullenagh.

With the absolute freedom of a man who had nothing to do (there is no higher form of liberty), I tracked the music to its source, Nagle's public house, a tiny, low-ceilinged, stone-floored place, riotously jammed this July Monday at three o'clock in the afternoon. The musicians sat on a bench in shadows along the wall near the front door: the pennywhistle player smiling with his eyes at the crowded room, the *bodhrán* player bowing and rocking over his pounding drum, the long-haired fiddler in a flat cap working furiously, nearly putting out the eye of the pretty redhead sitting next to him. All three young men looked as if they had recently seen some hard traveling. After every tune, they were joined by new players: a farmer with a Jew's

257

harp, a boy making do with spoons, a young American backpacker welcomed with his guitar.

It was my first day back in Clare in eleven years. I had returned with apprehension and not a little dread. Eleven years. Worried that a place I had loved would be changed. But this part of Ireland doesn't change—at least, nothing more than the paint on the farmhouses, crisp and bright in good times, a little shopworn in bad.

Eleven years earlier, my wife and I had come to this part of Clare to save money and to prove the theory of certain city friends that Dublin was not Ireland, and vice versa. Knowing nothing about the place, we had rented a good, sound house on a cliff overlooking the sea outside the village of Lahinch, two miles from Ennistymon. Seventy-five dollars a month. There we spent the winter, and I worked on a novel begun in Dublin. We would travel to the big city occasionally in our battered death-trap Mini, happy as farm kids off to the bright lights, but were always happiest when we would take the long, lovely drive from Ennis to Ennistymon, knowing that when we saw the ruins of the church on the highest hill of Ennistymon, we were home.

Standing against the wall of Nagle's now, watching the road-weary musicians play their pagan, soaring music, I felt no dread, no loss. I simply wondered why I had ever gone away. I'd come back to see the Burren (from the Irish "*bhoireann*," or rocky place), the landscape of limestone mountains, fields of stone and rocky valleys that stretch over one hundred square miles of northwest Clare. It had always had a hold on me, especially through the years I was away from it.

In the novel I wrote that year in Lahinch, I had set a chapter in the Burren and described it as a place that "lies brooding along with the sky, a place that seems too old, too full of secrets, to be interested in anything except its own strange self. Remote and cruel, it is a separate country within the pastoral land of Clare."

Time for confession. I had never been, as the locals say, "out on the Burren." We had driven through it on our way to Galway and gone deeper into it on our way to Doolin, the village on the sea where the best traditional music in Ireland is heard. Riding home at night, with moonlight on the limestone fields and shadows cast from boulders, the child in me would receive a spooky thrill.

After spending a few days on the Burren, I saw I was partly right in my intuition. It is certainly old, fiercely so, and it does have many secrets. But I had been dead wrong in my belief that the Burren is cruel. I had never seen, for example, the beauty and variety of its wildflowers, the astonishing flora that grows from the limestone fissures, mysterious alpine, Mediterranean and tropical plants that flourish side by side in the west of Ireland.

The Burren is a place that on first sight lets you take from it what you need. I had needed a cruel landscape to describe a character's battle with cruelty. One of Oliver Cromwell's men, Ludlow by name, had needed something else. He wrote "... savage land, yielding neither water enough to drown a man, nor a tree to hang him, nor soil enough to bury." In the employ of the noted religious maniac and mass murderer of the Irish, Mr. Ludlow was looking at the Burren in terms of practicality. And so had I. One of the mysteries of the place is that your initial response to it describes yourself and not the landscape.

* * * *

I had asked a friend in Ennistymon, Pat Wall, to recommend someone to guide me through the Burren. "Well," Pat said, "no matter what you're looking for, Christy Browne will help you find it."

We met in the lobby of the Falls Hotel one morning, and, over coffee, Christy described to me the geologic history of the area. The limestone of the fields and mountains was created from sediments of a sea in the Carboniferous period that had been compressed into rock and, when the sea level changed, formed and re-formed by tide and erosion. Two hundred and seventy million years ago, the movements of the earth's crust threw up the Burren as a plateau, and then the Ice Age finished the job, sculpting the Burren into rounded mountains and valleys of limestone and shale, leaving the "perched boulders," some as high as fifteen feet, dominating the fields. The three Aran

Islands, off the coast of Clare, were once part of the Burren, until millions of years of rain, wind and Atlantic surf separated them.

More than 5,000 years ago, when the first settlers arrived, they saw the land as something easily cleared and the grass growing out of the limestone as rich feed for their cattle. They also learned that limestone is a natural heat retainer and, like few farmers in the world, drove their stock *up* the mountains to spend the winter. Their descendants do so today.

When we went out on the Burren, this sense of continuity, of landscape and people, was easily understood. A true pleasure of the Burren is that in the quiet, under a huge bowl of changing sky, you feel a sharpened sense of time, and of timelessness. Tim Robinson, the author and cartographer, who has mapped the Burren, described such a moment when I saw him a week later at his home in County Galway. "I was on the Burren one autumn day, an absolutely still, sunny, perfect day. I was climbing, when I saw men above me, on a different track, driving their cattle up the mountainside to winter pasture. Their cries, the yapping of the dogs, the sounds ringing to and fro, gave me a sense of the wholeness of the place."

Spending time on the Burren will make a mystic of even the most skeptical. Fifty million years ago. Five thousand years ago. As near as a moment ago.

* * * *

The whole history of Ireland can be read in the Burren's ruins. Christy and I went to see some of the "wedge tombs," mausoleums made of enormous flat sheets of limestone and shale, and also saw Bronze Age "cooking places." These are horseshoe-shaped stone containers that would hold up to one hundred gallons of water, heated by hot stones. "Throw a joint of meat in there," Christy said, "a little wild thyme found over here. I'd say twenty minutes to the pound."

Later, I followed Christy out across a field toward the ruins of a ring fort. Solemn cows looked up at us and then grazed on grass lying in

patches among the limestone. Christy was telling me about the Celts
when he interrupted himself to point out a small yellow carpet of
plants growing in the fissures: lady's bedstraw, once dried to stuff
mattresses. He bent to cup in a hand a purple hybrid orchid. "I took a
man out here last spring, a retired tea planter in India who'd settled in
County Cork. The only thing he wanted to see was orchids. Nothing
but orchids. He had no interest in anything else."

"Mad for orchids," I said.

He rose and smiled. "Or just plain mad. Now look here," he said
and walked over to the fort and what remained of a defensive band of
sharpened spikes of stones set perpendicularly to the ground around
it. These were *chevaux-de-frise,* close enough to allow people on foot
to squeeze through and escape from an attack by cavalry. Beyond them
were the ruins of the Celtic fort, probably constructed about the time
of the birth of Christ. With walls eighteen to twenty feet thick and
entrances sometimes underground, they were sound protection in an
age of tribal warfare.

The Celts were a people who migrated from somewhere in Eastern
Europe with a distinct language, culture and religion. They introduced
iron, a much more durable metal than bronze, to Ireland and were a
people enthralled by the arts of poetry, sculpture and jewelry design.
Their religion was a sort of pantheism. "That," Christy said, pointing
to a perched boulder, "is where a divinity lived. That," pointing to a
stunted hazel tree, "is holy. God didn't just live in the sky, but in the
rocks, wells, flowers."

The Celts were also enchanted by war; and because cows were
money, they were constantly involved in cattle rustling. One of the
greatest epic poems in the Celtic language (still the primary language
in parts of Kerry, Galway, Donegal and the Aran Islands) is *Táin Bó
Cúalnge,* or *Cattle Raid of Cooley*. A prime example of Irish
exaggeration of the mundane into art.

The Celts have been described variously as intuitive, reckless,
impulsive, mystic, melancholy. Listen to the speech of the people who

love to turn the language on its ear, and see that mysticism and melancholy in nearly everyone you meet.

* * * *

We drove along a ridge of a valley and there, beyond rolling limestone hills, changing color under the shift of clouds, was Galway Bay, a bright blue, seeming to hover in the distance. Lipstick-red roses grew wild in the rock walls at the side of the road. These walls are constructed to let the savage Atlantic gales blow through with no damage. I asked Christy why these sights, from megalithic to medieval, were in such good repair.

"Respect," he said, driving his van in the wild-West fashion: expertly, full-bore, nonchalant. "Certainly respect for the past. But also superstition. That old fort we saw, some people refer to them as 'fairy forts.' Now, we're not talking about Tinkerbell. But beings that are mischievous, at best. Evil, at worst. Farmers wouldn't cut a bush, move a stone, afraid of the power of the fairies. A lot of superstition has died out, and a good thing. When I was a boy, we were told to stay away from certain people, usually the odd duck, because it was said they went out at night to be in league with the fairies. And, even today, old beliefs exist. Some people out here won't start a new enterprise on any day but a Friday. They won't spend or lend money on a Monday. The superstitions are so old, they don't even know where they come from."

Ahead, half a mile or so, was Corcomroe Abbey, set at the base of a gray Burren hill, commanding a long view of the "dry" valley ("dry" because, with few exceptions, the rivers and streams of the Burren are underground). It is a magnificent sight, founded for French Cistercian monks in 1194 by the king of Limerick. Walking around and through the place, Christy noted various styles of pillars, different because of the different artisans who had built them, each adorned near the top with stone-cut Burren flowers. Most beautiful were the long windows, framing a stretch of treeless Burren mountain, shifting by the minute from homely gray to black to purple and then a dazzling white.

The monks christened this place *Sancta Maria de Petra Fertilis*—
Holy Mary of the Fertile Rock. They brought education of a high
standard to the region and were a vital part of the life of northwest
Clare until the abbey was dissolved in the seventeenth century by what
is known as the Penal Laws. This legislation was aimed at destroying
the Irish language and the Catholic faith. At the former, the laws were
successful; the latter only bound the people tighter in their hatred of
English rule. Catholic education was illegal; Catholics were forbidden
to buy land, mortgage what they had or rent it for profit. Catholics
could not vote, be elected to office, keep a gun or a horse worth more
than £5. Priests were ordered out of Ireland and if caught returning,
faced the penalty of being hanged, drawn and quartered.

These laws had a profound effect on the history of the land. The
historian Robert Kee wrote: "This division between Catholic and
Protestant, which was to shape for so long the whole character of Irish
society, heightened an even more fundamental and obvious division
common to every society: the division between rich and poor …

Catholicism and all the older traditions of Ireland, including the Gaelic language, now coloured poverty with a special identity, making the poor, even more than in most countries, a nation of their own."

Christy and I stood in the churchyard among the ancient Celtic crosses, wildflowers at their bases. No people could be seen down the whole valley, no sound except for a breeze in the hazel bushes. Who maintains this place?" I asked, looking back at the strong walls of the abbey.

"It maintains itself," he said.

* * * *

We stopped for a pint in the town of Ballyvaughan. I had remembered it, from eleven winters before, as a bare, run-down, boarded-up sort of town, but now in high summer it was prosperous-looking, spruced-up and crowded with travelers. Most of these were young European backpackers, stopping off before journeying north to Connemara, in Galway, or heading south to Kerry. It seemed they had no interest in the Burren, which is just as well.

We were the only patrons at O'Lochlen's pub, a small (as are most pubs in the towns of the West) and beautiful place, with an old monument of a cash register and, in the doors, glass the color of tarnished gold, decorated in swirling, coiled Celtic designs. The publican O'Lochlen served us and sat in the gloom on a high stool behind the bar, talking with Christy across the room about local politicians and the sudden death of a young man from the town. I sat at the bar, looking out the door, across the narrow road to a stone wall and, beyond, O'Lochlen's cows grazing in a green field.

After learning I had lived in Lahinch, the publican asked if I had ever known a certain man. It seemed the man had an expensive and tall flagpole erected in front of his house and would run up the Irish tricolor now and then. It wasn't a daily occurrence, but seemed to be done on a whim. Then someone discovered a pattern. Saint Patrick's Day. The anniversary of the signing of the Anglo-Irish Treaty. "The

Fourth of July, your day of independence. His own birthday. His children's birthdays. Oh, it was the talk of the town when his flag would go up. We were all detectives, figuring it out," said Christy with a smile. One day, after months of an empty flagpole, the town woke to see the flag flying. Calendars were brought out, the date discussed by everyone, but no one could connect it to an event.

"Finally," O'Lochlen said, "it was decided that the night before, your man had had a bit of success with his wife in bed."

* * * *

I went out alone the next day, carrying a pack with a picnic lunch, and wandered around the east Burren, up to the top of a hill crowned by a wedge-tomb. A megalithic structure, in excellent repair and, like all the treasures of the Burren, just there, in a field, with no signpost, no fence, no words on a plaque. Maintaining itself.

There were whole worlds of flora blossoming from the limestone, purple and yellow accents in soft green carpets of grass. I took time to look at flaky limestone pavements, layered as fine as pastry, and shoe-sized depressions in the pitted rock.

It took a while before I found the abandoned village. Christy had given me directions, but I was happily disoriented and decided I'd ignore them and just follow my nose. I walked up a switchback lane and came to a farmhouse, where a young mother, baby on her hip, told me the village was "just above. But you're on your own, you know." I said yes. If I fell and cracked my skull, I couldn't sue her.

The lane narrowed as I climbed higher, and at the last curve a tree sheltered the entrance to the village. The backs of two roofless stone houses formed a gateway to a pavement of rain-and-wind-polished limestone, colored here and there by flowers. There were ten or twelve deserted houses, most of them three rooms, nine by twelve feet, some covered in ivy and bramble: the town of *Cathair Bheannach,* or the Fox's Den. As John Feehan, author of "The Secret Places of the Burren," wrote, "It is impossible to walk amongst these ruins without

feeling at one with the people—with their misfortune, their anguish, their pain."

The misfortune of the villagers was the Great Famine of the 1840s. The poor of Ireland lived on a variety of potato that today, some people say, would be unsuitable for livestock. When a blight hit the potato, the people either starved to death or left, if they could, for America in what were called "coffin ships," so many died on the journey. In 1841, the population of Clare was 286,394. The famine killed half of that number.

The catastrophe was not just an act of cruel nature but a crime. George Bernard Shaw said, "When a country is full of food and exporting it, there can be no famine." Cattle, sheep and grain were raised and exported throughout the Great Famine. There were reports of boatloads of grain, brought in as relief from British Quakers, passing boats full of Irish grain on their way to English markets. An English officer, Captain Wynne, reported viewing a turnip field: "I confessed myself shocked by the extent and intensity of the suffering I witnessed, more especially among the women and little children ... devouring the raw turnips, mothers half-naked, shivering in the snow and sleet, uttering exclamations of despair whilst their children were screaming with hunger."

I spent half an hour alone in the abandoned village, the buzzing of bees making the quiet more profound. There is no memorial for the dead of Clare, no statue, no sculpture, just places like *Cathair Bheannach* that are hard to find and, once discovered, pound you with emotion.

I walked back down the lane, and as I passed the farmhouse, the baby began crying, a long wail that made me shiver in the warm summer sun.

* * * *

By chance, I found a "green road" that Christy had pointed out the day before. Green roads are rock-walled tracks that are used to move cattle. The road I walked ran high along a ridge over Galway Bay, and from the height I could see ribbons of green in the blue water. The mountains of Connemara were in a purple mist, thirty miles away.

I went into a field and had my picnic of cheese, apples and red wine. There was a scent of the sea mixed with mountain thyme, sage, the heady perfume of wildflowers. Silence, and cloud shadows moving slowly over the bare Burren hills. I stayed until suspicious cows entered the field, all staring at the stranger lying in the grass. It was time to go home.

Chapter 44
Falling For Florence

For The Washington Post, *February 2004.*

Before you go to Florence, people who have been there will inevitably say, "Oh, Florence is beautiful." You won't be the first to wonder upon arriving what they're talking about. Aldous Huxley couldn't wait to split, writing to his brother that the place was "a third-rate provincial town," and D.H. Lawrence was equally blunt. "I don't much like the place; never did." Dylan Thomas thought it was "a grueling museum," and Dostoevsky went absolutely nuts in Florence, entering the Uffizi and then immediately running wild-eyed out to the street. Totally off his head, he forgot that he was the great champion of suffering humanity, being nasty to waiters to the point where one man said, "Don't you realize that I'm a human being, too?"

Of course, Lawrence and the Russian master are two of the bigger cranks in literature, and Dylan Thomas was sick from Chianti—but still, you might wonder at first what the fuss is about. The Duomo and Giotto's bell tower are jaw-dropping in their gaudy marble, the Baptistery an example of the school of design whose manifesto is that a thing worth doing is worth overdoing. But beautiful?

Looking to the heights surrounding the city, you might wish to be up there and not down in the dun-colored town walking in hive-like streets swarming with mopeds driven by maniacs. (It's no accident that "Vespa" in Italian means "wasp.") But relax, take it slow—an easy thing to do here, since despite immediate impressions, Florence is one of the more comfortable Italian cities. The old maxim about the impossibility of getting a bad meal in Italy stands true, and also, if you're willing to pay in the mid-price range of hotels, it's difficult to land in dreadful accommodations.

The capital of the Renaissance is the most welcoming of any Italian city to English speakers. This is due to the Anglo-American invasion of Florence in the latter part of the 19th century and the beginnings of the 20th, when aesthetes, fed up with the clunky pomposity of Victorian art and mores, dreary winters, hideous fashion and ghastly food, came to rediscover the lightness, color and sensuality of the Italian Renaissance. In the early 20th century, there were roughly 500,000 residents of Florence, and one in five were either Brits or Yanks. (Besides the lofty ideals of culture, it was also dirt cheap to live there.)

The tradition continues today, with dozens of American and British universities having satellite campuses in Florence.

Once you've decided to stay, take a second look at the maniacal mopeds. First, a tip on how to avoid being run down or getting freaked by the demonic bikes. In the narrow medieval byways it's often necessary to abandon the crowded sidewalks and take to the street. Your first experience of this can cause panic as you hear the imbecillic squeal of mopeds bearing down on you. But just keep walking in a straight line, don't look back (because for sure they're gaining on you), and they will pass you. Pass you in a blur, but they will pass. We live in hope.

When you start to think, hey, it must be a serious blast to buzz around on one of those things, then you've made peace with the place. The moped in many ways represents the spirit of Florence, which is the spirit of the adventurous young, dating to the time of Lorenzo the Magnificent. Look closely and that spirit will attach itself to you, no matter what your age, if you'll let it.

An example: a young woman hanging around outside an art school housed in a 15th-century building on a narrow street, talking to a friend, backpack slung over her shoulder. Seeing a garbage truck coming down the street making periodic stops, and realizing that once it passes her she'll be stuck behind it, she quickly double-kisses her friend, shouts "Ciao!" and jumps on her moped at the curb like a circus bareback rider, kicks it into gear before the seat of her stretch jeans touches the saddle, cranks the accelerator wide open and is gone in a gray mist of smoke, leaving only the admiring smile of the driver of the truck, which has just missed her, and the joyful shout of his colleague, hand on heart, beseeching the beautiful rider to come back to them.

You have time before going blind and crippling your feet in the museums, so take a tall seat in the back room of Mariano's on Via Parione and linger over a plate of cheeses, dried fruits and nuts, sweet and sour mustard dip, and a glass of wine. You'll be remembered when you go back, which you will.

Wander the flower, food and clothing market of Sant'Ambrogio (a stand-up guy, from all accounts) and then go to the antiques and flea market on Piazza dei Ciompi nearby. Have coffee in even the most dubious café with a jam-stuffed doughnut, and you'll stare at your cup and think: I've never had coffee until this moment.

Now, it's probably time to devour some culture, which is why you came. You'll go to the Galleria dell'Accademia, of course, to see the big naked white guy. About 18 feet high, David is the great cliché, the most famous statue in the world. But standing before it in its own skylighted gallery, you'll be overwhelmed at the scale of the thing, the nakedness, the drama in the stone, that here is David before battling Goliath. Made when Michelangelo was all of 29, David is young, the killer before the killing, but his stance and expression tell you he is far from innocent.

Seeing it in the flesh (and the enduring and seductive mystery of classical and Renaissance sculpture is that marble has become naked flesh) allows one of Italy's gifts, Humanism—the belief that the divine is within us—to shine.

If mystery is a component of all worthwhile art, then modern art's mystery is in its content, but in Renaissance art it is found in technique. How exactly do blocks of stone take flight, or the folds of a garment have three dimensions, texture and motion in oil on canvas? It's no surprise that artists along with pharmacists in Florence were part of the *speziali* guild, not just because they ground pigments instead of herbs, but because they too were sophisticated magicians.

You'll experience the magic with every Donatello, Giotto or Gaddi you stand before, but to discover how these alchemists were formed, visit the neighborhood of Santa Croce and follow a narrow winding street past an alley lined cheek-by-exhaust-pipe with mopeds to a nondescript building where artists are taught the way they were centuries ago.

"When I was in art school I didn't want someone trying to teach me to be an artist," said Daniel Graves recently. "I wanted someone who'd teach me to draw. Tradition has been broken in the instruction of making art." Graves, an American who came to Florence in the early 1970s to learn the technique and trade of painting — "About 30 of us migrated here. It was like something out of 'Close Encounters'"—is the founder and director of the Florence Academy of Art, a school with 76 students and teachers from 25 different countries. Last year there were 100 applicants to fill 10 spots.

Recently, he and fellow American Susan Tintori, secretary to the academy, sat in Graves's office and spoke of a movement of art that has come out of the school (and other ateliers) and been called the "New Realism." The movement had a recent major retrospective at the Panorama Museum in Bad Frankenhausen, Germany, which also published a handsome full-color 200-page catalogue. The Century Gallery in Alexandria showcased 60 of the works inspired by the Academy last year.

"We're cutting edge," Graves said, smiling, as he walked through the school with cubicles marked off in black cloth and teachers working with students on how to control, block and focus light. North light is the traditional light of the atelier, Graves explained. "It changes the least, you can work all day, which is why many 19th-century factories had north light."

The school's curriculum is intense, with long days. The first year is given over entirely to drawing still lifes, nudes from life, and classical casts, using charcoal and graphite. "You have to control charcoal, there are no accidents, so when you move to pastels there's no problem," Graves said. After a year (or sometimes two) of drawing, oils are taught, but only shades of gray, and the student doesn't receive a full palette of colors until Year Three at the earliest. There is also a full program in sculpture.

Tintori led the way into the small but very fine gallery of students' and teachers' works. "The staff here is teaching and instilling a sense of beauty in art which, when I was in school, was considered weird. Anything realistic was considered taboo, without 'imagination' or 'soul.'"

A visit to the gallery, with its black cloths, softly falling light and hushed intensity of the artists, will allow you a peek into something unchanged for 500 years, a glance into the Renaissance of Florence that will be as clearly defined as the masterpieces you will go to venerate.

Time to climb the Duomo. Don't go if you're claustrophobic or have a bad heart. Everyone else, get to the south door of the cathedral, pay the $10 and take your time on the straight-up hike through a spiraling labyrinth of 463 stone steps. There are a couple of places where you can stop and rest, including one on a balcony encircling the base of the dome where you become an eerie part of the magnificent 16th-century frescoes by Vasari and Zuccari. Even when you know your heart is coming through your skin, your efforts will be rewarded when you reach the marble "lantern," more than 330 feet above Florence, in the open air, with your fellow heroes.

The city is yours, spread out in its valley. There's the Arno, cutting nobly toward the Ponte Vecchio, and there, rising beyond, the Palazzo Pitti and the Boboli Gardens. You can see where you had coffee near Sant'Ambrogio, and find your hotel in the silent, sand-colored town, decorated with red-tiled roofs.

If the word "beautiful" comes to your lips, don't be surprised.

Chapter 45
Amsterdam

For GQ, *January 1987.*

One January my wife and I went to Amsterdam for two weeks. I went to do research for a book, and Mary came along to get out of town. People who had been to Amsterdam said three things: The weather will be awful, the canals are something to see, and don't miss the red-light district. I knew what winter was like in that part of the world, I'd seen pictures of the canals, and I was convinced red-light districts were no place to tour with your beloved.

What we found was a city of church bells, water, wind, framed by deep skies, a city completely without pretensions. The canals and the neighborhoods they flowed through had that sense of silence, order and calm one sees in certain schools of Asian art. The main canals ringed the center of the city like a mandala, the humpbacked bridges the spokes of the great wheel. Cocky little mallards shared the reflective water with the quiet barges. In the middle of a workday, in the center of town, the canals were still as a temple. Church bells tolled clearly. The tall, narrow houses seemed to be meditating on the beauty.

The red-light district, that tangle of tiny streets near the Dam, what the Dutch call the *walletjes* (the wharves), was a shock. I had expected something wicked, or something on the order of American sin strips, with the atmosphere of a hospital ward where the patients are engaged in working out various forms of mental illness. Instead, it was a safe, clean neighborhood where you could buy groceries, get a good meal, talk to a cheerful cop, see homes of families. The women, in their odd aquarium windows right off the little streets, seemed to be like everyone else: honest business people. Even the red lights above the windows were not prurient but charming. The pornography shops sold what can be found on any New York newsstand.

As an American who has lived in St. Louis, Chicago and New York, I'd given up defending my love of cities. The critics are right, of course. American cities are violent, foul, and nothing works. Of late, my response to this has been a New York shrug and a defiant, "So what?" In Amsterdam, though, I found something the writer Ian Buruma defines as "the City, meaning modern learning, politics, social mobility, cosmopolitanism ... everything in short that ought to lead to freedom and independence of thought."

I returned to Amsterdam the following September for ten days. I looked forward to seeing again the places my wife and I had been, the good restaurants, the civilized cafés, the little lanes we had walked. I didn't find them. I'd forgotten that travelers never really find what they're looking for. What they expect is never there. Returning alone to a place I'd shared produced in me an enjoyable sense of melancholy, that peculiar emotion raised to art by the cultures of northern Europe. I rambled around, looking for places. Instead, I found people.

* * * *

Holland is a dream, monsieur, *a dream of gold and smoke—smokier by day, gilded by night.* —Albert Camus, "The Fall"

There is a man who lives in a café in Amsterdam. That is what he tells you when you meet him. "I live in this café. I take all my meals here, I entertain friends, this is the phone number I give."

He is a trim little Scot named Alastair MacLean, just this or that side of 50. And his home is the Café DeSchutter (The Archer). It's located in Voetboogstraat, a long name for a short alley.

Most mornings Alastair arrives around eleven, feeds the cat, has fresh orange juice, sits at one of the plain tables near the windows and does the crossword puzzle in *The Guardian*. It is done quickly. Although Alastair has been and is many things—businessman, actor, producer—his true vocation is conversation. The crossword puzzle is like stretching exercises for the marathoner.

The puzzle decoded, he then has coffee and reads the paper. Around noon, he has a glass of beer, takes out a small plastic bag of hashish, heats one end of a piece with a match, crumbles it into some Drum tobacco and rolls it up. His cigarette finished, he takes his position at the end of the bar, a place where he can see whoever enters, close to the pinball machine, which he calls, "flipper." (To play flipper with him, and, worse, to bet with him, is a trip to the cleaners.)

Every hour or so, he orders something called *Unterberg* to go along with his beer. This is a miniature bottle wrapped in brown paper, with a green cap. It is 44 percent alcohol, the color of blood, and gives off a sinister odor of cloves and other spices. The only effect the hashish, the beer and the vile concoction produce in him is that his smile becomes more like the Buddha's and, after a while, it never leaves his face. Everything amuses him. His talk is fluid, ceaseless, opinionated.

Amsterdam has been home to him for ten years. "Do you believe in love at first sight? I do. The first instant I saw this city, I was in love." He had been a successful businessman in London, owning his own computer-software firm with two friends. He gave it up after coming to Amsterdam, and has since been an actor with ESTA (English Speaking Theatre Amsterdam) and is founder of the Amsterdam Playwrights Workshop. What attracted him? "Freedom. A country where there is organization without regimentation. Now, that is a neat trick, wouldn't you say? But here they've done it. And the feeling, the atmosphere of the city, suits me. The Dutch have a word for it, *gezelligheid,* which, loosely translated, means 'coziness.' It's a very bourgeois city, with all the virtues of the bourgeoisie: respect and love of knowledge, order, safety, cleanliness. Do you know the Dutch have at least eight words for 'bourgeoisie'? But they have none of the vices of the bourgeois. No intolerance, no repression of ideas, no meddling in the individual's affairs."

It is no accident that Camus set "The Fall," that funny, bewildering monologue of a novel, in Amsterdam. His protagonist, a washed-up French lawyer, has exiled himself to Holland and spends his days in a bar, explaining himself in detail to anyone who will listen. I don't compare Alastair with Camus's burned-out case. The point is that Amsterdam is a haven for exiles, and always has been. Whether you run from religious persecution, political bullies, the law, or from yourself, Amsterdam takes you in, welcomes you, leaves you alone.

Luigi Barzini wrote in *The Europeans* of this tradition, listing examples: "Spanish and Portuguese Jews escaping the Inquisition, German Jews escaping Nazis, Protestants from Catholic countries, Catholics from Protestant countries, Belgian, French and German merchants and bankers fleeing the paralyzing shackles of mercantilistic control. Books forbidden in other countries were printed in Amsterdam and smuggled across the borders. This tradition enriched the Dutch morally, culturally, and financially."

In the Sixties and early Seventies, hippies came to Amsterdam to take advantage of the liberal drug laws. Today, Tamils from Sri Lanka, escaping the civil war at home, are arriving in large numbers. And people like Alastair, who want to live the life of the cafés in peace and quiet, continue to come.

The old city doesn't change, but rather it transforms the newcomers. *Gezelligheid* can be translated as "coziness," but it is something more. Look at Dutch painting, especially the work of Vermeer, and go beyond the initial pleasure of appreciating light, color and other painterly concerns. See the scenes, the stories in the art. A girl pouring milk into a bowl, a garden party for two, an old woman sweeping her doorstep in a little street. They tell you that the Dutch revere life, even (perhaps especially) at its simplest. Peace is more than a word or a concept; in Holland, it is a way of life achieved through tolerance, respect and guaranteed privacy.

* * * *

Marijuana and hashish are sold openly in many coffeehouses. Usually you can tell if a place is selling by a painted marijuana leaf on the window. Or you can buy *Mellow Pages: A Smoker's Guide to Amsterdam*—a sharply produced, hilarious booklet that reviews between forty and fifty accommodating cafés. Kip, its author and publisher, told me, "I know a narcotics officer who recently said he'd caught a fellow importing 500 kilos of hash. They kept him in jail for two days and then sent him home."

Jan Winkel, a police official, said, "We are not concerned with anything unless it has a connection with heroin and cocaine. And we have never found any connection between soft and hard drugs."

Kip's real name was known by everyone I met in Amsterdam, but he refused to allow use of it for publication. He enjoys cloak-and-dagger and was disappointed that friends told his name to a reporter. He is a soft-spoken Englishman in his thirties, with a handsome hawkish face. Eight years ago, he left his home and his job of making and repairing musical instruments to come here and work at odd jobs. Two years ago, while looking through *The Agenda,* a sort of what's-on-in-Amsterdam, he noticed ads for cafés marked with a marijuana leaf. "I knew the places, of course, but here they were *advertised.* So I trundled off to the police, gave them details on what I wanted to do. They just shrugged. *Mellow Pages* was born."

At the front of each edition Kip warns about hard drugs, in heavy capitalized print, in violent, obscene language. "You know, he said, "It's easier to buy heroin than grass in Britain."

Does Amsterdam have its own heroin problem? "Wherever that shit is, you have a problem. But I've seen the problem lessen since grass was decriminalized. Somebody who wants to get high can go to a nice café, smoke a little and be happy. Go to one of the cafés I reviewed, spend a little time and then go to the Zeediik. See the difference."

I'd been to the Zeediik. It is a tiny fourteenth-century street that meanders from the Nieumarkt to Prins Hendrikkade, and is one of the very few streets in Amsterdam to avoid. The police used to allow heroin dealing on the Zeediik, hoping to control narcotics by limiting it to one area. But it didn't work, and in the spring of 1985 the police shut it down. The city has purchased the buildings on the street and has plans for a luxury hotel. But the junkies are still there, blade thin, walking quickly when they're trying to score, or sleepwalking when high. It was just like home.

The cafés take some getting used to. When first witnessing one full of teenagers, motionless as lizards, the air sweet with high-octane hashish fumes, you begin to think deep thoughts about tender lives being given over to getting ripped two or three times a day. The feeling is that maybe the Dutch have gone too far. But then you recall the scenes of American shopping malls, where teenagers drift, as stoned as any Dutch kid in a café. What is the difference?

"Here," Kip said, "you don't worry about kids smoking crack when they can't find pot."

* * * *

At a café on the Spui, I met the author Harry Mulisch. The Spui is a little square that borders the Athenaeum kiosk and bookstore. By chance, Mulisch had picked the café where I had coffee every morning as the place for our meeting. It was quiet there in the mornings, and I would sit outside in a wicker chair under the green awning, feeling suitably European and depraved, watching the young women floating by on their bicycles.

Mulisch is one of the best-selling writers in the Netherlands, the author of "The Assault," a story about the occupation of Holland during World War II. The movie based on the book won an Academy Award in April for best foreign film. In the Netherlands, the book has sold over 250,000 copies, an extraordinary number anywhere, incredible for a country of 14 million people. Mulisch has said, speaking about himself, "The writer has become a kind of pop star, he's visible, he appears on TV." I understood his celebrity when he walked into the café one rainy afternoon and sat at my table. The waiters, who knew me from my morning coffee and voyeurism, had always treated me with a typically Dutch attitude of distant courtesy and silent cordiality. With Mulisch at my table, they beamed, bringing my beer with a "There you are, sir! Everything all right?" They almost bowed to Mulisch, bearing his small glass of orange juice regally on a large tray. To be a writer in Amsterdam is not a bad life.

Tall, with a full head of salt-and-pepper hair, Mulisch, at 60, looks fifteen years younger. He is an intense man, and speaking with him gives you the feeling that both of you are involved in some sort of conspiracy. One of the first things he said to me after getting out of his raincoat was, in a whisper, "See those men over there?" I looked at three workingmen, standing at the bar, laughing. "Jokes," Mulisch whispered. "We Dutch can only communicate with jokes. I'd like to tell them. 'Enough joking! Be serious for once in your life.' Sorry, I just finished work, and I'm still in my preaching attitude. What would you like to know?"

I asked him to explain the phenomenal fact that nearly everyone in Amsterdam speaks English. "We're a country of linguists. It's got to do with being a trader nation, but also the fact that little Holland has always been surrounded by large, aggressive countries, Britain, just across the water, and France and Germany." He smiled. "Knowing what the other fellow is saying, especially when he has a weapon in his hand, can help."

How was success treating him, I asked.

"Fine. No problem. If you're a writer in Holland, and you're halfway competent, you won't starve. The state will subsidize you. The only thing strange about selling all those books is I don't know who is reading them. When I sold 6,000 copies, I had a fairly good idea. But a quarter of a million copies? Who is reading my book? Everyone?"

I asked if the war and the Occupation were still important to his countrymen. "Absolutely. We are on the site of one of the greatest crimes in history, here in Amsterdam. How can you forget?"

On May 10, 1940, Germany invaded neutral Holland, and the Occupation lasted five years. Amsterdam was liberated at the same time as Berlin, while the rest of Europe had been freed nearly a year earlier. During the final winter of the war, known as the Hunger Winter, starvation and disease ruled the city. Of approximately 110,000 Jews living in Holland, 100,000 were murdered during the war.

The people of Amsterdam resisted in every way. Because there was so little anti-Semitism in the Netherlands (unlike most of Europe), people of every class joined in the Resistance. An example of this is what is known in Amsterdam as the February Strike. In late February 1941, the dock workers rose up and went on strike, not for better wages or working conditions but to protest the treatment of their Jewish neighbors. The strike was settled by German machine guns, firing squads and deportations to the death camps in Eastern Europe. Amsterdam has not forgotten. At the head of the Waterlooplein open-air market stands a huge, rough gray-green stone statue of a man, known as "The Docker." His feet are solidly planted, his hands pull imaginary rope. His face is calm, eyes downcast. He stands, officially nameless. But everyone calls him "The Docker," and everyone knows what he represents.

"How can you forget?" Mulisch repeated. I asked him why he wrote. "What did Samuel Johnson say? Anyone who writes for any reason except money is an idiot. Something like that. But, seriously, I write to get rid of things. Things that I have to get out. *The Assault* was written for that reason. To get rid of what happened to me and my family and my city." He paused. "Sometimes I don't succeed."

* * * *

"Do you think people travel just so they can go home again?" Scott Rollins asked me ten minutes after we'd met.

"I don't know. But since I've been here, I think of New York all the time."

"You can't compare them, though, can you? It doesn't work. New York is a place of doers. Amsterdam is a place of thinkers. Neither is better, or worse. Just different."

We were in his office at the Foundation for the Promotion of the Translation of Dutch Literary Works, a state-supported organization that is exactly what the name implies. The foundation is located on the Singel, one of the main canals, in a beautiful old canal house. Rollins had greeted me in his stocking feet. "I just bought some new shoes and they're killing me." He was dressed in jeans, a loose red shirt and a black vest. On the back of his head was a small black hat.

"What kind of hat is that?" I asked. He took it off and looked at it. "Felt. Black. I don't know. Fellow stopped me in the street yesterday and asked what religion I belong to."

His clothes looked as if they had been purchased at flea markets. That is where the students of Amsterdam buy their clothes, and Rollins, at 35, still has the sensibility of the student. He looks like a thinner, younger version of Jack Nicholson, with the thinning hair and sharp Celtic features. Raised in Connecticut, Rollins went to Syracuse University, and in his junior year went for a year to Holland as an exchange student. He's lived in Amsterdam ever since. "Fifteen years," he said. "Sometimes I wake up in the middle of the night and think, Good God, I've been away for fifteen years."

What kept him? "Hard to say, I loved the coffeehouse culture. The neighborhoods, all separate but connected by little bridges. And you're not in cultural isolation here. It's a world village. When I first got here, I was struck by the friendliness, the concern of my contemporaries. In those days, it was like coming to the promised land. It still is."

Not long after arriving, Rollins and two friends started an English-language literary magazine called *Dremples (Doorways)*. "Oh, it was fun. We had our café, battles, manifestos and all that. It was the kind of magazine that came out when it came out. We were always broke, starving ourselves so the magazine would live."

Fourteen years ago, he came to the foundation to ask for funds for *Dremples.* He was given money and, five years later, offered a job. Besides his position at the foundation, he is a translator, an editor and a publisher with his own imprint, Bridges Books, which produces high-quality paperback fiction, poetry and essays.

We went for a drink at a noisy café where a little man was operating a barrel organ on the terrace. These are amazing contraptions, painted the colors of kindergarten classes, and heard in every Amsterdam neighborhood. And the sound is part one-man band, part oompah, part the sound track of a Fifties movie. Later, Rollins asked, "Do you like Lebanese food? I know this great joint in my neighborhood."

We collected his bike, and Rollins taught me how to ride on the back. You let the rider start, and then you hop on, sidesaddle. You dismount before the bike stops. After several drinks this can be an adventure.

The bicycles of Amsterdam look, at first sight, like old clunkers, the kinds of bikes harvesting rust in garages all over America, hopelessly out of fashion. But they are stripped down, quick, durable, without gears, the brakes in the pedals, the handlebars and seats positioned so the cyclists can make good time while sitting down. Most are tan or black, and all have the chains enclosed to protect them against rain. Bicycles are important in Amsterdam, and it's delightful to see and hear the morning and evening rush-hour swarm of wheels.

Rollins lives in the *pijp*, a neighborhood so-called because the streets, unlike those in the rest of the city, run as straight as a long-stemmed Dutch clay pipe. As we ate, he talked about the city as university. "Here, the notion of students is totally different than in America. Being a student is a profession, and a respected one. And being a student really has little to do with attending classes or taking tests. Here, a young person comes to the city, is associated with a university in some way, lives in a neighborhood of like-minded people and studies. That means reading, going to galleries, hearing music and, most of all, spending hours every day talking with people. In this way, the whole city is a classroom, the whole city is a culture you study."

After the restaurant thinned out, the owner took down a guitar from the wall and gave a syrupy rendition of "The Girl From Ipanema." When he finished, he handed the guitar to Rollins, who tore into "Statesboro Blues." People drifted in, and the guitar was passed to anyone who wanted to play. A group of English people bought drinks for everyone. One woman who knew Rollins vaguely was surprised to learn he was a publisher. "You're in books? And here I thought you were just another bum." It is a remark Rollins treasures.

Diana Blok, a young photographer, sang Chilean folk songs in a haunting, fragile voice. Born in Uruguay, she has lived in Amsterdam for more than ten years. Several of her pictures were on the wall. Her work—strange erotic scenes, nudes, intriguing abstract studies—can be seen at the Marcuse Pfeifer Gallery in SoHo, in New York.

Why, I asked her, do you live here? "I don't know. I try to leave all the time, but I can't. It's an easy place to live if you're a foreigner. In Amsterdam, no one is considered foreign. It's a good, fair, open place."

I had a long walk back to my hotel. At three in the morning the city was as quiet as a museum at closing time. The canals were lovely, the arches of the bridges illuminated by rows of white light bulbs. Behind me, I heard the whir and clank of a bicycle. Turning, I saw a face that you carry with you forever. She was dressed in a long blue sweater and baggy green pants. I don't even know if her face was beautiful, but it was composed, serene.

She went up the cobblestoned lane next to the dark mirror of the canal, her posture perfect, and turned into a little side street, gone.

Chapter 46
Belfast and The Wee Man

For GQ in March 1985, a trip to Belfast and a prizefighter profile. When this was written, and for many years after, I thought the war in the North of Ireland would never end. There was too much history, too much blood, too much hatred, too many people in control who are easily the most dangerous members of the species—young men who have nothing to lose.

I was in Ireland that Good Friday of 1998 when the referendum that brought peace was passed. It was as if spring, that spring, had brought something like a permanently fresh, bright morning to Ireland.

This piece gives some idea of what it was like without that light.

As the train slowly left Lisburn Station, bound for Belfast, twenty minutes away, you could see him clearly standing in the alley, a boy of 11 or 12 in a dirty, man-size sport jacket. Under close-cut auburn hair, he had that distinctive Irish face—small nose, small, thin lipped mouth, paper-white complexion—a face that can be described as either impish or savage. Waiting patiently, he held half a brick in his hand.

He picked his spot carefully and let fly, pitching the brick off his ear, full overhand, not changing his impassive expression even after his throw had shattered the plate glass of the buffet car. He turned and walked up the alley, walking, not running, in his hand-me-down jacket. He rounded the corner and was gone in the white and yellow fog and coal smoke.

"Ireland has her madness and her weather still," W.H. Auden wrote, and those are two realities the visitor can count on after being away from Belfast for a while. It is still a city of secrets— "whispers" in Ulster parlance—and secret armies. After looking around the shattered old place, you see nothing much has really changed. One of the countless ironies of the place is that the setting of the city is still beautiful, surrounded on three sides by dark hills and the fourth by the Belfast Lough. At times that beauty beyond what you see in front of you, and a wicked gallows humor heard everywhere, is all that seems to be holding the place together.

The violence continues, coming and going according to timetables set by the paramilitary groups that run the neighborhoods. On the first day of the visitor's return, a British soldier was shot and seriously wounded in the Divis Flats area of West Belfast by an IRA sniper using an Armalite rifle. South of the city, down along the border in County Fermanagh, a soldier in the Ulster Defence Regiment (a regiment composed entirely of Northern Irishmen) and his girlfriend were killed instantly when his car was blown to pieces by a bomb on a quiet country lane.

He was 19 and she was 18. They had planned to marry in the summer.

The British Army seems to be everywhere, cruising in gray armored cars, or patrolling on foot in four-man squads, walking the ruined streets of Republican neighborhoods. Turn a corner in the Falls Road or Andersonstown or Divis Flats, and what had seemed to be just another poor Irish city changes to a city at war, as soldiers come toward you. In combat fatigues and regimental berets, holding automatic rifles, they slowly walk, stopping now and then in doorways on either side of the narrow street, checking rooftops, checking every face they see. In a guerrilla war, anyone, everyone, could be the enemy. The day after one of their own has been killed, the young soldiers seem a little more jumpy, their faces a bit more surly.

BELFAST SAYS NO reads a huge banner, in red letters, hanging high on City Hall, declaring to the casual traveler the province's wild, never-ending pessimism. To those in the know, the banner is the response of the Unionist majority to the Anglo-Irish accords signed in November 1985, which allow Dublin, for the first time since partition in 1922, a voice in the affairs of Northern Ireland. The banner means that Reverend Ian Paisley, Ultser's most famous man, is still very much in control of his tribe.

If the old city is still mired in the vile little war now entering its seventeenth year, and Paisley is still, unfortunately, Paisley, one thing at least has changed. Belfast is home base for one of the finest prizefighters in the world. Training at Eastwood's Gym on Castle Street is Finbarr Patrick McGuigan, WBA Featherweight Champion of The World, "the Clones cyclone," or as the people in the North lovingly call him, "the wee man."

Fleet Street journalists and American television, which has broadcast three of his fights, have decided that the wee man, a Catholic, is a "unifier" of the people in the North because of his marriage to a Protestant woman and because he draws his fans from both communities.

American TV's love affair with McGuigan might be more realistically explained by the fact that he is one of only two non-Blacks or non-Hispanics holding any of the twenty-seven championships of the WBC and WBA.

Presenting the defense of his title in Dublin on February 15, ABC seemed to get a little out of hand, going more for cliché than research. There was an interview with the champion. Then a reporter, Al Trautwig, was seen in a Dublin pub wearing an Aran sweater, drinking Irish coffee. The same, of course, as dressing in a kimono and drinking sake to broadcast a sumo match from Tokyo.

There was file footage of a riot in the North, with Trautwig's voice-over solemnly intoning, "Barry knows the animosity in Northern Ireland between Protestant and Catholic, North and South, Loyalist and Unionist." The last two have no animosity toward each other because they are one and the same.

Barry's father then sang "Danny Boy" in the ring before the fight, and there were shots of young men in the pub listening or singing along, teary-eyed, a bit sweaty, lost in sentimentality and booze. Anyone with any sense of being Irish had to feel that the poor sods had again been turned into a joke, that saddest of stereotypes, the stage Irish. One could almost hear, as the lads wept in their beer, the swish of a thousand lace curtains being closed on a thousand parlor windows, from Sydney to Boston to Bantry. Embarrassed again, dismissed again.

The fight itself, ably called by Al Michaels, was superb. McGuigan is good on television, not because of hype but because his fights are always good. And that, the well-fought bout, is one of the rarest events in sports. You can see ten fights, and three will be bicycle races and the rest between ill-trained and out-of-shape athletes. The one fight worth watching will be a match with a fighter like McGuigan. In shape, skilled, aggressive, hungry and with heart.

That February weekend, the networks broadcast three other fights with quality boxers (Livingstone Bramble, Mike Tyson, Wilfred Benitez). None could match ABC's ratings with McGuigan. The networks might have a gold mine if McGuigan can move up in weight, while still retaining his punching power, and challenge the charisma of fighters like New York's Hector "Macho" Camacho. There is certainly no doubt of McGuigan's popularity in his homeland. People have responded to him first because of his talent and second because of his polite, country-boy demeanor. And to the Irish, North and South, Protestant and Catholic, he is "Our Barry," a champion, the boy who went out and made good and commanded the world's respect. But unifier?

McGuigan has not discouraged the label. "I'm an inspiration, a bit of hope," he has said. And offered, on television, his vision of a solution to the war. "I feel, if the younger people started today and forgot about yesterday, these Troubles would be over in ten years." His manager,

Barney Eastwood, has said, "While they are in the hall, they are Barry McGuigan United. The wee man could walk up the Falls Road or the Shankill Road any day, and not a man would lift a hand to hurt him."

All true, and yet the people of the North have always felt that way about prize-fighters, attending bouts and rooting for the home boy, no matter his religion. It's the same as an American bigot who is also a baseball fan cheering the play of a black center fielder. The boy can play, and that's that.

* * * *

Over on Castle Street, black Austin taxis, the mass transit for the Catholic poor of West Belfast, are lined up in the rain, waiting to be filled with passengers, each paying 30 pence to ride up the Falls Road. A red neon sign, "Eastwood—THE BEST BET," sits atop a two-story building. On the first floor is a large betting parlor crowded with men, smoke as thick as a fogbank hanging near the ceiling, and there is not one smile on a hundred faces. Outside, near the wall, trying to stay out of the rain, is a skinny boy standing in a ragged coat, begging.

Around the corner, a long temporary wooden stand is loaded with fruits and vegetables. A woman calls out, "Fresh bananas. Lovely fresh bananas." A man in a raincoat, near a partially closed shutter, watches the street. When asked where the gym is, he looks the visitor up and down. "You the Yank, then?" And opens the shutter, revealing a narrow stairway.

It is a bright, tiny blue-carpeted gym, seemingly too clean for a fighter's workroom. There is a slightly elevated ring, three heavy bags, one speed bag on a low platform. And, at eye level, fight posters and photographs covering all four walls. David McAuley, a dark-haired, 21-year-old flyweight, undefeated in twelve pro fights, is pounding a heavy bag under the direction of trainer Eddie Shaw. Two well-built young men dressed in jeans and turtlenecks are at the far end of the room, leaning against the wall. They have the stillness, the resigned expressions, of policemen which, in a way, they are—here to protect the champion, who is changing in the locker room. For one used to the chaotic, filthy gyms of New York, Eastwood's is like a well-run office at lunchtime.

Shaw comes over to chat in the delightful accent of Ulster, an up-and-down chant, the working marriage of the brogue and the burr. He is a merry little man of 40 or so from the Falls Road area. "Apache country," he says with a smile. He has been training McGuigan since his first pro fight, in May 1981. An undistinguished bantamweight, Shaw tells you of his best night, a knockout on the undercard on a Sonny Liston fight. "Ah, the size of that fella" Shaw says. "He shook my hand, and by Jesus, my arm disappeared up to the elbow." He is complimented on the gym. "Aye, a good place. And what's better is, there's no politics here. Any boy who talks politics, either side, is gone."

Shaw then goes to fetch "the boss," Looking at the photographs, the visitor notices that there are many that include Barney Eastwood —"B.J." or, to the people who work for him, "Boss." All except McGuigan, who has always referred to him as "Mr. Eastwod," never failing to thank him after a fight or an interview. This has been the inspiration for a popular comic record in Ireland by comedian Dermot Morgan called "Thank You, Mr. Eastwood," on which mimicking McGuigan, he thanks the boss for everything—his life, his career, his future, has next breath, everything.

Here, near the speed bag, is a poster for Miss Lovely Legs (Northern Ireland Heat), who is sponsored by the B. J. Eastwood Organization. Next to it is a poster for Miss Betting Shop of 1983. "How's life?" you are asked, and as you turn around, Barney Eastwood is shaking your hand. He leads you away, showing you other photographs: of Ken Buchanan, the great Scottish lightweight champion; of Jimmy Watt; of Eastwood shaking hands with Muhammad Ali in London. A pay phone rings near the doorway, and Eastwood sits you in a chair and answers it. "Yes, Hello, Bob. How's life?"

He is a good-looking man in his early fifties with a pleasant intellectual face and light-blue eyes, as shrewd as you'll ever encounter.

Even when he laughs or is negotiating on the phone, they don't change. One of the wealthiest men in Ireland, he has made his fortune as a bookmaker. His eyes tell you that there is an edge to everything, that he is a man who finds it first and is there waiting for you, ready to give odds. He is not liked in Ireland (what Irishman would ever like a bookie?) but is well respected. "A good friend, a worse enemy," a sportswriter has told the visitor, adding that there has never been a whisper of scandal or corruption concerning Eastwood or his organization.

McGuigan comes out, followed by Shaw, and walks quickly to a heavy bag, bantering for a minute with McAuley. Dresssed in a T-shirt that says "The Clones Cyclone," gray sweatpants and blue-and-fluorescent-yellow boxing shoes, McGuigan begins to shadowbox in front of a mirror. Five feet six and a half inches tall and 126 pounds, the champion has a long reach, perhaps the longest of any ranked featherweight. Much has been made of this gift, but a long reach helps only a boxer, a man who can fight standing straight up, jabbing from a distance, hooking from a distance, and be gone when the opponent tries to counter. McGuigan's style, however, is that of a toy Joe Frazier, fighting from a crouch, always moving forward, pursuing, with power in either hand, the classic banger, the infighter who wants to clip you with short, crisp hooks to the body, corner you and string together combinations.

Having recently turned 25, McGuigan has a record of thirty wins and one loss, which came by way of decision in his third pro fight. Of the thirty wins, twenty-five were knockouts. He has never been in trouble in the ring, with the possible exception of the ninth round against Juan LaPorte in February 1985. The slick former champion caught McGuigan coming in with an overhand Sunday right, a bomb the Irishman never saw coming, and lifted him off his feet. He survived the round and went on to outpoint LaPorte. Two fights later, in London, McGuigan easily whipped Eusebio Pedroza in fifteen rounds for the world title. On his return to Ireland, 100,000 people jammed O'Connell Street in Dublin to cheer him.

There are two clichés attached to Irish fighters: They mature late, and they can be hit. Both seem to apply to McGuigan. As an amateur, he was raw, clumsy, seemingly without any skill. Once he turned pro, he became a tiger—a clever, vicious counterpuncher—his hand speed improved, his ring knowledge blossomed.

He has had the advantage of a generous manager who has gone out and acquired talented and expensive coaches, like the legendary Bobby McQuillar. McQuillar taught the young Irishman that, no matter how well trained an opponent is, he can never get his liver in shape to take a left hook. Watch McGuigan in a fight, and see him, at least twice every round, pound a left to the side of the body, just at the beltline. It is not a tap, but a looping hook thrown as hard as he can throw. Twenty of those and most fighters are looking for a shower and a warm bed.

He has always had great stamina, or, as they say in Belfast, "he can fight to the end of the day." But he can be hit. Just look at his nose now as he makes the speed bag sing. It doesn't look too bad, maybe a bit flat, giving a rugged character to his handsome altar boy's face. Closer up, it is the nose of a fighter who is always coming in, willing to take three shots to land one.

McGuigan nearly gave up a career in the ring after he knocked out an African fighter named Young Ali in London in June 1982. Ali died a few months later, never waking from a coma. McGuigan went home to Fermanagh and did no training for seven months. He spent days walking the hills around his home, refusing to talk about fighting, closing himself off to everyone. "It was," he said, "the most important thing that ever happened to me." After months of persuasion by Eastwood and by his family, McGuigan returned to fight. After the Pedroza victory, he publicly dedicated his championship to the young African.

Shaw puts gloves, a protector and headgear on McGuigan as Eastwood rubs liniment onto his forearms. McCauley and the champion touch gloves in the center of the ring and they begin to spar. For the first round, clocked by Shaw, McGuigan doesn't throw a punch. He moves in against the lighter boxer, slipping jabs, stepping side to side, catching hooks on his shoulder, blocking with his gloves. In a corner he waits for McAuley to follow and then feints right, steps left and is gone, bouncing in the middle of the ring, waiting.

Shaw directs McAuley with a finger, telling him which way to circle. There is no sound except for the grunts of the fighters, the smack of leather on leather, the shuffle and squeak of shoes on canvas. Eastwood and Shaw, standing on the apron, watch closely, grim-faced.

They break for a minute and then have another round, with the champion absorbing punches, slipping jabs and practicing his foot work. McAuley's hand speed is impressive. He has a sneaky jab, but of every ten he throws, only two or three connect. At the end of the three minutes Eastwood comes over to stand next to the visitor. "He'll open up this round," he says. McGuigan comes out, bangs both gloves together and in a flash is all over the lighter flyweight. He hooks off his jabs, doubling, tripling, on the hook to the body. He crosses with his right and is in again, hook to the body, hook to the head, a straight right hand, a left uppercut. McAuley is weaving, confused, and Shaw calls it off. McGuigan and McAuley stand together, headgear touching, speaking quietly, McAuley laughs and touches the top of McGuigan's head with a glove.

Standing on the ring apron, just a few feet away, the wee man, all 126 pounds of him, does not give the impression of smallness. The impression is of power, speed, remarkable energy and movement. The visitor thinks again of "Smokin' Joe Frazier."

After four three-minute rounds of rope skipping, four rounds on the speed bag, four rounds of sit-ups and four rounds of shadowboxing in the ring, McGuigan is finished for the day. He is weighed, with his manager and his trainer watching, and goes to the showers. In the locker room McAuley sits, legs spread, head back against the wall. The champion, in a towel, is signing boxing gloves to be auctioned off at a charity event. He's congratulated on the birth of his daughter ten days ago. He looks up, smiling, speaking in a light, sweet voice. "She's a darlin.'"

"What's her name?"

"Danika Katherine. Danika's a name my wife, Sandra, came up with, Katherine is for my mother. And Sandra had a niece named Katherine, She was blown up in Newry six years ago. Nine years old she was."

What is there to say? McGuigan stares, expressionless. His bright blue-green eyes are hard, intense, in his handsome, heart-shaped face.

Before you is a young man who, like most champions, has never had any profession except that of fighter. He is rare in his trade in that he has no entourage, doesn't care for nightlife and has saved his money. His family, he says, "is everything. They support me. They surround me." His one indulgence is a new black Mercedes, which he drives on the narrow rural roads of Ireland the way he fights: with no respect for his health. Eastwood says, "It's absolutely terrifying to drive with him. I always say to myself, 'The wee lad has the best reflexes in the world, why worry?' But then I start on my prayers."

McGuigan is asked about the "Thank you, Mr. Eastwood" record.

"Funny as a Mass card," he says, grinning.

McAuley laughs and says, "He does your voice better than you, Barry."

"The bugger. It's a pity to take the mickey out of me for thanking someone. You know, if he'd donate some of the money he's makin' to Band-Aid or somethin', it'd take away a wee bit of the soreness."

Watching him sign the gloves, you are struck by the size of his hands. They are a heavyweight's hands, and McGuigan comes over to show you. He looks at them proudly. "When I was a boy, we had a game called crackers at school. Rapping each other's knuckles it was. Now, down in Monaghan, I played with the big lads, big country lads; their hands were regular carrot crunchers. But I always won."

How long will he fight? "Two years, maybe three. I'll make me money, and then I'm away. I don't want to be a brain-rattled old man of 30."

How many times has he heard that from other fighters?

McGuigan says, "Three years, tops."

Will he miss the crowd? "The crowd. I don't even hear them when I'm in there. I'll tell you what I'll miss. The training."

"He's a fierce one for the training," McCauley says. "How many miles did you do Christmas Day, Barry?"

"Eight."

What will he do when he retires? "I don't know. My brother suggested marathon running. That might be a way to go. I enjoy being a champion." If he were a challenger, how would he fight McGuigan? Without a pause, he says, grinning, "I wouldn't show up."

Born in the Republic of Ireland border town of Clones, McGuigan moved just a few yards into British territory and took British citizenship not long after he turned pro. He did this so he could fight for the British Championship. Only the radical Republican leadership seemed to mind. It dubbed him "Barry the Brit" in its newspaper, *An Phoblacht*.

At Sinn Fein headquarters on the Falls Road, a press officer has refused to talk to the visiting reporter about McGuigan. "Barry the Brit? He's an example of what the Brits think of the Irish. Give us bread and circuses. And fuck all bread."

Across the road, in a pub made of concrete blocks and a chicken-wire mesh on the front façade to catch Molotov cocktails, the patrons will gladly discuss McGuigan. In the long, stone-floored room, men are crowded in, drinking pints. It is two o'clock in the afternoon, but the men have little to do except come and drink. We are in a part of West Belfast where 60 percent of the workers are unemployed.

It is the worst slum in Europe, a warren of tiny streets, bricked-up buildings, blown-out bars, full of children who look as if they hadn't had a square meal in years. Beyond the rotting little network of streets are fields of destroyed buildings, scorched timbers and rubble.

A squad of the King's Own Scottish Borderers, called Kosbies here, pass by on the street. Their flat, sand-colored berets with pom-poms would seem comical on anyone but these tough veteran Scots, pointing their weapons at a young woman who is razzing them in a harsh voice. She is in a queue of other women and young children holding boxes of food, waiting in the sleety rain for a bus that will take them to Long Kesh Prison for visitors' day.

In the cold pub, the men talk of boxers, of when Belfast was a great fight town. They speak to the visitor and one another in the curious Belfast barroom method: One man stands, holding his pint, looking at the floor, while his mate shouts in his ear, so close his nose often touches his friend's face. "Do ye hear what I'm tellin' ye?" he shouts, and the friend nods. Move away and the shouter will follow.

"Ah, then there was Spider Kelly," an old man tells you. "Beautiful. A dancing master he was."

His friend shouts in your ear, "He took a punch like a bloody dancing master, too."

What do they think of McGuigan?

"The best of the lot, and we've seen some good lads."

John Caldwell, a former flyweight contender, is brought over to talk. A grizzled little man, he tells you stories of his meeting with Sugar Ray Robinson, of nights on the town in New York when he was in his prime. Caldwell is now an unemployed plumber. "I'd go to America in a minute, but no one would claim me."

The old fighter looks around the room. "Every man here would get out if he could. How can you not love the wee man? He could get out with the money he has, but he stays here, trains here. He's one of us."

The next day there is a press conference at Eastwood's Gym. Swiss television is on hand, a crew from CBS News, a reporter from *The Boston Globe* and forty or so Irish and English journalists. They are here to see McGuigan spar with two Mexicans and a Panamanian Barney Eastwood has brought over to train with the champion.

McGuigan rocks the first Mexican with a wicked hook in the middle of the first round and then eases off for two rounds. The second Mexican is no challenge either, and McGuigan simply boxes him. But the Panamanian, Manuel Mejia, is a classy, strong counterpuncher, and he gives the Irishman a three-round war. Mejia is managed by Luis Spada, Roberto Duran's manager, and he has Duran's style, appearing wild, a bit out of control, concealing his expertise. Mejia backs

McGuigan up, lets him come forward and clocks him with a straight right.

The stiff punch wakes the champion up, and he closes on the Panamanian. Two, three, four lefts to the body drive Mejia to the ropes, and McGuigan corners him, winging a right off the forehead. The bell rings, and Mejia is happy to touch gloves, saying to McGuigan, "*Bueno. Muy rapido.*"

Standing at a distance, beyond the television lights, is an old Irish sportswriter, on the road for the first time in years. He has stayed in a pub across the street a pint too long and is clearly enjoying himself now, speaking with his photographer. They are not interested in the sparring. They are speaking of a friend's generosity. "Generous, is he?" one says to the other. "Christ, he wouldn't give you the steam off his piss."

McGuigan bounces into the locker room as other fighters let him pass. He still has the same fierce look of being in the ring with a man in front of him. He is asked about the sparring partners. "The Mexican boys have a lot to learn. Nothin' but bazooka hookers. But Manuel, now he's slick, he knows what he's doin.'"

He is asked about that other Panamanian, Duran. "The best." He stares. "Ever." His eyes are angry.

It doesn't seem to be the time to ask about New Orleans, Sugar Ray Leonard and "*no mas.*"

"The best ever?"

"Ever. Leonard was good. Duran was great." He turns away, and Shaw begins to take off the gloves.

Twenty minutes later, McGuigan sits on the ring apron and takes questions. This being two weeks before his February '86 title defense against Danilo Cabrera, he is asked how he feels about fighting in Dublin for only the second time. "Good. I'd like to take half of Belfast down with me. But, if I can't manage that, three quarters will do."

He is easy with the press, a man enjoying the spotlight. When asked about the "Thank You, Mr. Eastwood" record, he says, "Funny as a

Mass card." And then mentions Band-Aid. He's an excellent performer, lines memorized, giving people exactly what they want.

"Ah, he's a cute one," the old sports writer says. "Country cute. You can't come from the border without acquiring a bit of cuteness."

* * * *

Is there a spookier part of the world than the border between Northern Ireland and the Republic? It is miles of open green fields, country lanes, a beautiful place of hills and quiet farms. It is also a violent place. A modern, mechanized army is here on patrol, seeking to engage a guerilla force that strikes quickly and then vanishes, or picks out individuals and hands down rough country justice in the form of knee capping, car bombing, sniping.

The route the border takes has been described as the path a drunken man takes in a dark room. A masterpiece of gerrymandering, it separates six counties of Ulster from the rest of Ireland. The six counties make up only one sixth of the landmass of the island but contain one third of its population. To Irish Republicans it is an obscenity. To the British and Loyalists it is something to defend to the death. Writing in 1922, Winston Churchill, commenting about how World War I changed institutions, toppled empires and changed the map of Europe, said, "But as the deluge subsides we see the dreary steeples of Fermanagh and Tyrone emerging once again. The integrity of their quarrel is one of the few institutions that has been unaltered in the cataclysm which has swept the world."

That "quarrel," these "troubles," continue today along this border. Yeats put it more economically: "We pieced our thoughts into philosophy,/ And planned to bring the world under a rule,/ Who are but weasels fighting in a hole."

Drive south out of Belfast and you will pass Long Kesh Prison, or, as the British term it, "the Maze." From the road it looks like a concentration camp, complete with barbed wire and tall gun towers. Here, in 1981, ten young men starved themselves to death for a cause.

Low, flat prison buildings in the distance seem out of place on a plain surrounded by gentle green hills.

It is a typical Irish day in that there are four seasons in an hour's time, with bright sunshine, then a cloudy sky, snow and finally light rain and rainbows. In the late afternoon the moon appears in a patch of clear sky, and there is an eerie shine on the wet black road. Round a bend and there is a soldier in camouflage fatigues standing in the middle of the road a hundred yards ahead. At the side of the road are two other soldiers, standing in a ditch, their weapons trained on your car as you stop. All their faces are blackened, and the whites of their eyes are startling, ghoulish.

Later that day you learn there has been a twenty-minute gun battle in Crossmaglen, over in County Armagh, between a British platoon and the IRA. A friend says, "No wonder the border was so tight."

To the people of Ireland, events that happened 300, 500 years ago are spoken of as if they occurred last week. The Irish are a people penned in by their history, which is as real to them as their humor and poetry, as real as their misery and grief. A prizefighter cannot change that. The appalling reality is that it is unlikely that any person can unite them or move them toward peace and reconciliation.

In the village of Clones, just over the border, turf smoke drifts through the wet streets, bringing a sweet smell of earth. At McGuigan's grocery store, Laura McGuigan, Barry's sister, takes you on a tour of the burned top floor, where the family used to live. The night Barry won the world title, five camera crews descended on Clones, plugged into the store and living quarters, overloaded the ancient wiring and set the store on fire. "The price of fame," says Laura, a pretty girl, who, with her bright eyes and black hair, could be her brother's twin.

Back in the shop, she shows you McGuigan T-shirts and sweatshirts and bags of potato chips with the champion's face and name. Has she seen his fights? "Almost every one of them. It's a cruel thing, a prizefight. But it's his life. It was his way of expressin' himself. It was his way out."

Does she ever want to leave? "Oh, aye, I have already. I was down in Dublin two years. But I'm back now. It's quieter." She pauses. "There's nothin' to do. The best you can say is it's home."

McGuigan's father-in-law, Jim Mealiff, runs a small hotel across the road. As his 14-year-old son pulls pints in the bar, the proprietor is asked how business is. "Without you fellas, the writers and photographers, I'd be in the street."

Mealiff is a sly man, and his business doesn't look as if it depended on itinerant writers. What of the idea, he is asked, of "cuteness" being a way of life for border people? "Of course. You're living here under the gun. You're living with two sets of rules. You grow up fast here. You learn to live with people, to keep your counsel, to find out what the other fella wants and then give it to him."

He grabs a pint of Guinness and sets it before you. "There now, that's what *you* want."

If McGuigan had been born somewhere else, would he have been a champion? "Look," Mealiff says. "That lad is a *fighter*. There's been loads of cow flop written about him, about how he brings us all together and all that other carry-on. And for the night of a fight, aye, maybe it's all true. But he's just a fighter. The best in the world at his weight. In a year's time he'll be the best in the world, pound for pound. There's no stoppin' him. He doesn't duck anybody, he's never taken an easy payday. If he was to lose his championship, the easiest money you'd ever make would be to bet on him gettin' it back."

Mealiff pauses and takes a sip, looking around the bar, counting heads, directing another of his sons to serve a quartet of farm boys in the corner. Turning back to the visitor, he says, "He's a fighter, not a bloody politician. Now drink that down and listen to what I'm gonna tell ye. The Pedroza fight, it was the fourth round, and the wee man came out with fire in his eyes ..."

Chapter 47
Irish Cooking: A Culinary Quest

For The Washington Post, *March 2008.*

The world's shortest volume: "Irish Cooking." Only one recipe: root vegetables and meat boiled several stages beyond exhaustion.

But all is changed utterly, say the Irish hospitality industry and foodie buzz. The Irish have become prosperous and, of all things, European. I decided a food safari was in order to smell what was cooking. Here is a chronicle of some meals during my recent visit: a sampling of the new and old, a search for the best seafood chowder in the West, and how I came to love the blood of pigs.

Mary and I start the hunt at Galway City's Elles Café, a modern place advertising "certified organic coffee." Alas, a "classic" omelet has the lightness of a paving stone, with slices of bubble-gum-colored ham fresh from shrink wrap, and pieces of greenish tomato with a hunk of stem still attached. The coffee is certifiably appalling.

Ah, but lunch. Now we know what they're talking about. On Quay Street, a pedestrian-only street of this medieval college town dedicated to fun, we find Trattoria Pasta Mista. It's a true trattoria, like those found in every town in Italy, down to murals of local sites committed by an enthusiastic amateur, moronic Euro-pop, crisp and professional service, and sensational food: plump mussels posillipo with fresh tomatoes, mopped up with toasted spears of Tuscan bread. Scarlet carpaccio on a nest of baby arugula topped by broad shavings of

Parmesan. Prawn and crab ravioli topped by sweet sun-dried tomatoes strewn with bitter olives, creating an opposite-attracts love affair.

The next morning, at Darry Ryan's B&B in the heart of town, breakfast is a feast. Eggs over easy fried in bacon fat, two small mild sausages, a grilled half-tomato garnished with fried mushrooms, white toast in a rack, brown bread, strong tea.

There's also black pudding, which I eyeball carefully. You can't have a proper Irish breakfast without black pudding, a sort of sausage that uses pig's blood as its dominant ingredient. Added to the blood are oatmeal, milk and bread. It's baked and then cut in thick circles and fried.

The texture is dense; ditto the taste, heavy and unpleasant. I drown it with tea.

"You don't have to eat that," says Mary, slathering toast with rough-cut marmalade. She had tasted a small morsel once and immediately pushed the pudding to the side of her plate, stared at it and said, simply, "No."

Hold the Curry

The 16th-century severity of Churchyard Street hosts a lively farmers market circling through fog around the Collegiate Church of St. Nicholas. Delicacies bump into each other, Galway Bay oysters next to dozens of farmhouse cheeses.

Organic farmer Martin Korek offers his specialty, wild garlic pesto, "made last night." He holds out the flowers of the garlic, a gentler scent than the bulb. Here's a small, perfect pumpkin. Korek notes that in the past, the Irish raised big pumpkins suitable only for watery soup. "This, just slice and bake, a little salt, a little honey. Delicious."

Steps from the market is Griffin's, a traditional Irish bakery here since 1876, with jaunty, white-capped shopgirls working the counter. New Ireland is around the corner in the form of the Gourmet Tart Co., a spare gallery that lets the art do the talking, with glittering confections posing like museum pieces.

Pubs now offer oddities such as curries or pasta, but stay with sandwiches and soup in the labyrinthine rooms packed with fans glued to a soccer match from England. At the Front Door Pub, Mary deems the seafood chowder "nice."

One grilled chicken salad, one grilled ham with butter and stinging mustard, washed down by pints, served up by a merry staff, is nicer. As nice as the stranger explaining the offside rule and the blindness of the referee, poor man.

That evening it blows half a gale through the black streets. We duck into Monroe's Pub, go behind the bar, dodge the bartenders, through a narrow door to the Pizza Cabin. Place our order, tell the server where we'll be in the pub. God's own hot, crisp, cheesy pizza arrives 10 minutes later.

Next day, a ramble away from Galway finds us in Westport, the elegant provincial capital in County Mayo. At noon the churches are full, the pubs closed. As an excuse to get out of the rain we stop in O'Cee's Coffee Shop. The coffee passes muster, but a fat scone—suitably crusted, with a soft cake interior, here-and-there currants and a bit of butter—makes the moment deliciously complete.

Another foodie proverb: The best Indian food beyond the subcontinent is in London. Now add, astonishingly, Westport. We find it at the Everest, run by Jivan Timalisina, born in Nepal. The recently opened restaurant is in an old stone chapel on the tree-lined quay of the Carrowbeg River. The green, maroon and white decor shines, overlooked by a spectacular image of the Anapurna range. Lunch is a bright chicken tikka and sizzling lamb kebabs laid across grease-free onions and peppers, with a riata of yogurt, mint and parsley. Curries have a blush of tomato. Nutty basmati rice balances the heat. (Choices are mild, medium or hot, but go for hot—do you really want to live forever?) Cobra beer, as bitter as it is cold, is recommended.

Business is good, Timalisina says, and not just for wandering gourmands. "We're getting a very good local following," he says.

It Only Gets Better

Connemara is a land of mountains springing from flat moors, ebony lakes changing to blue along with the vault of sky. Mary says, as we approach every turn of the road, "Are you ready?"

In the town of Clifden, set above an estuary leading to the sea, a place where hikers and cyclists make base camp, lunch is at E.J. Kings, a pub of stone-flagged floors and food either simple or full of flair. The Guinness is creamy, and an open-faced crab sandwich on brown bread, with no mayonnaise but just oil, gives a straightforward tang of the sea. Just as good is a BLT, with crispy rashers (bacon), sun-dried tomatoes, caramelized onions and a sharp farmhouse cheese making every bite satisfyingly complex.

But the star is the chowder, based in rich stock, laced with sherry, cream, onions, potatoes and salmon that adds a touch of pink to the creamy whiteness.

After a day spent walking the empty, mountain-shadowed moors, enchanted by the innocence of nimble Connemara lambs—woolly, black-faced, with slender black legs—we decide to eat one.

The pleasantly eccentric Marconi Restaurant offers the old peasant food with remarkable changes. Colcannon—baked cabbage, mashed potatoes and butter—is updated brilliantly, just with lemon. The rack of lamb is crusted outside, lusciously pink inside. And there are three kinds of potatoes: mint-roasted, mashed, and a quickly disappearing mound of sea-salted fries.

Sweets for the sweets: three scoops of hand-churned ice cream in a caramel-and-brandy-spun basket afloat in a pool of English toffee sauce.

The next morning at The Quay House, in the sparkling conservatory of vines climbing and crisscrossing overhead, the breakfast is superb, especially a counter of freshly squeezed orange juice, grapefruit wheels, apricots, rhubarb and syrupy plums next to a bowl of thick yogurt, the best tasted outside Greece. But the black pudding? It's ... never mind.

If travel is the search for the perfect experience, we've found it at Roundstone Beach, with a picnic on an island of boulders on a stretch of empty sand. We settle into stone benches carved by wind and tide. Sea pinks—delicate flowers like pompoms—flourish in the fissures. The beach is watched over by a cemetery rising on a bluff with Celtic crosses against the ever-changing sky.

At the Connemara Hamper, we had packed our rucksack with salami, an Irish brie, olives in their own oil, two rolls and a bottle of Sicilian red, which stands up to the salami and the Atlantic's breeze. The rolls stuffed with cheese and sausage are moistened with the oil. Surf crashes accompanied by the screech of one gull, which finally goes quiet and politely keeps its distance.

Later that day, in the rugged little town of Kinvara, hugging a wide harbor of fishing boats accompanied by an aristocratic yacht, we bag the best fish chowder of the cuisine safari at Keogh's, a pub with prominently displayed pictures of hurling teams going back to the 1960s and a tape playing Elton John profundities. The chowder is more like a creamy fish stew, with hunks of hake, cod, salmon, clams and a sherry-less stock so vibrant that the bounty of Kinvara's fishermen needs no tarting up.

Asked about the chowder, a teenage girl brings more brown bread and says, "Ah, we make it every day." And that's that.

Chapter 48
The Little Bighorn:
A Battle Turned Into Myth

For the St. Petersburg Times, *June 1985.*

Old battlefields are like cathedrals. Both are places of power and irony: holy ground, yet tourist attractions, sites that offer a visitor a walk into the past surrounded by modern life.

Out on the high prairie of southeastern Montana, the National Park Service administers a battleground that was the site of a conflict more written about, painted, filmed and discussed than any in our history. Most Americans know little of the great battles of our wars. Even battles where thousands of Americans died and fought bravely, where whole armies pitched into each other, are largely unremembered.

Mention Yorktown, Shiloh, the Ardennes, and most Americans will come up blank about commanders, terrain and tactics. But a fight where less than 250 American soldiers died is known, in some way or another, by almost every citizen. It is a battle with two names: Custer's Last Stand, the Battle of Little Bighorn. Fought 109 years ago this month, it has achieved the status of an American myth, immortalizing the names Custer, Sitting Bull, Rain-In-The-Face, Crazy Horse.

Hundreds of books about the campaign and hundreds of biographies of the participants have been published. Hollywood films have been made (including one with an actor named Ronald Reagan playing Custer, heroically, of course) and countless sculptures and paintings have depicted what went on that hot June afternoon. Even Americans who got all their information from the corner tavern were educated by a large painting given free by the Anheuser-Busch Co. to bars all across the nation depicting (inaccurately) the Last Stand.

But what actually happened? It was a simple battle, really. George Armstrong Custer, with a troop of 600 men, entered the Little Bighorn Valley looking for Sioux and Cheyenne "hostiles" to engage and force back on to reservations. As always, Custer and his beloved 7th Cavalry were looking for a fight and a great victory. Last in his class at West Point, Custer had been ready when the Civil War came. He was made a major general at the incredible age of 25, fought in all the great campaigns, conducted hundreds of cavalry charges, emerging without a scratch.

He believed in an army legend, "Custer's luck," but had great talent to go along with it. Ambitious and clever, he had made himself one of the most famous Americans of the day, cultivating friendships among newspaper editors, congressmen and the Army hierarchy of Sheridan and Sherman. He was sure he would, in a short time, be president. A victory over the Plains Indians, in the summer of the centennial of the republic, would insure it.

Sitting Bull, when asked years later about his adversary, responded: "Custer was a fool. He rode to his death."

On the morning of June 25, 1876, scouts of the Crow Nation (implacable enemies of the Sioux), under Custer's command, sighted a large Indian village lying along the Little Bighorn River. Some say Custer underestimated the number of warriors in the camp, which is odd because it was three miles long, three-quarters of a mile wide and contained 15,000 people, 5,000 of whom were Sioux and Cheyenne warriors. It was the largest gathering of Indians in the history of the West. Sitting Bull, the great spiritual leader and politician, had brought together no less than six tribes, all determined to be harassed no longer, to fight to the death to preserve their traditions and culture.

After sighting the village, Custer made the first of many mistakes by dividing his command into three battalions. He kept five companies for himself and sent Maj. Marcus A. Reno with three companies across the river with orders to charge the southern edge of the camp. Capt. Frederick W. Benteen was sent far off to the left flank to block an escape from the camp while Custer rode along behind the cover of high bluffs to attack the northern end of the village. It was about three in the afternoon. His troops had covered 90 miles in three days. The temperature was about 100 degrees.

Reno charged the village but was met by 1,500 Indian fighters. He tried to form a skirmish line, but was soon being overwhelmed. He then ordered a retreat into a stand of cottonwood trees near the river, where the fighting was intense, but at least his troopers had cover. At this point, Reno's scout, standing next to him, was shot in the head and blood and brain matter spattered over the major. Reno panicked, gave contradictory orders and the men made a disorganized flight from the trees, piling their horses into the river and up a steep hill with the Indians in pursuit.

Reno was the first to crest the hill. He was soon joined by Capt. Benteen, who had hurried up after receiving a written message from Custer: "Benteen. Come on. Big village. Be quick. Bring packs. P.S. Bring packs."

Benteen had his hands full. He took command, fortified the hill, rallied the troops and was indefatigable throughout the day and most of the next before another column, sighted by the Indians coming down the valley, forced their exodus toward the Bighorn Mountains.

Where was Custer? The only account of what happened to him and his men came from Indian sources, long unbelieved by historians until recently when archaeologists, in extensive digs at the site, confirmed the chiefs' accounts. It seems he rode along the bluffs until he was attacked and surrounded four miles away from Reno's and Benteen's position.

There probably was no final, glorious charge. Indians led by Crazy Horse on the left, Lame White Man in the middle and Gall on the right executed a classic pincer move. It was quite by accident. Indians fought with only two tactics: decoy and ambush. There was no need for decoy. Custer rode straight into them. The pincer was coincidence, but it was coupled with the odds of 50 Indians to one trooper. Custer never had a chance.

How long did the battle last? One Sioux warrior said, "As long as it takes a hungry man to eat his lunch." Not long. Two Moon, the Cheyenne chief, said, "The shooting was quick. The smoke was like a great cloud. We circled all around them, swirling like water around a stone." Chief Gall, through the smoke and dust and heat of the battle, saw the Great Spirit, mounted on a black pony, riding with his men.

The five companies under Custer were annihilated. Because of Benteen's courage and cool, the rest of the 7th lost only 47 men, with 52 wounded, fighting the same odds Custer faced.

It seems every generation, since the battle was fought, turns back to the Little Bighorn. Thomas Berger's brilliant novel, "Little Big Man" (a historical figure, a Crow scout who stayed with the pack train that day), and the Arthur Penn film of the book, gave the 1960s generation a new, less heroic, more realistic version of Custer and the Indian wars. In 1976, the novel "The Court Martial of George Armstrong Custer," by Douglas C. Jones entertainingly investigated minutiae of the battle, showing gross mistakes on the part of the command that led to folly and destruction. And late last year, Evan Connell, a novelist and essayist, came to the Bighorn party with his book, perhaps the best of the lot, "Son of the Morning Star."

The story of this book's publication gives every writer a certain gleeful satisfaction. It was presented to several eminent New York publishers. The reaction was the same everywhere: Cut it, re-form it, re-think it, write a biography of Custer instead of a history, punch it up because who, today, is interested? Connell took the manuscript to a small house in Berkeley, Calif., North Point Press, which accepted it immediately. North Point produced a handsome volume and, at this date, 160,000 hardcover copies are in print. Paperback rights have been sold for $210,000. NBC has purchased film rights and will produce a mini-series. Somebody, the big shots in New York publishing notwithstanding, was very interested.

Connell brings the novelist's touch to his history. He concentrates on both an analysis of character and a detailed account of the events leading up to June 25, 1876. We learn of the culture clash that began with the settling of Jamestown by the English and ended two centuries later at Wounded Knee. This 200-year war between a pantheistic people of great pride and ferocity and a modern, Christian industrialized race, equally proud and warlike, is presented in calm prose: The tragedy dawns slowly on the reader. As the shameful list of broken treaties, massacres, enslavement and dispossession mounts, and heroic men like Sitting Bull and the mystical, charismatic Crazy Horse fight bravely for a culture, we understand the horror, not just of bloody fights, disease and starvation, but worse, the certainty of doom, the death of hope.

Today, the battlefield is preserved on the high plains. In the clear air you can see details on the Bighorn Mountains 50 miles away. Marble markers show where troopers fell on the bluffs above the river. An iron-fenced pen near the top marks where Custer fell with 50 or so soldiers. Above that is a granite monument where all are buried in a mass grave. Below, in the ravines, other markers show where men died, and it is especially frightening to go down into the gullies where you can see that these young men were completely cut off, seeing only an enormous, indifferent sky, and approaching warriors.

Almost all of the U.S. soldiers were mutilated after the battle. Heads were smashed to jelly, arms and legs and genitals severed. Indian women, coming up the bluffs after the battle, reported that some men were still alive while being scalped, while others turned their weapons on themselves. Cries of "Oh, John," the soldiers' name for every male Indian. "Oh, John, no," were heard.

Custer was stripped, like all the rest, but he was not mutilated. Some say it was because the warriors respected his great medicine. Others say that he was protected by a young woman he had known who was living in the village. A Cheyenne warrior cut off the tip of a finger, but that was all.

Connell finds it hard to portray Custer as the beast some modern Americans would have him. He was the type of soldier America has always produced: fearless, brash, daring, a man who has no doubts about his cause or his abilities, with many interests, a lover of life involved in the business of death, enchanted by war. He was a professional, hired by us to fight our wars.

With that in mind, it is good to stand on Reno Hill today, in 1985, near evening, and look out over the beautiful valley, the huge sky rolling overhead, the Little Bighorn cutting through the cottonwood trees puffed with summer, and watch fat magpies chattering, chasing each other through the ravines. or sitting on the marble headstones watching a freight train moving off beyond the river.

Consider in this place the idea that battlefields are kin to cathedrals. It can't hurt to offer a prayer in such a place. An appropriate one, perhaps more a challenge than a prayer, was said by the great Ogallala Sioux prophet Black Elk, and is written on the Visitors Center: "Know The Power That Is Peace."

Chapter 49
Dipping Into the Finger Lakes

For The Washington Post, *June 2002.*

At the end of "Tender Is the Night," F. Scott Fitzgerald dooms his hero, Dick Diver, formerly of the Riviera and Paris, to wander New York's Finger Lakes. After spending some time here, my only reaction is that we should all be so lucky.

It's a simple place —villages, towns, orchards, vineyards, corn and dairy farms sprawled on hillsides, dipping into glens. Serene small towns are set in landscapes mostly free of billboards or roadside attractions.

The area's borders are, roughly, Lake Ontario to the north, Syracuse at the eastern end, Rochester to the west and the town of Elmira to the south. A line of 11 slender lakes, all running north to south, define the region. These are exceptionally deep lakes (Seneca is more than 600 feet to the bottom). Stands of birch thrash in the wind, bordered by meadows, and the land rolls away to the silvery shine of waterfalls.

Vladimir Nabokov fell in love with America while living in Ithaca, the college town at the foot of Cayuga Lake. He taught at Cornell and set his novel "Pale Fire" in Ithaca, which he renamed New Wye and moved to Appalachia. The fictionalized region was apt; the country surrounding Ithaca has hollows, streams, dirt roads, the 1984 Pontiac rusting next to the beleaguered porch that someone didn't quite get around to.

Ambrose Clancy

"Ithaca Is Gorges," say the bumper stickers. That's right on both counts, and a good place to start for a two- or three-day drive around the area. The downtown pedestrian Commons is clean, quietly funky, without chain stores or "Clockwork Orange" attitude. The Saturday farmers market has ragamuffin kids running free past stalls selling everything from Cambodian food to Hawaiian shirts patterned with 1940s bathing beauties. Slow rags and jump blues are played by blissed-out musicians. Most vendors look as if they came to school here in 1970 and never left.

Gorges are everywhere throughout the Finger Lakes, and to explore one cutting directly through the heart of Ithaca, start at the corner of Court and Linn streets. In the distance is a waterfall with a path sliced out of rock leading up to it. This is Cascadilla Gorge. Like its countless mates and the 11 lakes, it was formed—the Iroquois have it on good authority—by the Great Spirit who blessed the country by laying on his hand, creating the fingers of water. Some people don't believe this but insist that 550 million years ago glaciers pounded through north to south and, when they thawed, carved out a singularly American place.

The waterfall is about an hour's hike up through the broken light of Cascadilla, and on late mornings it's rare to encounter another person. Within minutes you feel as if you're in wilderness, the town gone and forgotten, and find yourself whispering when the gorge flattens to water moving as slow as syrup past high walls of shale. Approaching falls and rapids at the next bend of the stream, you have to shout to be heard. Smells of moss, grapevine, wet sandstone stay constant up to the top, where a wooden stairway leads to the lip of the gorge and a sudden, startling reality worthy of Nabokov: bicycles, cars, buildings, reversed baseball caps and backpacks. Cornell University.

After your hike, stay healthy and have lunch at the Moosewood Restaurant. Yes, that's the same Moosewood beloved by hippies and vegetarians, the same people who produce the best-selling cookbooks. It is an unpretentious place with an attentive staff of college kids. The curried egg salad and vegetable soup with wild mushrooms is delicious with a glass of the local Riesling.

As you drive up the eastern shore of Cayuga Lake, the country opens out with lush farms and tall white silos anchored to weathered red barns. (Although Cayuga is the longest lake, it is only 40 miles south to north, so you can easily meander along its shores, then visit Seneca Lake, and make it to Canandaigua Lake by late afternoon.) Past the town of Aurora, a narrow road rises to a brick plaza next to a converted dairy barn high over the white-capped lake. This is MacKenzie-Childs, where 240 artisans create pottery and furniture in a style where country inn meets the Casbah.

A tour takes you through workshops where you can follow raw clay and rough wood making their way through skilled hands to brightly finished products. The restaurant's ceiling looks like the Sistine Chapel, if Michelangelo had used found objects instead of paint: chairs, dolls, desks, bird cages, Coke bottles, tasseled pillows. Outside are gardens and livestock, including a herd of shaggy Scottish Highland cattle, four-legged representations of the MacKenzie-Childs idea.

The lovely drive along Cayuga, tracking hills rising and falling next to lake coves, can remind you that it's difficult to go anywhere in America, even the most idyllic spots, without traveling over a strata of tragedy. In August 1779, Gen. John Sullivan came this way, carrying a brief from George Washington to make total war on the Iroquois and "lay waste all the settlements around so that the country may not only be overrun but destroyed." It was the end of the Iroquois confederacy of six tribes, a centuries-old organization that kept peace among themselves, one so successful that New York Gov. George Clinton named them the "Romans of the West." Sullivan's men massacred or put to flight everyone in their path and burned everything to the ground.

In the 19th century, the Finger Lakes area was called the "burned-over district," not in memory of Sullivan's rampages but because of the fiery religious passions the place inspired. Joseph Smith went into the

woods surrounding Palmyra and came out as the first Mormon. Other groups, who believed in celibacy for all members, weren't thinking too many moves ahead. There were Perfectionists burning for converts along with Spiritualists, as well as Jemima Wilkinson, who changed her name to Publick Universal Friend. Born of this spiritual heat were earthquake social movements, including abolition and feminism, the latter celebrated in Seneca Falls by the National Women's Hall of Fame and the Women's Rights National Historical Park.

Poet Deborah Tall, who has lived in the region for more than 20 years, understands the catastrophic history and palpable sense of mysticism that seems to rise organically out of the landscape as easily as mist on morning lakes. "Everywhere I go now, I see things no one else sees," she writes in her beautiful book "From Where We Stand." "One eye on the road, one eye on the invisible, I straddle the here and there, the now and then, and feel surprisingly at home."

Finger Lakes weather is often a series of dramatic gestures, such as a storm gathering one recent afternoon in high skies over Geneva, at the top of Seneca Lake. Twenty miles to the west, in the countryside outside Canandaigua, we could see the storm flashing and rumbling up the lake from Lisa Herrick's upstairs porch at her B&B, Villa Bianca. When the rain finally swept down on the hilltop house, it was time to go inside through dark velvet curtains at the porch door. A chenille throw lay on the four-poster bed and Herrick had set a plate of mozzarella, basil and tomato on a table next to two wineglasses with a basket of freshly baked bread.

Of course, we allowed some time for vineyards and wineries, an easy task with close to 80 sites to choose from. In the heights above Keuka Lake, Konstantine Frank, a European immigrant, proved 40 years ago that *vitis vinifera,* the classic European grape varieties, could thrive in Upstate New York. Two hundred years of conventional wisdom had said that winters were too cruel for the aristocratic vines. Frank, who had managed estates in Ukraine, knew better, and persevered to the point where the winery bearing his name produces truly superlative vintages, by any standard. His son Willy and grandson Fred continue to improve the tradition. Their quality reds consistently beat French and Napa offerings at blind tastings.

"Wow," said a visitor, setting down a glass of pinot noir. Willy Frank nodded and said, "Of course, wow. Now try this Chateau Frank Champagne. It's better than wow."

Stopping for lunch in Penn Yan (a town named for its original population, Pennsylvanians and Yankees), we found another version of Finger Lakes picturesque, at a place called Holly's Red Rooster—

Dwight Yoakam on the jukebox, waitresses who call you "honey" and "doll," trays of fish sandwiches, coleslaw and iced glasses of draft Genesee beer.

Afterward, heading for Hammondsport, we missed a turn and ended up on a dirt road that bumped down through woods, curved and rose up to a crossroads. Sun shadows fled across the fields toward the lake. Time passed. We were in no hurry to check a map.

Chapter 50
Ireland's Warm Cold Season

For The Washington Post, *January 2005.*

Winter in Ireland? Right. Wait until August to go to Alabama. Be sure to mark your calendar for the rainy season in Chiapas.

But hang on, there might be something to this.

One of the key differences that define the Irish, as opposed to the other nationalities in the British Isles, is that Rome, that source of civilization, order and homogeneity, settled Britain but decided to leave Ireland be, naming the place on their maps Hibernia, the land of wintry weather. But some people, even Italians, now actually prefer Erin in winter. There's no accounting for taste, said the man who kissed the cow.

Kevin Myers, a columnist for *The Irish Times,* is one who sings arias to Ireland in the winter months. "The nights are cold now, and they are longer, but the shortness of the days is offset by their beauty. The hedgerows are losing their leaves with the reluctance of people undressing in a cold bedroom, and around them the great broadleaf trees are touring the colors of the rainbow before going naked for the season which becomes us best: winter. Summer in this country is a fraud ..."

Myers, it should be disclosed, is never happier than when standing *contra mundi,* a wit who will never be out-curmudgeoned in a country filled with razor-tongued misanthropes. But he's right on this score—

if you pick your spots. Avoid the flat Irish Midlands, which in winter can remind you of horror film sets. You wouldn't be surprised to come upon a Black Mass over the next rise or a mad dog howling on a hilltop.

No, go to the West. Take long lovely drives where the towns of Castlebar, Westport and Sligo Town are safe harbors in the sea of moor, bog and mountain. Out of season, when the coach tours are gone and the days shorten, the West seems haunted with melancholy, that feeling of sweetened sorrow the Irish have a lock on. It is a place where landscape rules emotions. It can be grotty, cold and drizzly, but you can spend June in Ireland and have the same weather.

The light at times, late or early in the year, is highly polished, scoured clean and hallucinogenic, providing fragility to things as rooted and ancient as stone. The seasons slipping away from summer turn the land shades of maroon and heather to complement the eternal green. People sometimes are an afterthought here. It's a place Seamus Heaney describes as "the empty amphitheater of the West."

Airlines practically pay you for flights to Shannon and Dublin, and you can get great deals on car rentals and hotel rooms in the larger towns. Once there and rambling around, you will be seen as an individual, not part of a battalion of mass tourists besieging the place. Many attractions and museums will be closed in the small towns, as well as many small-town restaurants, but you will never go hungry. Many pubs in the West serve three meals a day, and the food is good. Europe's feeling for food has even penetrated the locals of small towns. Sometimes it will be plain, but there will be plenty of it. And in the pub, as opposed to chic restaurants, you won't go hungry for Ireland's second most popular indoor winter sport, conversation.

Take some time to spend in Dublin, that most hospitable city, where all the attractions and museums will be open. The Fair City, along with New York and London, has the best theater in the English-speaking world. Those chic restaurants are there, too, and in the cold months it's easy to book a table after the play. It's a cozy place in winter, with pubs serving rich soups for lunch, and soda bread as dense as cake.

In the chilly streets of Dublin there is the comforting smell of rashers and bread in the morning, and coal and turf smoke in the evenings.

It's the time when ghosts are most at home. Laugh, but Irish people are not so quick to disparage people who believe in spirits that reside in places other than bottles. After all, the pagan Irish invented Halloween, the night when there is only the thinnest of veils between this world and that of the dead.

Myers's idea of summer being a fraud has to do with Ireland as a place more than a postcard, and long lingering twilights, salmon jumping though the mist and all the rest of that flapjaw toora-loora-loora. When the short days come, dominated by high rushing skies and a sharp perfume of sea and bog, then what you see, hear and smell teaches you an essential lesson of what makes the Irish separate from most people. It has to do with an unembarrassed belief that there is another, richer life occurring simultaneously with all this fiddle.

W.B. Yeats, Ireland's greatest poet, living or dead (say that in a pub in Ireland and be ready to defend your position, and sometimes your person) firmly believed that spirits roamed the world and that you could talk to them and they'd bend your ear back. Edna O'Brien, daughter of County Clare, has written, "You are Irish, you say lightly, and allocated to you are the tendencies to be wild, wanton, drunk, superstitious, unreliable, backward, toadying and prone to fits, whereas you know that in fact a whole entourage of ghosts resides in you, ghosts with whom the inner rapport is as frequent, as perplexing, as defiant as with any of the living."

In the winter you'll be spared the most odious traveler outside the wine snob, the literary cannibal who will happily knock you down on pathological quests to find the last pencil shavings of the master.

Find your way to Gort in County Galway and follow the signs to Yeats Tower and Coole Park. The Tower, at Thoor Ballylee, is a perfectly preserved square Norman fortress rising next to a river above the unspoiled landscape. The interior is closed until May, but it's worth a drive and a ramble around to see it. Sometimes the only observers will be you and a wise-faced donkey hanging his head over a rock fence, with 20 sheep grazing, woolly heads all coming up at once as you approach.

Here, the poet began the final and most productive stage of his career with his much younger wife, Georgie. (His friend Ezra Pound, who lived for verse and sarcasm, called the tower "Ballyphallus.") There is a plaque near the door:

I, the poet William Yeats,
With old mill boards and sea green slates,
And smithy work from the Gort forge,
Restored this tower for my wife George;
And may their characters remain
When all is ruin once again.

Here, Yeats noted where all of us are, have been or are moving toward:

What shall I do with this absurdity —
O heart, O troubled heart—this caricature,
Decrepit age that has been tied to me
As to a dog's tail?

Just a few miles away, in County Galway, is Coole Park, where Lady Augusta Gregory had her country house and vast estate. She, too, was a founder of modern Ireland, through her collaboration with Yeats (who spent long visits happily sponging off his friend) creating a national theater, The Abbey, still one of the great companies of the world.

The woods and grounds at Coole are magnificent, and you will probably have them to yourself. Look for the Autograph Tree with names cut into it by house guests (who sometimes stayed months): Yeats, his great artist brother Jack, Sean O'Casey and George Bernard Shaw, among others.

Continuing an out-of-season Yeats pilgrimage, head just north of Sligo Town to the village of Drumcliff. Here is Yeats's grave, set in a serene, lovely churchyard next to a small and very fine Protestant church. Words live in Ireland, you'll agree, when you see the tombstone and read the world's most famous literary epitaph, written by the poet himself:

Cast a cold Eye
On Life, on Death.
Horseman, pass by!

Save time to take the waters. Kilcullen's Seaweed Baths, in nearby Enniscrone, are right on the Atlantic, where they've been since 1912. The Edwardian baths are reviving, sensuous, strange and, for many, hilarious. Singles or doubles are welcome, and taking the baths with a companion is highly recommended. First, you sit in a wooden box with only your head exposed. In the box is a wooden handle by which you control steam rising from below. After you feel parboiled, slip into warm seawater and long wide slippery strands of seaweed. Have the guts to then stand up and pull the overhead chain for an ice-water climax.

Short, bright, cold days and windy clear nights in the empty and beautiful West will allow you to stare into a fire, sip a hot whiskey and decide, after all, that dreaming instead of doing is not a bad way to pass the time.

Chapter 51
Bath: An English Treasure

For The Washington Post, *February 2001.*

Sixty years ago George Orwell, in a valentine to his native land, wrote about the experience of returning home from abroad. "When you come back to England from any foreign country, you have immediately the sensation of breathing a different air. Even in the first few minutes dozens of small things conspire to give you this feeling. The beer is bitterer, the coins are heavier, the grass is greener ... The crowds in the big towns, with their mild knobby faces, their bad teeth and gentle manners, are different."

Today's traveler has these identical impressions. Take a flight, for example, into Bristol Airport, a clean and quiet place that is closer to a library than a modern airport (teeming hells of garbled announcements, poisonous food, headaches and apprehension). Walk outside and you breathe Orwell's air. Across the way there are cows in a field, solemnly ripping away at green grass.

Drive east through the beautiful order of rural England, and see signposts for villages with names out of Monty Python: Chew Magna, Wootton-Under-Edge, Chipping Sodbury. Soon you arrive in a city of noble architecture made of golden stone, set in the Somerset Hills above and along the River Avon, a place that is another uniquely English experience. Ancient, lovely, founded nearly 2,000 years ago for comfort and pleasure and still holding those pursuits as its flag: Bath, Queen of the West.

This is a small city of sumptuous hotels and inns, elegant and eccentric shops, antiques markets, galleries and bookstores. There might not be a more musical city in England, certainly not one that places performances in more delightful frames. Even the buskers who perform in front of Abbey Church have more panache, and better acoustics, than any other street artists. Voices reflect easily off the facade of the church, with its stone angels and sinners climbing, as they have for five centuries, on stone ladders, some panicked and falling, others doggedly ascending to their reward. On a bright afternoon a young Irish tenor laments "The Leaving of Liverpool," while a stoic fiddler is clever enough to include his bright-eyed terrier in the act.

Mozart, Schumann and soprano Barbara Bonney are beautiful anywhere, but never more so than in the Georgian splendor of the Assembly Rooms, the restored building that was once the center of Bath social life. Five blazing chandeliers proceed down the long, high-ceilinged room. They dim as the singer, in a saffron silk gown, enters with her accompanist. Forty minutes after the concert, La Bonney swans into Woods, a restaurant behind the Assembly Rooms. Now dressed in black, still holding her encore bouquet, she leads her entourage to a center table. Diners look on with discreet pleasure. But no one applauds, no one asks for an autograph. It is an expected, quite normal event, a final act to the performance.

The first pleasure of Bath, though, and the last thing you take away when you leave, is the effect the architecture has on your visual and emotional senses. Sandstone from around the valley was mined, not quarried, so views from the city are of tree-crowned hills. The stone is soft and, when first used, was white in color. Anne Elliot, Jane Austen's heroine in "Persuasion," was uncomfortable with "the possible heats of September in all the white glare of Bath." (Divine Jane also showed her curious dislike of Bath with a typically wry touch. She has the vain twit Sir Walter Elliot become convinced that in Bath "you may be important at comparatively little expense.") The whiteness fades over time, producing a golden tone that becomes more complex and subtle in the West Country's changeable light, in rain or wet fogs.

The stone speaks, but so does the Georgian idea that architecture must be an echo of reason, classically ordered, and work not just for the comfort of the resident but to communicate with the spirit. And Bath's Georgian avenues that turn into streets leading to squares and laneways offer something more, the concept of surprise. Walking up the steep hill of Gay Street, you're unaware of one of the marvels of world residential architecture until you're two or three steps away. It appears you're heading toward a park with tall trees. Suddenly you're in the King's Circus, finished in 1769. (Bathonians drop the royal modifier.) A perfect circle of 30 attached town houses, 42 feet high, 1,000 feet in circumference, with only three narrow streets for entrance and exit. Classical columns, parapets, tall windows and portholes, moatlike areaways and basements, stone acorns sprouting at the top, all looking in on a park with five towering plane trees.

Today there are businesses here, but it is still home to some fortunate people. Notable residents have been William Pitt, David Livingston and Thomas Gainsborough, who set up house and studio and began making a living by low-balling the established Joshua Reynolds for portrait commissions.

There's another surprise if you take narrow Brock Street off the Circus. Ahead, where the short lane stops, is a park sloping away to the left. But then, at the end of the block, the magnificent Royal Crescent appears. Finished in 1775, it is a long arc of town houses guarded by 114 Ionic columns looking out on a wide flagstone walk and the park falling away. Make your way up the hills though the steep streets and another wonder awaits you: Lansdown Crescent, a mirror image of its sister below, where black and white sheep keep the grass of the park neatly clipped.

Bath began in pagan myth, became history through Roman energy and engineering, and was more or less completed at the end of the 18th century, the high-water mark of the Enlightenment. The legend

starts with Bladud, a prince of a Celtic band who was not only unhappily named but also a leper reduced to the profession of swineherd. And not just any swine for poor Bladud; he was given animals who were as diseased as he was. When his pigs wandered into a marsh of hot mineral springs, they were immediately cured. Bladud had the wit to take the plunge and found in short order that he was in rude health as well.

The Romans arrived in A.D. 43, drained the swamp and built a spa, creating a large bathing pool, saunas and a temple. It's significant that the conquerors made Bath a place of R&R, not a garrison town. The arts flourished and the empire builders met the locals on levels far removed from the point of a sword. Relaxation was more than just a hot bath, taking a little steam and a rubdown. Throughout Rome's 500 years in Bath, there were dispatches from the capital to enforce the rule of gender-segregated bathing and to stop the constant carrying on.

The Roman Baths are faithfully preserved and the museum at the site contains many first-century treasures, including a horrific Gorgon's head and fine mosaic floors. The great bathing pool can be seen from a terrace built by Victorian architects, who also added their notions about the classical period by including some moldy statues. Underground it is warm and humid from springs that have never ceased rising at nearly 300,000 gallons a day, at about 115 degrees Fahrenheit.

The Baths are a must-see, and also a favorite destination of school outings. Depending on your morning mood, it can either be charming or excruciating to be among quick-moving teams, with sketchbooks the size of shields, crying, "Miss, Miss, who was Bladud again? Miss, Miss, can we have the meal now?"

By the early 17th century some "aquatic doctors" (we owe our word "quacks" to these gents) were suggesting that good could come from drinking the water as well as splashing around in it. A certain Dr. Oliver also prescribed a biscuit of his own recipe that, when taken with the water, would cure every affliction thinkable, including "the itch — noise in the ears, running of the ears, sharpness of urine, wounds, ulcers, piles, numbness in any part and all special diseases of women." Men suffering venereal diseases came for treatment, but Bath was a place where it was easier for a rake to contract one than find a cure.

It's not surprising people returned for the waters. Most felt better after a few weeks of a restricted diet and flushing themselves out several times a day. Those who rejected the offer of a "Bath chair" (a sort of enclosed rickshaw) and actually walked the steep streets did even better. People still drink the waters in the Pump Room, and it is still a place where Bathonians meet, especially in the off season. Go for mid-morning coffee or afternoon tea to see and be seen as a professional trio plays classical melodies and show tunes. This is the "new" Pump Room, opened in 1795, a place of tall gleaming windows, wedding cake molding and a high square ceiling. The tablecloths are starched, the flowers at each table fresh, the silver polished to reflect the light of the chandeliers. Behind a rail, a man in 18th-century livery will serve you a glass of the mineral water flowing from the three spouts of the pump.

It is said that you must not leave Bath without consuming three things. The first is Dr. Oliver's biscuit, which is not bad. The second is a "Bath bun," a plump, delicious muffin with just a hint of sugar and a few currants on the top. (Ask for it toasted.) The last is the Bath water, which is warm and tastes filthy. But it contains 43 minerals, people will say. Maybe, but it still tastes like someone has put old rocks in your glass.

For the connoisseur, Bath is one of the great antiques centers of Britain. Many museums would envy the furniture and jewelry in the hushed atmosphere of the beautiful shops along Bartlett Street. But something not to be missed, if you're there midweek, is the dawn market at Paragon Antiques and Bygones. The market is just across from the Slug and Lettuce, at Broad Street and York Buildings, and open only on Wednesdays from 6:30 a.m. to 3 in the afternoon. At Paragon there is no pretense or formality, and the dealers themselves, in their dawn rituals, seem to be the real treasures.

It looks like a shipwreck. There is a wide assortment of good silver, porcelain, old prints, military collectibles and musical instruments sharing space with a lot of homely junk. On two floors 60 dealers show their wares, and whatever you're looking for, there are bargains for those on the dawn patrol. The proprietor, Tom Clifford, stands quietly amid the growing chaos. "I've owned this place for 22 years. For my sins." He points to a large, two-handled brass tureen. "Any interest in that? Great for soup. Or bathing small children. Go on then and get your breakfast," and he points at the small café that is part of the market. Twangy West Country accents are calling out breakfast orders and bantering. "You dodgy sod, you. You'd sell Styrofoam as antique if you could." An old bit of advice is remembered while looking at steaming mugs of strong tea, plates of eggs, bacon, sausage, tomatoes, mushrooms, beans and toast: Eat what the country does best, so in England eat breakfast three times a day.

There is a feeling of some old method of commerce and community here in the early hours as the ancient city sleeps. There is a sense of privacy, but also good fellowship among the dealers, who have mild knobby faces and gentle manners. They have, like their city, an easy appreciation of beauty, and a serene confidence that comes with being on good terms with the past.

Chapter 52
Artful Dublin

For The Washington Post, *January 2002.*

Someone has crafted a dense, human-size spider web in a 17th-century baroque chapel. At the center of the swarming thread, a longhaired woman lies in a hospital bed, sheet to her chin. Silence, light filtering from stained glass, and her stillness trapped in the maze reminds the viewer of some old dada wisdom—any work of art that can be completely understood is the product of a journalist.

Down the hall, in a large room, a young German is rushing around in a white jumpsuit. He alternately plays with toy airplanes and bakes cakes in a microwave, which every hour on the hour he blows up.

These exhilarating works of art from Chiharu Shiotta and Frank Werner were at the Irish Museum of Modern Art in Dublin recently, part of a show called "Marking the Territory." The images were compelling enough, but the real strangeness was that they were happening in Dublin at all. For centuries, the visual arts in Ireland ran a distant second due to the superiority of the Word. But no longer. "This is an ideal place for an artist to be," Paolo Canevari said. The young Roman was represented at IMMA by "Differences," seven people on a bench on whose foreheads he methodically rubber-stamped religious denominations. "The Irish aren't jaded. There's no boredom with art."

Even Dublin's humor, a style distinguished by an urchin's allergy to the sentimental and a duty to bring everything down to street level, has softened toward the public art of the city. The statue of the River Liffey, personified as a woman in a fountain, is still known as "The Floozy in the Jacuzzi," and a realistic sculpture of two middle-age women taking a rest from shopping will forever be "The Hags With the Bags." And what else could a giant metal spike proposed for the north side be called but "The Stiletto in the Ghetto?" These days, however, all landmark slang is said with affection and pride.

Every nation prizes creativity. But countries such as Ireland, which for so long had little but creativity, revere it. It is now museums, galleries and artistic work that are embraced, and not just the theater, pub wit and the writer. One of the engines of Dublin's artistic boom is IMMA, only 10 years old yet housed in one of the most magnificent 17th-century buildings in the world, the Royal Hospital, Kilmainham. Formerly used as a warehouse and steadily declining into dereliction, the place has been brilliantly restored. Bright galleries of dazzling art surround the cobbled courtyard. You can refresh your eye by strolling outside, through the extensive formal gardens, wide sloping lawns and parkland. The museum and grounds command the top of a hill with views north across the river to Phoenix Park, and to the east the spires of Dublin, under ever-changing Irish skies. To go to Dublin and miss IMMA would be like going to New York and missing the Cloisters and the Museum of Modern Art.

A Surprise in Temple Bar

After you've been to IMMA, walk east, always keeping the river on your left, until you hit Dame Street—where, if you walk toward the Liffey, you're in Temple Bar. This part of town has a reputation as the place where young foreigners, lured to Dublin by cheap airfares and favorable currency exchanges, can come to drink in the street, bellow and throw up on their shoes. But it has also, since its renewal some years ago, been an oasis for the arts.

Aileen Corkery curates video and performance art at Meeting House Square in Temple Bar, a box of open space in the lanes and alleys crowded with galleries and boutiques that map the district. "Dublin is a fresh, sexy scene," Corkery, a transplanted Yank, said recently as she took in the buzzing Saturday market of the square. Food from every culture is sold in open-air stalls, as well as Irish organic produce and cheeses, leather and jewelry, all accompanied by a lone saxophonist gone in a Coltrane meditation.

Corkery described the two tracks of Irish art today that a visitor can explore: the old lions getting their due and the young ones being recognized. "The Dublin scene is confident," she said. "We're no longer a backwater. Money is flowing in. No one wants to say that visual arts is the newest thing, but it is. There are some great galleries around now, really great. And, of course, tons of cowboys selling pretty pics to people with too much money."

Managing the difficult stunt of taking chances while making money is the Kerlin Gallery, located in a grotty alley of Dumpsters and cracked pavement. (Around the corner is Davy Byrne's, the pub where Leopold Bloom had the rarest of Dublin lunches, a Gorgonzola sandwich and a glass of Burgundy. Go around 10:30 in the morning, before the mob, so you can look at the lovely, subtly erotic murals by Cecil French Salkeld. Perhaps the murals have attracted those having coffee or eye-openers at this hour, smartly dressed couples appearing stuck in the sad but still exciting moments of illicit affairs.)

At the Kerlin not long ago, Dublin-born Sean Shanahan, 41, opened a show of new work. The striking monochrome, monolithic paintings divided the wine-sipping crowd into the befuddled or the delighted. "A case of the emperor's new clothes," someone muttered, while his companion responded, "All your taste is in your mouth."

Transported Studio

Shanahan was asked why Ireland excelled in the written arts at the expense of the visual. "There are many reasons, I would think. Writing and reading are such private endeavors, and Irish psychology is an inward thing. You don't need a lot of money to write, it's self-taught. But now there is money here. And people like Barbara Dawson, bringing Bacon's studio to Dublin, that creates excitement."

A couple of months earlier, in the most stunning event in European art circles in years, Dawson, director of the Hugh Lane Municipal Gallery, transported artist Francis Bacon's studio intact from London to Dublin. Born in 1909 in Dublin, Bacon was, as Shanahan said while looking at a portrait of one of his screaming popes, "easily one of the best painters of the 20th century." The startling, at times terrifying, portraits, once glimpsed, are unforgettable. They were created over a period of decades in Bacon's studio, a famously chaotic jumble of paint, clothes, empty cans, champagne bottles and broken furniture that never had the benefit of cleaning, or even straightening.

Bacon's sole heir gave the complete contents of the studio to Dublin. It was meticulously recorded, disassembled, packed, transported and reconstructed in the Hugh Lane—which, under Dawson's leadership, has become one of the fine small museums of the world.

Looking at the riot of color and trash at the transplanted studio, Shanahan said, "Harrowing. It's like looking inside his head."

"Oh," Dawson said, "but beautiful as well," noting the bright pigments worked on the door and walls, which the artist used as a palette.

Part of the exhibit is a state-of-the-art database that is easy and comfortable to access, along with some of Bacon's last drawings and works in progress. "Michelangelo couldn't have done better," Shanahan said, looking at one the charcoal sketches.

Portrait of the Actor-Artist

"It's energy, not money," said Noelle Campbell-Sharp when asked why the Dublin scene is jumping. "Ireland's energy has been released! Here, have a cocktail," she said, liberating a tall glass from a passing tray at an opening at her gallery, the Origin, a town house in the Georgian splendor of Harcourt Street.

The Origin was launching an exhibition of paintings of Dublin pubs by Andrew Painter, an Englishman who lives in France. "Yes," he said, surrounded by his accomplished and witty work, "a painter by name and nature."

Most openings provide wine. The Origin doesn't stoop to such mundane fare, but serves Jameson's mixed with seltzer and apple juice. Sounds appalling, but it goes down smoothly enough, and within minutes the art grows in appreciation. (A tip on how to get to Dublin's heart immediately: Check the local papers for openings at galleries and show up at the appropriate time. No one in this most hospitable of cities will check a list; you'll be introduced to artists and can revel in Dublin's greatest virtue, the gift of gab.)

Campbell-Sharp runs the friendliest gallery in the city. How did she choose the name? "Well, because of 'The Origin of Species,' obviously."

Obviously.

The top floor houses her extensive collection of Napoleona. "Why Napoleon? My dear, forgive me, but that's another rather stupid question."

The best gallery for emerging Irish artists is Green on Red on Lombard Street. Photographer Clare Langan shows here, as well as Corban Walker, who has exhibited all over Europe and is, many critics say, the best young sculptor in Ireland. (He is also an actor, appearing in the 1995 film "Frankie Starlight" with Gabriel Byrne and Matt Dillon.)

At his studio in an old firehouse on Dublin's north side, Walker spreads out intricate architectural drawings of a staircase commissioned for a Tokyo skyscraper. Everything he does is highly finished, austere and pertains to image and space, like a series of sculptures in front of a police station in the suburb of Clondalkin.

Slender steel columns rise from the pavement and out of a running stream nearby, some impaneled with neon. They are reminders of Celtic standing stones arranged in ancient times to mark the seasonal progression of the year. There is a sighting hole in one that looks toward its mate, but the 10-foot column appears only four feet high from this vantage—exactly the height of its creator.

"I comment constantly on my condition," Walker says, "and a world that is not made for me. Even sitting in a chair is difficult, sometimes painful, somehow wrong. That's why I made 'Have a Seat,' an oversized chair in which a person of normal height can sit and see and feel things from my perspective."

Standing next to a mysterious and beautiful sculpture of wood and glass in the courtyard of his studio, someone mentions that the piece is almost exactly his size. The artist's only response is a wry smile and a nod. "Ireland can accept art now as human expression, not just something hanging on a wall," Walker says. "Bitterness, begrudgery, whatever you want to call it, is going. We're opening up and out. It's liberation."

Chapter 53
Cheltenham

As promised, a bouquet to the town. For The Washington Post, *August 2001.*

Have you seen that Madonna video where she's hanging in the back of a limo with some outre pals, chugging bubbly, dressed in a fly cowgirl rig, all fashion clues indicating female pimp? Makes you wonder if she changed her outfit when, it's rumored, she showed up to register her little girl, Lourdes, at Cheltenham Ladies' College.

The motto of this serene, immaculate Regency town, set in a Cotswold valley a couple of hours north of London, is *Salubritas et Eruditio*—Health and Learning. Once a spa town of mineral springs serving husband-hunting debs, broken and bored aristocrats, and Eurotrash circa late 18th/early 19th centuries, it still retains the latter virtue of its motto. Some of the finest secondary schools in Britain are here, which explains why, Fleet Street maintains, Madonna will be willing to pay about $22,700 a year, the freight at Ladies' that will turn Lourdes into a Cheltenham town and gown girl.

The school, in the heart of town, is an early-Victorian masterpiece, domed observatories, carved staircases and a 1,500-capacity Gothic hall. Director of Development James Carpenter, opening an oak door leading to a corridor paved in black and white marble, is asked if Madonna's girl will, in fact, be attending when she's ready for junior high.

"Rumors," Carpenter says, smiling. "I can't be expected to comment." Open windows give on to the quadrangle where a magnolia tree shimmers in full bloom. A Brahms melody comes faintly from a music lesson as girls in emerald uniforms drift across the grass. (Cheltenham's more sedate residents refer to them as "the green peril.") Looking at a copper beech framed by red brick dorms, Carpenter adds, "If true, one would quite look forward to parent meetings."

His remark belies Cheltenham's reputation as being the most conceited town in England. Only the unimaginative or shortsighted would consider this small, beautiful, civilized city stuck-up merely because it embodies the England of mandarin politeness, desert-dry humor and discretion. It's refreshing to come to a corner of Britain not publicly wringing its hands over present-day problems. The Guardian newspaper recently announced that the United Kingdom is "a country on the verge of a nervous breakdown."

But Cheltenham will have none of that.

A World of Silence

An advantage for the traveler here is that you won't be bumping into many other tourists; most visitors to the Cotswolds give Cheltenham a miss, concentrating on the villages. It is a good, centrally located base for day trips around a part of England that is comparable to the Lake District for sheer rural splendor. Wooded hills lead to hollows opening to valleys following running streams. On good days, when not besieged by coach tours, the Cotswolds is a world of natural solemnity— "a world of silence," English poet Laurie Lee writes, where the villages are "like ships in the empty landscapes."

Cheltenham will give you a city's jump but within the comfortable limits of a town. There are opulent parks, chic restaurants, boutiques to match London in theatricality, and shops where a bell jingles above the door when opened, announcing your entry into the 18th century.

In the summer of 1788, a visit by King George III to take the waters (two pints three times a day) established Cheltenham as a spa town and created a building boom for the court and other aristocrats.

George the "mad king" is known for losing the North American Colonies and his marbles, and for conducting matters of state while lying under a couch.

Cheltenham water has a laxative effect, so poor George was always on an excitable search for "the necessary," and looked even more off his chump than usual. At times he would spring himself from the prison of court and roam solo, resulting in cases of mistaken identity and endearing him to the people of Gloucestershire. He once rode across the hills talking to a farmer about breeding and pasturage. The farmer asked if he'd ever seen the king, and what was his style of dress. "As plain as you see me now," George is said to have replied.

By 1830, a French visitor thought Cheltenham was "London in miniature," which was not an altogether good thing for some. Tennyson lived here with his mother and thought Cheltenham "a polka, parson-worshiping place." As well known for his hypochondria as his lyricism, the poet relished the harebrained cures on offer. One regime he submitted to was exquisitely off the wall: Get yourself wrapped chin to toe in wet sheets, then walk up and down outside until dry, becoming entertainment for kids taunting, "Shiver and shake, shake and shiver."

A Regency Jewel

A good place to begin a tour of the town is in Suffolk Square, a Regency jewel, as crisp and proud as it was in the 1820s, when it was planned and built. Regency is a broad term for a good deal of buildings erected from the 1790s to the 1850s, when the new, more baroque Victorian style came into vogue. It shares the sublime symmetry of Georgian methods along with the belief that harmony provides pleasure, but it is less rigidly ordered. Regency often has distinctive wrought-iron balconies on the facades, like the Suffolk Square row houses, decorated with shiny black metal hearts and honeysuckle against the vanilla stone. The three-story terraced houses are balanced by St. James Church at one end, and all look in on high hedges concealing a green, home of the Cheltenham Bowling Club. Usually a member will let you in and show you around.

Inside, the hush is occasionally broken by the click of brown and black woods colliding on the billiard-table smoothness of the green.

The solid mass of houses looking in are mostly cream, but here and there you see a pale lemon or pink, proving that the charm of English understatement applies not just to speech. In Suffolk Square, all drama is left to the vault of sky, which seems to have been included in the design. On fine days, it is a sea of endless blue with sailing clipper ship clouds.

Past St. James on Norwood Street, outside David Allan's Bespoke Tailoring and Alterations, a woman steps off the curb without looking—and literally stops traffic. She is tall, slim, with wheat-colored hair that matches her cashmere sweater, in butter-colored leather pants and high-heeled boots, nose tilted, well aware of how good she looks. As you watch her floating across the street past the striped awning of Trowbridge Antiques, writer Martha Gellhorn's comment comes to mind: "The English don't give a damn. They're certain they're superior to everyone else, so they couldn't care less what others think."

All eyes follow her as she swings her way toward Montpellier. This quarter consists of a long island of buildings between two streets that curves down to the great pile of the Queens Hotel. Across from the wide, tree-lined lanes of Montpellier Gardens, fronting the shops, are 32 white terra-cotta figures of shapely women in loose gowns. These are the caryatids, based on statues from the Erechtheion in Athens, and they give the area an *élan* not seen in other Midland towns. (The sculptures look identical, but some have their right knee forward, others the left.)

Cafés and Cut Flowers

All shops, cafés and restaurants on the island have entrances to both streets, including a miniature square that opens onto Montpellier Arcade, built in 1832. It took its name from the French spa town, where slow-to-act British aristocrats were happily interned during the Napoleonic Wars. The area is known as the "continental quarter" because of its sidewalk cafés and un-English appearance. A wooden stall of cut flowers is open for business outside Casa, where

Cheltenham's youth (including members of the green peril) pose in the window over untouched espressos, practicing ennui.

A lovely green dome tops Lloyds Bank at the head of Montpellier. This was once the Pump Room, built in 1824. The interior of the dome is extraordinarily beautiful. Looking up can give you a sense of flight from the planned optical trick of elevating panels of dove gray and pale green with scalloped molding. At the very top is a white and sand colored blossom on a field of vivid red, a perfect setting for what was once one of the most extravagant meeting places in England. The Rev. F. E. Witts, churchman and diarist, visited on occasion: "It is used as a promenade, and Fashion now consecrates it as her throne. Speculating matrons, chaperoning fair and slenderly endowed nymphs with tapered waists, and elderly bachelors with injured livers and bilious complexions smile their approbation."

Lloyds keeps the amazing room in first-rate condition, but the people working here could be in a windowless tomb. It is a bank, after all, and so all is somber and silently energetic. There's the sense that little has changed from Rev. Witts's day; for some, there is nothing remotely more serious than money. Take your time to look at the curious early 19th-century prints on the curved walls, some set next to graphs of current interest rates, others behind potted plants.

And take time to visit Burton Bass at his shop, Montpellier Clocks, at 13 Rotunda Terrace. Bass is a tiny, fit man in his eighties who, like a lot of Englishmen of his vintage, appears to have dressed in the dark: checked jacket, orange and red plaid shirt, paisley tie audible from 50 feet. He, unlike many of his countrymen, genuinely likes Americans. He served on an American-built destroyer in World War II and will thank you and your country for keeping him dry while facing the German navy in the North Atlantic.

In the high-ceilinged front room, "long case" clocks (not "grandfather," please) line the walls like sentries at attention, broken only by a fireplace sporting a vase of pussy willows. Bass points out a 1705 clock with a painted ivory face and made of applewood. "I could let you have that for 18,000 pounds [$25,000]. This clock, like its mates, will last many more hundreds of years. They're made to be repaired, not like today's clocks. It's as good as the day it was finished."

He has just made tea. "From bags, I'm afraid. Will you join me? I have a 1750 clock in the back with Turkish numerals made here in England for a sultan. I suppose you've never seen one of those?"

Cheltenham Abloom

Montpellier ends at The Queens Hotel, a faithful 1838 copy of the Temple of Jupiter in Rome. Just across the way from Ladies' College, it was quarters for Bass's comrades-in-arms, American Army officers. The older girls at Ladies' were often greeted by coos and whistles until the headmistress found out, requested a meeting with the commanding officer and read the riot act. The wolves were immediately tamed.

The Queens and the Victorian Town Hall, which hosts Britain's oldest literary festival every October, are sturdy bookends for the Imperial Gardens, a great greensward with blooming flower beds. Close to 25,000 bedding plants produce incredible floral exhibitions throughout spring and summer. It is another place to linger, along with at least four more formal gardens, in what has been called "a town within a park."

There is an old English expression that says, "You are closer to God in a garden." And in Cheltenham, you are always close to England's past and spirit. Even on one of the more modern streets of burger joints and supermarkets, there are narrow spaces between the buildings that lead to the 13th-century St. Mary's Church and its courtyard, a place of medieval quiet and green shadowy lanes. This midland town will always be, in the words of poet/philosopher George Santayana, "charming, clement and eminently habitable."

Chapter 54
Galway City

For The Washington Post, *April 2001.*

Pasha's Rug Store in Galway City is one of many shops in the Bridge Mills, a 17th-century building rising beside the Corrib River. Cathriona Kilgarriff takes a silk rug to the window for better light. The Corrib is madly rushing past, white-water ribboned brown. She's asked if it is always so wild.

"Only when it rains," Cathriona says. And then her smile slowly grows, wicked with irony. A smile that could be the image of this jaunty old city, full of young people, facing the Atlantic.

Rain, oh God. The Irish language (heard more here than in any other Irish city) has, it's said, as many words for rain as the Eskimo has for snow. Spend some time and you'll get all varieties. But with rain comes what forecasters call "bright spells"—sun showers and heart-stopping rainbows, often double, that arch over the town and melt into Galway Bay.

With a population of 60,000, this is one of the fastest-growing urban centers in Western Europe, and here everything is fast, everything is changing, everything is growing. But in this vivacious town, the pentimento of an older Ireland shines confidently through the slick modernity.

Galway has always been different, always a center of education, business and culture. The Vikings, who settled Dublin, Waterford and

Wexford, sailed into Galway Bay in the 9th century. They stayed just long enough to take sport in sacking a monastic site, murdering some people near the Corrib and scaring the wits out of the rest. (The Norsemen preferred, for inexplicable reasons, to put down roots in Limerick.)

Galway's unique character begins with the coming of the Normans near the end of the 12th century. (Even in some current histories, Irish memory of subjugation still insists on calling them "land pirates.") The Normans figured out quickly what was beyond the Vikings' perceptions: a deep, natural harbor, fresh water from the Corrib, a gateway to inland lakes and the splendors of Connemara. There were unending supplies of salmon and shellfish, suitable grazing for livestock, a conquered people to exploit.

Norman architecture and engineering, and a concentration on trade with the Continent and not just England, made Galway a separate Irish place. Seven hundred years after the Normans settled, a 19th-century visitor observed that it "did not seem to belong to any part of Ireland that I have seen; it seemed to belong only to itself."

The independence is still here, along with beautiful galleries and shops, a university of 11,500 students, two of the most innovative theaters in the country, music everywhere, and a long tradition of celebration. "A festival city," says Tom Kenny, owner of Kenny's, Ireland's finest bookstore and the best art gallery in the West, a cultural event every morning he opens shop. "We fairly lurch from one festival to another."

Galway writer William J. Hogan has noted, "If any man lives long enough he becomes a stranger in his own place." Maybe, but it wouldn't take him long to find his way home. Take, for example, the enduring rituals of the Irish Sabbath.

There's Mass in the morning, of course. But Ireland is quickly becoming post-Catholic, in some part due to the growing disenchantment with the clergy concerning ongoing scandals of abuse and thievery. Galway's own Bishop Casey fathered a son and used church funds to educate him in the United States. His St. Nicholas

Cathedral, built in 1965, is cheerfully considered by almost everyone in Galway to be ugly in the extreme, described by one old-timer to a recent visitor as "a bloody heap of stones."

The Sunday midday meal, called "dinner," is still observed throughout Ireland with plates full of meat, gravy, potatoes and vegetables cooked to the fatal point of mush. Here in Galway, however, it can be proper curries or bowls of *al dente* pasta with fusilli or ziti, marinara or alfredo. But expect an Indian or Italian meal to also come with fries. Don't be surprised if you're asked if you want boiled or mashed spuds, as well.

After dinner, it's time to walk it all off and take the afternoon air. Few places can beat Galway as a city for a stroll, due in large part to the banning of cars in the tangled, medieval streets south and west of Eyre Square. New Ireland is in the fashionable young crowds walking the old cobblestone roads past stone buildings, some of them here when Columbus visited. Towering construction cranes, vulgar reminders of the new economy, are Sunday silent, motionless against the rushing western sky, and seem like Celtic crosses in forgotten cemeteries.

As people promenade, window-shop and greet friends, there's music on the street, the sound of a guitar coming from one corner blending with the melodic wisp of a penny whistle played by a bright-eyed young woman near Lynch's Castle. A superb 14th-century building with carvings of flora, gargoyles and merchant's marks, the ground floor is now a bank. On Sunday afternoon, the ATM lobby (or BankLink; those near pubs are called "DrinkLinks") is crowded with young people in two queues, almost all chattering on cell phones. If you're over 35, you raise the median age dramatically of any room you enter, but everyone is welcome. Galway is the rare place where youth is not wasted on the young.

And, with youth at ease in the Castle, a kind of Galwegian irony is at work. The verb "to lynch" comes from this solid mass of cut stone. In 1493, as the story is told, James Lynch Fitzstephen, the mayor of Galway, tied one end of a rope to a stake in a room on a high floor and

the other around his own son's neck, and flung him out the window. (The son allegedly murdered a man over a woman.) Apocryphal, current historians say, but no matter; it is a tale every Irish person knows and takes meaning from. Today it's a lesson in Hibernian karma—youth triumphant, welcomed to the child-murdering Lynch's to do business.

Pubs are different on Sundays. In the afternoon, families with kids come in to eat their big meal and watch soccer from Scotland. Rowdiness is frowned upon. The old idea of the pub as communal meeting house is respected. The Lisheen Bar on Bridge Street is a rambling cavernous place (like many pubs here) with room leading to room ending in a café where on Sunday breakfast is served all day. It is a bright place, crisply painted, with clean wooden floors. Some important Irish pleasures are entertained here: talk, drink and music.

Multi-channeled TV and computers have debased the Irish gift of conversation, but in Lisheen's, it crackles from table to table, bringing to mind the Irish word "craic," which means a good time. In Galway, turning the language on its ear is still one of life's permanent joys.

On the bar, pints of stout settle, "cascading" in sheets, brown turning black creating the white collar—the only beer that is performance art. Hot whiskeys steam in glasses. A treat on a raw day: a shot or two of Irish, some sugar, three or four cloves, a slice of lemon, boiling water poured on top. (Ask to go easy on the sugar and wait a minute or two before tasting to let the cloves and lemon do their work.)

In the front room, musicians sit in a booth and play for most of the afternoon. Flute for melody, concertina for harmony, guitar for bass and fiddle for madness. Between tunes there's no applause, and when asked why, the cryptic response is, "Ah, it's our own, you know."

Late afternoon, in the less chic part of town, Sunday is even more subdued. Eglinton Street will remind a visitor of Irish cities when the Celtic Tiger economy was a fool's dream. Here the clothing stores are closed, their dusty windows advertising a fashion dictated only by keeping warm and dry. Simple pharmacies, small bakeries and the Booze Brothers Off License are next to dubious "nite" clubs.

The second-floor snooker parlors are just opening, and outside the turf accountant, men in torn sweaters and flat caps chant their doom in age-old cadences.

"And how'd the big bay run yesterday?"

"Like the dog food he's soon to be."

In the quiet pubs, some old men stare through their pints while others turn the newspaper to "the Irish sports page"—the obituaries. Ask them the time and be prepared for a history of the sundial.

Toward evening, a good place for coffee and pastries is the restaurant in Bridge Mills. Upstairs, Bill Doran is sorting out his tiny shop, Country Folk Arts. He specializes in handmade treasures of the West: vintage linen, needlepoint, crochet and fine lace. His most recent linen is from the 1960s, the oldest made more than a century ago.

He apologizes, saying, "It's like a bomb hit the shop," as he pulls down a beautifully embroidered ecru cotton bedspread. "This was used to 'dress' the bed after a birth when the mother received visitors. Or when any important visitor called. Have a feel for the weight of it. This would be several years in the making. Women spending time at night working together, the way your traditional quilts were made."

He displays napkins the size of hand towels made by serving girls at big estates, and exquisitely worked pillowcases. "It's heritage, history, beauty created by so-called simple people who were anything but. In Ireland women didn't inherit land, only possessions. They put their pride in this cloth, their hearts and souls, preserved it and passed it on."

By 9 o'clock, Monroe's on Dominick Street (which might just be the best bar in the world) is filled with country people up from Clare, in from Connemara, from as far away as Leitrim and Roscomon, to dance with Galway housemaids, students, mechanics. This is "set" dancing, the originator of American square dancing, but worlds away from school gymnasiums, cornball patter or polite steps. Blazing reels are danced at an extraordinary pace, whirling, riotous, two-men, two-women teams who fly around the floor as the pub fills with high-pitched shouts, the ancestor of the rebel yell.

Whoever believes there is no eroticism in Irish life, besides reading Brian Merriman, Edna O'Brien or James Joyce (whose wife Nora, inspiration for Molly Bloom, was born here), should catch the happy pagan rites at Monroe's. Tall beauties in tight jeans and sweaters swing from partner to partner, rocking the wood floor with boot heels, faces given over to joy.

"There's music here seven nights a week, 363 nights a year, every night but Christmas and Good Friday," says the young owner, Gary Monroe, after sitting in with the *bodhran*, the goat-skinned Irish drum. "But the set dancing draws the biggest crowds, you know. It's all about the old saying: 'Live till you die, and live with the light in your eye.' "

Monday starts slowly. There are just a few old women attending early Mass at St. Mary's, not far from the Wolfe Tone Bridge in Claddagh (from the Irish for "rocky beach"). This was a fishing community that was thriving centuries before the Vikings murderously swept down out of the northwestern sea.

It's here that the ring of friendship, two hands offering a crowned heart, was created. Here is the place the sentimental old ballad speaks of seeing "the moon rise over Claddagh" and "the strangers came and tried to teach us their ways," a song that has embarrassed not a few Irish American children hearing some sloppy rendition.

Now Claddagh is a modern, working-class neighborhood, but something distant and pure remains if you follow the Corrib out some morning as it thunders to the bay. In a protected nook of the stone harbor, hundreds of swans, ducks, gulls and cormorants float peacefully together, out of the wind, as ragged clouds stalk the horizon. Looking back at the green and brown dome of the disparaged cathedral, you can see a bright spell settling over the town.

Some of the sea birds are already in flight.

Part V
GIMME SHELTER

Doing the North Fork piece (see page 120) for *The Washington Post*, I got in touch with Troy Gustavson, publisher of the Times Review Media Group, which includes three weekly newspapers in eastern Long Island, and interviewed him about the area. After the piece appeared, I sent him some clips, looking for a job. We met and Troy offered me a reporter's position with a start-up weekly, the *North Shore Sun*, that the company was preparing to launch. It was the best experience of my professional life.

Best, and euphoric, September 6, 2002, the morning the first edition ever of a newspaper we had created from scratch, appeared on newsstands. Something from nothing, except maybe hard work, talent, perseverance, and spirit. I was blessed to be thrown in with brilliant and hilarious people who provided all the qualities just listed. Thinking of you, always, Greg, Nicole, Matt, Mike, Denise and Meg.

We eventually all went our separate ways, and 10 years later I learned that the post of editor of one of Times Review's papers, the *Shelter Island Reporter*, was open. I applied to Andrew Olsen, the current publisher, and executive editor Grant Parpan, and got the job.

An island between the North and South forks of the East End, reached only by ferry, it has large tracts of the land preserved from development, and a long, and not always heroic history. Mashomack Preserve, which covers a third of the Island has more than 2,350 acres of mature oak woods, wetlands, meadows, with more than 11 miles of unspoiled coastline. The Island, which some residents fondly call "The Rock," has a year-round population of about 2,500, which swells to more than 10,000 in the summer.

In the summer of 2012, we were living in Greenport, the little port on Peconic Bay, which looks across to Shelter Island. A month or so before I learned about the *Reporter's* job opening, our friend Sheila was visiting from England, and one evening Mary and I took her to dinner on the Island. We were living just a block from the North Ferry dock, and so we walked onboard and stood outside for the crossing. As the ferry eased away, lights in Greenport were just winking on behind us. The sun was almost set, lighting up the sky and catching the peaks of the soft harbor swells. Approaching Shelter Island, the last of the light was lingering in the tops of trees on the bluffs of the Heights.

We walked up a hill following a path bordered by flowering hedges so lush with summer they almost met overhead, and had a meal outside at a restaurant. After dinner, coming down the hill to the ferry, the moon was rising over the harbor spread out before us, and Sheila, using one of her signature phrases when encountering beauty, said, "Prepare to gasp."

I got hooked on the romance of ferry crossings—which has not faded, and I hope never will—those short intermissions in our days, being carried from one shore to another. Those who don't live or work on an island often just get a vague sense of something deeper in the mundane chore of leaving and returning, but the ferries are bright markers of those simple events. Sometimes on those crossings it's impossible not to be reflective of things more important than simply travelling from one map point to another. Anthony Cronin captures the idea in "Living On An Island."

What happens here often seems unreal.
But what happens over there does not really matter ...
People here seem slightly daft.
But people over there seem deficient in understanding.

I grew up in a small town. If that sounds Mellencamp-ish, it is. John grew up in Seymour, Indiana, a bit north and east from my hometown, Mount Carmel, Illinois, a little town on the Wabash. That's where our similarities end. (I have never called myself "Cougar.") I don't have illusions about small towns. I grew up in one. I also have the perspective of being an adult living in an Irish village, and in cities, such as St. Louis, Chicago, New York and Dublin.

One of the first people I met on Shelter Island asked if I had a thick skin. "You're going to need it," he said. Well, it's not rhino-class, but it's thick enough. After working for the paper for only a couple of weeks, someone wrote to me privately that I should do everyone a favor and drown myself, and then on our letters page an editorial of mine was called malicious, smug and vindictive—and that was the nice part. I enjoyed the letter writer's rhetorical skill, especially his suspicion that calling out my politics would bounce off pre-thickened skin, but attacking my prose style would cut deeply. (Thanks, David Olsen. Honest.)

I knew Island life wouldn't be all summer evenings of moonlight and flowering hedges. It's all been a bit unreal, to steal Cronin's line. Which leads me to give the poet the last word:

On the night sea
And above the clouds
You realize that
Here or there
Though everything after all is finite
Nothing after all is final.

Here are some pieces published in the *Reporter*. Note, there will be references to "the Island," meaning Shelter, not Long, since Islanders truly believe there is only one.

Chapter 55
To the Manor Born:
Slavery on Shelter Island

January 2023.

As the hot August night wore on in the attic of the old house, she decided she couldn't take it anymore. It was growing more stifling by the minute and in the claustrophobic space made of rough boards, there was a squeaking sound of scurrying mice somewhere in the dark corners and moving across the floor. She said her goodbyes to her companions and walked down the steep, narrow stairs to the main floor of the old house. Outside, finally, there was a breath of air as she stood on a hill looking out on a sliver of moon hanging in a mist over the still water of Gardiners Creek.

"I was aware I had a choice," Katrina Browne said recently about her experience in the Sylvester Manor's attic in August 2015. An accomplished filmmaker, activist and teacher, Ms. Browne was participating in an event sponsored by the Manor and The Slave Dwelling Project, which spends overnights in slaves' dwelling places with the goal of identifying the places enslaved people lived and then assisting property owners, governments and agencies to preserve them.

Ms. Browne (her brother Whitney is on the Manor's Board of Directors) made the award-winning documentary "Traces of the Trade: A Story from the Deep North," chronicling her Rhode Island family's involvement in the slave trade. She said the night under the Manor's roof was an insight into what enslaved and indentured—

slavery that legally had an end date—people of Sylvester Manor suffered.

The Slave Dwelling Project had made its point in real terms. "The heat, airlessness, sleeplessness and the anxiety of mice crawling over me could be relieved because I had a choice, the power and privilege to retreat from those conditions," she said. "They couldn't."

White Oak, White Gold

In 1652, an Englishman named Nathaniel Sylvester sailed with his wife Grizzell from his family's sugar plantation in Barbados and landed on Shelter Island. He, along with his brother and two other investors, had purchased the Island from an English aristocrat to create an 8,000-acre estate as a "provisioning plantation," servicing the sugar plantations of the West Indies.

Since sugar, or "white gold" as it was known, was a cash crop of immense proportions in the 17th century, every available inch of land in the Caribbean was sown with sugar cane. Almost everything else, including wheat, meat and other foodstuffs, and the wood to make barrels to transport the sugar, had to be imported.

Since the Sylvester's arrival, the Manor had been held in private hands until it was recently incorporated as a nonprofit organic farm and educational facility.

Sylvester and his partners had been attracted to the Island's forests of white oak to harvest and manufacture the sugar barrels, plus the Island's easy access to the Atlantic. Along with their household provisions, other property arrived with the Sylvesters—an enslaved family owned by Mrs. Sylvester of Jaquero, his wife Hannah and their daughter Hope, the first Africans to set foot on the Island.

By 1680, there would be close to 30 enslaved people living at the Manor, which, according to the historian Ira Berlin, was the largest population of slaves in New England.

How seemingly "civilized" people could participate in the ownership of others is explained by legal documents, where a horrific crime is spelled out in supposedly rational, legal terms. Sylvester's will, archived in the East Hampton Library, notes that Jaquero, Hannah and Hope were the property of his wife. But the enslaved couple's second daughter, Isabel, belonged to Sylvester, because she was termed "increase," having been born on his property.

It's unknown precisely what cruelties the enslaved and indentured people suffered at the Manor, but most experts agree it wasn't the same as the barbaric conditions people endured in the South, the Caribbean and South America. "There may have been degrees of hardship and horror, but we don't know the degree of cruelty or mistreatment," said Donnamarie Barnes, curator/archivist of the Manor. "But they were enslaved and isolated on an Island. That's the baseline."

Ms. Barnes said she gets a hint of the suffering through her research and her own perceptions of the people and the place. "Sometimes when I walk the grounds and the woods, I get a sense of desolation in the face of so much beauty," she said. "You can't escape the feeling of being enclosed and trapped."

As Mac Griswold, author of "The Manor: Three Centuries at a Slave Plantation on Long Island," wrote: "Everything is simultaneously ghostly and absolutely present."

Final Rest

Above a dirt road near the Manor's gates is a cemetery under pine trees surrounded by a slatted wood fence that looks like an old comb missing some teeth.

It's an unusual cemetery in many ways, not least that it has few headstones marking graves, just stones. Anecdotal and scientific evidence says there could be as many as 200 people buried here. At the foot of the hill is a massive stone with words, weathered by time, cut in the rock that read: "Burial Ground of the Colored People of Sylvester Manor."

Stephen Mrozowski, an anthropologist/archaeologist at the University of Massachusetts, has visited the Island with teams of students and scientists for more than 20 years to uncover the 300-year life of the Manor, and done extensive research on the burial ground.

He's excavated all parts of the grounds, finding a cultural mix of Native American, African, Dutch and English lives, and was one of the people who spent the night in the attic in August 2015 as part of The Slave Dwelling Project.

In scholarly journals he's noted that the Manor is a living, archaeological laboratory to study the interactions of the various cultures, enslaved and free, which were here in the 17th and 18th centuries. Mr. Mrozowski's research is one testament to the Manor's commitment to bring to light the history of slavery on the Island. "I'm very proud of the way we've approached the subject of slavery and incorporated it into our narrative and the honesty that we deal with it," Ms. Barnes said.

One of those buried in graves marked only by a stone, is a man named Comus who was bought in 1762 and died in 1820, according to records of the Shelter Island Historical Society.

By all accounts he was an imposing presence, well over 6 feet tall who worked with livestock, threshed wheat and harvested apples. He also had a sense of pride that got him into trouble with his owners, as a letter in the Historical Society archives states: "... Commo (sic) will be a plage [plague] to you & I suppose you intend to Sell him there."

Comus was never sold, according to Ms. Griswold, but lived and died enslaved on the Island. Ms. Griswold reports that when he was in his 70s, he was admitted into the Shelter Island Presbyterian church "along with another manor slave, Matilda. He paid pew rent as a full subscriber ($2.50) but he sat in the four short rows reserved for his race at the back of the church."

Heartbreak and Hope

Several years ago, during partial construction work at the Manor, a "spiritual cache" was found in the enslaved people's attic living quarters, a hiding place for talismans in West African religious belief, said Maura Doyle, a former Manor historic preservation coordinator.

The enslaved people would take a brass button that fell to the floor, a slate picture frame, a used candle, or other everyday articles and bundle them together and hide them away to ensure, for example, a successful birth.

But what is most striking in the attic, inspiring a mixture of heartbreak and hope, are etchings of sailing ships on a wooden beam near a narrow attic window. You can see a progression in the work, from a suggestion of a ship to finely drawn images of sails and intricate renderings of ropes and riggings. The etchings speak of an indentured boy's need for expression and freedom.

The drawings—probably etched into the wood by a nail—were made by William Pharaoh, a boy of African-American and Indian heritage, who came to the Manor when he was eight. William lived in the spaces under the eaves in the 1830s with his brother, Isaac, who was five when they arrived.

Ms. Barnes, in her research, found a letter written in August 1840 that began, "William has run away."

The letter, Ms. Barnes said, recounts how William and Isaac had gone to Greenport on errands one day and were seen speaking to the captain of a sloop that was bound for New London that night. "The boys came home and had dinner," Ms. Barnes said. "But the next morning, William and his things were gone."

Further research by Ms. Barnes carries William's story a bit further. Recently she came upon his name in a database, whalinghistory.org, which revealed that after arriving in New London from Greenport that August day 182 years ago, he signed on to the Superior, a whaling vessel.

He lied about his age (and apparently his indentured status), saying he was 21, when he was 19. The ship's manifest spelled his name "Faro," and other log information noted that he was 5 feet 9 inches tall, "an Indian from Long Island."

The Superior was bound for the South Atlantic and hunted whales for two years. When it returned in July 1842, William signed on as a crew member of the Jason, which went whaling off the tip of South Africa and into the Indian Ocean. The ship's logs, Ms. Barnes said, record the Jason sailing to the island nations of Madagascar and Mauritius, returning to New London in May 1844.

Whaling in the 19th century was an enormously profitable industry, and working on the ships was a meritocracy, so no matter who you were or where you came from, you could advance in the seaman's trade and be free. On the East End and throughout New England, hundreds of men of color—Native Americans and free black men—signed on to ships and plied the world's oceans, often on voyages lasting more than three years.

"It is not a very well told story that men of color were such a big part of the whaling story," said Sandi Brewster-Walker, who grew up in Amityville and is of Montaukett heritage on her father's side. She has done extensive research and has written about Native Americans and free black men who worked in the industry.

As Times Review Executive Editor Steve Wick has written, "Before oil was pumped out of the ground in Pennsylvania in 1859, the oil of oils, the best of the best, was the pure oil found in the head of a sperm whale. Thousands of whaling vessels sailed the world's oceans in search of whales to kill. On Long Island, Sag Harbor and Greenport were the main whaling ports, with small operations in New Suffolk and perhaps Jamesport. The industry made ship owners and captains wealthy, as is evidenced by the beautiful homes they left behind on the East End. Crew members received tiny portions of the overall value of oil."

But the meritocracy meant that, if you were hardworking, you could move up the ranks of a ship's crew, no matter your race or class.

"In terms of dollars, the whaling industry brought in huge amounts of money," said Michael Butler, general manager of the Sag Harbor Whaling Museum. "It was the main center of employment and the main funding for the local economies. It made a lot of people very wealthy—in today's dollars, hundreds of millions. We also know that probably 30% of whalers and sailors were people of color."

The rest of William Pharaoh's story remains to be told, Ms. Barnes said. New information about him following his dream of going to sea "is an incredible finding, and that there are many great stories waiting to be told," she added.

William's brother, Isaac, she said, stayed at the Manor for the rest of his life and was laid to rest down the hill in the burying ground.

Chapter 56
Remembering Chris

From February 2023.

Perhaps the finest accolade I've received in 10 years as editor of the *Reporter* was a statement by Chris Lewis at a public function not long after she retired from the Town Board in 2017. One of the joys of retirement that she was looking forward to was, she said, that, "I won't have to pick up the phone at 7 o'clock in the morning to answer questions from Ambrose Clancy."

That short sentence sums up Chris. The use of a wry phrase to make several points at once; the inclusive smile to those who get it; her sense of public service; and the Midwestern wit of making a pleasure sound like a chore.

I'd call her at 7 a.m. for several reasons. I knew she'd pick up the phone. I knew she'd answer (mostly) my questions about the town government and the issue of the moment. And I'd start my day with the benefit of her sense of humor—her conversation was never far from a smile—her optimism, clear thinking and a dedication to doing something to make where she lives a better place.

News of Chris's death on Wednesday, Feb. 1, was a shock. This might seem strange, to be shocked by the death of an 88-year-old person. But she was among those rare people who, no matter their age, or debilitating illness, cause you to be momentarily brought up short when you hear the news. It's because they are the ones who seem indestructible, the ones who have a character that is strong, anchored to an idea of service to young and old and all income levels, and a *joie de vivre* through struggles. Her spirit, intelligence and dedication made her the conscience of the Town Board and beloved among her constituents. During 12 of her years on the Board, she was also the deputy supervisor, and previous to her terms at Town Hall, she spent 12 years on the Board of Education. Adding to that significant record of public service, Chris volunteered with the Senior Citizens Foundation and became its president.

But her accomplishments as a professional—she worked as a registered nurse for many years—and as an elected official, are secondary to the life she led as a wife, mother, grandmother, and friend. Again, that's why it's a shock that she is no longer here. But the shock evaporates, and you receive, after the ache of grief eases (just a bit), a gift if you're lucky: The knowledge that the loved one is not truly gone. They're with you, always.

Chris was one who, in newspaper-speak, "knew how to play the game." Meaning she would talk to us, professional-to-professional, and once you got to know each other, person-to-person. She was unlike the many elected officials on every level of government who deal with you with the unspoken vibe of—"Why don't you get a real job?" Seeing her around town she was always bright, serious when a topic required it, and a jaunty observer of the wider world and its problems. At Town Board meetings, she was the wise one in the midst of sometimes chaotic characters.

It's hoped that the opera produced by some actors over the issue of affordable housing will fade away, ever so slightly, as did the full-scale *Gotterdammerung* productions going on at work sessions at Town Hall around "dark skies" and short-term rentals. During those months of shouting, innuendo, sarcasm and bile, Chris stood out for her reserve and wisdom. When some characterized simple enforcement rules for proposed town ordinances as "gestapo tactics," Chris calmly noted to her colleagues that "most people will follow directions and do the right thing … Most people don't drive drunk or invade other people's houses for purposes of burglary. But laws are for people who absolutely refuse to do the right thing."

Or when a colleague went on the attack against this newspaper and fellow Town Board members, Chris, her voice calm, but her eyes flashing, said, "Don't diminish people you're opposing, it's just necessary to state your point of view. In the future you might consider that ... This is not the schoolyard."

And for a girl raised in the feet-on-the-ground world view of Indiana and Illinois, and a woman working as a nurse in hard-headed New York City, she could also stop you with a Zen koan worthy of a monk in a monastery. Once, in a long discussion at a Town Board meeting on an issue that kept circling back to its beginning with no resolution, Chris said, "Every problem doesn't have a solution. Sometimes you just have an outcome." Walking out of Town Hall that late afternoon after Chris had laid that on her colleagues and the few audience members in the room, a friend said, "What the hell is she talking about?"

I said I wasn't sure. "But it makes sense. Somehow."

My friend was nodding his head as he headed for his car. The next morning at 7, I asked her about a few details on an unrelated issue, some background on others, and then, before saying goodbye, said, "That stuff about solutions and outcomes? What did you mean?" Without a pause, Chris said, "Got you, didn't I?"

I laughed. And she said, "Keep thinking about it." And I have, especially since I heard the news of Chris's death.

Farewell, my friend. I'll stay in touch.

Chapter 57
A Shelter Island Mystery:
Homicide Case Still Unresolved

From February 2023.

With the fifth anniversary coming next month of the most shocking and brutal crime ever committed on Shelter Island, it still remains unsolved.

The case of Rev. Paul Wancura, an 87-year-old retired Episcopal minister, who became only the second recorded homicide victim in Island history, has produced no arrests, and no suspects have been identified. The Shelter Island Police and the Suffolk County Police departments have designated the crime as a home invasion, burglary—several items of jewelry were stolen—and a homicide. Both departments say the investigation is "active." Shelter Island Police Chief Jim Read said, "As we approach the fifth year of Rev. Wancura's death, the case and investigation remain active for our department and Suffolk County P.D.

Suffolk County has the lead in this investigation, but both agencies continue to collaborate on all sources of information and feel confident we'll solve this case. We remind our community that, should you have any information that could assist in this investigation, you can call the Shelter Island P.D. at 631-749-0600 or SCPD Crime Stoppers at 800-220-TIPS."

A law suit filed two-and-a-half years after the homicide, charging the minister with sexual abuse decades ago, is still unresolved.

The homicide came to light on a bright, windy, March day in 2018, when Father Charles McCarron of St. Mary's Episcopal Church went to check on his elderly colleague, who had been out of touch for several days. He thought he was prepared for the worst. But what Father McCarron discovered was a horrific and heartbreaking scene.

"It's been kind of like a PTSD event for me," Father McCarron said.

He had gone to Rev. Wancura's home in Silver Beach, where the minister lived alone, because he had been absent for Sunday services at a church in West Islip where he had assisted most weekends.

He entered the waterfront house on Oak Tree Lane, the one-lane road that leads to Shell Beach, through the garage door, which Rev. Wancura had a habit of leaving open. "Knowing his age, I was prepared to find that he might have fallen, or was ill," Father McCarron said. "But not what I found."

The elderly minister was in a bedroom, trapped in a corner in a heap between the bed and a wall, with his wrists so tightly bound the circulation in his hands were almost cut off. It was determined that he had been in that state from three to seven days, Chief Read said.

Rev. Wancura was airlifted to Stony Brook University Hospital and placed in the intensive care unit. After enduring multiple blood transfusions and the amputation of his left hand, the priest succumbed to his wounds on April 16, 2018, just short of a month after being found.

The official cause of death was sepsis, which is a system-wide infection, often caused by injuries.

He was lucid and his own personable self during his time in the ICU, Father McCarron and others said, receiving friends and colleagues at his bedside. At times he rallied, giving hope he'd pull through. But being tied up for days, immobile against a wall, had been too much for the nearly 90-year-old man.

A visitor to the hospital, a veteran of Vietnam, said he had never seen such serious wounds since his service in the war.

Adding to the mystery is that soon after Father McCarron's discovery of Rev. Wancura, the police reported another burglary on

My Life In Pieces

Oak Tree Lane they estimated occurred on the afternoon of March 4, when the owners "returned after being away for an extended period of time," Chief Read said at the time. "Detectives are exploring the possibility that the burglary and the discovery of a burglary two weeks ago in the same area might be connected."

The chief added that the second incident is "broadening the scope of looking at suspects."

Chief Read, within a few days of the reports from Oak Tree Lane, said it was "not a random incident." Detective Lieutenant Kevin Beyrer, commanding officer of the Suffolk County Police Department's homicide squad, confirmed that assessment.

"There were elements of the crime that led us to believe that, whoever did this, planned it and knew what they were doing going into it," Det. Beyrer told the *Reporter*. "We don't believe that the person or persons who did this thought they were going into an unoccupied house."

One of Rev. Wancura's friends, who had visited him in the hospital, said that he had told him it was not "persons" who had committed the crime, but one man. When this was mentioned to the detective, he confirmed that the victim "did speak about one person, but we don't want to limit ourselves. We want to keep our options open." The officer said his department has "looked at hundreds of people, everyone he had contact with," noting that a clergyman "has contacts with hundreds of people."

About a month after the first reports of the incident surfaced, the police released a description and photograph of one of the items stolen from Rev. Wancura's residence, a Lucien Piccard Seashark watch.

A $10,000 reward for information leading to the arrest of the killer or killers has been posted. Anyone with information is urged to phone 1-800-220-TIPS.

Rumors were part of nearly every Island conversation in the weeks after the homicide, and still circulate today. One that stuck was that an employee on a crew working on bulkheads in the area could be counted as a suspect. Det. Beyrer is aware of the theory, but said it is just that—a theory.

It's in no way a cold case, he said, even though lately, tips on information have been few and far between. In the beginning of an investigation, especially one with the notoriety of the Wancura case, the police receive a lot of tips, he added.

"People come up with theories," Det. Beyrer said. "Different ideas, things we might not have seen."

But over time, the rate of the public's contact with the police providing information drops, he said. "We've run every lead down, and everything that comes in, we run it down," the detective said. "We want to bring this in."

A Community In Shock

After the crime became known, a sense of fear flooded through every Island neighborhood, affecting people of all ages, but especially senior citizens. The Island had been that clichéd place where people didn't feel the need to lock their doors at night.

The incident on Oak Tree Lane inspired the town supervisor at the time, Gary Gerth, to sum up what was on the minds of many residents: "This has shattered the innocence of Shelter Island."

The only other homicide case in the Island's 300-year history occurred in 1998. Kenneth Payne III was arrested for killing his neighbor Curtis Cook, with police reporting that Mr. Payne was angered by threats Mr. Cook made to his girlfriend and daughter, and a belief that Mr. Cook was guilty of child molestation charges that were pending against him.

Mr. Payne was sentenced to 25 years to life in an upstate prison, but released after six years when the State Court of Appeals determined he had been sentenced on a wrong charge.

Reports of the Wancura case of an elderly minister assaulted, bound, left alone and subsequently dying from the attack, in a small Island town, attracted extraordinary attention. There were stories in media outlets as far afield as Britain.

Lawsuit

On Aug. 13, 2021, a North Carolina man filed suit in New York State Supreme Court against the Episcopal Diocese of Long Island and two Long Island Episcopal parishes for $20 million, alleging that when he was a boy, he was sexually abused by Rev. Wancura from 1978 to 1985.

Rev. Wancura had assisted with services in several Episcopal parishes, including Holy Trinity in Greenport and Caroline in Setauket. It was there that Lew H. Crispin III of Buncombe County, N.C., alleges in the suit that Rev. Wancura abused and sexually assaulted him on a "regular and ongoing basis for a period of approximately seven years, beginning around 1978, when Plaintiff was about eight years old, and ending in or about 1985, when Plaintiff, then about 15 years old, was baptized and confirmed and then immediately ceased attending Caroline Church, never to return."

The suit claims church officials were aware, or should have been aware, that Rev. Wancura was a sexual predator of children.

Represented by his attorney, Gil Santamarina of Manhattan, Mr. Crispin is seeking $20 million in damages that the abuse, he claims, "caused and will continue to cause Plaintiff to suffer severe and permanent damages, including but not limited to physical injury and mental and emotional distress."

Since the original filing, the three suits have been consolidated into one before a State Supreme Court in Manhattan, where the main branch of the Episcopal church oversees the Long Island congregations. The church has filed a motion to dismiss all the charges.

Asked last week about the status of the action, Mr. Santamarina said, "We're still waiting for a decision on the dismissal. I don't think they will succeed with their motion. Unless they define success as delay. If so, to that extent they succeeded."

The diocese has had no comment since the suit was filed, and reiterated their position last week. Denise Fillion, director of communication for the Episcopal Diocese of Long Island, responded to a request for comment via email, stating that Bishop Lawrence Provenzano, the leader of the Episcopal Church on Long Island "cannot provide any further comment on this for the time being. I will be in touch if that changes as the case proceeds."

Wancura Remembered

An Episcopal archdeacon of Suffolk County, Rev. Wancura served in many roles throughout the Diocese of Long Island, including, for a decade, serving at the Church of the Holy Trinity in Greenport.

A graduate of Queens College and the Columbia University Graduate School of Business Administration, he held a Master of Divinity from the General Theological Seminary in New York City.

He had also served with the U.S. Army Counterintelligence Corps in Austria and France, before finding his vocation in the Episcopal priesthood.

Rev. Wancura was interred in the cemetery of the Caroline Church of Brookhaven in Setauket on April 23, 2018, where he had served as pastor for close to three decades. He was laid to rest alongside his wife, Helena, who died in 2007.

At a memorial service held at St. Mary's in April 2018, his friend, Islander Twoey Brayson, remembered Rev. Wancura as a man of "keen intellect," who was versed in history and theology, who "liked to dance, sing, enjoyed a good cigar and a wee dram of Scotch ... He was still a student. He never acted old ... He loved Shelter Island for its natural beauty but also for its peacefulness ... Paul is truly missed by all who knew him, loved him and were enriched by having him in their lives."

As of publication date, the mystery is still unsolved.

Chapter 58
The Power of the Press

From March 2014.

If you picked up the *Reporter* this week, the paper you held in your hands was created by the editorial, advertising and production staffs over a week's time in our office on North Ferry Road.

Around three o'clock on Wednesday afternoon it was sent via mouse click to a building in Shirley in the middle of the Pine Barrens. There, in the early evening, printers with Atlantic Color Corp. began working with our one linked computer file.

In the "prep room" two printers were overseeing the loading of aluminum plates into a laser machine, which burned images of eight newspaper pages per plate. These then would be loaded into the press down the hall. It was quiet, the room filled with the purring of the plate imaging machine.

One example of technology outpacing the printing industry was right in front of you in the prep room, where just a few years ago there would have been eight workers shepherding this step of the many it takes to make a newspaper. Now there were two.

In the corridor just off the huge press room was a free vending machine dispensing orange ear buds that will dull—almost—the clanging bells and racketing roar of a machine printing 21,000 "books" (newspapers) an hour. In one corner was a hill of giant spools of paper trucked from Canada and in a far corner were four silos filled with ink—blue, red, black and yellow, which with the printers' skill and help from computers will make every color in the book.

Two circular vents hanging from the ceiling were emitting what looked like steam. "Not steam," said Plant Manager John Markel, "that's misting water to humidify the room. Paper's made out of water, right?"

Mr. Markel, broad shouldered with a gait suited to a pitching deck, has been a printer for 35 years, starting at age 15 helping his father. His role requires him to manage and work multiple jobs all over the plant. But standing in the middle of the pressroom, he said, "This is my house. This is my comfort zone."

Comfort, but sometimes on Wednesdays, when all the East End weeklies, plus several newspapers farther up-Island go to press, it sometimes seems like "standing on a cliff," Mr. Markel said.

Four printers in dark blue coveralls running the press had ink up to their elbows, confirming the old adage that printers have to go on vacation to discover they have fingernails.

One young printer walked a catwalk above the floor, working on the four "towers" of the press. Printer Rich Valek was all over the press room floor: here at a central computer console using a touch screen, there at the towers getting a close-up of the run, back down the line checking ink, taking pages from the line to see if the green of grass in an ad was true or the blond hair of a woman in a photo looked genuine.

The continuous running belt is an industrial trapeze act performed at blinding speed, the endless paper flowing up, down, through, around and back again. Even though you've seen this in a hundred movies, it's still a mesmerizing, stop-you-in-your-tracks sight.

But how much longer the awesome and beautiful power of a press will continue to roar is a question everyone involved in the newspaper business debates openly and within themselves, when cornerstones of American journalism are cutting print editions to three days a week and newsrooms everywhere are making do with skeleton crews.

The digital transformation has put printers at risk, with the U.S. Department of Labor predicting that over the next several years close to 13,000 of them will be looking for work. Eight out of 10 people surveyed by Pew Internet Research said they received news from local TV, 60 percent said they got information online and only 17 percent reported getting news from a national newspaper such as *The New York Times* or *USA Today*.

The late Ray Bradbury's prophesy back in 1953 of a "post literate populace" may be upon us. In his masterpiece, "Fahrenheit 451," Bradbury has a character say: "I remember the newspapers dying ... No one wanted them back. No one missed them." But nothing is that dark. Pew's research found half of all people surveyed read a local newspaper. And newspapers in one form or another continue to attract people, including Americans 18 to 24. According to Nielsen, almost 60 percent of them read "content" on a range of devices, just not on paper.

The printers working in the press room weren't hanging funeral wreaths. They were too busy, working with efficiency, skill and silent pride, putting the deafening machine through its paces. Mr. Markel said that printing was in danger of becoming just factory work, but then he pointed to a young printer and said, "That guy can make or break your day." He was standing next to one of the enormous rolls of paper feeding into the machine, with another roll of paper behind it. With flawless timing, he guided the last few feet of paper from the diminishing roll onto another, splicing it perfectly so there was no break in the press run.

The team didn't speak, but made only slight gestures and had a kind of telepathy about what needed to be done. The machine, though computerized in most processes, has to be tended by human hands, knowledge and experience.

The press was dialed up to run at 2,300 papers an hour. Then it was throttled back as one printer near the end of the long belt was bent over timing the paper flow. He drew a finger across his throat. The press, like a thoroughbred, slowed to a trot.

Mr. Markel took a *Reporter* off the line. "Here's your paper," he said.

Chapter 59
All American

From April 2017.

Last Thursday, the family was up before 5 a.m. and Lydia Martinez Majdišová was pleased the kids didn't have to be cajoled and hassled to get out of bed like most school days.

Emma, 13, and Sebastian, 9, were sleepy but happily excited and Lydia felt the same. They were all nervous, but what surprised Lydia was her husband Pepe Martinez. When facing something new and challenging, he never shows nerves or expresses his emotions, she said. But today was different. He was as keyed up as his wife and children and showing it.

They were all in their Sunday best. Pepe asked Lydia more than once if he looked all right, if his tie and coat were right, and he was worried about being on time. Breakfast was a quick stop at STARS Café in the Heights, which Pepe and Lydia own and operate. Coffee for the parents and bagels for the kids, with Emma having her favorite bagel with avocado.

Almost every day of the week Pepe is at work at this time, in the basement baking, getting the coffee ground and brewed for the early birds, while Lydia wrangles the kids out of bed, feeds them and gets them off to school.

On North Ferry and the drive to Central Islip, it was pouring rain. The family was early for their 8:30 appointment, battling wind-driven rain across a wide plaza with the federal courthouse looming above them. At security, all electronic devices, including cell phones and cameras, were taken and registered to be picked up later. Lydia, anticipating the security, had left her bag in the car.

On the second floor, the federal courtroom is spacious, high ceilinged, filled with light and warmed by walls of light brown wood. The family separated, with Pepe going forward beyond a low wooden barrier with 152 other people, all scheduled to take an oath and be sworn in as American citizens. Families and friends made up more than twice that number sitting in rows behind them.

The whole world was in the room. People from 38 countries, according to Immigration and Customs Enforcement at Central Islip. A court official said there was to be no eating or drinking—except bottles of water—no hats allowed except for religious exceptions and no gum chewing. In a soft voice, the official added, "This isn't a movie theater. This is a federal courtroom."

It was an atmosphere reserved for far too few public events in American life. People were dressed up for a life-changing occasion. There were no loud voices, but only a hush of people speaking, the massive space and wood walls making it sound like distant surf. No one looked at screens.

The morning dragged on, with those to be naturalized completing final paperwork. Emma and Sebastian, on either side of Lydia, leaned in to their mother. An hour and a half after arriving, an immigration official said it was taking longer than expected and friends and families were told to leave the courtroom and go to the cafeteria on the first floor. They would be informed when the proceedings would begin.

On the first floor, Lydia realized her cash and credit cards were in her bag in the car. Then, above them on the balcony, they heard Pepe's voice. He'd remembered the family was without cash and dropped down a rolled-up bill. Emma retrieved it. "It's a hundred dollar bill," she said with some amazement.

Emma paid for breakfast. She had a banana and Sebastian dug into cereal. Waiting was something Lydia and Pepe were used to, she said. Born in Tampico, Mexico, as a young man Pepe entered the United

States illegally to work picking fruit in farm fields. He came to the East End in the 1990s and managed to sort out his immigration status to get a green card to live and work here legally.

But then, seven years ago, Lydia took the children to Slovakia, her native country, for an extended visit and Pepe went over to spend Christmas and then returned to the States alone, while Lydia stayed on for a while. "I'll never forget that phone call," she said in the cafeteria. "I was in a doctor's office with the kids. It was Pepe, who started by saying, 'I don't want you to get freaked out.'"

Going through immigration at JFK, he had been taken aside, questioned and then told to make an appointment with a judge. When he did, he was taken into custody and held for six weeks in a New Jersey immigration facility. "There I was, with two little children," Lydia remembered. The six weeks felt like an eternity "because we didn't have a clue how long it would take. Horrible. But he had a persistent lawyer who was daily annoying the heck out of the judge and the immigration officers."

With the financial and emotional support of several Islanders— Marie Eiffel was heroic in helping Pepe—and Island institutions, especially Our Lady of the Isle parish, the family pulled through. On his release, Pepe immediately began the process of becoming a citizen. The long process was made longer when Superstorm Sandy and a federal government shutdown canceled appointments with immigration authorities.

Emma remembered driving with her father, and a CD of a woman instructing applicants for citizenship was always playing. "I couldn't listen to any music," she smiled, adding that she grew weary fast of the sound of the woman's voice. She also commented on her father's memorizing the Pledge of Allegiance, and substituting "allegiance" with "alliance," and how she, who had the pledge memorized from kindergarten, would correct him.

Back in the courtroom, it was another wait of nearly two hours before United States District Judge Joseph Bianco entered and told those about to become citizens to rise and repeat the Oath of

Allegiance to the United States. It begins: "I hereby declare, on oath, that I absolutely and entirely renounce and abjure all allegiance and fidelity to any foreign prince, potentate, state, or sovereignty ..."

The judge then led the applicants in the Pledge of Allegiance. "Fellow citizens," he greeted them, to applause. He noted that they must remember and "hold close to your hearts" the countries and culture of their births. "But now, this country embraces you."

Judge Bianco told a story many Americans have heard in one form or another, of his grandfather arriving from Italy in the 1920s, "with nothing, nothing, and becoming an American, and living an American life. What would he say, if when he arrived, he would be told his grandson would be a federal judge?"

Before he left the courtroom, and officials began handing out certificates of citizenship, the judge said, "Now, don't go to work. Call your bosses and say the judge ordered that you can't go to work but must celebrate."

Pepe was one of the last to receive his certificate before being reunited with his family in the aisle of the courtroom. They all had their arms around each other. There were tears.

"I've never seen immigration people so nice," Pepe said with a slight smile.

He wished he could have had a chance for a few words with Judge Bianco. "I wanted to thank him," he said. "I'd tell him this is not just for my benefit. It's for the benefit of my family."

They took the judge's advice and went for lunch at Viva la Vida, a Mexican restaurant in Oakdale. A perfectly named place to celebrate a perfect day.

Chapter 60
Fish Story

From August 2022.

That old idea about regrets is dead on: In retrospect, it's not what you've done that really hurts, but what you didn't do. And summer is passing and I haven't gone fishing.

When I was smarter, I used to go party boat fishing out of East End ports three or four times a summer with Delaney, my guru and mentor. Party boat fishing is not for those expecting to see the sailfish dance and having your man run you a piña colada every hour. It's also not standing in a stream wearing waders, casting and dwelling on Life, Nature and Man. Party boat fishing is smelly, messy and an opportunity to slice up your hands on hooks, knives and fish spines. It's fun, for all that. It's also fun, many maintain, to be in God's own sunshine with a perfect excuse to drink beer at nine in the morning.

A few years back we saw a brochure for three-day codfish trips out of Montauk. There was some kind of bizarre appeal to this. After a day fishing I've had it and am ready for dry land and a shower. This would be Extreme Party Boat Fishing. Delaney, reading the brochure, said, "Three days. What kind of people would do this?" He looked up. "Except, I mean, people like us."

Sometimes I wonder about Delaney. Soft-spoken, the most laid back of men onshore, there is more than a little Ahab in him when it comes to cod fishing. He has a large codfish refrigerator magnet. His rod is detailed with a cod skeleton and the legend: "Death From

Above." When we decided to go extreme fishing, he pronounced, gloomily, "It'll be great. Or awful." It was both. We had perfect weather, saw three sunsets and two sunrises at sea, battled monsters, had a blast. I also crippled my guru and brought all fishing to a halt. Our extreme voyage ended in an emergency room.

O'Hara decided to ship out with us. It was apt we sailed on the Viking Starship, because O'Hara *is* a Viking. Tall, broad, with long blonde hair, he loves the water and playing the wild fool—sharing a beer with caught fish, apologizing that he will have to eat them, etc.

At Montauk harbor, on a velvety evening, we loaded our gear on board. The Viking Starship is a 140-foot boat with rails to fish from running bow to stern, a cabin of bare wooden theater seats forward and a galley aft. O'Hara was lashing down our coolers as we sailed past a sliver of beach catching the last of the sun. We passed the swinging beam of Montauk Light and were out in the open sea.

What kind of people would do this? A group of young guys who were fishing for a living. They all had buzz cuts, sunburns, ear studs. A separate tribe. A guy from Hong Kong who collected every fish head caught—"Good for soup."

I met a chain-smoking 80-year-old man along the portside rail. When I said it was a beautiful evening, he let loose a stream of indecipherable vehemence. He seemed to be denouncing me, or the evening, or both. The only thing I could make out were obscenities. He spit on the deck to punctuate a thought as I moved away.

At the stern I asked two men in their 50s if they'd ever done this before. "Many times," said Jake, a weather-beaten Norwegian holding a label-less bottle of clear liquid. His buddy was named Tony, Jake told me, "And he don't talk much." I noticed Tony fingering a fish billy, a short club used to brain the poor beasts. He would look solemnly at the billy, then the boat's wake, and back to the billy.

"You got it here?" Jake poked me in the gut. Before I could answer he grabbed my shoulder, laughing, holding up his bottle, shouting either a blessing or a curse, it was hard to tell.

The mates were, like most men who work the boats, cheerful, patient, expert. The captain, like the master from "Moby Dick," didn't appear among us right away, making his appearance in the afternoon of the first day. But it wasn't anything metaphysical with our captain. He had a DVD player in the wheelhouse and a collection of Goldie Hawn discs.

Ten p.m. up on the bow we stared at constellations riding directly overhead as a bottle was making the rounds along with extremely complicated dirty jokes. Dawn was pink and gray, seabirds working low along the soft swells and then the sun blazing up out of the horizon.

Fishing all day for tile fish, none of our crew had much luck. It was difficult fishing. The tile is a big-headed bruiser who lives at 600 feet. You need a 5-pound weight to keep your hook on the bottom and dragging that up through two football fields of water is no fun.

During an afternoon lull, the rolling ocean seemed to be breathing. Someone pulled in the inedible and seriously ugly sea robin and threw it back. O'Hara compared the fish to an alien-obsessed true believer on a podcast, telling the other fish when he gets to the bottom, "They captured me! Took me on their vehicle!"

There was commotion up the rail, shouts and curses as Jake and a mate tried to get Tony away from a huge tile fish flopping on deck. Tony was wild-eyed, yelling, scrambling in a crouch after the fish with his billy. They calmed him down, convincing him the fish was dead. "All right, Tony," Jake said, giving his gasping friend a hit from the bottle. Tony clutched his bloody club, nodding. The mate said, "Once more and I'm gonna use the hose on him."

The sun, banded like Jupiter, set quickly, leaving yellow stripes glittering in the blue waves. Dinner was not a success. O'Hara had been in charge of provisions and thought he'd done a good job, but all he'd brought was peanut butter and onion pitas. We all slept deeply, as the captain headed for a new fishery 60 miles off Nantucket, where the sun rose the way it had set, with purple stripes across the middle, powering up out of the sea.

We fished all morning and caught cod on every drop, many of them wanting to pull us in with them. Shouts all morning up and down the boat. Catching two and three cod on the same line. The mates were gaffing fish non-stop. The guy from Hong King rushed around collecting heads. Tony was a windmill.

Delaney stopped fishing for awhile. It was then, near noon, that I brought him, and the fishing, to a stop. He was standing behind me while I fought two cod. I swung the fish up over the rail as Delaney said, "Man, you hooked me."

One of the 9-inch "whale cod" hooks was buried deep in his forearm. He was calm, but his eyes showed pain as the mate cut the jig and tackle off and worked on the hook. But it was too strong and in too deep.

Jake got a pair of rusty cutters from under an old bait box. Booze was poured over the crusted slime and rust of the cutters as Jake and Tony staggered up to Delaney. "No," the mate, the voice of sanity, said. "We'll take him home and get him to a hospital."

Home was a 10-hour sail away. A crowd grew around Delaney, who stoically sat inside, bearing it. After the adrenaline rush wore off he was shivering, so O'Hara got a cushion and Delaney lay down on the deck, a blanket over him. The mate said to me, "First hour is crucial. If he doesn't go into shock he'll be all right. If he does, we'll get a medevac helicopter."

It was like a really bad toothache in his arm, he said. Since he was tough, we became tough. Guys would ask, "How's your buddy?"

"Him? No sweat."

Then the stories came. One guy took a hook in the back. Yeah, I know a guy took a hook in the *eye*. So? How about my buddy, took one *here*, he grabbed his crotch. Guy *died* on this boat once. We boxed him in ice and kept fishing.

An ambulance with a police escort was waiting at Montauk. At Southampton Hospital they shot Delaney's arm full of lanacane and since the hook was so strong, had to call in the maintenance man and borrow his pullman line pliers to cut and push it through. Later,

Delaney had a perfectly rendered whale cod hook tattooed over the scar. He lives for the moment when someone asks about it.

"Well," he says, "there's a story behind that."

Chapter 61
Food, Friendship and Comfort

From November, 2022.

At 7:30 on the Friday morning before Thanksgiving, Chef Carl Cosby was in the kitchen off the Shelter Island Presbyterian Church Hall, going over the menu he had prepared for the day, and organizing ingredients.

Over the next several hours, he would prepare about 60 meals of cheese quiche, spinach, corn salad and a dessert of sliced fruit. Joined later by the Town's Nutrition Site Manager Sara Mundy, and the kitchen aide Alison Binder, they were a smoothly operating team, turning out meals for the sit-down Dinner Bell program for seniors later in the morning, and packing up home-delivered meals for the Meals On Wheels program.

As Chef Cosby sliced pie segments of the golden quiche quickly and expertly and placed them in segmented aluminum trays, Ms. Mundy was spooning in healthy portions of spinach, and Ms. Binder was placing containers of salad, slices of bread, plastic cups of juice and milk in insulated bags, ready for delivery. "Quiche is definitely a favorite," Chef Cosby said. "Right up there with shrimp scampi and stuffed flounder."

"Meat loaf," Ms. Binder said.

"Oh, yes, meat loaf," Ms. Mundy said, and the trio smiled.

Another favorite for sit-down dinners is brownies and marble cake for dessert, the chef said.

The Town's Dinner Bell program, where meals are served in the Hall—brightly decorated for Thanksgiving—and Meals On Wheels are funded by The New York State Office for the Aging, Suffolk County and the Town, Ms. Mundy said. At the twice-weekly, sit-down meals, Ms. Mundy will make announcements, and provide information that, "I believe is helpful about activities throughout the week or the weekend at the Senior Center and the Library." There is also music, provided by Linda Betjeman at the piano, and sing-alongs.

The county provides strict nutritional guidelines, and Chef Cosby works to put together balanced, healthy meals, he said, without forgetting that they have to taste good and appeal to the folks receiving them. He has experience cooking for seniors, having worked as a dietary supervisor at a Southampton nursing home and at San Simeon in Southold.

Meals delivered to residences across the Island are often split in two by the recipients, Ms. Mundy said, with half for a midday meal and half later, providing a nutritional boost twice a day.

On The Road

In the church's parking lot, Diane Anderson was chatting with Margaret Koller about a purple knitted headband Ms. Koller had given her. They were comparing notes on knits and perls when Chef Cosby came up with a large cooler and placed it in the back of Ms. Koller's Volkswagen Tiguan. Ms. Anderson said goodbye, ready to make her run. Meals On Wheels would provide 33 meals today, by three different volunteers. All told, there are nine volunteer drivers in the program. Ms. Koller would have 10 stops, and travel about 25 miles on her run. Volunteers use their own vehicles and pay for their own gas, Mondays, Wednesdays and Fridays. Ms. Mundy said, simply, "They are the reason this program is able to work. We deliver through rain, snow, you name it." She also noted that there are two main volunteers who help with the in-person meals served in the Hall. Any senior can apply to get the service, Ms. Mundy said, but most are homebound, or can't drive, and some, through dementia, disability or frailty, can't cook.

Ms. Koller, who has been volunteering since 2016, took a clipboard with all her stops noted. She usually has the same route and sees the same folks. Putting the VW in gear, she turned onto North Ferry Road and said, "This is really more food for the soul than the body. Some of the people are starved for company." Asked why she volunteers, she paused, and said that, of course it is providing a needed service, but she also receives a benefit. "It makes me feel good, and I make connections, which is important."

Individuals Within the Group

At her first stop on North Cartwright road, Ms. Koller took a meal from the cooler and put it in a basket, along with a flyer with information about the free Thanksgiving dinner open to all—families included—at the Center Firehouse at 2 p.m., Thursday. (Sponsored by the Lions Club, the Fire Department and the Senior Center, those who need transportation to the Firehouse can call 631-749-1059 to arrange it, and to get more information. Those unable to come to the dinner will get deliveries.)

Audrey Norris and her home aide, Vinette Olinkiewicz, greeted Ms. Koller with smiles in Ms. Norris' pleasant, well-kept living room and, after handing over the meal, she stayed to chat. Asked about the meals, Ms. Norris said they were "always good, really delicious."

Visiting a few senior citizens at home, it immediately becomes clear that the elderly are not a homogeneous group, but individuals as varied as any demographic cohort. You see homes that are dark, difficult to navigate because of cluttered doorways and rooms, either through hoarding, or not being able to clear and clean. And then there will be spotless places, open and light-filled. Some folks don't want to engage, and insist that the meals be left on porches or in garages, but almost all enjoy the frequent connection to Ms. Koller, a bright presence, who quietly questions them on how they're doing.

Checking up

"It's not just about the food," she said again, back behind the wheel, and it's not just about personal contacts, but the visits are also well-being checks. Everyone involved in the program has a story, most of them recent encounters, where an elderly person has been helped.

Chef Cosby, filling in for a driver, recently knocked on a door and got no response. He kept at it until, "I heard the lady saying she had fallen." She shouted the code to open the door—it took a while—and he finally gained access. "She told me she'd been on the floor since the night before, but she seemed to be O.K," he said. "I called a neighbor and then an ambulance. We had to convince her to go to the hospital, just to be safe."

Driving through the Island, Ms. Koller now and then would note a place where she had once delivered meals, remembering the people she had come to know. They had, she said, either passed away, or gone to places where they could receive greater care. She hasn't forgotten them.

At each stop, Ms. Koller was greeted as a friend with smiles, conversation and mild laughter. Peter Gulluscio met her at his front door on Midway Road. She asked if he had received the scarf she'd knitted for him. He said he had, and Ms. Koller told him the best way to knot it. Asked how he was doing, Mr. Gulluscio said he was feeling all right. "I sleep really well," he said. He pointed across the road, saying that when he was a boy, there were 60 to 70 horses in the field. "Now if there's one or two that's a lot," he said, and there was small talk about how times had changed.

As Ms. Koller said goodbye, Mr. Gulluscio said he was looking forward to the meal, and would see her soon.

Chapter 62
Remembering Richard

From February 2021.

Before certain circumstances and then COVID-19 changed everything, one of the best parts of my week was Thursday morning at the *Reporter's* office on North Ferry Road. I was almost always the first to arrive, greeted by bundled stacks of the paper we had put together over six days and had sent to the printer on Wednesday night. A daily newspaper is called by its employees "the daily miracle," and we could justifiably call our work "the weekly miracle." Seeing the bundles of newsprint was proof miracles happen.

I'd cut the plastic strips around the bundles and place a fresh copy on each of my colleagues' desks, load up the paper in the enclosed news box outside, and the one inside the newsroom next to the door. And then the bonus to my favorite morning would be the arrival of Richard Lomuscio. We'd greet each other and he'd say, picking up a copy of the paper, scanning the front page, "What's new?"

"Read all about it, my friend."

Richard would, of course, first turn the pages to find his byline (just like every journalist ever born) and gently, but with enough force to make his point, ask why I hadn't used the photo he'd sent to accompany that week's "Richard's Almanac." When I always responded that it was a matter of space he, in turn, with a wicked grin, would ask why I didn't cut something less essential to *Reporter* readers, such as that week's editorial. He had a point, since I was fairly certain that after the police blotter, Richard's column was the most popular part of our paper.

Then he'd turn to the front page and quickly scan pages as he spoke about the issues on the minds of Islanders and throw in an anecdote of an earlier time related to a story in that week's paper. We'd turn to talk about state and national news. He didn't always agree with my interpretations—and vice versa—but it was a lively conversation with humor as the connective tissue of our disagreements. And he had a wonderful exit ramp when all had been said and repetition was just around the conversation's corner. He'd look aside and say, "Oh, well."

Richard was the rare person who had an effortless charm, a sense of civility and commitment to be involved in every encounter, a genuine interest in you and what you had to say. His humor was the product of a delight in the unexpected, the quirks and imperfections of the world and in all of us, and often in his own eccentricities. I'd run into him around town, and would find myself standing in the IGA parking lot talking for half an hour about Trump, or town government or hilarious tales of Bob Dunne, the editor Richard had worked for when Dunne ran the *Reporter*. I cherish a memory of sitting outside Stars Café on a spring afternoon, as he asked me about my life before Shelter Island.

His death was a shock. His engagement with life and living was so visible in his many passions, from cars to poetry to travel, and above all, his family. His vibrant sense of life was obvious to anyone who knew him and, for those who didn't know him personally, had a nearly identical understanding of him through his weekly column. To speak of his professionalism as a journalist would have embarrassed him. Meeting every deadline, and knowing that writing a column required empathy as much as information and entertainment, was something you just did. And when I assigned a straight news story—Richard never hesitated to accept—I knew it would be done impeccably, with no bias, and a cleanly written sense of who, what, when, where and why.

His final column on Feb. 19 was headlined "Carpe Diem," and opened: "The headline of this column is a Latin expression for 'seize the day' and it's applied to themes often found in lyric poetry—to enjoy life's pleasures while one is able."

Mary and I and all who knew you take your parting advice to heart. We will remember it as just one of the many gifts you've left us.

Chapter 63
Church Bells in March

From March 2017.

One day last week I decided to ring some church bells.

I've had this feeling before. The last time was more than 10 years ago when I asked if I could ring the bells of Orient United Methodist Church, and the sextant obliged me. Call me crazy.

Church bells have always stopped me. Literally, if I'm walking and hear them in the distance. Or if I'm driving and hear their music on the breeze, they stop my thoughts. The solemn beauty of the bells, sounds giving texture to the air, always call me back to something that doesn't allow for expression, because I can't quite connect the feeling to words. Sometimes an act expresses an emotion more clearly than words. Sometimes, the more you use words to discover something within you, the further away you get from it.

I met Father Charles McCarron at St. Mary's Episcopal Church on a wet, chilly afternoon. Father McCarron said he had never been up in the bell "chamber," a separate space at the top of the bell tower, and welcomed the opportunity to go exploring. From the tiny vestibule of the church, a door opened to a winding wooden staircase as steep as a ladder. Father McCarron said St. Mary's had two bells, a funeral bell that tolls—single notes—and a larger bell that rings "joyously" and is rung twice a week on Sunday before the 8 a.m. and 10 a.m. services.

The bell also rings out at the annual 10K Run/Walk in June as the runners come up the hill to St. Mary's.

The bell surely tolls for thee, but more likely than not these days the church bell is rung by a computer chip of recorded sounds. It's as rare today for a bell to alert the community to a crisis as it is for an actual person to ring a church bell. On the Island, Our Lady of the Isle has no bell and never has, Father Peter DeSanctis said. Union Chapel has a bell, but the bells of the Presbyterian Church are recorded.

Above the winding stairs was a small, dusty space. It was dark and the damp day brought forth a rich odor of old wood. In a corner was an actual ladder that we climbed to the bell chamber.

Bells first came into use as early as 400 A.D. by Christians to call people to prayer, note the death of a parishioner and to alert the community to danger. It wasn't until the 15th century that Flemish master bell makers discovered a process to tune bells and make them musical instruments. In the Catholic tradition, the Angelus bell is rung in the evening, three notes a beat apart, followed by silence. The series is then repeated three times. The purpose is not just a call to prayer, but for the listener to stop and reflect on the day that is passing.

When it comes to religion, I'm a weddings and funerals man. But I've always liked churches, and learned through 16 years of Catholic education that they're more than religious venues; they're places of art, theater, architecture, language and music. Culture with a capital C.

One Sunday morning when I was 14, my sister Liz shook me and said it was time to get up for Mass. "I'm not going," I told her and turned over. My mother shook my shoulder next and said I had to get up and I told her the same thing. Why? she asked. I told her I didn't believe in it any more. I was awake staring at the ceiling when my father came in. "What you believe or don't believe has nothing to do with this," he said. "Get up and get ready. You're not going to break your mother's heart."

There was no arguing with him, ever, but I thought later that he had given me an enduring gift, one of many I cherish. My beliefs were my own. I was entitled to them. (I didn't break my mother's heart until I was 18.)

My father was the kind of man who wore a hat and lightly touched the brim whenever he passed a Catholic church. That was the only show he made of his religion. He followed the rules, mostly. He would give up drinking for Lent, but claimed he had a dispensation from the bishop for March 17. We had trouble, like many fathers and sons. But more than 20 years before he died, all was resolved.

He died on a March night in Florida, where he and my mother were vacationing. He'd had a heart attack a week before and I went down to be with them, spending every day in the hospital with him and going with my mother to church, the first time in years. He had a good death, if there is such a thing. Peaceful, himself to the very last.

I remember the tolling of the bell at Our Lady Queen of Martyrs in Queens as the pallbearers carried the casket out that March morning. I continued to go to church after his funeral, but gave it up after a few months.

St. Mary's bell chamber has louvered shutters to allow the sound to flow out. The funeral bell is small, with an iron clapper, like a hammer, bolted beneath it. When the rope is pulled from below, the clapper rises to strike the bell once and then comes back to rest.

Next to it is a large bronze bell green with age with a clapper hanging within it. It's hung on a wheel that swings the bell when the rope is pulled. Words are inscribed in the weathered bronze surface. Father McCarron, drawing close to see the words in the gloom, read them aloud: "In loving memory of Jarvis Bonesteel Edson. Born April 30, 1845. Died January 26, 1911. An upright, honorable man and devoted father and husband."

We didn't speak. What was there to say?

Down in the vestibule I pulled on a thick, braided yellow rope and nothing happened. Father McCarron smiled and said to give it another try. I put my back into it, bending my knees, giving it a strong pull as the bell sang out. I had to let the rope slip through my hands or it would've pulled me off the floor.

In a corner of the vestibule was the thin, white rope of the funeral bell. It was easier to pull. I felt the deep tone of the bell tolling high above running through the rope into my hands.

Chapter 64
Baby of The Family

From Memorial Day 2016.

He was the man I never knew, the man who gave me my name.

He was brought closer to me through a phone call I got one afternoon. An editor at *The Washington Post* phoned to say a man who lived in the D.C. area had called and wanted to know if I would contact him. The name Timothy Donleavy didn't ring a bell, but I called, and when a man answered I identified myself. He asked if I was related to an Ambrose Clancy who had grown up in Ridgewood, a neighborhood straddling the Brooklyn-Queens border. My uncle, I told Mr. Donleavy.

"I didn't think there were too many Ambrose Clancys around," he said. "When I saw the byline last week, I thought I should try to get in touch with you."

My uncle, my father's brother, had been the youngest of five, just like me. But to me, Ambrose was just a framed high school yearbook picture on my grandmother's dresser of a smiling, handsome teenager. He was real for me only as quickly spoken, affectionate memories, related mostly by my mother.

My father, who had been the oldest in his family, rarely spoke of him. But his name, said by my mother as she recalled him, always produced a bright smile from my father, but little more. He did tell me how his youngest brother, "the baby" of his family, hated that designation as much as I did. Another connection was his nickname,

Amby, which I inherited and also hated by the time I was 11 or so. By 16 no one called me that at my surly insistence, except my father, who got a pass. The sound of the nickname was different in his voice, something tender, more intimate. My father said the name to me on his deathbed the night before he died—just that, with no other words attached.

For my mother, Ambrose was a wild, good-hearted boy, a brother-in-law 15 years younger than she, who was always around the house, she said, an eager babysitter for her three little ones. (My sister Liz and I came along later, so Liz never met Ambrose, either.) It was obvious from my mother's stories that Ambrose, who adored his older brother, had also been more than a little in love with his vivacious sister-in-law.

Mr. Donleavy said he had grown up with Ambrose in the old neighborhood, elementary school boys at Our Lady of the Miraculous Medal in the 1930s. Then both boys got scholarships to Regis High School, the private, Jesuit college prep in Manhattan, where some gifted Catholic boys from all over the city got a free ride. The long subway trips to Manhattan bound the two even closer, Mr. Donleavy told me. "He was my best friend, the one who makes you laugh, who cheers you up, who shares difficulties with you," Mr. Donleavy said.

The scholarship boys also went to Notre Dame together, in the fall of 1943, but their academic careers were cut short. "Along with a lot of other fellas our age, we felt we had to be in it," he said. "It" was World War II. "So, Amby and I enlisted in the army together on the same day." They were sent to basic training at Camp Upton in Yaphank. Mr. Donleavy laughed at the memory. "The fellas thought he was crazy. He never moaned about basic to them. But he did with me."

The two boys shipped out to England in early 1944, where they were finally separated, with Ambrose going into an infantry regiment, and Mr. Donleavy headed to a tank company. Ambrose went into France on the second day of the invasion. A month later, Mr. Donleavy got a letter from him. "It was upbeat, but near the end, he wrote, 'I hope you never have to come to this place.' By the time I got the letter he'd already been dead a few days."

Timothy Donleavy served with honor, fighting all the way to the Rhine, until the defeat of Germany. After the war, he moved away from Ridgewood, and my family went to Illinois. Connections were lost.

My father, my mother told me years later, became a bit unhinged at his baby brother's death. He maniacally pursued government officials to find out, in every detail, exactly how Ambrose had died. He was making plans, at great expense with money he didn't have, to get his body back to New York for re-burial, but my mother finally convinced him to stop. In the early 1970s, my parents and Liz went to Paris one winter for a week and took a long day trip to the American cemetery in Normandy to visit Ambrose's grave for the first time. Liz, in her early 20s, said the experience produced one of the shocks of her young life.

My mother had spent the train trip to the cemetery recalling happy memories to cheer up my father, who was trying to be good company, but had finally retreated behind his copy of the International Herald Tribune. At the gravesite, my father did shed a quiet tear or two, but it was my mother's reaction that astonished my sister. "She was livid," Liz told me. "So angry. It was his grave, seeing his name, and all the crosses, the whole madness of wars." She raged on bitterly until they were on the train back to Paris, when my father's comforting finally took effect.

The shock was that my mother was consistently even-tempered. She never spoke of war or politics, except to give a brief shake of her head at the mention of either. That was my father's territory. But that winter day in the graveyard, my mother crossed a line. She grieved by spitting her fury at what had been done to her young brother-in-law, dead at 19, and all of his comrades buried around him. And then she stopped, and remembered him ever after for his optimism, his joy in living, his love and bravery.

This Memorial Day we remember the dead, and also the families, as we should, of veterans everywhere. Nowadays we sympathize with veterans and the difficulties they face: Fighting in ill-defined wars, and for too many, coming home to heartbreaking problems caused by their service. But we should also remember that finding a way to live in peace with others and yourself after combat isn't just the lot of many modern day veterans. That search has been there forever.

My uncle, though, was spared those troubles. The man I never knew, who gave me my name, will always be 19.

Chapter 65
Dignity, Respect and Comfort at Calverton National Cemetery

From May 2022.

Rich Hilts enlisted in the U.S. Army right after graduating from high school in upstate Rome. His first day of basic training was Sept. 11, 2001. "We didn't believe it," the program specialist, training and safety officer at Calverton National Cemetery said. "We thought it was a game being played on every recruit."

When the reality of the terrorist attacks became clear, it "reinforced my commitment," he said, as he made his rounds of the Cemetery last week on a day of pouring rain. That commitment was a 10-year army career with three tours of duty in Iraq. Hilts, 38, lives in Rocky Point with his wife Kathleen, where they're raising three sons, and is one of 96 Cemetery employees in Calverton. He had two comrades-in-arms who were killed in action and buried in Arlington National Cemetery. There are 137 National Cemeteries in the country, two on Long Island—Calverton and Long Island National in Farmingdale. All are maintained by the Veterans Administration, and most of the personnel are veterans.

Anyone killed on active duty or during training, or any honorably discharged veteran, is entitled to be buried in a National Cemetery, as well as their spouses and dependent children.

Hilts drove his work pickup slowly out of a winding roadway under the trees to open green fields and whiter-than-white marble headstones shining under a sky the color of ashes. The thousands upon thousands of headstones are exactly the same height, 28 inches from the grass once the stone is placed. You see no monuments, obelisks or elaborate mausoleums. Death is the one irrefutable equalizer for everyone, but it's a physical fact seen in these fields of polished stone. "Every grave is the same," Hilts said. "There are four-star generals buried next to privates."

The headstones are as trim and straight as a military formation. Keeping the stones clean and "plumb" from every angle takes constant maintenance, so that not even a hint of shoddiness is allowed to break the sense of order, completeness and pride. The sight hushes conversation; the beauty, silence and solemnity are moving reminders of sacrifices made. That feeling, Hilts said, "doesn't ever stop. Not even after seven years," noting that he celebrated his anniversary here this month.

Calverton's 1,045 acres holds the graves of more than 287,000 veterans and eligible family members, according to Executive Cemetery Director Anne Ellis, with an average of 5,400 burials a year. Ms. Ellis noted that the Cemetery has the highest "casketed" burial rate of all National Cemeteries, meaning others have higher burial rates of cremated remains.

After his discharge from the Army, Hilts went to St. John's University and graduated with a degree in Homeland Security, the first university, he said, that granted that degree. When he heard of openings at Calverton, "It just made sense to apply here."

The Cemetery is going through big changes, with infrastructure upgrades in the administration buildings and new burial fields being opened to inter more veterans and their loved ones. In a new field, two caretakers were excavating graves in the rain with a backhoe. One smiled and said, "This rain isn't so bad. Better than dust on a hot day." Steve Yanetta, a Marine Corp vet, and William Pearsall, an Army vet, served in Afghanistan and have now found their places at the Cemetery. Yanetta is a vehicle operator and grave digger and Pearsall sets headstones. Pearsall said that after being discharged from the

Army, he wanted to continue serving his country, and the Cemetery was a perfect fit.

Yanetta added, "I don't have that gut-wrenching feeling of waking up, thinking, "Oh, I've got to go to work,' I've found a good place here."

Ms. Ellis echoed that sentiment, noting that working at Calverton "is a privilege and a steadfast commitment to serve and honor veterans and their families every day. I couldn't be prouder of the professionalism and skill with which the Calverton team fulfills our commitment to those who have served and sacrificed for our nation."

Every day he makes his rounds, Hilts looks at the headstones, which note dates of births, deaths and military service. "I find stories in them," he said, remembering seeing the grave of a Korean War veteran, a sergeant. "And on the back it said, 'Holocaust survivor.' Think about that life. I imagined some Army humor, you know, some guy complaining in Korea, 'Sarge, this is really cold,' and the sergeant saying, 'Cold? You want to hear about cold?'"

Stopping at the edge of one field, Hilts points out the grave of Medal of Honor recipient Michael Murphy from Patchogue, killed in Afghanistan. Nearby is the grave of Tech. Sgt. Dashan Briggs of Port Jefferson Station, who died in a helicopter crash in Iraq. Tech. Sgt. Briggs was a member of the 106th Rescue wing out of Gabreski Air National Guard Base in Westhampton Beach. Another stop is at the grave of Colonel Francis Gabreski, who gave his name to the base. And Hilts points out, again, that rank, or type of service, is equal here, where the famous aviator and officer is buried next to Private George T. Becker.

Many of the flags lining the main roadway have been donated by veterans' families. These flags covered their loved one's caskets, Hilts said, and they will be flying this Memorial Day weekend. He stops by one of the "shelters," perfectly smooth, concrete-roofed places, open on all four sides in the woods, where families receive the caskets of loved ones who will be buried. They are elegant in their simplicity, set unobtrusively in nature, reached by walkways under the trees. "Serene," Hilts said quietly.

As a training officer, he coaches caretakers in dealing with families. "Everyone grieves differently," he said, some in silence, some more emotionally. "We always remember: Dignity. And respect. And comfort."

This Memorial Day, the veteran will be off duty at home. Nothing special is planned, he said. "It's going to be a day with the family."

Leaving the Cemetery, a slow-moving hearse followed by a long line of private cars was entering, headlights bright in the gray day.

Chapter 66
Remembering Nick

From May 2021.

At 7 a.m. on a Monday more than a decade ago, alone in *The Southampton Press* newsroom, I was paralyzed, staring at the computer screen. Hired a week before, I'd come in on Friday to learn the computer system, how to access and navigate the server, get templates for stories, photo captions and how to file articles and columns.

But I didn't listen to my instructor, who looked like she was still in high school. It wasn't her fault, though, since anything that has to be plugged in has always been a profound mystery, and explanations provided are heard as gibberish. After a while, seeing my blank expression, she said the words we tech twits dread: "You'll pick it up."

I heard someone come into the silence of the newsroom, but didn't look up, eyes locked on the screen, tentatively touching the keyboard, thinking: "Careful, when these things blow, they blow big."

There was a hand on my shoulder. I looked up and Nick Morehead said, "I'll be your Sherpa." He sat next to me and in 20 minutes I had it cold; what had been Everest was just two steps up to solid ground. It was a comic secret we shared when I worked for the Press and then when I knew him on the Island. He'd send me information about South Ferry, or the Shelter Island Preschool, or a letter to the editor, and always say, "If you need help formatting this ..." And once at the

Post Office, looking at mail I'd just taken from my box, I heard a voice behind me: "Can you figure that out? See, the top left address means ..."

I decided to arrive early for the Celebration of Life ceremony at Our Lady of the Isle on Saturday, figuring there would be a good-sized crowd. But I didn't expect a line of cars going bumper-to-bumper up into the Heights, parking 1,000 yards away for the first available spot, or getting the last two seats in the last row of pews in the church with my colleagues Jenifer Maxson and Charity Robey scooting in just ahead of me. People stood, lining both sides of the church, and two-deep in the back, crowding the foyer, and on a sweet spring afternoon, standing on the steps outside to hear.

It was only right.

I knew, but it was good to realize again, that I wasn't the only one who was touched by Nick's generosity, humor and warmth. The turnout at the church and a garden party hosted by Kathleen Lynch, Fred Hyatt, Patty Quigley and Mike Dunning after, were more than impressive. In some ways it was overwhelming, how so many friends, of all ages, wanted to express what Nick meant to them.

He died May 15, at age 46, after a long struggle with cancer, leaving his wife, Paige, and two children, Larkin and Cayman. But at the service and the party afterward, Nick was very much alive.

Saturday afternoon, Our Lady of the Isle was filled with stories, memories, grief and tears, but balanced by much laughter, joy, and even a rousing soccer chant. Music was provided by Katie Springer and Anthony Pennino, Katie's voice soaring on Leonard Cohen's "Hallelujah." Sitting in the church, I remembered Nick as a complete pro of our profession. Peter Boody was editor of the *Reporter* when Nick worked here and we spoke when we both learned of his passing. Peter said that Nick's time on the staff of the *Reporter* was his favorite of all on Shelter Island.

"He was terrific at his job," Peter said. "An excellent reporter and writer who kept the copy flowing, never missed a beat, never had an issue. Steady, reliable, talented. He was thoughtful and insightful and just plain fun to have in the office, with a great sense of humor that lightened everybody's spirits."

He remembered Nick teasing Archer Brown, copy editor extraordinaire, when she had questions on stories Nick had filed. "I can hear him saying 'Come on Archer, where's the love?'" Peter said.

When Nick left journalism to work at South Ferry—or, as Peter wryly noted, "wised up"—he was missed at the paper. "Through all these years since," Peter said, "I've thought of him fondly and often, always hoping to catch him for an impromptu chat on the ferry."

During the service at Our Lady of the Isle, when friends and loved ones from all parts of Nick's life spoke about him, I remembered the time I first got to know him at the Press. It was a happy newsroom. Steve Kotz, who was an editor then and is now, remembered a day when he came into the conference room of the paper for the weekly Thursday editorial meeting where next week's paper would be hashed out. Before he got to the office, he said, he'd pulled into the parking lot of the post office, and noticed he was parked next to Christie Brinkley.

"I gave her that little nod of recognition you'd give a celebrity who wouldn't know you from Adam," Steve said. "I was surprised when she returned the greeting with a nod of her own and a warm smile. When I got to the office, I told my story and added, 'Gee, do you think she's got something for me?' Without missing a beat, Nick looked up from his paper and said, 'Yeah, it's called a restraining order.' That's all it was, but whenever I think of it, I chuckle."

At the memorial service, Island resident Reverend John Moore of the East End Church of Christ, said, looking out at the standing-room-only church, "You don't fill up a building this size without being a good man."

And Nick's sister-in-law, Shelli Nicolet, in her eulogy, said, "He always wanted to know how to make other's lives easier ... He was the best of us."

Shelter Island has honored a favorite son.

The next five entries probably should have their own section, but since they initially appeared in the Reporter *in the mix of columns, features and news stories of our weekly editions, I've presented them here, where I hope they remain as comfortable as in their original, crowded home.*

One October at the North Shore Sun, *Greg Zeller, Nicole Cotroneo and I decided to each write a ghost story for Halloween. When I became editor of the* Reporter *10 years later, I continued the tradition.*

The stories that follow are fiction, with first-person narrators, some of whom bear a vague resemblance to an editor of a weekly newspaper in a small, island community.

Chapter 67
An Encounter

From Oct. 2018.

The steering wheel shuddered in my hands. Next I heard a thumping and felt the unmistakable wobble that signals a flat tire. I pulled onto the shoulder and put on the caution lights.

It was 5:30 a.m. at the top of the hill near Stearns Point Road. I was heading toward the Center, on my way to the office to get a jump on deadline day. But now the day had suddenly jumped me. Out of the car I saw the left rear tire crumpled. I'd never changed a flat on this car and had no clue how to jack it up and put on the donut. This was not going to be fun.

Shadows shimmered through a clump of trees with the moon, bright as a beacon, flooding part of the golf course falling away down the hill. The murmur of the wind was shattered by two screeches coming from Goat Hill above. Owls? Who knows? Not me, as I popped the trunk and began unscrewing the jack from its nesting place. Why hadn't I ever learned how to do this? The owner's manual wouldn't help. Every time I consulted it, I had the sense someone with an insecure knowledge of English had translated it from the original Korean.

But then Luca saved me. And left me with questions I still can't begin to answer.

I didn't hear him approach, just a soft "Good morning" directly behind me. The owl hadn't made me jump, but Luca's sudden presence certainly did.

"Oh, sir!" he said. "Sorry, sir, I didn't want to frighten."

I laughed from nerves and he gave me a quick smile, introducing himself — "Luca Spettro." A young man gripping an old suitcase, 30 or so, long hair curling from his watch cap, eyes as bright as they were warm. He suddenly looked away, staring at the flat, saying softly, as if a pet had gone lame, "Oh, a pity, yes, oh, a flat one," and set down the suitcase next to the car and squatted near the tire. He was dressed in a gray woolen jacket and rough gray trousers. When he ran pale hands along the tire tread, I saw he was a young man who didn't make his living behind a desk. The hands were scraped and nicked, with a couple of bulging knuckles.

"I help?" he looked up.

"Please. You know how to put the donut on?"

"Donut?" Luca asked, holding fingers to his lips. When I explained that it was the spare tire, he laughed, and went to work with the confidence and pleasure some people have figuring out a mechanical challenge. In the weak, shifting light, I couldn't quite see Luca's face, and when he looked up now and again he quickly glanced away. But he was friendly, answering my questions as he worked. A stone carver and mason, originally from Verona in Northern Italy where he had learned his trade, he now worked for a construction company in the city. He was on his way back to New York this morning after finishing an extended project building a stone arch on a property here.

"Finish," Luca said, working the jack, a touch of grief in his voice. "All over."

With the spare fitted to the wheel, I told him I'd give him a lift to the ferry. He took a step back, and thanked me, but said he had slept badly, was a bit stiff, and looked forward to the walk. I insisted. He politely refused.

When I reached into my pocket, Luca put a hand on my arm. "No," he said.

"Come on—"

"No, you'll help someone sometime."

He picked up his old bag and started down the hill. Passing him I honked the horn. He didn't look up. Eyes on the street, Luca held up one arm as a farewell. Why did he avoid my eyes? Why not accept a lift? Was he a burglar, slipping away? But would a thief stop and help someone?

I asked around that day about a New York company sending a stone carver to the Island, but no one knew about it. Someone said there was a beautiful stone arch leading into a walled garden on a property up on Serpentine Drive. That afternoon I went looking for the arch. It could make a nice feature for the paper.

The Island was dressed for Halloween. Pumpkins sat on porches, huge spider webs clung from trees and plywood ghosts haunted lawns. The light in the sky had softened and travelling clouds threw deep shadows on the road in the last hour of daylight.

I hit pay dirt quickly. Taking a switchback turn there was a pebble driveway leading to a grand house looming high over the bay. To the left was a cottage and next to it an arch with carved stone turrets set in a high brick wall. I parked and walked over and touched the pale stone, fine as sandpaper. It wasn't Luca's arch, I thought. This was weathered; its original white faded to gray.

An elderly woman in a broad-brimmed hat was directing a landscaper tending to a row of bushes within the walled garden. When she saw me she came forward and we introduced ourselves. I took her hand. It was so light it felt like holding a piece of cloth. "I was admiring the archway," I said.

"You saw him," she said. A statement, not a question. She looked away, out at whitecaps below in the bay catching the light. "We should go inside."

I sat on a sofa and she in a wing chair near a window in a room that wouldn't be out of place in Victorian times, and Julia told me a story. She was the oldest of four, growing up in this house. Her mother died when Julia was 19. "In those days—well, as the oldest girl it was expected I'd take charge of the children and the house," she said.

Her father, who had a business in the city, left all responsibilities to her. "He depended on me for everything and loved me very much," she said, and when he decided to build the walled garden—something his wife had always wanted—she was left to organize it. "That was how Luca came here," she said.

It had been a long day. I felt that fuzziness of thought that fatigue brings. And understood the expression of "someone walking over my grave."

Luca had arrived with a crew of two workmen and they were quartered in the cottage near the garden. He became part of the family; the three little ones adored him. She raised her folded hands from her lap and opened them, a gesture of resignation: "We fell in love."

Luca dismissed the workers after a while to complete the arch on his own and when her father would stay in the city—sometimes as long as a week—the two lovers would have time for each other in the cottage.

"That's where my father found us one night when he came home a day early," Julia said.

It was a horrific scene. "My father said he would get his pistol from the house and no court in Suffolk County would convict him of shooting Luca dead," Julia said. "He was to leave immediately. I saw him on the road out there as he was leaving," she paused. "He promised to write, to come back. But he never did. We were so in love."

She got up slowly and went to a carved oak desk and took something from a drawer and handed it to me. It was a newspaper clipping, yellowed, encased in plastic.

—SOUTHOLD, October 29, 1955
A good Samaritan was killed early Friday morning on Route 25 when a delivery truck struck and killed him at the side of the road.

Luca Spettro, a native of Italy employed in New York City, was looking for a lift when he began helping Mr. Ken Stukeski of East Marion, who had a flat tire. The truck, driven by Jonas Warshah, struck Mr. Spettro, killing him instantly. "I never saw him in the darkness," Mr. Warshah said.

Police are investigating the incident further.

"You're not the first to have seen him," Julia said. "But I never do. It's as if he can't come all the way back here, or gets here and turns away. The people he helps—and he always helps them in some way—they, like you, have found their way here."

She never married, never moved away. Her younger siblings come summers and holidays with their children. In fact, a crowd was due this weekend for Halloween.

"Oh, this time of year," Julia said, in a melancholy tone suited to the dimming afternoon.

People ask if I believe in ghosts. I say no, a similar response to the way I distrust memories—even my own—from long ago, and don't believe every story I hear. But not believing in the reality of memories or stories has nothing to do with the reason they stay with us.

As I walked out of the house I knew two things for sure. Luca's arch was there in the shadows. And the donut was securely fastened to the left rear wheel as I drove away.

Chapter 68
Haunted Tales of Sylvester Manor

And here, in the roll call of fictional ghost stories, is a feature article, with real people and a real place, that shows that maybe ghosts are not just the product of make believe.

She had just started working at Sylvester Manor as a housekeeper, now almost 40 years ago, when Rose Wissemann came in touch with something one afternoon that still haunts her.

She recently recalled that unforgettable day when she had been doing some work in one of the smaller houses on the Manor grounds. As suddenly as a shadow shifts across a floor, an unsettling feeling stole over her. It was a sense that even though she was alone in the place, something—someone?—was with her. She stood still in the room. More than one presence, in some kind of terrible distress, was very near.

Being practical and levelheaded, Rose went about her work and kept the eerie experience to herself. But a few days later she was passing the time with Eben Case, the master carpenter, who was repairing the staircase in the main house. Rose was saying what a happy house the Manor was and then began to tell Eben about her few disconcerting moments in the other building.

As she spoke, she was struck by Eben's lack of surprise. He just nodded his head and waited until she was finished before he spoke. Rose was not the first to encounter something otherworldly in that

409

particular building. Eben, whose roots on Shelter Island go back to the 18th century, put down his tools and told Rose a tale of terror, flight and the finding of a safe harbor from torment. It had long been known, he said, that Quakers who had been driven out of New England by Puritan elders, after being beaten, tortured and dispossessed of everything for their beliefs, were given shelter by the Sylvester family in that building.

Eben asked Rose how anyone could be surprised if their tormented souls lingered in the place where they had found sanctuary.

The ancient Celts believed during harvest revelries in late October there came a night when only the thinnest of veils separated the world of the living and the dead. Whether one believes this or not, there's no doubt that everyone loves ghost stories. Rose Wissemann's story of the Quaker souls is just one of many that has been collected by the staff at Sylvester Manor over the years.

Another tale from the Manor involves a mahogany and gilt mirror dating to the 1750s. It's said that if you happen to look into the mirror when the light is just right—ideally on a late fall or winter afternoon as darkness finds the corners of the room—a woman in a long white dress will appear in the reflected background. Is this Mary Burroughs Sylvester, another exile, who suffered from mental illness and spent years in treatment, far from the Manor?

No one can say for sure. But historic documents do help round out the tales.

"Every one of our ghost stories actually happened and we know that person existed and has some place in the narrative here," said Maura Doyle, the manor's former historic preservation coordinator, during an interview. "We do not judge. I myself have never had a paranormal experience, but many other people have. What's fascinating is that there are references to some of these experiences in the family archive that is now at New York University," she said. "That's 10,000 documents that include wills, ledgers and correspondence."

At nearly 400 years old, the Manor has had more than its fair share of history—and ghost stories. Some of the stories can be traced to specific items in the house, like the haunted mirror, while others relate to other parts of the property that visitors can see for themselves.

Along those lines come reports of a female spirit allegedly haunting a section of woods near the Manor House. "She flits in and out of the trees," Ms. Doyle said. "The story goes that she was an indentured servant from Ireland. She is seen around there because her toddler drowned in a nearby pond where they used to water the livestock."

It's also been said that on certain moonlit nights, a man can be seen rowing a boat silently across Gardiners Creek. More than one person has sworn the man at the oars is headless, a ship's captain and murderer, doomed forever to row for his sin.

Could it be the infamous and largely misunderstood Captain Kidd or perhaps one of his victims? One tale claims that Kidd, a rumored pirate, murdered two shipmates on the premises who now haunt the grounds.

"Captain Kidd was genuinely involved with Sylvester Manor," Ms. Doyle said. "He took goods from the Manor to market and would take a consignment fee for doing this."

Another more mythic tale of the Manor involves the devil himself. The story claims there are three large stones on the East End: one in Orient, another in Montauk and a third at Sylvester Manor. All three stones bear a similar mark or depression that appears to be the "Devil's Footprint."

According to legend, God forced the devil out of Long Island and Satan left by taking three giant steps—in Orient, on Shelter Island and finally in Montauk—before disappearing into the ocean. The Journal of American Folklore of 1898 reads: "This footprint is that of a right foot. The impression of the heel and instep is deep and well-formed but the toe-prints are lost where the rock slopes suddenly away." Folklore says that anyone who makes a wish while placing a foot in the footprint for the first time will find it comes true. Do it again, however, and you will receive only calamity for your efforts. It's also said that horses would not pass the rock without being seized with terror.

"I found out recently that the stone from Orient is now at the Brooklyn Museum. I'd like to find out if that's true," said Ms. Doyle. "Ours is still here out by the windmill."

Chapter 69
The Rose Garden

From October 2014.

In those days we were living out in the country, about 10 miles from town in an old rambling ark of a house. It had looked charming and eccentric when we moved in June, but now in October, I realized that taking it had been a mistake.

It was just the two of us, my 11-year-old daughter Nora, and I. The job I had committed to in the town didn't begin until September. The two of us were getting over the death in the spring of Anne, and felt like shipwreck survivors. Shattered, lost, but bound closer than ever, grateful to have each other.

It was a good summer together. We had a couple of horses and explored the lovely hill country that surrounded the house. I even went out alone riding sometimes in the middle of the night in a battle against insomnia and grief. The riding would tire me for sleep later, and by focusing on controlling the horse through dark landscapes, I could replace dwelling on Anne, and what Nora and I had lost.

The grounds around the house were pretty, especially an old and elaborate rose garden, almost all gone to seed, but still producing the occasional saucer-sized pure white rose. The autumn brought work, school, and isolation, and the beginning of the short days brought a sense of oddness with just the two of us in an old house that could have comfortably housed a family of ten. The girl was lonely, I knew, and I was kicking myself for not taking a house in town. When she asked if we could have a Halloween party, we both threw ourselves into the planning and decorating. There would be some life and laughter in the old place, and Nora could get closer to the kids she was just beginning to make friends with at school.

The party was a success, with kids in costumes feeding and watering the horses, playing music and games in the candle-lit house, listening to ghost stories from me and other parents, devouring pizza, macaroni and cheese, hamburgers and oceans of soda. At one point I was sitting on the front porch with my neighbor George from the next farm over, looking out on the chilly, moonless night. "They say this place is haunted," George said.

I laughed. He was the chief of the volunteer fire department, and seemed to be the most serious and sober man I'd met out here. "Oh yeah, haunted by a crazy old coot years ago who killed his wife here," he continued. "Some kind of accident when he was trying to protect her. Her pride and joy was that old rose garden."

George was pointing into the darkness. "The old widower went a little nuts and hanged himself from that tree next to her garden. They say he haunts people who love each other, making mischief."

"And you believe that?"

There was a pause. I couldn't quite see his face in the shadows. "Boo," he said finally. "Happy Halloween."

Cleaning up, Nora talked about everyone at the party. She stood behind me as I did dishes at the sink and put her arms around my waist, hugging. "This was the best Halloween," she said.

Near two I awoke, shaking from a terrible dream and couldn't erase the images from my mind. I crossed the hall to Nora's room where she slept peacefully. Trying to go back to sleep was hopeless, I knew, so I did what I had done more than once—went riding.

When I had first thought of it as an insomnia cure, months ago, I gently woke Nora to tell her my plans. The second time she sleepily said, "Dad, just leave a note, OK?"

I left a note on my pillow, locked the house and saddled the horse. As I rode away from the house, Nora woke shaking from her own terrible dream, seeing me lying injured at the crest of a hill that fell to a stream about half a mile away. When she checked my room and found only my note, she phoned George, waking him up, telling him I was hurt, and describing exactly where I'd be lying.

"But how do you know that, honey?" he asked, coming out of a deep sleep. Nora began to cry, and George said to calm down, he'd have a look.

He drove his truck out a farm road toward the stream and parked at the base of the hill and played his spotlight up and down the soft rise of ground. He was just about to drive over to our place to check on Nora when he swept the spot again over the hill, just as I came riding over the crest.

The sharp light caught my horse's eyes and spooked her. She reared and threw me to the ground, exactly where Nora had told George he would find me.

In the hospital a few days later I was given a painkiller to ease the discomfort of the traction the doctor said would knit the hairline fractures of my neck. In a dreamy state, I heard the nurse come into the room accompanied by a lush, almost overpowering odor.

"These were brought by an old gentleman who wouldn't give his name but said you'd understand," she said, setting down a bouquet of saucer-sized, pure white roses. "Aren't they beautiful?"

Chapter 70
An Autumn Gift

From October 2016.

It had been a few years since I'd seen Simon. When we worked it out and discovered it was almost a decade, we both laughed. Could it have been that long? He was one of those people you meet after a long separation and re-establish your old affection in a moment.

Simon and I were reporters at a newspaper on Long Island for five years and became friends in a hurry. He left to edit a community weekly in a small upstate town, and shortly after that I left. We stayed in touch with emails and the occasional phone call. When he called to say he was in the city at a conference with an afternoon and night free and would like to see the Island, I told him Mary was visiting relatives in New Hampshire so he would have to settle for just me.

"Then the hell with it," Simon said, fake anger in his voice. "If she's not there, what's the point?"

He had been widowed early and never remarried. Childless, he was a strong, independent man, who always seemed perfectly at peace with himself, some of the many qualities that made him a good friend.

I bought his favorite bourbon and red wine, and late in the afternoon drove to the ferry to pick him up. At home I held up the bottle of Jim Beam and a glass to Simon, but he said no, he was on the wagon, but not to let that stop me. Again, we laughed when I told him I was using the same transportation. I threw some dinner together, set the table and lit candles, remembering the advice that if you're cooking for an occasion and the food is next to inedible, turn down the lights and let candlelight lend ceremony to the meal.

After I cleared the table and spooned ice cream into bowls for us, Simon said, breaking the mood of happy reminiscing, "This is a rough time for me—late October." He said two years ago, near the end of the month, his mother had died. The grief in his face and his empty eyes said everything, I thought. But when he told me a story about the aftermath of his mother's death and meeting a woman named Lucia, I learned it wasn't grief alone that had him staring into the candlelight as if he was searching for answers within the flame.

"My mother asked for me, before she passed away, but I didn't go," he said, finally turning his eyes to mine.

Faith—his mother's name—was the most remarkable person he'd ever known. A single mother, she raised Simon and his sister Virginia, who is a year older, in St. Louis, working as a bookkeeper for a travel agency during the day and three nights a week waiting tables. Simon and Virginia both went to college and were launched on careers soon after graduation. "She did everything for us," he said, "and made our home happy in the bargain. She was so" —his voice caught— "proud of me. Of us."

Over the years he never missed a week in the spring with his mother who was living with Virginia and her family back in St. Louis, and spent every Christmas there. A week didn't go by when he wasn't in touch with her. When Virginia called to tell him that Faith—who had been bedridden—had taken a turn for the worse and had asked for him, Simon said he would organize flights and be there later in the day.

"But I didn't," he said. He started drinking, didn't answer texts or phone calls, and arrived two days later in St. Louis after receiving a final text from Virginia that said only: "She's gone." The expression of rebuke on his sister's face when he arrived at her house turned Simon mute. There were no words to explain. All he could do was weep. When she embraced him, it was worse.

He went home immediately after the funeral and stopped drinking. The small town was just starting to become aware of Halloween, and so was he. It had finally turned colder, with falling leaves scurrying ahead of the wind. For a few days, a pale half-moon appeared over the town every afternoon, glowing brighter as the days darkened.

Sleeplessness became a mocking enemy. During those October nights, he would get up and try to read, but eventually found himself in the pre-dawn hours at the office, a three-story house just off Main Street. Alone, he'd work, writing and editing stories, putting the paper together for the coming week. Every other morning or so, near dawn, Officer John Caldon of the police department would poke his head in to say hello. Other than that, Simon was alone, and back home by early afternoon, dreading the night to come.

He tormented himself: Why didn't he come when Faith called him? Was getting hammered an excuse not to go? Why had he denied his mother's final request?

Simon was brought out of his wee-hours solitude one morning by a knock on the front door of the old house. A young woman with a backpack, holding a cardboard cup of coffee, made a quick apology as Simon ushered her in. She was slight, about 30, with a serious but bright and warm expression. New to town, Lucia had been told the paper kept bound copies going back decades. She was researching a series of families from the area—she had learned she had relatives in the town—and wondered if she could look through some old issues. She wasn't the first person to come by to rummage through the recorded past; the "ancestry" craze was bringing many people to the paper's archives.

"I asked her where she got coffee at this hour," Simon told me, "and she said the truck stop out on the interstate. 'If I'm back tomorrow I'll bring you a cup,' she said with this killer smile."

He showed her the room at the back of the house where the bound copies were kept. An hour later she emerged and sat across from his desk. "Success?" he asked.

She was getting there, she said, and then asked why he was working at such an ungodly hour. He mentioned his insomnia. "And you, Lucia?" Simon asked. She wanted to get her research done before work, she answered. When he asked where, she pointed at the logo on coffee cup.

"I don't know who came up with the idea of eating where truckers go for the best food," she said with that smile, and asked if it was all right to stop by the next morning. She'd bring him coffee and some doughnuts, which was the only thing the truck stop did halfway decently. Simon thanked her, but said no.

"I'll bring them," Lucia said. "You'll want one after you see me chowing down."

She was right. The next morning the doughnuts and coffee—just milk, no sugar, the way he liked it—were delicious. Out of her backpack she took a small pumpkin and placed it on his desk. "Got to brighten this place up," she said over her shoulder as she went to the archive room. It was amazing, he thought, how healing can begin with the simplest acts.

They spoke later in the small office as the wind found several new entries into the old house. He asked about her research. She was close to finding what she was looking for, with one name leading to another, one person to another. "What are *you* looking for, Simon?" Lucia asked, offering half of the last doughnut.

He was surprised at not being startled by the question. She was an open, straight-ahead person of good manners, and he knew if he ducked the question she wouldn't pursue it. But he told her how he couldn't answer the question that robbed him of sleep and peace— why he had not come when his mother had called. "I'm afraid," he said, not caring that he was opening up to a stranger. Somehow he knew she had provided a way of opening up to himself. "Afraid I'll never get over this."

"Sure you will," Lucia said. "Did you ever think you didn't go was because you knew if you went she would die, and by staying home you thought she wouldn't? Some say you don't bury your mother in the earth, but in your heart. Would your mother want you to beat yourself up like this?"

He quickly changed the subject, saying that, yes, he'd split that last doughnut with her. It wasn't that she had crossed a line of intimacy—it was that Simon was speechless before the wisdom she had presented.

The window next to his desk began to turn from black to gray. The morning was taking the night by surprise. Lucia looked at her phone and said, lightly touching his hand, "Got to go. No rest for the wicked."

A few moments after she left, he heard voices on the porch outside. He was still half stunned at what she had said, and took his time getting to the door. There was Officer John. "Hey, Simon," John said, framed by the light growing on the street behind him. "Thought I'd drop by to keep you company for a minute. But I see you had that covered."

"Do you know her, John?"

"The old lady? Never had the privilege. Relative of yours?"

"She was with someone?"

No, the cop told him. There had been only one person going down the steps, a smiling, elderly woman. No one else.

"I went inside," my friend told me from across the table. "I don't know how long I held that little pumpkin in my hands. It was the most real thing I've ever touched." One candle had burned out with a thin thread of smoke.

"What do you make of that?" Simon asked me.

I shook my head, looking for an answer.

"A simple thing," he said. "A gift."

Chapter 71
Answering the Call

From October 2022.

On the highway toward the newspaper office, the landscape to the south changed for an instant from farm fields to a medieval walled city brooding in the distance under the sky.

Was I dreaming?

I took the next exit and that old-world vision from a moment ago revealed massive Victorian brick buildings looming in a park of trees and courtyards filled with triumphant weeds, trash and silence. Stone entrance steps lay crumbling to dust below a decaying balustrade. Dead vines were crucified to red bricks. On the first floor, the glass in the windows were long gone, covered with gray wood, and the windows on higher floors had been smashed jagged by vandals. Curtains stripped of color by time and the elements moved in the breeze through barred windows.

I spotted words cut in stone over one of the main doors: "Lake of the Woods Asylum." It wasn't the cold day, just a week or so before Halloween, which made me shiver. It was the last word that created the instant chill, sparking a memory I unsuccessfully try to hide from, of Colleen when I was five, and she, my sister, was 19.

Along with my aunt, she had raised me after my mother died when I was a year old. My aunt was good, but Colleen was my comfort and solace.

My father told me later that, after the voices only Colleen could hear became louder, and she was often missing from the house in the morning, having walked out only in her night dress, a well-meaning doctor suggested a place where she could get help. My father listened. She was taken to a place like this, not far from our Long Island town, and where I last saw her, when my father drove the three of us, Colleen silent, something within fortifying her solitude, as she sat with us.

I had never been more frightened.

And it is where she had died in a fire, that killed 10 other patients, a year after she was committed. Just a week before her death, my father had handed me the phone's handset to speak with her. I had refused. I loved her too much, I was too confused, too frightened to hear her voice coming from, as my father said, "the asylum." I ran from the room, shouting, "No! No! No!"

There's not a day passes that I don't think of my beloved sister. She comes to me in dreams sometimes, silent, her eyes closed. She haunts me. I've been lucky. I love and am loved. But my rejection of Colleen has stayed with me like a permanent injury.

I'd been at the Lake of the Woods Journal just a week. Retired, I came up from Long Island to the New England town to fill in for an old newspaper friend who had been put out of commission by a knee replacement. I was enjoying being back in a newsroom, and who could resist spending time in the dreamy golden days of a northern October, with the town dressed for Halloween.

At the office I asked about the asylum. Liz, a young reporter a year out of journalism school, told me a little about the place and that the complex of enormous, empty buildings was ticketed for the wrecker's ball. She had done a story on how teenagers now and then got in and had beer parties. She'd done follow-ups on the unsafe structure, and got no comments from the property owners or the county about securing it. "There's an easy way in," Liz said. She'd take me the following day. We'd share a byline for a story to ignite some official responses.

My intuition about the place was correct when I did some research. Terrible things happened there, as in other huge institutions, until new drugs freed the mentally ill to control their conditions at home through pills rather than being warehoused, where in many cases quacks dispensed "therapies" that caged human beings like animals.

The primitive methods of treatment included restraint devices unchanged since the dark ages, and procedures that drilled holes in skulls, reducing patients to cyphers.

When Liz and I arrived, I followed her to stairs leading down from the courtyard, which seemed to be blocked by plywood. But with a smile, she moved it aside and opened a door at the bottom.

We were in.

She had brought two flashlights, and we needed them in the half light. Stairs led up to a darkened cluster of rooms. Our beams bounced back to us from thick dust and fell on a solid oak chair with leather straps for arms and necks, a hole in the seat for a bucket below. In another room near an abandoned gurney with a stained cover were torn notebooks and beer cans.

"High school," Liz said. "Homework and beer."

She started sneezing, eyes running, and catching her breath, said, "Oh, God, my allergies." I was weeping, too, but not from the dust. Why was I punishing myself?

At the end of a hallway, we came to what had once been a reception area, with broken furniture. On a falling-apart desk was an old rotary-style phone with its cord dangling, torn from the wall. In the next room, Liz's sneezes wouldn't stop, and now she was coughing. "I've got to go," she gasped. I told her I'd see her outside; I wanted to make some notes. I heard her sneezing her way down the steps and the door closing.

In the silence, in the half-dark, I scribbled in my notebook. And then was struck breathless by a sudden sound. I willed myself not to hear it, but the ringing of a phone continued. With the powerlessness of a dreamer to change the dream, I followed my feet back into the dim, devastated reception area. All I could see was the old, disconnected phone, ringing louder at every shaky step I took. Unlike years ago, when I refused to hear a voice, I took up the handset...

Liz was standing in the windy courtyard, amid the trash and weeds. "You're smiling," she said, a bit astonished, and put her hand on my arm. "Are you O.K.?"

"Yes," I said, covering her hand with mine. "Yes. All good."

Chapter 72
The Choice

From October 2023.

It was around this time of year, a few days before Halloween, when Davis told me his tale.

I was in the common room of the rehabilitation center that morning, quite proud of myself for making it all the way to the self-serve coffee bar, doing the simple—but until lately, grueling—tasks of walking under my own power, getting a cup, putting a pod in the machine and returning without staggering in pain. Davis and other volunteers were decorating the bright room with corn stalks, pumpkins, and little bouquets of fall flowers sprouting from witches' hats.

I had been there six weeks and was about to be set free in one more. I was coming out of an 18-month torment of four surgeries, steel pins and rods implanted in my left arm, leg, and shoulder, and then the long education on how to walk, use a spoon to eat soup, or the remarkable feat of bending down to pick something up off the floor.

I asked Davis one day as he was helping me bathe if I would ever be able to forget the SUV rounding the corner of the road and not seeing me on my bike. "I hope not," he said, which I thought was a strange response. Like most of the staff, he was professional, encouraging and dedicated, but unlike the others he had genuine warmth, an understated empathy, a true connection.

Someone pasting paper ghouls to the bulletin board said she'd read a news story where an obscure legal term was used and asked Davis to explain. As he filled little bowls with candy, he gave her a clear, brief explanation that summed it up. "If I'm ever arrested, I'm calling you," she said, as others laughed. Someone said, producing another surge of the laughter, "You couldn't afford him."

Something clicked. His name. And as I looked closely at his profile, I knew who he was. An attorney, he was as famous as the clients he represented, such as movie stars in deliciously messy divorces, a U.S. Senator acquitted in a trial of corruption involving private planes and prostitutes, a scion of enormous wealth accused—and acquitted—of murdering his parents.

Later, as he gently coaxed me to lift weights attached to my ankles, I said, "Could I afford you?"

He didn't look at me, but smiled and said, "For you—pro bono."

"So—

"What am I doing here? When we finish, you'll have my deposition."

It took a few days of pestering before he said, sharing scones and coffee with me, "OK," with the resigned air of a man facing the most difficult item on a list. "Believe me, or don't," he said, looking at me squarely. "But here it is."

He had been visiting his daughter and her family in a small Midwestern town in late October a couple of years ago, when his youngest grandchild, Megan, 7, asked him to take her to the traveling carnival that came to town every autumn. He said her mother would take her, but Megan was fiercely determined, as only certain little girls can be, that he take her.

"We went in the late afternoon, just getting dark," Davis said. "It was what I expected. Oh, God, I've always hated those things." He described the cheap canvases and wobbly floorboards of makeshift stages where magicians in stained tuxedos wowed only those under the age of 8; the moth-eaten lion, the abused elephant, the terrified monkeys; the dodge-em cars piloted by undomesticated teenage boys crashing into you; the smell of grease, week-old popcorn, manure from the goat-petting pen.

At the edge of the carnival grounds was the "House of Horrors," another canvased structure made to look like (not even close) a decayed mansion. "Little Meg kept pulling me that way, and even after I distracted her by winning a toy at the shooting gallery and nearly poisoning us both with cotton candy, she still insisted on the house."

As candy-colored lights came on in the early evening, they mounted the platform and climbed into one of the two-seated cars on a track with an attendant securing them. It started with a jolt and they followed the car ahead through swinging doors into the darkness.

"Creepy music, and whenever a new car on the track entered the house it would light up the dusty floor, the cracked wood, and the—what would you call them, exhibits?—were hilarious," Davis said. "Bed sheets with holes cut for eyes and mouths on wires waving in front of you, right? Witches—oversize dolls on wires passing, one on a broomstick that was bent out of shape. But Meg was having a ball and I would go, 'Whooo!' which made her even happier."

But then, the life-changing moment happened.

Their tour was almost done. He could see the car in front of them breaking through the doors and out to the raised platform above the midway. Meg was looking to her right at the final ghost streaming by, when out of the corner of his eye to the left, something was moving toward them through shadows. "It was a man, in a shirt and jeans all stained with something dark, and blood on his face, nearly covering it, stumbling toward us, holding in one hand what looked like a phone and his other hand out, beckoning me. But it was his eyes! Pain, confusion. Beseeching."

And then they burst out through the doors and into the lights. In the moment before the attendant came to let them out, Megan looked at her grandfather and said, solemnly, "You said very bad words."

"I didn't realize I'd said anything, but I must have. I immediately went up in full alpha attorney mode to the jerk running the house, demanding to know what was going on. Was it part of the show? Was there a maniac loose in there? What? Everyone looked at me like I was nuts. 'Just a show, man,' the guy kept saying. Other people said they hadn't seen what I saw. 'Just a show, man.'"

And tugging at his hand was Meg, tears in her eyes, suddenly frightened of her grandfather and his incensed cross-examination. He led her away, apologized to her, and they left quickly.

Davis waited as I poured him a cup of coffee and broke off a piece of scone. "Strange, right?" he said. "But it got even stranger."

Two nights later he woke from a sound sleep. No dream awakened him; he was just immediately awake, a memory of 20 years past flooding him. "I was a terrible father—and not much of a husband either, ignoring the people I loved. Madly in love with myself, my work, my ego ... you know that person. That Halloween, my daughter—Megan's mom Claire—who was then 14, was going to be in the school play, playing the lead role in Cinderella. I promised to be there, and then the day of the play, I realized I had to write a brief and told her I'd have to miss it. Claire just stared at me. 'I hate you,' she said, and walked away. That cinched it. I had to go."

The night of the play he was late—he was always late—but thought he wouldn't miss much of the performance, speeding along, taking a short cut along a narrow country road in the darkness. Around a curve was a car crumpled against a pole, hood popped and crushed, one headlight beaming straight up through smoke, the front window a cobweb from the crash. And a young man in shirt and jeans, with dark spots on his clothes, his face covered in blood, a phone in one hand stumbling toward him. "And those eyes," Davis said.

He drove by, in fact went faster. "The only thought as I passed was: 'He has a phone. I don't have to help.'"

Davis arrived in the middle of the third act. He hugged Claire when he greeted her in the school auditorium after the show, her face beaming though her stage makeup.

"And I forgot every detail of that crash until I woke up that night years later after the Haunted House episode with my granddaughter," Davis said.

He began a series of consultations with psychologists and therapists. All agreed he had suffered dissociative amnesia, a condition that protects traumatic incidents from your consciousness by blocking them. "But I knew it was more," Davis said. "It was not the horror, it was my selfishness, my need to make amends with my daughter, to come off as the world's greatest dad, and leave the wounded there on his battlefield. I had to do something. I got in touch with the cops, the hospital, EMS, private doctors, tow truck shops. But ... not a trace, not a whisper of any kind of accident." He paused. "For the first time in my life I understood the word 'haunted.' And the consequences of making a choice."

That something he had to do came when he read a notice in the paper about the need for volunteers at the rehab center.

"Has it helped?" I asked. He didn't answer, standing and putting a hand on my shoulder. "Now look, I'll probably see you, but if I don't, you and the family have a really Happy Halloween."

Chapter 73
Word Play in 2019

Here's one of the columns that appears every December in the Reporter, *an end-of-the-year discussion on the state of American English.*

With a look back at 2019 slipping over the horizon as a smoking pile of bad rubbish (good riddance), let's turn our attention to the sunlit uplands of 2020 where we can think about what has happened to the English language.

Oh, my.

It was a year when phone calls became "perfect," some people were "woke," some had a platform and those who didn't were canceled and thrown under the bus, thought leaders had to grapple with optics to the point where you couldn't wrap your head around it for all the ghosting.

That last, uh, sentence, beyond not taking the advice that clichés should be avoided like the plague, contains some of the words that the cold-eyed (and hearted) language constables of Lake Superior State University (LSSU) have sent to the gallows in their annual "Words Banished from the Queen's English for Mis-use, Over-use and General Uselessness."

Other utterances that deserved a swift and merciless death, according to the Robespierres of LSSU are "eschew" because, "Nobody ever actually says this word out loud, they just write it for filler." And "wheelhouse," describing an area of expertise that is "an awkward word to use in the 21st century. Most people have never seen a wheelhouse."

Added to Merriam-Webster's dictionary this year is "dad joke," which reminds me: A misogynist, a billionaire and a Russian agent walk into a bar. The bartender says, "What'll you have, Mr. President?"

Speaking of jokes, we should mourn their passing as one more example of how storytelling is fading away in a blizzard of images, and sarcasm has become wit. Tell me a story? If you insist.

Bank manager realizes $9 million has gone missing. After an investigation all guilt points to a teller who is deaf and mute. Manager hires a sign language expert, brings in the teller and says, "Tell him to tell me where the money is." The interpreter signs, the teller signs back. "He says he doesn't know what you're talking about." Manager pulls out a gun, puts it to the teller's head. "Tell him I'll blow his brains out if he doesn't tell me." The interpreter signs, the teller quickly signs back with the exact location of the cash. "What'd he say?" the manager asks. The interpreter replies, "He told you to go to hell."

And did you hear about the insomniac agnostic who suffers from dyslexia? Poor man was up all night wondering if there was a Dog.

Where was I? Oh, right. "Words, words, words," as Hamlet responded to a question of what he was reading.

We can learn a bit about the state of the souls of English-speaking people in 2019 by dwelling on the most frequently searched words in Merriam-Webster last year. On the list are: cynical, apathetic, conundrum, ambiguous, integrity and pretentious.

There are no ... words.

As we do each year at this time, we asked David Lozell Martin, the journalist, editor, best-selling author of a dozen novels, as well as one of the finest American memoirs, "Losing Everything," to weigh in. The hanging judge of language—do not get on the wrong side of him over the serial comma—complied, releasing his holiday guide of, as he put it, "this year's writing outrages."

Below is Mr. Martin's dispatch from his fortress on the Delmarva Peninsula, named for the brave and noble Delmarva tribe. Sir, the floor is yours:

"Americans can't stomach phonies. We reserve a special level of gall for people who misuse the language under the belief they are coming across as grammatically superior. One example is the use of 'I' over 'me.' People hear, 'Johnny and me are going to town,' and they know that's wrong but, nevertheless, some misguided snoots assume that 'I' is generally more correct.

"'Please give your comments to Bill and I.' 'Join my beautiful spouse and I for a holiday party.'

"You don't have to know the official rules and reasoning for using 'I' or 'me.' All you have to do is take out the surrounding words and see if 'I' or 'me' sounds better when standing alone. You wouldn't say, 'Please give your comments to I.' Or, 'The award was given to I.'

"As with our appendix, the grammatical evolution of 'whom' has rendered the word vestigial. 'Who' refers to the subject while 'whom' refers to the object. But if you're going to make a mistake between these two words, err on the side of the common usage of 'who.' Don't put on airs with an ungrammatical 'whom.'

"'Whom do you trust?' Correct. 'Who do you trust?' Incorrect, but becoming acceptable. 'Whom do you think is a better worker?' Incorrect and snooty. Don't do it.

"'Begging the question' is a phrase people misuse thinking it makes them sound smart. It's often used these days to mean 'raise a question.'

"'The quarterback is out, which begs the question: can the team score points on Sunday?'

"No.

"'Begs the question' has a specific use in logic. You use 'begs the question' when a reply simply restates the question rather than answering it, or the reply is based on an unsupported premise.

"'Why is she so popular? Because so many people love her!' The answer 'begs the question' because it restates what's in the question.

"English is a beautiful language, and we should all strive to use it correctly. But if you are going to make a grammatical mistake, don't make one that gives the impression you're ignorant *and* a pompous ass."

Thank you, Sir.

Finally, we consulted the elves and gnomes of the Oxford Dictionary, beavering away in shadowy caves near the River Cherwell, who emerged, blinking into the light, to declare that their Word of the Year is "Vax."

It was chosen, they whispered, because after "our lexicographers began digging into our English language corpus data, it quickly became apparent that vax was a particularly striking term. A relatively rare word until this year ... It has generated numerous derivatives that we are now seeing in a wide range of informal contexts, from vax sites and vax cards to getting vaxxed and being fully vaxxed. No word better captures the atmosphere of the past year than vax."

Yes. Vax and fully vaxxed. Words to literally live by.

Chapter 74
Meeting Ms. Biddy

From August 2015.

I met Ms. Biddy yesterday at the Post Office. She was going through a stack of mail when she looked up and nodded as I unlocked my box. I said good morning and she returned the greeting.

The speaking part is a relatively new experience. Until just recently, when I'd see her at the post office, she'd stare straight through me, walking right past, as if it would be somehow inappropriate to speak to me. But the nods of recognition became more frequent and, like I said, we chat now and then.

I remember three years ago, when I came to the Island, being introduced to Ms. Biddy. Shaking my hand, she looked at me carefully, unsmiling, with an air that she knew something secret about me that she'd divined in just a few seconds.

Yesterday, I was just about to say something about the weather when, looking past me, she whispered, "Well, she's back on her feet pretty quickly." I followed Ms. Biddy's eyes to a young woman walking into the service area of the post office. "Was she sick?" I asked.

"*Sick?*" Ms. Biddy said, her eyes alight with malice. She went on to describe in detail some substance abuse problems the woman had struggled with recently. "If you call that kind of behavior 'sick,' then I suppose so," Ms. Biddy said, still whispering. She then told me about a relative of the woman who, just a few years ago, and it was all quite cleverly covered up, you know, but of course everyone knew, had to ...

Sometimes there's no hint of heartlessness when speaking about her neighbors, but instead she'll use a soft, worried tone that usually begins with, "Did you hear about poor So and So? Oh, yes, terrible, really, but he was found to be ..." In many ways the quiet, solicitous tone seems to strike deeper chords of cruelty.

Remarkable woman, Ms. Biddy, a good Christian who somehow missed Matthew 7:5.

Remarkable also in that she is a shapeshifter—I've met her on the Island as a younger woman and as a young and old man. Her husband, Mr. Biddy, waiting for his wife in the car, will often motion me over to inform me that the guy walking in to Schmidt's, and you didn't hear this from me, well, I bet you didn't know that he's really a ...

But the most remarkable thing about encounters with Ms. or Mr. Biddy, is my role in them. You see, at that first meeting, my sense that Ms. Biddy knew something secret about me was correct. She was silently telling me: "You may think you're not like everyone else, but you're deceiving yourself."

No argument, because there I am whenever we meet, hanging on every word.

To say the world is awash in gossip is not news. It's apt that social media platforms have been likened to a hive, with all of us buzzing like insects within. If someone makes a mistake, which is a good description of being human, there are millions to joyously let the world know every detail, and then millions more to comment about it.

It's not just stupid fun. We live in an age when young people have killed themselves because of gossip posted online. Most of us, however, if we're lucky enough to get past the age of 21, can tune out all that insect-brained buzzing. But face-to-face conversation is another story. I haven't seen any reader surveys for the *Reporter* lately, but it's a good bet the police blotter is one of the most popular features, and not just with readers overly stimulated by *schadenfreude*.

As the paper of record for the town, the *Reporter* is obligated to publish news of what the police are doing, including who they're arresting and ticketing. The police also want the community to know they're fulfilling their role of serving and protecting. If everyone who breaks the law and is caught isn't named, it's an easy temptation to choose who the police and the newspaper *will* name. Still, that doesn't relieve the unsettling feeling that someone's trouble is available to anyone with a dollar at the newsstand or a mouse to click. It's especially troubling for young people, just starting out in the job market, who make mistakes that become part of the public record. You hope that people in charge of hiring will remember the words of President George W. Bush who, when hounded by the press during a campaign about alleged drug use, refused to go into details. For a man not known for eloquence, he turned around the question perfectly, answering, "When I was young and irresponsible, I was young and irresponsible."

I think of my own life. Time and time again I've relied on the gambler's wisdom that it's always better to be lucky than good.

There are reports that say all gossip isn't bad. An article in the Atlantic Monthly last November stated that "gossip is now being considered by scientists as a way to learn about cultural norms, bond with others, promote cooperation, and even, as one recent study found, allow individuals to gauge their own success and social standing." Which says a lot about some studies and some scientists and might all boil down to the idea that paper never refused ink.

Is gossip more prevalent in smaller places than larger ones? It seems so, and it seems to hurt more deeply. I was speaking to a friend recently. He grew up in a small Midwestern town and currently lives in a small town down South. His take was that "small towns aren't *particularly* cruel—just that they are more transparent so we can see who is doing what." Another friend has recently been the subject of small town gossip. She said she was bearing up under the long looks, silences and whispers. "I felt better," she said, "after re-reading Shirley Jackson's 'The Lottery.'"

Author Jackson is "having a moment," as *The New York Times* reported recently, with a new collection out and a biography on the way. If the moment leads more people to the tale that ensured her reputation, only good will follow. It's recommended reading on lots of levels, but for those who live in a small town, it's required.

I held the door for Ms. Biddy as we left the post office. I asked her opinion of "The Lottery."

"Oh," she said, "I can't be bothered reading that kind of trash. Now, look, do you see him? His first wife ..."

Chapter 75
Remembering Jim

From August 2023.

We immediately got off on the wrong foot.

It was the second week I was editor of the *Reporter*, 11 Octobers ago. I was looking for a story, and went to Town Hall on Monday morning a little before 9 to cover a Community Preservation Fund meeting. I'd been introduced at the previous Town Board work session so had met the supervisor and a few other people, and, waiting for the Monday meeting to start, met a few other people. I was the only person in the audience.

When Supervisor Jim Dougherty arrived, he seemed a bit startled that I was there, and curtly, but with a smile, told me that no press was allowed. I said it was a publicly advertised meeting and, if the committee was not in executive session, the New York State Open Meetings Law disagreed with him.

He said, with a colder smile, "No press allowed. We have to ask you to leave." I said, fine, I would leave when escorted out by the police.

Someone said, "Come on, Jim," and he paused for a moment, and nodded, and as the saying goes, if looks could kill, I was wounded.

A few days later, I decided the better part of valor would be to apologize for coming on too strong. I'd have to cover him and the Board, after all, and wanted him as a source. Before a work session, I took Jim aside asking if I could have a word. As I started to speak, he said, "I was going to call you. I was a real [expletive] the other day. Sorry, you were absolutely right." I laughed and told him he'd beaten me to the punch.

We crossed swords now and then—and afterwards would say to each other, "You apologize first"—over the years when he was in office, a natural result of both of us trying to do our jobs. My respect for him never wavered, even when I thought his leadership style was too often like seeing every problem as a nail and he held the hammer. I saw his commitment to the natural world of Shelter Island and to the betterment of its people as strong, fierce, smart and practical. How much of Shelter Island would be paved over if not for Jim's never-flagging work to keep it green? Even though we disagreed on some points during the mini-Armageddon of the short-term rental debate, which consumed the Island for months, I admired his role as a champion for the Islanders who depended on the income of summer rentals of their homes to pay mortgages and allowed them to live in the place where they grew up and which they loved.

Jim worked to stop what could be a frightening endgame for the purity of our ground and surface waters. He also was a vocal leader on ending excessive aircraft noise—remember the summer weekends when the skies above the Island were like outtakes from "Apocalypse Now?" with choppers hauling the rich to the Hamptons—using his perch as chairman of the East End Supervisors and Mayors Association to push for regional solutions to the cacophony over the East End.

Even after snidely calling into question at public meetings the *Reporter's* coverage of something, or blistering us, when we met privately he was smiling, focused on me, and warm. Mary at times couldn't understand why I could be at odds with Jim. "He's such a charmer," she would say, after meeting him here or there.

Unfortunately, the nadir of his career was telling a "joke" about a woman who was raped and enjoyed it. And he told it at a State of the Town luncheon, no less. The *Reporter*, and many residents, called him out on it, and he made a mistake by initially digging in and not apologizing. A New York City TV network affiliate covered the story, and Jim apologized. Then, at a Town Board work session, he apologized, saying he never meant to insult women with a "lame joke." Resident Vinnie Novak, a constant Dougherty foil, immediately objected, saying it was much more than "lame," and Vinnie was absolutely right.

Then there was the time when Vinnie and Jim had played a two-hander in a bit of political theater over the safety of the water in Fresh Pond. Jim and others disparaged Vinnie for years, terming him a wacko and worse, about his call for something to be done about the dangerous water in the Pond. (Just wondering: Where are all of you now, who scoffed at Vinnie, when everyone agrees that Fresh Pond needs to be cleaned up?)

The stage for their drama (comedy?) was the Town Hall Meeting Room during a work session in September 2015, when Vinnie brought a sample of Fresh Pond's water in a glass jar and challenged Board members to drink it. Before offering the water to sample, Vinnie made the case that children, pets and people with compromised immune systems should be warned about swimming in the pond, noting that swimmers will inadvertently swallow some water that could harm them. Jim had announced the previous week that "the water's fine, come on in."

Vinnie responded by saying, "If people want to swim, I don't have a problem. I *do* have a problem with people not knowing the potential harm in store for them." Then he took the glass jar to the table where the Board members sat, saying, "I thought you guys might like to take a drink of this since, if it's good enough for kids ..."

Jim was the only one to take the challenge, calling Vinnie's bluff, pouring some water into a small paper cup. "Don't drink it, Jim," Vinnie said, as Jim put the cup to his lips. From about 15 feet away it was difficult for me to tell if he actually drank the pond water. Jim said it was essentially tasteless, "Like water from my tap." Vinnie later said that he had just pretended to drink it. Credit to Jim, however, for understanding the situation perfectly, while his colleagues didn't, that he could either fake a quick sip, or actually drink it, knowing a little taste was not going to cause him to pass out on the spot.

I asked him later if he had really taken a drink. Absolutely, he said. And then winked.

One of my favorite memories is coming out of the Center Post Office and seeing Jim in his blue MG on Thomas Street stalled out at the corner of North Ferry Road. When I asked what the matter was he called down the wrath of God on his beloved roadster. Since he was at the stop sign, I offered to push the car across the street and he could park in front of Justice Court before planning his next move. There was no traffic, and I was surprised how easy it was to push the little sports car with Jim at the wheel.

Safe across the road, he got out to thank me, saying, with a big smile, "I can see the headline now: '*Shelter Island Reporter* pushes Dougherty around—and he takes it.'"

Never, ever, Jim.

Chapter 76
American Fried

From October 2013.

Have you noticed the strange way some girls and young women are talking these days?

It's not what they're saying, but the way they say it, a low tone that begins by including you in some kind of conspiracy (even if the subject is the artistry of Ryan Gosling) and then at the end of a sentence their voices trail off to an even lower register, going from whispery to gravelly, almost a whine.

I was beginning to worry about myself so was much relieved to find out someone else was picking up on the phenomenon. And not just some guy with poor social skills going on about how eerie females are sounding when he's around.

Long Island University did a study recently of the speech patterns of 34 women aged 18 to 25 and found more than two-thirds were speaking in what has been termed "vocal fry."

It seems the sound of a dungeon door creaking open in a horror movie is the result of aping certain celebrities, which includes the Kardashians. But what's more interesting is that it's not only tween girls gone pop culture delirious, mixing in vocal fry with their normal speech pattern of North American Chipmunk. (This alarming sound seems to be the choice of all phone customer service representatives.) Many highly educated women's sentences are trailing off down the gravel road. I was watching an editor at a popular news website on TV the other night who at times sounded like Kim K. discussing shoes, even when she was talking about John Boehner.

Guys aren't immune from vocal impersonation. Listen to young White men greeting each other with, "Sup, dawg?"

Where are they from? Straight outta Smithtown.

When I was a teenager growing up in the Midwest, my buddies and I would never call cash "money." It was "bread," and there were guys and then there were "cats." A job was, of course, a "gig," which is now Standard English.

We didn't listen to jazz but talked like wised-up sidemen, even though our most adventurous experiences were limited to playing half court basketball and drinking beer in the woods.

We spoke like Dizzy Gillespie by picking up the argot from an older generation of small town White guys we venerated. They actually listened to the music and admired the flair of the artist-vagabonds' vocabulary, knowing at 20 that their own futures were life sentences of wife, family, home and paycheck.

Artists, musicians especially, have always had license to speak any way they wanted. Think of John Fogerty, the guiding spirit of Credence Clearwater Revival. John grew up in the back-of-beyond bayous of Berkeley, California. Or Bruce Springsteen's border-state drawl, picked up busting sods in Long Branch, New Jersey. Or Robert Zimmerman who, when he left middle-class Minnesota and became Bob Dylan, sounded like a dust bowl hobo.

Politicians can lose their aural roots and find newer ones. Hillary Clinton has been known to get down home and drop the "g" from the end of words. But the good Methodist girl from the tony Chicago 'burbs gets a pass after living for many years with the most persuasive Southern Baptist who ever lived.

Hillary's polar political opposite, George W. Bush, did grow up in Texas, but was educated at an eastern prep school and Yale. Why then is his "gol dang hit but Ahm bout to turn yew ever witch way but loose" accent so tortured it sounds like he's speaking with a broken jaw? Strange, but his siblings have the cultured Texas accent of privilege, with notes of Fifth Avenue tailoring and $1,000 cowboy boots, rather than W.'s Big Boy overalls and steel toe work boots.

A St. Louis friend of mine told me about his son coming home from his first day of fourth grade a couple of years ago. Asked how it had gone, the boy said his new teacher had a speech defect. Miss Maloney seemed like a good teacher and not everyone in the class privately made fun of her at recess. My friend told his son not making fun was the right thing to do. We all have to overlook someone's flaws and see the whole person.

Curious—and not a little concerned—my friend was anxious before meeting the teacher at the first parent-teacher conference. Turns out Miss Maloney's speech defect was because she was Long Island born and bred.

She didn't say—"Not just big, it's yooj, nome sayin? Like, I mean, y'know, we're all yooman beans, right?"—but there was no mistaking she learned English at her mother's knee in Yaphank.

It used to be if you had a thick accent and wanted some accelerated social mobility you'd change your way of speaking, afraid if you opened your mouth in front of influential people they'd immediately subtract 100 points from your IQ. But Mr. Bush showed it could help you get elected president and didn't hurt Miss Maloney getting a job teaching school.

It's a good sign now that an accent can add panache, since by many accounts regional accents are waning. This is due, some opinions have it, because of television, which has its own featureless accent, kind of Indiana flattened even more when spoken by someone who is all haircut and no brain.

Replacing that with vocal fry may not be the worst thing after all.

Chapter 77
Personal and Political

From August 2018.

Work long enough in journalism and odds are you'll get to know a Jarrod Ramos, the man who killed five staffers of the Annapolis, Maryland Capital Gazette in their newsroom on June 28. It's a sign of the times that until that day, our Jarrods never took their threats to the ultimate, murderous conclusion.

I met my Jarrod over the telephone one spring morning some years ago when I was working at a start-up paper. In the newsroom early to crank out a story on deadline, I got a call from a Suffolk County cop I knew saying there had been a two-car crash during the wee hours that killed a 20-year-old man. No alcohol or drugs were involved, he said. It was no one's fault, he added, and gave me a name. I found it in the phone book. A man answered with a shout and I immediately identified myself and asked if he was related to the young man. "My son," he said. I could hear air being expelled from his lungs in one long groan as he repeated, "My son."

I expressed my condolences and asked if he would speak to me on the record. "Yeah," he said. "You guys do a good job. But not those [expletive] from *Newsday*. They're on my lawn!" I told him to call the police.

"I've been talking to the cops since two o'clock this morning," he said "I don't want to talk to cops any more."

His son was a lover of cars, he said, since he was small, had a good job in a garage, was sweet natured and had never been in trouble. In a whisper: "I've been crying all night and all morning. I don't have any more tears right now ... but I will."

I went to the garage where the young guy had worked and spoke to his boss, who said he was one of the best employees he'd ever had. Two of his friends also spoke with me. Our story ran on Page One the next day, a bouquet to a fine young man who left his family and community in mourning. At 10 a.m., I got a call from the father—screaming.

"You better get a crash helmet" was the least violent thing I could decode from the full volume of his voice. "How could you say I had no tears for my son? When I'm finished with you ..." On and on until I hung up. Half an hour later he was in the newsroom, a short, brawny guy pointing at me, yelling obscenities. Greg Zeller, our editor, stood between us as our sportswriter, Mike Gasparino, was calling the police. Slamming the door, the father ran out into the parking lot. The police showed up and took statements. Later that day we were told they had spoken to him and told him to stay clear of us.

Insane with grief? Possibly. But then a few years later I heard he showed up at another newspaper, raving, until he was convinced to get out before he was taken away in handcuffs. Since then, he's been brilliant in his silence and absence.

But as I said, the times have changed. My man's problem was a personal thing. Jarrod Ramos' murders in Maryland can also be characterized that way. But some overexcited supporters of certain politicians, including President Trump, don't need it to be personal, since any reporter will do. Almost daily, the president tells us that the free press is "the enemy of the people," "disgusting," "dishonest" and "scum." Many Trump supporters scoff at people who take these statements seriously. It's only entertaining rhetoric, they say, it doesn't mean anything, the only ones upset at constant attacks on the First Amendment are liberal snowflakes. (Which reminds me of our columnist, Robert Lipsyte, who once identified himself in this space as "a snowball. With a rock inside.")

Part of the show at Mr. Trump's rallies is pointing to journalists separated into corrals as he defames them. Many reporters have written about revved-up Trump supporters physically threatening them, face-to-face. Remember the candidate for Congress in Montana who body slammed a reporter to the ground for asking a question? That wasn't an isolated incident. The Freedom of the Press Foundation has led a project tracking abuses inflicted on journalists. In the last six months of 2017 it found 125 "press freedom incidents," from the manly Montana man's attack to other acts such as being arrested, jailed, assaulted and harassed.

This was on display at a recent Smithtown rally for Republican Congressman Lee Zeldin, as reported by our Karl Grossman last week ("First Amendment violated in Suffolk County"). Some yahoos who showed up to cheer speaker Sebastian Gorka—a reactionary crackpot and presidential adviser until he became too shameless even for the Trump White House—hounded members of the working press and smacked down a photographer's camera. After the abuse, two credentialed journalists were ejected from the rally.

The congressman later apologized and asserted his fervent commitment to the First Amendment.

Why do people attack freedom of the press? Easy. Because they're encouraged every day to do it.

And they think they can get away with it.

Chapter 78
A Double Life

From February 2013.

Since Mary and I moved to Shelter Island more than a year ago, many things, all good, have happened.

But one thing ended after we arrived. I no longer receive the reminder, coming at least twice a month in the form of certain pieces of junk mail, of a time when I was once in some small way a different person. Well, that might be too dramatic. It's better to say I was just going under a different name.

Why the mail addressed to my double stopped could be the vagaries of our post offices here, or the fact that even junk mail, like those sea turtles that live for a century, has a finite life. So begins a tale, a cautionary one for sure, that might be titled, "Oh, the webs we weave ..."

Once upon a time, before the world was digitized, we were living in the city, and a video store renting and selling cassettes opened in our neighborhood. Mary went around and returned saying it was an amazing place, with racks of cool videos and a bright, young, energetic staff. She showed me her membership card in the name "M. Lydon," which we both could use. When I first went to the store, the owner, a Russian immigrant named Dmitry, introduced himself. After I selected a Japanese detective movie made in 1953, he took my card, looked at it and said, "Thank you, Mr. Lydon." Was there a trace of condescension in his voice? How could he know that wasn't my name?

Dmitry was Rasputin without the weird clothes and the thicket of beard. But he did have the Mad Monk's eyes, focused on me like laser pointers.

The bright, young, energetic staff Mr. Lydon-ed me to death whenever I entered the store. "Oh, Mr. Lydon, we have that Nigerian musical you asked for." "Mr. Lydon, we have a new print of 'Nights in Skopje' if you're interested."

Then came the day when Dmitry, staring at me slyly, said there was a new policy—everyone had to have their own card. He pulled one from a drawer, telling me he would set me up on the spot. "And your first name, Mr. Lydon?" I paused. He looked up and said, "First name?"

I stammered, "I think I'll just stick with M."

"I'm sorry, we must have your first name," Dmitry persisted. Was he enjoying this?

"Martin," I said. He filled out the card and I signed it. Walking home with a documentary about Taiwanese shrimpers, I thought: Martin? Where in the name of God did that come from?

Friends and family thought this was funny. My niece signed up Martin Lydon for a record club. A friend got Martin a free, trial subscription to "Guns & Ammo." The junk mail monster spawned as a joke birthed 20 years of free offers and never-ending, no obligations necessary for Martin. I was in Dmitry's store when I heard Mary calling out, "Oh, Maaarty," and looked around to see who she knew named Marty. She was smiling wickedly at me in front of the rack of Mexican bullfight films. A friend made dinner reservations and as we waited in the bar for our table, the hostess came in calling "Table for two for Mr. Martin Lydon." Then the charade became tragic in a hurry.

One day, when Dmitry went to get my reserved copy of "Bobby Cooley: King of Western Swing," I noticed a machine that rewound tapes to ease wear and tear on your VCR. "I'll take one of these," I said.

"Certainly, Mr. Lydon," the Russian said. I gave my credit card and was reading the instructions for the machine when I heard, "Mr.

Lydon, there must be something wrong, this card is for someone named Ambrose Clancy."

I stared at him. Felt sweat trickling down my spine. "Well, you see, I ..."

Dmitry's eyes drilled me, and a sort of smile came to his lips. Was he relishing playing spider to the fly? "That's my pen name," I managed to get out, and added, even weaker, as if apologizing, "I'm a writer."

One of the young clerks had come over. "Wow, what a cool pen name," she cooed.

"So you use your real name for the membership but your pen name on your credit card?" Dmitry said with the force and contempt of a hotshot D.A. cross-examining a miscreant. Mary thought this was hilarious when I told her. I said it wasn't funny. Just tell him, she advised. "Are you kidding?" I said, my voice rising. "I'm in too deep!"

The nightmare continued. I was returning "Inside Biloxi," when one of the clerks asked when I would return the other movies I'd rented. I told her I only took one. "No," she said. "It says right here, Martin Lydon, and you rented 'Naughty Nurses' and 'Gidget Gets Married.'" I said there must be some mistake, when Dmitry came over and said, "Oh, that's the other Martin Lydon. I always wanted to ask you if you were related."

At home, I told Mary and then, in true wonderment, said, "Amazing. What are the odds of having two Martin Lydons in the same video store?" She said, quietly, as if talking to someone perched on a bridge railing, "There's only one Martin Lydon, you damn fool, and it's not you."

Eventually, Dmitry couldn't make a living and announced he was selling out. I went around to see him on the last day. "It was always a pleasure, Mr. Lydon," he said. "Or should I call you ..."

I met his smile with one of my own, shook his hand and left.

Chapter 79
Losing and Finding
The Way in Mashomack

From October 2014.

It was one of the rare times you get lost and it doesn't matter.

Even with directions to the Nicoll Family Cemetery in Mashomack and several good landmarks to watch for, every one was missed.

The day itself might have had something to do with distracting the visitor. It had stormed all night, and now at mid-morning the fierce rain was just now-and-then showers drifting from an October sky the color of porridge. The wind, though, was still up, like strong surf, climbing and falling. All along the twisting, washboard road heading from Route 114 through Mashomack, light broke through the lumpy clouds, catching fallen leaves as they swirled and darted.

The search for the cemetery was started because someone said it was an active—an odd word for the subject—private cemetery, and there was mention of it in historians' Patricia and Edward Shillingburg's comprehensive chronicle of one of the Island's founding families, "The Nicolls of Sachem's Neck."

There are nine known cemeteries on the Island, according to the Shelter Island Historical Society. Two are on the grounds of Sylvester Manor. The Island churches, Our lady of the Isle, St. Mary's and the Presbyterian Church maintain almost all of them including the Nicoll Cemetery, cared for by the Presbyterians. A private association takes care of the Emily F. French Memorial Cemetery.

Two helpful women at the Manor House told the visitor he'd come too far and gave directions to go back about half way to Route 114, stop at a grassy spot, look for a split rail fence and a path leading up off the road. The path to the cemetery was missed, of course, but one of the advantages of being lost is the luck of discovery, to be in Mashomack on a day that's like a hinge on a door, swinging the season wide open.

It was a good walk up a hill, the sharp, vinegar smell of autumn on the wind. The sky broke with patches of blue peeking through as the path wound around a large meadow of pale grass and curved down to meet another path through the trees. After an hour's solitary hike of seeing no one, there was the startling sight of a walker appearing around a bend.

Holly Cronin smiled when asked if she knew where the cemetery was. "You're here," she said, pointing up a trail rising steeply to the right. "You can't see it from here, but it's right up there." Ms. Cronin said she walks in Mashomack often and has visited the cemetery on occasion. Looking at a meadow rolling away to a stand of yellow trees waving in the distance, she said, "You never get used to it. You still feel the magic."

The cemetery isn't seen until almost the last step at the top of the hill. Greeting the visitor are two, six-foot-high monoliths with rusted chains swung between them. A tall headstone topped by a cross stands inside the iron rail fence of the graveyard. Black letters are cut into granite on a stone table. Rainwater pooled in names and dates carved in the stone. Like most cemeteries, it's a place that brings a hush inside.

It seems only children and the childish think of cemeteries as depressing or morbid places. Samuel Beckett wrote about them, brightening his observation with a pun, "Personally I have no bone to pick with graveyards, I take the air there willingly, perhaps more willingly than elsewhere, when take the air I must."

The first Nicoll buried here is Joanna DeHoneur Nicoll in 1772. But is she? Which suggests another question: What's an old cemetery without a mystery?

"We don't think she was living here at the time," Ms. Shillingburg said when asked about Joanna. "We find it just a little weird that she was buried there. It's somewhat of a mystery. Her husband was spending much more time in Islip than he was here. One of the thoughts we've had is that her children may have put a tombstone in her honor."

Since 1772—or perhaps a bit later—Nicolls have been buried in the sheltered copse at the top of the hill. One of the last was Delancey Nicoll, whose remains were laid to rest here in the autumn of 2009, his daughter, Jessica Nicoll, said. Reached at home in Northampton, Massachusetts, Ms. Nicoll is the director and chief curator of the Smith College Museum of Art. Growing up in Bayport, she remembers going to Mashomack and the family cemetery on summer days.

"We'd go out and have a picnic, a real treat," she said, remembering the beauty of the place and her father's sense of "being anchored. We'd read the tombstones and think of the people and their times." Ms. Nicoll plans to be buried here.

Walking out and down to the main path, a dead tree bleached white by wind and rain stood like a stick figure of a man, with one arm raised, as if beckoning, bringing on the thought—not quite yet.

Chapter 80
The Many Lives of
Shelter Island Town Hall

From March 2016.

Shelter Island's Town Hall was once a funeral parlor. Provide your own punch line.

The building on the eastern rim of the circle across from the Shelter Island Library was also a place where Islanders endured teeth drilling and were physically examined. In its long life, the property at the Center's crossroad also hosted, at separate times, a pool hall—again, keep all ironic comments to yourself—a barbershop and a blacksmith.

Not so long ago, a journalist who had covered Brookhaven Town Hall—221,400 square feet and a meeting room with seating for 800— was stunned walking into the Island's seat of town government. The place announces its plainness at the entrance, nothing so grand as marble steps or Greek columns, but just a driveway. The public meeting room, immediately to the left of the main entrance, makes tall people instinctively want to duck. When 35 people are in the narrow space, it can correctly be termed "packed."

Humorous for some first-time visitors, the room delivers a sense of welcome and openness for regulars at town meetings. There's no place to hide for public officials and the audience, which can be a good and bad thing, just like the rest of the Island.

The town assessors—located in the house next door—have determined that the handsome main building was once a one-story saltbox built prior to 1850, with a second story added in 1875. Later additions included a long, low, one-story structure, which now houses the meeting room and, down the hall, the Town Clerk's office. The two spaces, divided by a wall, was once a wide room, separated at times by a curtain.

This was a "viewing room" where the dead were waked, at an establishment operated by mortician Ambrose Havey, who opened for business in September 1978 and built the addition. Town Clerk Dorothy Ogar, who has worked in town government since the early 1960s, noted that the public bathroom across the hall from her office was a "preparation room" for corpses. Down the short hall, where now there are town offices, was an organ to greet mourners with dirges.

Out back, where the Building Department resides, was space for storage and a showroom where the bereaved could select a casket.

A Caring Place
The Building Department's long, low building behind Town Hall was where Joseph Condon, the Island's blacksmith, worked at his forge in the last part of the 19th century. According to the Shelter Island Historical Society, the poolroom and barbershop operated after 1900.

The saltbox on the corner where the government now does business is known by residents with long memories as: first, "the McDonald house," for a family who lived there, and then, "the White house," not for any connection to government, but because the Whites—Frank White was a mason—resided there in the middle of the 20th century.

By the late 1960s the handsome house was, according to a *Reporter* story, "an abandoned and unsightly structure," but in the early 1970s, Vincent King and his family bought it and spent $40,000 making it livable again. Part of the house was leased to the town in 1975 as an office for Dr. Edgar Grunwaldt, the Island's resident physician, which was located where Supervisor Jim Dougherty's office is now. Dr. Grunwaldt was remembered in the pages of the *Reporter* as a doctor whose "care was all encompassing—from home births to midnight house calls to caring for the elderly and even the occasional dog with a fishhook caught in its mouth."

Dentist Vincent Stiles also leased space upstairs in the White house for his practice. When what is now the Medical Center on South Ferry Road was donated to the town by Clews Carpenter, Dr. Grunwaldt set up his practice there. Rented out to Shelter Island Realty in the late 1970s, the building was unoccupied for a short time, until a request by Ambrose Havey was granted by the Zoning Board of Appeals in 1978 so the building could be used as a mortuary. In September of that year, after buying the White House from the King family for $76,598, Mr. Havey opened the first funeral parlor in Shelter Island history.

'There was a need'

Mr. Havey, who had several funeral parlors in New York City and Westchester County, and his wife, Agnes, were pilots, often taking to the skies to discover new places to visit, according to their son, also named Ambrose, who spoke to the *Reporter* from his home in Lookout Mountain, Georgia.

The younger Mr. Havey, a retired minister who once operated the Shelter Island Funeral Home with his father, said his parents landed on a grass strip on the Island one morning in 1963. Like many first-time visitors, they were immediately enchanted. Not long after dropping in, they bought a summer home at Westmoreland Farm. In the late 1970s, Mr. Havey said, the family began considering opening a funeral home.

"There was a need to fill with no place here," Mr. Havey said. "How inconvenient and impersonal it was that people had to go away from home to mourn the loss of someone who had lived on the Island all their life."

Both father and son worked in the city and Westchester managing the other businesses and flew out for Island funerals.

"It wasn't economically sound to have a full-time funeral director on the Island," Mr. Havey said, "so we hired a young man, Jimmy

Walker, who lived in an upstairs apartment in case there was a death in the middle of the night and people wouldn't have to wait until morning to be attended to."

The Haveys soon found there was not enough space and built the addition for an expanded viewing room. But by the late 1980s, the business was headed for the red. "Any accountant will advise that you have to do 50 funerals a year to survive," Mr. Havey said. "And we were plugging along with 28 to 30 a year. We weren't making it."

The Haveys sold the residence to David DeFreist for $400,000 in 1989 to continue as a funeral parlor. Ten years later, Mr. DeFriest sold the White house to the town for $395,000.

Mr. Havey said he treasures his time living and working on Shelter Island. "I felt very torn," he said, "knowing I was leaving the Island and the funeral home."

A Good Move

"It was so cramped, we had file cabinets on top of file cabinets," Ms. Ogar said, remembering the old Town Hall building, also known as the "Town House" and now police headquarters.

From July 1932 until the move to the White house in 1999, the small, idiosyncratic building directly across from the Center Post Office was where the supervisor, the town clerk, the Town Board members and other town personnel were located. After a heavy rain, it was reported, the floor in the basement, where the Police Department was headquartered, would be waterlogged for days.

Although the town paid $395,000 for the new facility, it floated a bond for $425,000 with the balance of the funds earmarked to make the place suitable for town government. The spacious new digs were appreciated most by Ms. Ogar and her staff, since "this is where we live, we're here all the time," she said.

Is Town Hall haunted? Deputy Town Clerk Sharon Jacobs smiled and noted this wasn't the first time the question had been asked. "I always say, 'Ghosts would never haunt a funeral home,'" Ms. Jacobs said. She smiled again: "At least I don't think they would."

Chapter 81
February

From February 2022.

The smallest in the family, but unique among its siblings for much more than size. And the only changeling and magician, every now and then becoming larger, and then, presto!—well, a year later—returning to its small but distinct stature.

February, with its 28 days, once every four years adds on a day to make 29, the "Leap Year." The website MathIsFun explains that, "Leap Year [is] any year that can be exactly divided by 4 (such as 2016, 2020, 2024, etc.), *except* if it can be exactly divided by 100, then it isn't (such as 2100, 2200, etc.), *except* if it can be exactly divided by 400, then it is (such as 2000, 2400)." Got it? MathIsFunButGivesMeAHeadache.

Some call February a cheat and unfair, since rent and mortgages must be paid, when other months add two or three days extra for the same price of a roof over your head.

It seems that when the world was young (which with February-logic we call ancient) and the Roman calendar was on the drawing board, some sages came up with a calendar of 10 months, running from March to December. Seems January and February were not even worth a thought since there was no harvesting of anything in those 60 or so days, so it was kick-back time, pass the grapes and vino, and who cares what the date is?

But the adults in the room belted their togas and decided this had to be sorted out. They aligned the calendar to the lunar year, which took no breaks. Numa Pompilius (you remember him), the head Roman adult, added January and February, making each 28 days, but then changed this because some conspiracy theorist said that these numbers were unlucky.

Fake science! Finally, January was given 31 days and February remained at 28 days, superstition be damned.

February contains surprises. It has, dead center in its progression toward March, a day institutionalizing love, which might be a good or bad thing. Good, of course, because it's, uh, like, love. Bad, because it makes one of the most powerful, mysterious and rewarding emotional states shake hands with those who are over-amped to sell you something every February 14.

I once had an assignment to do a magazine story in February in a corner of northern Europe. I'd been in that part of the world in deep winter, and the words February attached to Belfast made me shiver just at the thought. I pictured cold rain, the kind that falls softly, but not soft enough to keep it from soaking through clothes on its way toward bones.

I spoke to a friend before leaving, already in complaining mode, and she said, "Oh, February can be beautiful. You just have to watch for it." She's right, of course. There are dazzling days amid gray stretches, where every object in the landscape catches part of the light, and a view of a field has trees standing out, gleaming.

There's beauty, if you watch for it, in short days of soft sun and polished steel mornings, when dawn doesn't make a series of dramatic gestures, but slowly seeps in from the night. It's easy to understand then that the month is named after the Latin word *februum*, or purification.

More surprises within the shortest month become apparent on Shelter Island, when privacy and silence seem like friends.

Chapter 82
An Anniversary

From February 2022.

Ten years ago this month, the morning after Super Bowl XLVI (Giants 21—Patriots 17) I gave up drinking. People asked why. That is, some people asked, and I said, "I've been drinking too much and feeling awful."

Others would say, "Not even wine?" No. Being an extremist, I just shut it all down. No wine, no beer, no hard stuff. I know myself. I'd have a glass before dinner and then, as Loudon Wainwright III wrote: "Drinks before dinner/And wine with dinner/And after-dinner drinks/Single-entendre,/help me Rhonda,/Look for my cufflinks."

For a while before the Super Bowl, I decided to only drink on weekends. Great plan. Except I had as much in three nights as I'd had in four. I started the weekend plan after a long, joyous poker night. A friend said the following day, "We were taking the local. You were on the express."

It was a great 2012 Super Bowl party. Lots of friends, some I hadn't seen in a while, a classic game—I'm not a Giants lover, but cheer every Patriots loss—plenty of good food and a bottle of Bushmill's, my drink of choice, and I did some damage to it. Driving home, I thought of something our host had said, that everyone who drinks regularly has driven drunk at least once. And for most of us, more than once. I'd been lucky in my life. No DWIs, no accidents, no arrests. But I'm still

460

ashamed of myself for recklessly endangering people riding with me and those strangers on the road.

An old genre with a new name, the "addiction memoir," has always been popular for several reasons, not least in reading about compulsion, falling to the lower depths and climbing back to health and balance. That isn't my story. I never lost a job, or a relationship, and never ended up in a hospital or a police station. Again, it might be the result of living a charmed life. For me, the story was that something was wrong in my life, and had to change.

The morning after the Super Bowl, feeling as if a slow moving truck had rolled over me and then backed up, I resolved—no more. There was no physical reaction from quitting. It was unlike—night and day, really—from when I quit smoking. I'd been reduced to puffing at open windows of our place because Mary couldn't stand the smell (she was also urging me to quit). One afternoon, inhaling at my window, Deirdre, who was then about 8, standing next to me, said, "You shouldn't smoke." When I asked why, she said, "Because it's drugs."

"Who told you that?"

"School."

My clever response was, "What kind of school are we sending you to?" She just stared, repeating, "It's drugs."

I quit then and there. It was shocking. Shakes, night sweats. I went to bed for three days, fighting my body's desperate need for nicotine.

I remember speaking once with Jimmy Breslin, the journalist, author and never a stranger to the glass in his hand, who had just stepped off the booze merry-go-round, and asking him if he missed it. "Of course I miss it," he said. "It was my only sport." I missed it, too, but a new emotion crowded out nostalgia. Not drinking produced an astonishing feeling of freedom, as if I'd escaped from something, and of course, I had. As someone once said in another context, it was like being handcuffed to a fanatic for years and finally being set free.

Drinking was one of the loves of my life that I'd fallen for when I was a teenager. I loved bars, and still do—honkytonks and juke joints from Memphis to Mobile, stylish lounges of low lights and dressed-up patrons, Phil's in Wading River, the Whiskey Wind in Greenport, Midwestern roadhouses, big city corner bars, pubs in County Clare reeling with fiddles and flutes and songs. They're all still as much fun— really—but I don't have to pay for it with a mortar-blast headache, queasiness, Sahara thirst, uncertain recollections of the night before— I didn't, did I?—and a brooding sense of guilt.

My brother, who gave up drinking—long before me—said that he didn't become less interesting. But other people did. He was kidding, but making a point. There are some people with a few drinks in them who project an absolute fascination with themselves. It's harmless, and in a way, charming, if you can find a way to escape them.

One of the loves of my life turned on me, and became a burden and no longer a delight. We have parted, amicably, now for a decade. I probably won't go to a Super Bowl party this month, trying to wait out Omicron. But I played poker right before the new variant emerged—another riotous game—and didn't take the local or the express, and had a blast. I got home safe and sound and woke up happy.

Chapter 83
Telling Time in November

From November 2022.

Passing a green field of turf shining in a gray day, I saw hundreds of sea gulls standing, beaks to the wind. One raised its head to let out raucous screams and barks. Mostly ignored by its comrades, it pompously ruffled its feathers and joined in the silence again.

It's a marker of November, when gales at sea inspire the clever birds to take a break from off-shore fishing and hunker down on dry land until the high winds blow through. And with Election Week now upon us, we can relate to the gulls seeking some shelter from storms.

Herman Melville typically set an opposite course from most people (or sea gulls for that matter), writing: "Whenever I find myself growing grim about the mouth; whenever it is a damp, drizzly November in my soul; whenever I find myself involuntarily pausing before coffin warehouses, and bringing up the rear of every funeral I meet; and especially whenever ... it requires a strong moral principle to prevent me from deliberately stepping into the street, and methodically knocking people's hats off—then, I account it high time to get to sea as soon as I can."

November, the ninth month in the Roman calendar (the Latin word for nine is *novem*) is something of an unwanted guest in the year's list, when flamboyant October packs up quickly and steals away, leaving some colorful reminders of its visit, and is replaced by the dour newcomer.

But November brings a unique light to the season, often complimenting the beauty of morning mists and ground fogs that linger in patches before being chased by a brightening day.

Bookended by All Saints' Day and Thanksgiving, November often forces people to get in touch with their stranger side. Take King Canute, who once presided over what was called the North Sea Empire, comprising Denmark, England and Norway (but you knew that).

It seems Canute, to let people know he was a man of the people and as human as everyone else, took his throne to the seaside on November 12, 1035 and commanded the waves to stop rolling in. Would the waves listen? Not a chance. See, he then told the gathering of curious onlookers and suspicious sea gulls, I can't do *everything*.

It's not known how many of his subjects left that cold northern beach peeking at their neighbors and mouthing, "WTF?"

Speaking of how November has an affinity for the odd, you can book travel plans now for Oklahoma City, Oklahoma, where on the 19th of this month there is something called the "Oddities & Curiosities Expo." Hard to say what will be on display, but last year in Richmond, Virginia, the event showcased "all things weird. You'll find items such as taxidermy, preserved specimens, original artwork ... handcrafted oddities, quack medical devices, clothing, jewelry, skulls/bones, funeral collectibles and much more."

I've decided to pass—I don't want to know what funeral collectibles are. To say nothing of "much more."

Along with its sister, March, November has institutionalized a national oddity, the daylight savings time edict of "gaining" or "losing" hours. For those inclined toward conspiracy, this looks like an effort to create circadian rhythm disorder for millions of Americans.

The fancy medical term refers to the body's inner clock, which first went haywire when the wide use of clocks came into fashion.

In the 17th century, when railroads started running, they had to have schedules, so people and goods knew reliable times to get on board, and people needed personal time pieces. Before that, most folks lived by getting up with the sun, eating when they were hungry and hitting the sack not long after the sun went down.

Daylight Savings doesn't seem to bother my rhythms, circadian or otherwise, except I do forget to change the clock in my car and have moments of losing it, looking at the clock and realizing I'm way late, or way early. The phone, laptop and the TV, of course, all change on their own, unseen in the depths of the night, and all at the same time!

Like funeral collectibles, I can't dwell on this without getting really spooked.

Time, no matter how you define it, whether living by the rhythm of the sun or the digital clock, or month to month, is always a bit baffling. Physicist Stephen Hawking had a saying when he came to a crossroads of a problem that brings some comfort: "Only time— whatever that may be—will tell."

November escorts us from autumn to winter, when one long night of wind and rain brings us to the destination, and leafless trees and frost, rather than ground fog and fiery leaves, become the order of the day.

In autumn, it's always a pleasure to be on the way home through blazing scenery. But how much better to be traveling home on a wild winter day of rushing winds, the mercury dying in the thermometer, the day hurrying toward night, knowing soon you'll be at the place where the heart is found.

Chapter 84
Love's Labors Found

For Valentine's Day, 2018.

Billie Holiday, in one of her more poignant lyrics, wrote that "love will make you drink and gamble, make you stay out all night long." Which leads me to conclude there are worse ways to kill a weekend.

But what Ms. Holiday was getting at is it's always prudent to remember on this annual Valentine's Day that not all good things come when love comes to town. Which is not necessarily a bad thing. Like love itself, all this can be baffling, but stay with me here. Show some patience, which is something love requires.

The traditional American song, "Careless Love," recorded many times but owned by Bessie Smith, speaks to what can happen when an accelerated heart rate combines with being struck suddenly blind staring at a light all around one person.

Love, oh love, oh careless love
You fly through my head like wine
You've wrecked the life of many a poor soul
And you nearly spoiled this life of mine.

This love-with-consequences theme goes back to the man who gives his name to today's feast day.

There are many legends attached to St. Valentine.

One story goes that St. Valentine believed in love so fervently he fearlessly married Christian couples in ancient Rome when doing so was a capital offense. He was arrested but was spared a dinner engagement with some lions when Emperor Claudius II took a liking to him. Still a fool for love, Valentine tried to convert the emperor, which didn't go down too well. The emperor had Valentine beaten with clubs, stoned and then publicly beheaded. Talk about careless love.

Ambassador of Love, yes, but also one of the most notable in a long line of fools for love, which, if you keep your head, is an admirable thing to be.

Some folks honor the martyr to love on this day by celebrating with trysts at motels where the bed is shaped like a heart, the tub is a giant cocktail glass and there's a complimentary bottle of uncertain vintage. The fortunate ones, at least.

The triumph of hope over experience has often been a definition of a second or third or Liz Taylor number of marriages, but it can also be a working explanation for love in general. I once did a business story for a newspaper that tried to go beyond the flowers/sweets/lingerie matrix and discovered that V-Day for divorce attorneys meant a happy spike in billable hours. It seems lots of romantics get hitched on February 14 and more marriages inevitably beget more divorces.

David Mejias, a partner at a Glen Cove-based law firm specializing in divorce, told me that after the glow of joyous emotions during Christmas and New Year's—when the love-intoxicated believe everyone is as blitzed as they are—many see Valentine's Day as "an idealized situation. They look at their own lives and think it might be time for a change," Mr. Mejias said.

(It's tragic to think of an April morning when the Valentine Day marriages are wrecked on the rocks of dubious bathroom behavior or alarming in-laws.)

But those are in many ways sad cases, and what we want to celebrate and remember is the battle-tested bravery of great lovers. They're the ones who have gone through the fire because of their commitment to each other and have a to-hell-with-you defiance to throw in the faces of society, parents, tribes or any convention that would dare separate them.

Think of Romeo and Juliet, Heloise and Abelard, Tristan and Isolde, Donald Trump and Donald Trump.

Except for the last couple, all the others had to fight for their right to party with each other.

Walter Benjamin, the great German writer, made a study of, among other things, German romanticism. Benjamin said, completely seriously—maybe a bit too seriously, he was German, after all—that the only way of knowing a person is to love them without hope.

His counsel to give your all to the love of someone with full knowledge there will be unpleasant or even dangerous consequences, and somehow putting all that from your mind, is one of the bravest acts a person can perform. That courage is truly what makes the world go 'round.

What is love? Love is like jazz, and not just when it's choreographed correctly. Remember Louis Armstrong's response to someone who asked him to explain his art—if you have to ask, you'll never know.

But Shakespeare did make a fine attempt: "Love is heavy and light, bright and dark, hot and cold, sick and healthy, asleep and awake—it's everything except what it is!"

Got it?

Happy Valentine's Day.

Chapter 85
Last Call

From March 2014.

We were talking in the newsroom about obituaries recently—"obits" in newspaper speak. Obituary: from the Latin verb *obire*, with several meanings, such as "to go to meet." Or, my favorite, "to cope with." And isn't it remarkable how people continue to die in alphabetical order?

One of the all-time popular obits was Osama Bin Laden's, which many people commented on, mistakenly quoting Mark Twain (it was actually Clarence Darrow): "I have never killed anyone, but I have read some obituary notices with great satisfaction." Twain once had the pleasure of reading his own obit, but whether he said, "The reports of my death are greatly exaggerated" is up for debate.

What do Brittany Spears and Ernest Hemingway have in common? Right, both great Americans. But they were also blessed to have read their own obits because of journalists' errors. After phony reports of a car crash, Britt was reported as dead, and Hem was declared permanently toes up in newspapers after a real plane crash in Africa. A friend reported that Papa kept his premature obits in a scrapbook and often read them in the morning with a glass of champagne. It's anyone's guess what Brittany is up to in the mornings these days.

Alfred Nobel was given another shot at his legacy after his premature obit. The inventor of dynamite and other explosives must have had a tough morning after reading: "The Merchant of Death is dead ... who became rich by finding ways to kill more people faster than ever before." Not long after, Nobel made sure a good part of his estate would be used to establish the peace prize.

Most large news organizations write obits when the famous haven't yet shuffled off, so they can run them on deadline when the celebrity is truly dead, and just cross the final "t," as it were. Recently, a respected veteran reporter landed the position as principal obit writer for a big daily. A dream job, I thought, not just for the fun of rummaging around in people's lives and asking questions, but because it seems to be one of the more honorable forms of journalism. Even a poorly written obit, even the ones that get some minor facts wrong, even the standard death notice that's emailed to community newspapers from funeral homes with surname, middle initial, first name, date and place of death and birth, residence, survivors, arrangements—even that flat tolling of a life is a sign of civilization.

It's coping. The same as the evolutionary leap the species took when we developed the instinct to be horrified when the dead aren't treated with grave—take the pun—respect. There's also another human aspect of the obit—the need to make order out of the random and inexplicable events of a life. A life's purpose and direction is a given once it's set into language, punctuation, paragraphs. When I was writing obits for a newspaper, it was a pleasure hearing people eager to speak about a loved one, or someone they respected and missed and who had influenced them, and would continue to influence them, until it was time for their own obituary to be written.

It's also not the worst thing to read obits, working under the theory that there's nothing like a death notice, the same as a death sentence, to help you concentrate on life. Sometimes knocking together an obit, I felt that a survivor (the perfect word) when talking with me, was pleased to have a chance to make amends, or, again, to add a trace of order to what may have been a messy life. The old expression applies to preparing obits the same as delivering eulogies: No one is under oath.

Journalism is the first draft of history, yes, and obits are the working notes of biography. Eugene Polley, another great American, died at 96.

Polley invented the TV remote during, according to *The New York Times*, such an ancient era that the obit writer, Margalit Fox, felt it necessary to explain to contemporary readers that previous to Colley's scientific breakthrough, there was something called a dial, "a round thing with numbers on it ... One did not so much surf channels in those days as ride their gentle swells with all due deliberateness."

Ms. Fox elegantly revealed the true spirit of the obit, providing insight into how our forebears had coped with life.

Chapter 86
Are You Superstitious?

From Friday, March 13, 2018.

Looking at the calendar today, it's important to remember some old common sense: Being superstitious brings bad luck.

Fear of this date is known as friggatriskaidekaphobia, pronounced frig-uh-trisk-eye-deck-uh-pho-bee-uh (I think) in tribute to Frigga, a Norse goddess. Why Frigga (I just like saying it) gave her name to freaking out over a date is lost in the blizzards of Scandinavian lore.

The tail end of that freight train of a description above is the fear of the number 13, and when the numerically squirrelly among us see that number coupled with a Friday, they take on an extra weight of dread.

Not only was Christ crucified on a Friday, but the number of diners at the table the night before he was betrayed at the Last Supper was 13. This has sent some hosts and hostesses who are wrapped too tight into a panic down the ages when they realize they will be entertaining 12 at table. "In France," author Douglas Hill wrote, "it's still common for a *quartorzieme*, or 14th diner, to be included at the spur of the moment to round out a dinner party."

President Franklin Roosevelt was surely not French, but he would never dine with exactly 12 others. His secretary Grace Tully recalled, "The boss was superstitious, especially about the No. 13." And so

Grace was on occasion drafted as a *quartorzieme*, and had the good fortune to take an impromptu seat at history's table.

Even institutions dedicated to science and reason succumb to the sinister power of 13. For example, most hospitals don't have floors numbered 13. Stony Brook University Hospital spokesman Greg Filiano, who takes the elevator daily at the hospital, never noticed the numbers, he said to me a while ago, and so was asked to take a ride to check.

After the 12th floor, and before the 14th, he got off at "MR," or Medical Records, he reported.

Believing Friday the 13th is ominous can truly bring bad luck, said a travel agent friend of mine, noting that some customers who've realized too late that they're traveling on Frigga's Day have changed their travel plans.

"They have to pay extra for tickets, stay an extra night in a hotel and their schedules are all screwed up," he said.

But times have changed, and he finds far fewer superstitious people these days than in days past. About the irrationality of the whole thing, my friend is philosophical. "The Italians have no fear of Friday the 13th," he said, but beware of asking them to do anything important on Friday the 17th, or a Spaniard on Tuesday the 13th.

To get to the bottom of this, I consulted with "Dr. 13," also known as Thomas Fernsler, associate policy scientist at the University of Delaware. "If you can figure out what the hell that tiltle means, please let me know," Professor Fernsler said, adding he's really a math teacher.

The mathematician has made a career of exploring the number 13, and the vagaries and mysteries of the Gregorian calendar. "I started looking into it in 1987, which had three Friday the 13ths," Professor Fernsler said.

He went on to discuss other months with exact date patterns and "numerical models," but I was drifting away like Frigga in a storm of numbers. Professor Fernsler brought me back by remembering a math teachers' conference he once attended in Philadelphia. "It was scheduled over a weekend, and I was to speak on Friday the 13th," he said, adding he got to Philadelphia the night before and checked into a hotel. And was assigned room 1417.

"Room 1417 was of course a room on the 13th floor of the hotel," he said.

Math teachers obviously entertain themselves in hotel rooms differently than normal people because Professor Fernsler started playing with the number of his room, finding that 1417 evenly divides by 13. "It goes in 109 times. And if you add the digits of 1417, it equals 13."

Is he superstitious?

"Absolutely not," the professor said in his gravest associate policy scientist's tone. "But every time I fly on a commercial airliner, I wear the same socks and shoes, same pants and shirt and same underwear. And my lucky cap."

Chapter 87
Night and Day

From February 2019.

I get up early.

I mean *early*. Early enough to hear roosters announcing the morning as I unlock the back door of the *Reporter*'s office, with Orion striding across the black sky above me. Sometimes there's moonlight so bright you can read by it, and other times I'm cursing in the dark, fumbling to find the right key.

Getting up early means I go to sleep early, because one of the things I'm good at is sleeping, so I want to log eight hours in the sack. There are a lot of people going to sleep early these days and waking before cockcrow. This happens when the calendar turns to February, according to research collected in a large British study.

One reason for cashing it in early this month, researchers have found, is that during the low tide of the year, less daylight means the hormone melatonin is increased, triggering a chemical reaction telling us it's a school night every night of the week. Less energy, less light and over-heated rooms are other February factors creating a month-long sleeping potion.

Cursing or praising the hour before dawn, I sometimes remember that once at this time of morning I was just finishing a night of work.

On the Island in February, the only night shifts are done by police officers, who take tours from 3 p.m. to 11 p.m. and 11 p.m. to 7 a.m.

The Fire Department answers the call no matter the hour, but no volunteer is stationed at the firehouses, and the Highway Department will be out in pre-dawn hours when it's storming. Other than that, the Island sleeps in.

There's a separation between the two worlds of work. One morning, knocking off after a night driving a cab in the city, other drivers and I went to a bar, which had opened at 8 a.m. There were five of us along with several poor wrecks who had awakened and thought the first thing to do was order a shot and a beer from a half-asleep bartender.

Coming in off the rush-hour street was a young woman, dressed for work in an office. She asked the bartender for the ladies room, and when she came back out she gave us a look that still, in my memory, freezes me—pity mixed with disgust, that healthy young men were drinking at 8:15 a.m. I wanted to run after her and say, "No, you've got it wrong. We've been working all night, this is our 6 p.m." But then she probably would have yelled for a cop.

Three in ten Americans suffer from insomnia, according to The National Institutes of Health, and one in ten have trouble during the day with relationships and work because they've suffered a bad night's sleep. That was me when I was younger, but now, like I said, I'm an accomplished sleeper. I do tend to act like I'm sprinting from something when I'm zonked out, pumping my legs now and then, I'm told, but ... I don't want to talk about it.

These winter mornings, alone in the *Reporter's* office, the roosters give way to the quarrelling of turkeys. After a while, out my window darkness is melting and light is finding its way into the tops of trees on North Ferry Road.

Another day.

———— ◆ ————

THE END

Acknowledgments

First, my gratitude goes to my two publishers, John T. Colby Jr. of Brick Tower Press, who had the idea for this collection, and Andrew Olsen, publisher of Times Review Media, who I've worked with on and off for more than 20 years—totally on for the past 12.

Andrew has shown an unfailing dedication to producing three community newspapers in economic and cultural climates that seem determined to kill the business of local journalism. His excellent, award-winning newspapers bear witness, week in and week out, to his fortitude and leadership.

My thanks to a friend of more than four decades, who covered a few of the stories—for other publications—included in this book, David Lozell Martin, a journalist, editor, and best-selling author of a dozen novels, as well as one of the finest American memoirs, "Losing Everything." David has been an intellectual companion, as well as a close companion on less high-minded pursuits, since the day I met him. And I will be forever grateful to him for introducing me to Lester and Delbert Sluddums.

To Kirk Condyles, whose many photos grace this collection, a friend and colleague whom I've depended on. And Gregory Zeller, who has been my editor at two newspapers and my friend for more than 20 years—cheers, Doctor Z.

To the people at the *Shelter Island Reporter*, especially Julie Lane. Julie and I have worked together for more than a decade. Rare in temperament, never rattled, never expressing frustration or anger, Julie is indefatigable. She is not just an irreplaceable resource for our paper, but for the community she covers. Julie is invested in both, and strives every time to get every story right, and make every story count.

And thanks to all who now and in the past have made the *Reporter* run every week: Archer Brown, Susan Carey Dempsey, Peter Waldner,

Charity Robey, James Bornemeir, Robert Lipsyte, Karl Grossman, Christine Kelly-Smimmo, Maria Gennaro, Charles Tumino, Eric Hod, Robert Harris, Larry Winston, Michelina DaFonte, Jenifer Maxson, Nancy Green, Cindy Belt, Jim Colligan, JoAnn Kirkland, Joanne Sherman, and the late Richard Lomuscio.

To the Staff of the *North Shore Sun*, who carried me every step of the way: Gregory Zeller, Nicole Cotroneo Jolly, Matt Bodkin, Michael Gasparino, Denise McKeon, Megan Karaptis, Scott Brennan, Kirk Condyles, and Ashley Hadjoglou. Sunnies forever!

At Times Review: Grant Parpan, Joe Werkmeister, Jeff Miller, Tara Smith, Steve Wick, Denise Civilleti, Tim Gannon and Tim Kelly.

At the *Southampton Press*, thanks to Joe Shaw, Dana Shaw, Frank Costanza, and Bill Sutton.

At *Long Island Business News* (is it possible to have a happy newsroom? Yes), the late John Kominicki, David Winzelberg, Gregory Zeller (again, always), Michael Samuels, Ross Daly, David Reich-Hale, Henry Powderly III, Claude Solnick and Laura Glasser.

In Ireland, my gratitude goes out to the late Peadar MacGiolla Cearr and the late Dick Walsh, two *Irish Times* staffers who schooled me, and became my friends. Thanks, to Niall Kiley, also of *The Irish Times*. And thanks to the sui generis Jim Murray. Also, Marilyn Roantree, Jane Touhey, Laurie Cearr, Colette Delaney, Myles McWeeney, and Carmel Carey. To my teacher and friend, the late Christy Browne, and to the late Pat Wall, who welcomed us to County Clare and became our friend.

Thanks to my editors: At *The Washington Post*, Craig Stoltz and KC Summers, and to Tony Lioche at the *Los Angles Times*, Eliot Kaplan at *GQ*, John Mancini at the *Long Island Voice*, and John Leonard at *The Nation*.

Finally, to the ones I hold closest: Elizabeth Clancy, Deirdre, Cadence and Cordelia Weatherston.

And Mary Lydon. The one who has loved, helped, inspired, and been my heart every step of the way.

About the Author

Ambrose Clancy is the editor of the *Shelter Island Reporter*. He is the author of the novel, "Blind Pilot" and, with the photographer Peter Donahoe, "The Night Line: a Memoir of Work."

Mr. Clancy has been awarded numerous awards for columns, news and feature writing from the New York Press Association. In 2023 he received top honors from the National Newspaper Association for columns and feature writing.

For sales, editorial information, subsidiary rights information
or a catalog, please write or phone or e-mail
Brick Tower Press
Manhanset House
Shelter Island Hts., New York 11965, U.S.
Tel: 212-427-7139
www.ibooksinc.com
bricktower@aol.com
www.IngramContent.com

For sales in the U.K. and Europe please contact our distributor,
Gazelle Book Services
White Cross Mills
Lancaster, LA1 4XS, U.K.
Tel: (01524) 68765 Fax: (01524) 63232
email: jacky@gazellebooks.co.uk